Sex For Dummies
2nd Edition

DR. RUTH SAYS

Be spontaneous

- ♥ Drop in at work with a picnic lunch.
- ♥ E-mail each other love notes.
- ❀ Send flowers just for fun.
- ♥ Put sexy Post-it Notes where they'll get the most attention.
- ♥ Slow dance at home by candlelight.
- ❀ Read erotic literature aloud to each other.
- ♥ Sing an operatic aria.
- ♥ Attempt to paint or sculpt your lover in a provocative pose.

Dr. Ruth's Rx
For Real Romance

DR. RUTH SAYS

Be loving

- ♥ Speak, don't shout.
- ♥ Request, don't demand.
- ❀ Listen, don't tune out.
- ♥ Keep talking.
- ♥ Be gentle.
- ❀ Be kind.
- ♥ Be faithful.
- ♥ Be honest.
- ❀ Compromise.
- ♥ Share jokes.
- ♥ Share tears.
- ❀ Share troubles.
- ♥ Show respect.
- ♥ Share laughter.
- ❀ Share pajamas.
- ♥ Make time for each other.
- ♥ Make time for sex.
- ❀ Compliment each other.
- ♥ Say thank you.
- ♥ Don't use up all the hot water.
- ❀ Hold hands.

DR. RUTH SAYS

Be playful

- ❀ Plan a trip together.
- ♥ Buy two tickets to the ballgame and feed each other peanuts.
- ♥ Take a bubble bath together.
- ♥ Play a game of strip poker.
- ❀ Buy a new feather duster and use it on each other.
- ♥ Take dance lessons together.
- ♥ Feed each other a plate of spaghetti with sauce — naked.
- ♥ Play hide-and-go-seek.
- ❀ Go roller blading.
- ♥ Visit an amusement park and ride the carousel.
- ♥ Go skinny dipping.

For Dummies: Bestselling Book Series for Beginners

Sex For Dummies, 2nd Edition

Cheat Sheet

DR. RUTH SAYS

Be naughty

- ♥ Buy an item at a sex shop or browse a sex-toy catalog.
- ♥ Watch an X-rated video together.
- ♥ Visit a motel for two hours on a Sunday afternoon.
- ♥ Bring home edible underwear for dessert.
- ♥ Whip up some cream and lick it off each other.
- ♥ Put satin sheets on the bed.
- ♥ Set up a video camera in the bedroom for an evening and play act.
- ♥ Watch the video that you made.
- ♥ Set the alarm for 4 a.m. and make love in the sunrise.
- ♥ Make up code words for sex terms to use in public.

Dr. Ruth's Rx For Real Romance

DR. RUTH SAYS

Be romantic

- ✿ Go for a sleigh ride or a sunset cruise.
- ♥ Snuggle up by a fire.
- ♥ Reenact your first date.
- ✿ Massage each other's back.
- ♥ Take a long drive in the country.
- ♥ Help out at a soup kitchen together.
- ✿ Feed each other grapes.
- ♥ Go for a long walk by starlight.
- ♥ Have dinner at an intimate restaurant.
- ✿ Find the biggest stuffed animal you can and have it delivered.
- ♥ Play sensuous music.
- ♥ Share a bottle of champagne.
- ✿ Give each other sponge baths.
- ♥ Wear your tux to the dinner table.

DR. RUTH SAYS

Be surprising

- ♥ Take the kids to give your spouse a break.
- ♥ Compose an erotic poem or letter.
- ✿ Clean the bathroom together naked.
- ♥ Arrange a surprise party.
- ♥ Send a singing telegram.
- ✿ Watch TV together without channel-surfing.
- ♥ Spend an evening at a karaoke bar.
- ♥ Visit a nude beach.
- ✿ Send a balloon bouquet to the office.
- ♥ Learn to belly dance (men too!).

Hungry Minds™

For Dummies: Bestselling Book Series for Beginners

Universal Praise for Bestselling Author Dr. Ruth K. Westheimer

"Dr. Ruth Westheimer is the Stealth fighter of sex education."

— *San Jose Mercury News,* 1995

"Her image is synonymous with sex . . . ."

— *Time,* 1987

"Dr. Ruth writes the way she talks — enthusiastically, nonjudgementally and informatively . . . ."

— *Booklist,* 1994

"Her energy level is higher than that of a charged particle."

— *People Magazine,* 1985

"She can seemingly say things on the air that no one else can. This could be because she is short and sweet and takes her job seriously . . . ."

— *New York Times,* 1985

"America's star sexologist . . . ."

— *TV Guide*

"Her manner is down-to-earth and reassuring . . . she tries to make people feel better, value themselves, trust their instincts . . . ."

— *Ladies' Home Journal,* 1986

"If height were measured in courage, determination and hard work, this little lady would be 10 feet tall."

— *Newsday,* 1987

"Her name and the distinctive thrill of her voice have become inextricably linked with the subject of sex."

— *New York Times,* 1992

"This textbook style resource is comprehensive and easy to use. Accessible and up-to-date, it focuses on basic sexuality information and education for adults."

— SIECUS (Sexuality Information and Education Council of the United States) on *Sex For Dummies, 1st Edition*

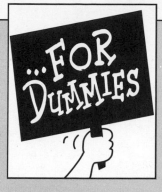 TM

References for the Rest of Us!®

BESTSELLING BOOK SERIES

Do you find that traditional reference books are overloaded with technical details and advice you'll never use? Do you postpone important life decisions because you just don't want to deal with them? Then our *For Dummies*® business and general reference book series is for you.

For Dummies business and general reference books are written for those frustrated and hard-working souls who know they aren't dumb, but find that the myriad of personal and business issues and the accompanying horror stories make them feel helpless. *For Dummies* books use a lighthearted approach, a down-to-earth style, and even cartoons and humorous icons to dispel fears and build confidence. Lighthearted but not lightweight, these books are perfect survival guides to solve your everyday personal and business problems.

> "More than a publishing phenomenon, 'Dummies' is a sign of the times."
> — The New York Times

> "A world of detailed and authoritative information is packed into them..."
> — U.S. News and World Report

> "...you won't go wrong buying them."
> — Walter Mossberg, Wall Street Journal, on For Dummies books

Already, millions of satisfied readers agree. They have made For Dummies the #1 introductory level computer book series and a best-selling business book series. They have written asking for more. So, if you're looking for the best and easiest way to learn about business and other general reference topics, look to *For Dummies* to give you a helping hand.

Hungry Minds™

1/01

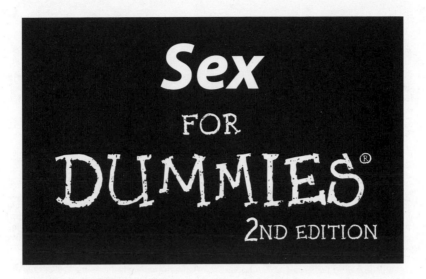

Sex
FOR
DUMMIES®
2ND EDITION

by Dr. Ruth K. Westheimer

Hungry Minds™

Best-Selling Books • Digital Downloads • e-Books • Answer Networks • e-Newsletters • Branded Web Sites • e-Learning

New York, NY ◆ Cleveland, OH ◆ Indianapolis, IN

Sex For Dummies,® 2nd Edition

Published by
Hungry Minds, Inc.
909 Third Avenue
New York, NY 10022
www.hungryminds.com
www.dummies.com

Library of Congress Control Number: 00-109414

ISBN: 0-7645-5302-X

Printed in the United States of America

10 9 8 7 6

2O/SY/QT/QS/IN

Distributed in the United States by Hungry Minds, Inc.

Distributed by CDG Books Canada Inc. for Canada; by Transworld Publishers Limited in the United Kingdom; by IDG Norge Books for Norway; by IDG Sweden Books for Sweden; by IDG Books Australia Publishing Corporation Pty. Ltd. for Australia and New Zealand; by TransQuest Publishers Pte Ltd. for Singapore, Malaysia, Thailand, Indonesia, and Hong Kong; by Gotop Information Inc. for Taiwan; by ICG Muse, Inc. for Japan; by Intersoft for South Africa; by Eyrolles for France; by International Thomson Publishing for Germany, Austria and Switzerland; by Distribuidora Cuspide for Argentina; by LR International for Brazil; by Galileo Libros for Chile; by Ediciones ZETA S.C.R. Ltda. for Peru; by WS Computer Publishing Corporation, Inc., for the Philippines; by Contemporanea de Ediciones for Venezuela; by Express Computer Distributors for the Caribbean and West Indies; by Micronesia Media Distributor, Inc. for Micronesia; by Chips Computadoras S.A. de C.V. for Mexico; by Editorial Norma de Panama S.A. for Panama; by American Bookshops for Finland.

For general information on Hungry Minds' products and services please contact our Customer Care Department within the U.S. at 800-762-2974, outside the U.S. at 317-572-3993 or fax 317-572-4002.

For sales inquiries and reseller information, including discounts, premium and bulk quantity sales, and foreign-language translations, please contact our Customer Care Department at 800-434-3422, fax 317-572-4002, or write to Hungry Minds, Inc., Attn: Customer Care Department, 10475 Crosspoint Boulevard, Indianapolis, IN 46256.

For information on licensing foreign or domestic rights, please contact our Sub-Rights Customer Care Department at 212-884-5000.

For information on using Hungry Minds' products and services in the classroom or for ordering examination copies, please contact our Educational Sales Department at 800-434-2086 or fax 317-572-4005.

Please contact our Public Relations Department at 212-884-5163 for press review copies or 212-884-5000 for author interviews and other publicity information or fax 212-884-5400.

For authorization to photocopy items for corporate, personal, or educational use, please contact Copyright Clearance Center, 222 Rosewood Drive, Danvers, MA 01923, or fax 978-750-4470.

Hungry Minds™ is a trademark of Hungry Minds, Inc.

About the Author

Dr. Ruth K. Westheimer: Dr. Ruth Westheimer is a psychosexual therapist who helped pioneer the field of media psychology with her radio program, Sexually Speaking, which first aired in New York in 1980. Within a few years, she had built a communications network to distribute her expertise that included television, books, newspapers, games, calendars, home videos, and computer software.

Dr. Westheimer received her Master's Degree in Sociology from the Graduate Faculty of the New School of Social Research and her Doctorate of Education (Ed.D) in the Interdisciplinary Study of the Family from Columbia University Teacher's College. Working at Planned Parenthood prompted her to further her education in human sexuality by studying under Dr. Helen Singer Kaplan at New York Hospital–Cornell University Medical Center. She later participated in the program for five years as an Adjunct Associate Professor. She has also taught at Lehman College, Brooklyn College, Adelphi University, Columbia University, and West Point. She is currently an Adjunct Professor at New York University.

Dr. Westheimer is a Fellow of New York Academy of Medicine and has her own private practice in New York. She frequently lectures around the world, including at universities, and has twice been named "College Lecturer of the Year." In June 2000, she received an Honorary Doctorate from Hebrew Union College—Institute of Religion for her work in Human Sexuality and her commitment to the Jewish People, Israel, and Religion.

Dr. Westheimer has written 18 books. Some of the others include *Dr. Ruth's Encyclopedia of Sex, Dr. Ruth's Pregnancy Guide For Couples, The Art of Arousal, Dr. Ruth Talks to Kids,* and *Rekindling Romance For Dummies.*

Dedication

"The reticent do not learn; the hot-tempered do not teach."

Chapters of the Fathers 2.6

To the memory of my entire family who perished during the Holocaust — I am thankful that they had the opportunity to instill in me the much cherished values of the Jewish Tradition before they were lost to me. And to the memory of my beloved late husband, Manfred Westheimer.

To my wonderful family of now: my daughter, Miriam Westheimer, Ed.D; my son-in-law, Joel Einleger; my grandson, Ari Einleger; my granddaughter, Leora Einleger; my son, Joel Westheimer, Ph.D.; my daughter-in-law, Barbara Leckie, Ph.D.; and my granddaughter, Michal Leckie!

Acknowledgments

I am grateful and appreciate the tremendous contribution in writing this book made by Pierre Lehu. Pierre and I arc now entering our twentieth year of working together! He is the best "Minister of Communications" anybody could wish for. A special toast to Pierre and to many more years of cooperation.

I have so many people to thank it would require an additional chapter, so let me just mention a few: Martin Englisher; Richard Freese; Cynthia Fuchs Epstein, Ph.D. and Howard Epstein; Gabe Erem; Josh Gafni; Ellen Goldberg; David Goslin, Ph.D.; Amos Grunebaum, M.D.; Alfred Kaplan; Steve Kaplan, Ph.D.; Ronnie and Michael Kassan; Bonnie Kaye; John Kilcullen; Larry Kirshbaum; Marga and Bill Kunreuther; Rabbi and Mrs. William Lebeau; Lou Lieberman, Ph.D. and Mary Cuadrado, Ph.D.; John and Ginger Lollos; Sanford Lopater, Ph.D.; Jonathan Mark; Dale Ordes; Henry and Sydelle Ostberg; Bob Pinto; Fred and Ann Rosenberg; Cliff Rubin; Jonathan Sacks; Tim Satterfield; Rose and Simeon Schreiber; Daniel Schwartz; Amir Shaviv; Richard Stein; Hannah Strauss; Romie and Blanche Shapiro; John and Marianne Slade; Greg Willenborg; and Ben Yagoda.

To the Hungry Minds staff: What a terrific, hard working, competent, and expert group you are to work with! Thanks especially to Kathy Welton, who "conceived" the idea and went chasing after me, and to Stacy Collins, Tracy Boggier, Kathy Cox, Allyson Grove, Joan Friedman, Corey Dalton, and Jennifer Young. Thanks also to Dr. Mitchell Reider for his professional reading of this manuscript and to Dr. Michael Rosenberg and Dr. Diane Brashear for their expert advice on the manuscript of the first edition.

Publisher's Acknowledgments

We're proud of this book; please send us your comments through our Online Registration Form located at www.dummies.com.

Some of the people who helped bring this book to market include the following:

Acquisitions, Editorial, and Media Development

Project Editors: Allyson Grove, Joan Friedman
    (Previous Edition: Kathleen M. Cox)

Acquisitions Editor: Stacy S. Collins

Copy Editor: Corey Dalton
    (Previous Edition: Shannon Ross)

Managing Editor: Tracy L. Boggier

Technical Editor: Mitchell W. Reider, M.D.

Editorial Managers: Christine Meloy Beck, Jennifer Ehrlich

Editorial Assistant: Jennifer Young

Cover Photo: T Stock Int'l / Index Stock Imagery / Picture Quest

Production

Project Coordinator: Emily Wichlinski

Layout and Graphics: Amy Adrian, Clint Lahnen, Kristin Pickett, Brent Savage, Jacque Schneider, Brian Torwelle, Jeremey Unger, Erin Zeltner

Proofreaders: Andy Hollandbeck, Nancy Price

Indexer: Liz Cunningham

Special Art: Kathryn Born, Medical Illustrator

Hungry Minds Consumer Reference Group

Business: Kathleen A. Welton, Vice President and Publisher; Kevin Thornton, Acquisitions Manager

Cooking/Gardening: Jennifer Feldman, Associate Vice President and Publisher

Education/Reference: Diane Graves Steele, Vice President and Publisher

Lifestyles/Pets: Kathleen Nebenhaus, Vice President and Publisher; Tracy Boggier, Managing Editor

Travel: Michael Spring, Vice President and Publisher; Suzanne Jannetta, Editorial Director; Brice Gosnell, Publishing Director

Hungry Minds Consumer Editorial Services: Kathleen Nebenhaus, Vice President and Publisher; Kristin A. Cocks, Editorial Director; Cindy Kitchel, Editorial Director

Hungry Minds Consumer Production: Debbie Stailey, Production Director

Contents at a Glance

Cartoons at a Glance

By Rich Tennant

page 5

page 63

page 337

page 259

page 193

page 121

Fax: 978-546-7747
E-mail: richtennant@the5thwave.com
World Wide Web: www.the5thwave.com

Table of Contents

• •

From the desk of Dr. Ruth

Dear Reader,

I have to start by saying that, when I was first asked to do a book called *Sex For Dummies*, I wasn't thrilled with the idea. Even though for years I've been saying that we must eradicate sexual illiteracy — a phrase that I thought appropriate for a college professor like myself to use — writing a book for people who considered themselves to be sexual dummies just didn't sit right with me.

But then I began to think

- ✔ of the tremendous number of unintended pregnancies we have each year in America (of which more than one million are teenage pregnancies).

- ✔ of all the women who do not have orgasms and think that they can do nothing about it.

- ✔ of all the men who are premature ejaculators and who think that they have an uncorrectable physical problem instead of a learning disability.

- ✔ of all the couples who expect so much from sex but who don't know the importance of foreplay and who neglect afterplay.

And so, you know what?

I decided that there are a lot of people having trouble mastering the sexual basics who need a book that clearly addresses the root of the problem.

Once I came to that realization, something else dawned on me. I've written many books about sex, and the bookstores are filled with other books on the subject — as are magazines and television shows — yet the message still doesn't get across correctly. "Why is that?" I asked myself. The research has been done. Good sex can be available to everybody. So why do so many people go without having truly pleasurable sex?

I think that many people have trouble sorting through the mass of sexual information and sexual imagery that they get each day. Much of this information is not clear, and some of it is contradictory. In the face of this, many of you begin to think of yourselves as sexual dummies — caught between conflicting sexual views — or at least as people not capable of performing up to par.

Now a lot of people had given up on learning to use a computer, something that I think is a lot more complex than sex. Many people were afraid to buy a book about Windows or DOS because they thought they wouldn't understand it. Then along came the *For Dummies* series, which stuck with the basics and used everyday words with a frank, humorous style, and those same people — you may be among them — have now become computer whizzes. So I decided if other writers can do it for computers, I know that I can do it for the subject I know best — sex.

So here I am with the second edition of *Sex For Dummies* — a book made for those of you who want great sex, but who may have had difficulties getting it "right." You can get it right. Just keep on reading.

Dr. Ruth K. Westheimer

Dr. Ruth K. Westheimer

Introduction

● ●

*T*he main problems that we have in dealing with human sexuality most often come directly from ignorance — both the not-knowing kind and the not-caring kind.

You would think that after "doing it" for thousands of years, we all would have found a simple and effective system for passing on vital sexual information from generation to generation. But sadly, here we are in the 21st century, and we adults continue to do a lousy job of educating ourselves and our young people about sex.

Part of the reason is that, in American culture, we're often embarrassed to talk about sex, especially when it comes to talking with our own flesh and blood (who wouldn't even be here without it).

As parents, many of us avoid the subject entirely. Often, even when we do work up the courage to have a heart-to-heart talk with "the kids," we don't do much more than pass on the bare-bones basics, concentrating on how to avoid pregnancy and scaring kids with the threat of sexually transmitted diseases.

These issues are certainly important points to cover. But what about issues of good sexual functioning, such as how to have an orgasm, or how to be the best lover possible? Is that ever on the agenda? After listening to the couples who come to see me in therapy, I don't believe these topics are talked about in the vast majority of families.

Direct from the Playground

So where did most of you learn about sex? You learned a little bit from your parents and a little bit at school. But because much of this information was, rightfully, passed on before you were really ready to use it, it may not have meant all that much to you, and so it didn't totally sink in. Later on, if you had another class, you probably felt the need to act blasé, as if you knew it all, and you may not have bothered to listen.

It's this Catch-22 that makes having good sex so difficult — you get the information before you need it, and you forget about it by the time you do need it. Or you get it so confused that it's not helpful to you.

Our children are the same way. Often, despite our best efforts as parents, kids are more likely to pay attention to what they hear on the street or in the locker room or at a pajama party. How much of this information is accurate is anybody's guess.

But even though some of this information is true, because it does not match the sexual myths that are also out there, the new information leads only to more confusion. And when you're confused, don't you often end up not paying attention to anything you've heard — preferring to trust your instincts?

Unfortunately, in sexual matters, trusting your instincts can often lead to problems.

In the end, you let trial and error become the teacher of last resort. And when that happens, not unexpectedly, you can often make serious mistakes — such as becoming pregnant when you don't intend to be, or catching a sexually transmitted disease, or, at the very least, having a less-than-satisfactory sex life, or going through your entire life never having terrific sex.

In the 21st century, this process of misinformation and confusion cannot continue. In the past, we had rules in place to guide us so that, even if we didn't understand human sexuality all that well, as long as we followed the rules and got married before having sex, we couldn't stray too far.

But over the past 30 years, these rules have begun to disintegrate badly. Some people would say the results — millions of unintended pregnancies, millions of single parents, vast numbers of people with sexually transmitted diseases — were predictable.

Marriage, Morality, and Sexual Safety

Let me say something about my philosophy at this point.

- ✔ I am old-fashioned and a square.
- ✔ I believe in God, I believe in marriage, and I believe in morality.

But, because I cannot dictate to you how you should live your life,

- ✔ I believe that I must give you the tools with which to conduct yourself as safely as possible.

That's why I believe in giving you information so that, even if you do have premarital sex, at least you have a better chance of not causing unintended pregnancies and not catching a sexually transmitted disease.

Do I encourage people to develop a relationship before they engage in sex with another person? Absolutely. And I'll say it again and again throughout this book.

But even if you're having a one-night stand that I don't approve of, I still want you to wake up the next morning healthy and safe. And I look at this book as an important tool in reaching you and others of all ages to help you discover more useful information on this important subject.

Icons Used in This Book

Sex For Dummies, 2nd Edition is intended to give you a start on a healthy approach to sexuality. It follows the *For Dummies* format that has proven so successful for computer and business topics. Important information is highlighted with little pictures, called icons, lurking in the margins. Here's what the ones used in this book signify:

This icon alerts you to a useful tidbit of information.

This icon points out tips to enhance sexual pleasure (so you won't have to put sticky tabs on the pages).

This icon is the "men's locker room" stuff that guys especially need to know.

This icon highlights "girls' night out" stuff that women need to know.

This icon points out stories from therapy sessions or likely scenarios involving individuals and couples that can help you cope with similar situations.

This icon points to practical advice and my personal thoughts on today's sexual dilemmas.

You'll see this icon next to medical descriptions of your anatomy or physical conditions.

This icon highlights some of the things you may think you know about sex that are false or misleading.

This icon signals behaviors that could cause trouble, either for you or someone else, and tells you when to look before you leap to stay clear of pitfalls to your relationships.

Starting Now

Whether you consider yourself a Don Juan, a Lady Chatterly, or a sexual novice, the first piece of advice I have for you is that everybody can become a better lover given the proper instruction. And because we are all sexual beings, whether we like it or not, why not get the most out of the pleasures our bodies are capable of giving us? So relax and read on. I guarantee that, by the end of this book, you can take the dunce cap that you may be wearing off your head and perhaps replace it with a condom somewhere else!

Part I
Back to Basics

The 5th Wave   By Rich Tennant

"NOW, THAT WOULD SHOW HOW IMPORTANT IT IS TO DISTINGUISH 'FERTILIZING PRACTICES' FROM 'FERTILITY PRACTICES' WHEN DOWNLOADING A VIDEO FILE FROM THE INTERNET."

In this part . . .

In this part I give you basic information that you need to master in order to fully enjoy good sex. And just because you're not a virgin, don't think that you can skip over this section. No matter how much experience you may have in the bedroom, to become a great lover you still need to spend some time in the classroom. Sexual illiteracy is often the cause of sexual problems; increase your knowledge, and you increase your chances of enjoying good sexual functioning.

Chapter 1

Making Babies: A Natural Outcome

The English language is a rich one because it has borrowed heavily from so many different tongues. As a result, people use a variety of words to describe the same thing — especially if that thing involves sex. (I'm sure you're familiar with some of these words, but, being polite, I won't mention them.) What never ceases to amaze me, however, is how often people who engage in the act of sexual intercourse forget that what they're doing is directly related to procreation, propagation, continuing the species, conception, pregnancy, MAKING BABIES!

Some unlucky couples must go through a great deal of trouble to have a family, and some can't manage to do it on their own at all, so they turn to medical science for help. But for most people, the process is relatively easy — at least until the baby actually arrives. The man needs only to place his erect penis into the woman's vagina and ejaculate. A baby may not result the first time — though it can — but eventually one of the man's sperm will unite with the woman's egg, and, voilá, a baby is conceived.

Because baby making is so easy, many women find themselves pregnant without intending to be. So here's my first of many tips:

If you absolutely, positively don't want to make a baby, then don't have sexual intercourse — be abstinent.

Yes, I know there are ways of preventing pregnancy from occurring — I talk about them in Chapter 7 — but none of these methods is foolproof. Believe it or not, in at least one recorded case, the man had a vasectomy, the woman had her tubes tied, and she still became pregnant. So remember, *the only method that works 100 percent of the time is abstinence.*

Ignorance Isn't Bliss

Now I'm pretty sure that most of you reading this book are not abstinent — at least not voluntarily — and that you bought this book to discover how to become better lovers, not to find out how to become parents. And, anyway, you probably think you know everything about the process of making babies, so you're tempted to skip this chapter.

Before you give in to that temptation, try this little quiz:

1. How many sperm do the testicles manufacture?

    A. 5,000 a day

    B. 50 a minute

    C. 5 million a year

    D. 50,000 a minute

2. After a woman has ovulated, the egg remains fertile for approximately how long?

    A. 12 hours

    B. 24 hours

    C. three days

    D. one week

3. The sperm and the egg usually meet where?

    A. at the entrance to the fallopian tubes

    B. inside the fallopian tubes

    C. in the uterus

    D. in the vagina

The answers are D, C, and B.

Unless your wild guesses were lucky ones, I bet that you didn't know the correct answers to these three questions. In addition, I bet that you are unfamiliar with other parts of the baby-making process. And don't argue; yes, you do need to know what making babies involves.

"But Dr. Ruth," I can hear you asking, "will knowing all the details about the birds and the bees really help my sexual functioning? After all, I don't know how my car works, but it still gets me around."

Good question. The best way that I can answer it is by giving you some examples of cases I see in my private practice that stem directly from ignorance.

First are the men and women who make appointments to see me because they don't enjoy having sexual intercourse. Their problem often turns out to be an underlying fear that the woman may become pregnant. Even if they know about contraception, or think they know, deep down inside they have misgivings. Their concern that having sexual intercourse will cause the woman to become pregnant affects their enjoyment of sex. Let me illustrate:

Kenny and Vera

Kenny and Vera had been living together for several years, and their sex life was fine. Before they were married, they used condoms, but after they got married, Vera began to use a diaphragm. Right away, their sex life began to deteriorate. At the time they came to see me, both Kenny and Vera thought that their sexual problems had something to do with the fact that they had gotten married.

After speaking with the two of them separately, however, I guessed what the problem might be. I explained it to them so that they'd realize what was happening. Even though Kenny knew that Vera was using a diaphragm, he did not feel the same sense of assurance that he did with condoms. He could no longer see the birth control device, and he had nothing to do with putting it in place.

I suggested that, instead of Vera inserting the diaphragm by herself in the bathroom, Kenny insert the diaphragm with her as part of foreplay. Seeing the diaphragm placed inside Vera's body restored Kenny's confidence that having sex with his new bride wasn't going to make her pregnant, and their sex life returned to normal.

In another example from my practice, some men believe that, because cavemen had to reach their orgasms quickly to impregnate their women before some wild animal got to them (no one knows for sure whether that story is true), premature ejaculation has been encoded into their genes. These men think that they can't do anything about being premature ejaculators. That presumption, of course, is a myth. Premature ejaculation is a learning disability, not a physical problem. When a man understands this, he can usually do something positive about it. (I discuss the treatment of this sexual problem in Chapter 20.)

Some Myths about Making Babies

Myths about things such as premature ejaculation get in the way of terrific sex, but myths about making babies have also caused people a great deal of hardship. For example:

- The notion that a woman can't get pregnant the first time she has intercourse is a myth. (She can.)

- The idea that a woman can't get pregnant if she "does it" standing up is a myth. (She can.)

- The belief that douching with a soft drink or vinegar after intercourse will prevent pregnancy is a myth. (It doesn't do anything.)

- And then you have the one myth that has caused more unintended pregnancies than all the others combined — the idea that if a man pulls his penis out of the woman's vagina before he ejaculates (the *withdrawal* method), she can't get pregnant. (She most definitely can! You can find out more about this myth in Chapter 7.)

Even if you've never fallen for any of these tall tales, you may have picked up some other myths along the way. I recommend that you start right from the very beginning — the process of making a baby — to be absolutely sure that you have your facts straight.

The Truth about Making Babies

The process of making a baby has not changed since Adam and Eve discovered sex: A sperm from the man must meet an egg inside of the woman (test-tube babies notwithstanding). When the sperm and the egg unite, the egg becomes *fertilized*.

Both the sperm and the egg are very special cells; they have only half of the genetic material (chromosomes) that other cells have. All cells need chromosomes to provide the instructions on how to divide and create an individual.

The process of fertilization mixes the chromosomes and genes of both partners together by combining the chromosomes from both the sperm and the egg into one single cell, called a *zygote*. As a result, instead of an identical copy of one of the parents (a clone), fertilization creates a unique individual that shares features of both parents. So now you know the reason you have your father's nose and your mother's feet: At least once in their lives, your parents mingled their genetic material.

Setting the stage

Female humans differ from nearly all the rest of their gender in the animal kingdom because, rather than wanting sexual intercourse only when they can conceive (that is, when they are *in heat),* women can want sexual intercourse at any time (provided they don't have a headache). Despite this difference, female humans do share with other female mammals the trait that enables them to make a baby, or *conceive*, only at certain times — in most cases, from one to three days a month.

Just because a woman is fertile only a few days a month, don't assume that those are the only days that unprotected sexual intercourse can make her pregnant. A woman's reproductive organs are much more complicated than that, as I explain in Chapter 7.

Unlike a man, who continually makes sperm (more than 26 trillion a year!), a woman has all her eggs already inside her at birth. These eggs — about 200,000 of them — reside in a woman's two *ovaries* (see Figure 1-1). About every 28 days, a fluid-filled sac in the ovary, called a *follicle,* releases one of the eggs. When a follicle releases an egg, many women feel a dull ache, known as *mittelschmerz,* in the area around the ovary.

Becoming aware of when mittelschmerz occurs is a good point of reference for anyone practicing *natural family planning.* I talk more about family planning in Chapter 7.

Figure 1-1: The egg begins an incredible journey in search of a sperm to produce a child. No wonder sex has been called "making whoopie"!

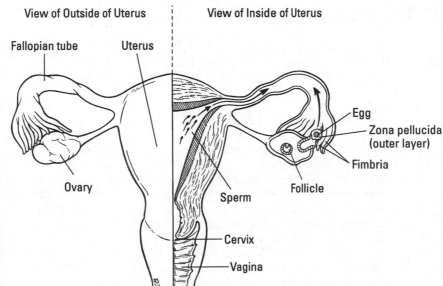

View of Outside of Uterus

View of Inside of Uterus

Fallopian tube   Uterus

Ovary

Sperm

Cervix

Vagina

Egg

Zona pellucida (outer layer)

Fimbria

Follicle

Getting the egg and sperm together

Everyone's talking about what happened last night at Club Fallopian. Mr. Sperm bumped into Ms. Egg, and now they're really stuck on each other!

Just as people have to meet each other before they can form a relationship, the process of fertilization can't begin until a sperm gets up into the *fallopian tubes* and meets the egg. This introduction takes place as a result of *sexual intercourse,* which is defined as a man placing his penis in a woman's vagina. When the man has an orgasm, he releases millions of sperm into the back of the woman's vagina. These sperm bind to the cervical mucus and swim right up through the entrance to the uterus, called the *cervix,* through the uterus itself, and then into the fallopian tubes — each sperm hunting for an egg. And if an egg happens to be floating along, the fastest sperm takes the prize.

You should always keep in mind two very important points about sperm:

 ✔ Sperm can live from two to seven days inside a woman after being ejaculated by the man. So, although the egg may have only a short time during which it can be fertilized (see the quiz earlier in this chapter), sperm that a man deposited in the woman up to a week before can still fertilize the egg and cause pregnancy.

 ✔ Even before a man ejaculates, his penis releases some liquid (called *Cowper's fluid,* because the Cowper's gland produces it), which serves as a lubricant to help the sperm go up the shaft of the penis. Thousands of sperm live inside the Cowper's fluid. Although that number is less than the millions of sperm in the ejaculate, how many sperm does an egg require for fertilization? One fast one.

Because of Cowper's fluid, a man deposits sperm inside a woman's vagina before he has an orgasm. That's why the pull-out, or withdrawal, method does not work as a means of preventing pregnancy.

Going for a ride

Little finger-like appendages on the end of the fallopian tube called *fimbria* lead the egg into the tube, through which it makes its way down into the *uterus.* If, during this trip, the egg encounters some sperm swimming along, then the first sperm to reach the egg and penetrate the hard outer shell, called the *zona pellucida,* will enter the egg and begin the life-creating process called fertilization.

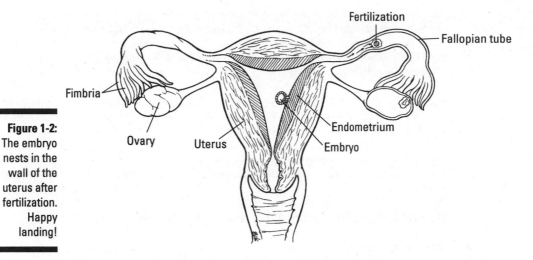

Figure 1-2:
The embryo nests in the wall of the uterus after fertilization. Happy landing!

Labels on figure: Fertilization, Fallopian tube, Fimbria, Ovary, Uterus, Endometrium, Embryo

A fertilized egg continues down the fallopian tube on a journey that takes about three days. During the first 30 hours, the chromosomes of the egg and the sperm merge, and the cells begin to divide. This new entity is called an *embryo*. When the embryo finishes its journey and enters the uterus (see Figure 1-2), it gets nourishment from uterine secretions, and the cells inside it continue to divide, causing the embryo to grow. Approximately six days after fertilization, the egg "hatches," emerging from its hard shell and then burrowing its way into the uterine wall, or *endometrium*.

The embryo releases a hormone called hCG. When the hCG reaches the mother's bloodstream, it signals that she is pregnant and causes the ovaries to continue producing the hormones estrogen and progesterone, which are necessary to maintain the pregnancy.

If the egg is not fertilized, it passes through the uterus. About two weeks later, the uterus sheds its lining, the endometrium, in a process called *menstruation*. A new lining then begins to grow, ready to receive a fertilized egg the next month.

Giving birth

After an embryo burrows its way into the endometrium, it grows until it has a human shape and all its organs — a process that takes about 12 weeks. At this point, the embryo is renamed a *fetus*.

The fetus grows inside the uterus until approximately nine months after the egg was first fertilized. Then, in a process called *giving birth,* a fully formed baby comes out of the uterus and through the vagina into the world (unless doctors have to remove the baby surgically, which is called a *cesarean section,* or c-section).

So an important possible consequence of sexual intercourse is the making of a baby that will be born nine months later. Of course, giving birth to a baby is only the beginning of providing the care a child requires. Having a child is a very big responsibility — not one to be taken lightly, and certainly not one to be ignored when having sexual intercourse.

Making babies makes good sex, too

One more thing about sexual intercourse and its pleasures: As great a feeling as you get when having an orgasm during sexual intercourse, I think that most couples will tell you that they got even more pleasure from the intercourse they had while trying to make a baby. You get an extra kick from knowing that the possible result of this union between two people who love each other is another little human being.

Chapter 2

Tuning the Male Organ

Sexual intercourse occurs whenever a man puts his penis into a woman's vagina. When the penis is in its normal, flaccid state, this feat is difficult (though not impossible) for a man to accomplish. However, when the penis becomes erect and hard, most men learn quite quickly the technique of inserting the penis into the vagina — sometimes too quickly (for more about that, see Chapter 20). This chapter is all about how and why a man gets an erection.

The Penis: Inside and Out

How a man gets an erection is relatively, ahem, straightforward. But to fully understand the process, you need to first examine a man's basic apparatus: his penis.

The three sponges (Not Larry, Curly, and Moe)

Basically, a penis is composed of three structures (see Figure 2-1), which are made of a sponge-like material that can fill with blood.

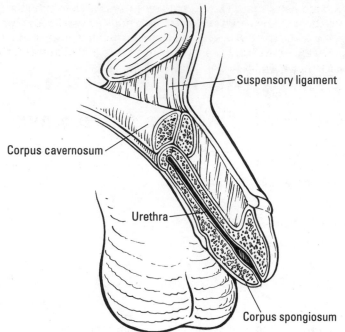

Suspensory ligament

Corpus cavernosum

Urethra

Figure 2-1:
The penis:
not as
simple as
it looks!

Corpus spongiosum

> ✔ The two *corpus cavernosa* contain the central arteries and lie on the top half of the penis. They are cylindrical tubes and are larger than the other spongy structure.
>
> ✔ The *corpus spongiosum*, which is under the two *corpus cavernosa* and which surrounds the *urethra*, is the pipeline for both urine and sperm.

When a man becomes excited — and I'm not talking about watching his team score the winning touchdown here — the nerves surrounding his penis become active, causing the muscles around the arteries to relax and more blood to flow into the penis. The sponge-like material then absorbs the additional blood, making the penis stiff and hard, or *erect*. This erection tightens the veins so that the blood cannot leave the penis, enabling the penis to remain erect.

At the base of the penis, the two corpus cavernosa split to form a Y, where the two ends connect to the pubic bone. This ligament controls the angle of the erect penis. I get many questions from men, each asking me if something is wrong with him because the angle of his erect penis is not straight out, parallel to the floor. I tell all of them not to go hanging any weights in an effort to change the angle, because they have nothing to worry about!

Penises become erect at all different angles — and the angle doesn't have any effect on the way the penis performs. As a man gets older, the ligament at the base of his penis stretches, and the angle changes. A man of 70, for example, may have an erection that points downward instead of upward, the way a young man's erection does.

At the head of the class: The glans

The head of the penis, called the *glans,* is shaped like a cone (see Figure 2-2). The opening of the glans is called the *meatus,* and at the base of the glans is a crown-like structure called the *corona.*

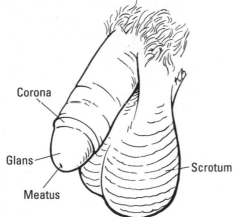

Figure 2-2: The glans brings it all to a head.

Corona

Glans

Meatus

Scrotum

The glans serves several purposes:

- ✔ The glans is a little thicker than the rest of the penis, particularly around the corona. This extra thickness serves as a seal to keep the ejaculated semen inside the vagina, near the cervix, after an orgasm. This is nature's way of making sure that the chances for fertilization are high. The glans also contains the greatest number of nerve endings.

- ✔ The glans also creates extra friction, which, in this case, produces "good vibrations" that help promote ejaculation.

- ✔ Men aren't the only ones who benefit from the glans. With all the thrusting of the penis inside the vagina that goes on during intercourse, the woman's cervix may get damaged if it weren't for the glans, which acts as a shock absorber.

For all you ladies, I suggest that the next time you see your lover's glans you give it the proper thank you it deserves. I leave the choice of how to do this up to you.

The foreskin: A real cover-up

At birth, the glans is covered by the foreskin, a sheath of skin that opens at the top. In an infant, this opening is very tight and usually cannot be pulled back (or *retracted,* to use the medical term). Usually, the foreskin loosens up as the baby grows older. When a male has an erection, the foreskin pulls back entirely to fully reveal the glans. The skin of the glans is very sensitive, and the purpose of the foreskin is to protect it.

In the Jewish and Muslim cultures, the foreskin is always surgically removed in a procedure called *circumcision.* Circumcision has also become popular in many Western societies because the penis is easier to keep clean without the foreskin. Because of today's better hygiene, some parents and physicians believe that circumcision is no longer necessary, although the debate is not entirely over. Figure 2-3 shows the difference in appearance between an uncircumcized and a circumcized penis.

Figure 2-3:
The penis on the right is uncircumcized, while the one shown on the left is circumcized.

Small glands underneath the foreskin secrete an oily, lubricating substance. If these secretions accumulate and mix with dead skin cells, a cottage-cheese-like substance called *smegma* forms. In an uncircumcised man, this smegma can build up and lead to infections and, sometimes, even more serious diseases. An uncircumcised man should always take special precautions when bathing to pull back the foreskin and clean carefully around the glans.

If a man happens to be bathing with a friend, pulling back the foreskin may be a pleasurable task for him to assign to his partner. Some women, who've seen the piles of dirty laundry stuffed into a corner of a bachelor's apartment, have general doubts about the personal hygiene of the average male. This can be one reason that they avoid performing oral sex. If oral sex is something that a man wants, but his partner has avoided, having his partner make sure that his penis is absolutely clean may be one way of changing her mind. Even if it doesn't change her mind, at least he'll have a very clean penis.

Circumcision and sexual performance

Because the skin of the glans of a circumcised male grows tougher and less sensitive than that of an uncircumcised male, people often wonder whether circumcision affects sexual performance.

Some men who aren't circumcised believe that, because their skin is more sensitive, they are more likely to have premature ejaculation. I've even been asked by adult men if they should be circumcised to cure them of this problem. (Because premature ejaculation is a learning disability that you can overcome — see Chapter 20 — I don't recommend having this surgery performed later in life.)

I also get asked by men who have been circumcised if a way exists to replace their foreskin. These men feel that, because the skin of the glans has been toughened, they are missing out on certain pleasures. I tell them that, as long as they are having orgasms, this is not something that they should be worrying about.

Size and sexual performance

Of course, when considering the penis, what concerns a great many men the most is the size of their sexual organ. They think that bigger is better.

Because men are more likely to get turned on by what they see, physical appearance is very important to them. That's why men are so concerned about penis size — just as they are concerned about the size of women's breasts. To men, the more there is of a body part that attracts them, the better. (Sadly, thighs, which all women seem able to enlarge with ease, no longer fall into this category. Where is Rubens, who painted such magnificent, voluptuous nude women, when we need him?)

Now, if men asked women how they feel about penis size, they'd get another story. Some women are actually frightened by very big penises, and many women just don't attach very much importance to the issue. But these men who are all hung up about the size of their penises can't seem to get that straight — and, because many of them are also stubborn, convincing them otherwise is a difficult job.

Measuring up

You can measure a penis in several different ways, and a man usually chooses the method that makes his penis seem the biggest. Although the basic penis measurements are length and circumference, the mood of your penis at the moment you pull out that tape measure is a key factor.

Even if two flaccid penises look about the same size, they may be very different in size when they become erect. (And a man may have different-sized erections depending on how aroused he is.) In the locker room, the man with the biggest flaccid penis feels the most cocky; but the real proving ground is in the bedroom.

One of the reasons that a man may think his penis is too small is the way he looks at it. (And no, I'm not going to suggest that he put on rose-colored glasses.) Most of the time, he looks down at his penis, and when he does that his eyes play a trick on him called *foreshortening,* the result of which is that his penis looks smaller than it appears to someone else looking at it. To see his penis the way his partner does, all he has to do is stand in front of a full-length mirror and take in that view — I think he'll be surprised. If he takes a look both before and after he has an erection, I'm sure his ego will get a nice boost.

Although you can't deny that men have different-sized penises, does the size of the penis make any difference where it really counts — inside the woman's vagina? In most cases, the answer is a very big no — the size of the penis makes no difference inside a woman's vagina.

The vagina is elastic; it has to be to allow babies to be born vaginally. So a woman's vagina can accommodate a big or a small penis. Because most of a woman's nerve endings are concentrated at the entrance to the vagina, the sensations that a bigger penis may cause aren't all that different to her from those caused by a smaller penis.

Obviously, if a man has a minuscule penis, a woman may not feel it very much, which is a slight problem. But, as Chapter 11 explains, most women need direct clitoral stimulation to achieve an orgasm. Because no penis can do that trick while performing intercourse, the issue of size becomes even less important.

Men ask me all the time if some way exists to make their penises bigger. I know of only one way to do this, and I'm passing it on only because it actually also promotes good health. Although most of the penis is visible, part of the penis is buried beneath the skin and is called the *crus.* If a man has a lot of fat in his pubic area, then more of the length of the penis is buried beneath the skin. With weight loss, a man can reverse this trend so that a greater portion of the penis becomes exposed; thus, his penis can "grow." The approximation doctors use is one inch of penis length gained for every 30 pounds of excess weight lost. (Sorry to all you skinny guys, but losing extra weight won't help you.)

Some surgical techniques can enlarge a man's penis. One technique can make most of it, except for the head, fatter, which leaves the head looking disproportionate. The other technique makes the penis longer, but requires the doctors to cut certain ligaments so that the penis does not point as high as before, which can cause the man to lose sensitivity. These side effects, as well as other risks, greatly reduce the value of these procedures, which is why very few surgeons perform them. In my estimation, the risks make such surgery not even worth considering. If you are intent on learning more of the gory details, however, make an appointment with a urologist.

Getting direction

The proportion of crus (penis under the skin) to exposed penis can cause variations in the direction that a penis points during an erection. Men with a shorter crus, and thus a longer penis, are more likely to have an erection that points downward, while an erect penis that has a longer crus will probably point outward, or even straight up.

Frank

When Frank came to see me, we spent half an hour talking without broaching the real reason for his visit. He admitted that he didn't go out with women, but he blamed that on all sorts of things that didn't make sense to me. I could feel that more was bothering him than he was letting on, and I told him straight out that I thought he wasn't being truthful with me. That's when he told me that he was afraid of dating women because, if he got close enough to them to have sex, they would notice that his penis was misshapen.

Because I am not a medical doctor, I do not examine patients, but I did ask him to describe for me what his penis looked like. He said that, when he had an erection, instead of sticking straight out, as did the erect penises he'd seen in some porno films, his penis had a very large curve in it. To me, his description seemed to be within the bounds of normalcy, but I sent him to a urologist to make sure.

When I next saw him, he was a new man. The urologist had confirmed what I had thought, and knowing that he wasn't going to be made fun of gave him the confidence to start dating. The next time I heard from Frank, about a year later, he called to tell me that he was engaged.

Occasionally, a man tells me that he is concerned because his penis points in a certain direction when it is erect. As you can see from Frank's situation, this phenomenon is not unusual. Some men have a more pronounced curve than others, and sometimes the penis also bends to the left or to the right.

Because I am not a medical doctor, my first piece of advice if you feel that your penis has an abnormal shape is to go to a urologist to make certain that this curvature doesn't indicate some problem.

In the vast majority of cases, the curve falls well within the norms of most men, and the concern is just a case of sexual ignorance. In other words, the man did not know that most penises are curved to some extent. Once in a while, a man does have a more pronounced curve than most. Even the majority of these men don't have a problem in bed, although a few may have to adjust the positions that they use. In some cases, however, a man may have *Peyronie's disease,* a condition that can make sex impossible (although, rest assured, in most cases the disease goes away on its own after a short while, as I discuss in Chapter 20).

In any case, this problem is mostly in the minds of the men who come to me with concerns about the appearance of their erect penises. Because they believe that their penises look unusual, they are afraid to date. They worry that, when the time comes to undress, their partner will react negatively.

You have one simple way to avoid worrying about how a new partner will react to the shape of your penis, and this applies to the vast majority of other doubts that people have about their sexual abilities: Wait until you have established a strong relationship before you have sex with somebody. I don't say you have to get married, but you will find the experience of making love much better if you are in love and you integrate sex as an expression of your love rather than as a form of recreation.

So, whether your penis looks like a boomerang or is straight as an arrow, remember that the three little words "I love you" are far more important to your lover than the direction in which your penis points.

Getting on Better Terms with Your Testicles

Although a man may not understand the inner workings of his penis, outwardly, he is at least on somewhat good terms with that part of his anatomy. But, when it comes to testicles, too many men know almost nothing about them.

Be forewarned: By the time you've finished with this chapter, you will not only be seeing testicles differently, you'll also be feeling them in a whole new way.

Making the descent

As a baby boy develops inside his mother's womb, his testicles are still inside his body. During that last few months before birth, the testicles poke their way outside, or descend, into the *scrotum,* a sac of skin located at the base of the penis. Occasionally, one or both of the testicles don't make the descent.

Some of these undescended testicles are of the hide-and-seek variety, meaning that, during the first year or so, they kind of come and go. As long as they make an occasional appearance, everything will be just fine, and eventually they'll get up the courage to stay where they belong.

A testicle that remains inside the body will not function properly because the temperature will be too warm. A boy who has this problem may also be embarrassed by his appearance. For these reasons, medical intervention is usually called for, which may be a type of hormonal therapy but more likely will involve surgery.

Manufacturing hormones

In addition to testicles' vital role in the continuation of the species, men require functioning testicles for the hormones they produce, most importantly testosterone. *Testosterone* is called the "male hormone," and that name truly fits. If a boy is born without testosterone, his scrotum forms as the outer lips of a vagina and his penis as something akin to a clitoris.

Even if only one of a boy's testicles fails to form properly, a partially developed uterus and fallopian tube will develop inside him. This is because he will not have enough of another hormone normally released by that testicle, *MIS*, which inhibits the growth of female organs.

Producing sperm

Despite the fact that a variety of contraceptive methods have allowed people to disconnect sexual intercourse from reproduction, the main purpose of having sex, from an evolutionary point of view, is still to make babies. But, although the penis is required to penetrate the woman's vagina for the best chance at success, the man needs seeds to place within her to accomplish this important task. These seeds, called *spermatozoa* (or more often by their nickname, sperm), are manufactured in the testicles.

Sperm are rather amazing little creatures. They are the only parts of the body that do their work outside of it. You see, sperm don't survive well at high temperatures, particularly the temperature inside our bodies. This is why the testicles lie outside the body where they can be cooled by the soft summer breezes (at least for those of you who favor kilts or loincloths).

For the sperm to be successful at their task of making babies, they have to overcome many obstacles after making a long journey. You may well recognize their final shape — an oval head with a long tail that helps to propel them along — but sperm do not start out that way (see Figure 2-4).

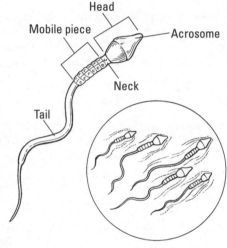

Figure 2-4:
The sperm: hydro-dynamic, a good swimmer, and a heckuva guy.

From humble beginnings

Early in their life cycles, sperm are called germ cells. (In this case I think most people would have preferred a nice, long Latin name; but rest assured, these cells have nothing to do with what we commonly associate the word germ.)

Germ cells are produced in the *seminiferous tubules,* which are long, spaghetti-like tubes that are connected to each other, packed into a tight ball, and surrounded by a tough membrane. This package is called — drumroll, please — a *testicle.* (Between these tubes are cells that produce the male hormone testosterone.) As the germ cells travel along the tubes, slowly but surely they turn into sperm.

Their metamorphosis complete, the sperm leave the testicle and head for the *epididymis* on their way to the *vas deferens.* (If you haven't already done so, at this point I strongly suggest you look at Figure 2-5, because you may get lost without a map, and you can't stop at a gas station to ask for *these* directions.)

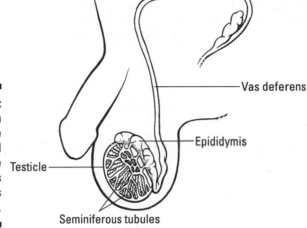

Figure 2-5:
The sperm
leave the
testicle and
head for the
epididymis
and vas
deferens.

Vas deferens

Epididymis

Testicle

Seminiferous tubules

Meiosis: Small division

Now that you've had a chance to look at the diagram and can picture in your mind's eye the journey that the spermatozoa take, I have to tell you about one more important transformation that they make.

All our cells have the complete code of genetic material, called *DNA* (the long term is deoxyribonucleic acid, but DNA is much easier to say), unique to each individual. But while the germ cells start out with all this DNA, along the way they undergo a process called *meiosis* (pronounced "my-*oh*-sis"). Here are some of the important effects of meiosis:

✔ When a germ cell undergoes meiosis, it forms two new cells, each of them having only half of the DNA code: 23 bits of genetic material (called *chromosomes*) instead of the normal 46.

When a sperm teams up with a female egg, which also only has 23 chromosomes, their genetic materials intertwine, and the resulting baby ends up with a package containing a total of 46 chromosomes that is a mixture of both the mother and the father.

✔ When the male germ cells divide, the sex chromosomes divide also. The male has one X and one Y chromosome; the female has two X chromosomes.

Whether the sperm that reaches the egg first has an X (female) or Y (male) chromosome determines whether the baby will be a girl or a boy.

All you macho men out there may appreciate knowing one more thing about a *spermatozoon* (a single, fully developed sperm; spermatozoa is the plural): Not only can sperm move around on their own outside the body, but they're also fully armed, like little guided missiles. Over the head of the sperm lies the *acrosome,* which is full of enzymes that help the sperm penetrate an egg if it should be so lucky as to meet one on its journey.

When they're ready, the sperm leave the *testes* (another name for testicles) and enter the epididymis, which is a series of tiny tubes that lie on top of the testes. (For those of you into amazing statistics: If unfurled, these tubes would reach 60 feet in length.) During their journey through the epididymis, sperm learn to swim. They enter the epididymis with useless tails and leave it as little speed demons.

Vas deferens

If you go back to Figure 2-5, you see that the sperm's next stop on their voyage is the *vas deferens,* a tube that ejects the sperm into the urethra. In the urethra, the sperm are mixed with fluids from the seminal vesicles and the prostate; then they make their way out into the world through ejaculation.

The combination of these fluids and the sperm is called *semen.* The amount of semen ejaculated during sexual intercourse is generally around a teaspoonful, though it varies depending on when the man last ejaculated. The semen is whitish in color, has a distinctive smell, and is thick when it first comes out. Sperm only comprise about 5 to 10 percent of the volume, but they are the only part of the semen that can cause pregnancy.

Too few sperm (male infertility)

Just because your testicles look normal does not mean that they are fully functioning. If a couple tries to conceive but can't seem to do it, one of the first things that doctors look for is a problem with the man's sperm. The most common problems are a low sperm count (which means that the man is not producing enough sperm) or the sperm he is producing lack sufficient *motility*, the ability to swim to the egg. The basis for the problems may be abnormal sperm production, which can be difficult to treat, or a blockage somewhere along the line, which may be corrected through surgery.

Interestingly enough, most semen analysis is done by *gynecologists*, specialists in the female reproductive system. A gynecologist is usually the first person that a woman consults when she has problems getting pregnant. Commonly, the gynecologist asks that the man's sperm be analyzed. Then, if the tests reveal a problem with the sperm, the man is sent to a urologist for further evaluation.

Why boys wear cups

Despite the fact that so many men adopt a tough guy, macho image, the heart of their maleness, the testicles, is highly sensitive. The testicles are so sensitive that men may experience some pain down there just by thinking about the pain that occurs when their testicles are struck by an object.

If a boy has never had the sensations caused by a blow to the scrotum, then he may not see the need to wear a cup over his groin area when playing rough sports. But no man who has suffered this agony would hesitate for a minute to protect himself with a cup.

At risk for testicular cancer

Even though the testicles are easily accessible, most men don't pay all that much attention to them (apart from trying to protect them from getting kicked). That can prove unfortunate, because testicular cancer can be deadly if you don't find it in time. Although rare, testicular cancer most often appears in men from ages 15 to 35. In fact, it is the most common form of cancer in men in their twenties and thirties. Luckily, the disease is also easily curable — if a man finds it in time.

Because the testicles are outside the body and available for examination, men can easily feel testicular cancer if it is present. And the best news is that, because the testicles are so accessible, men can spare themselves the trouble of going to a doctor for the examination (as we women must do with cervical cancer) by examining their testicles themselves.

Check for lumps

Testicular cancer usually begins as a painless lump. The sooner you find such a lump, the better your chances of having it dealt with without any serious medical consequences.

To check for lumps:

- ✔ Gently take each testicle and roll it between your thumb and forefinger to see if you detect anything different about it than the way it felt the last time.
- ✔ Your testicle should feel smooth and firm with a slight softness, a lot like a grape.
- ✔ As a guide, compare your two testicles to each other.
- ✔ If you do find something that feels different, pick up the phone right away and make an appointment to see a urologist.
- ✔ Do this test once a month.

Remember that the epididymis sits on top of the testicle. Some men examining themselves for testicular cancer mistake it for a strange lump. They get a real fright before a doctor explains to them what it is. So what you need to have clear in your mind is that you are checking your testicle — the hard ball. The lumpy epididymis, which lies on top of the testicle, belongs there and is supposed to be lumpy.

Testicular cancer can hit any man, but men who had one or both undescended testicles at birth (see "Making the descent" earlier in the chapter) are at higher risk. So if either or both of your testicles had not descended when you were born, make doubly sure that you perform this exam.

Sometimes a minor injury to the groin area may cause some swelling. This swelling can mask the presence of an undetected cancerous growth. This is why a monthly checkup is necessary — so you know what's normal for you from month to month, and what's not.

I know that many of you are squeamish about medical things, particularly when it comes to something in your genital area. But this testing is important so please don't be lax about it. Early detection and immediate medical attention are the keys for successful treatment.

If you really don't like the idea of examining yourself, and if you have a partner, maybe you can ask her to complete this exercise. I don't know if she'll like doing it any better than you would, but you both may profit from the side effects.

Testicular pain

Men don't usually talk about private matters (especially when the matter pertains to anything hanging between their legs), but feeling a twinge of pain from time to time in the scrotum is quite common. If a man experiences this sort of pain and it disappears after a minute or two, he doesn't have to worry. On the other hand, if he has any continuous pain, then he should go to see a urologist immediately.

The Prostate Gland

In addition to their testicles, another problem area that men should have checked — and all too often don't — is the *prostate*. The prostate gland, located below the man's bladder, produces some of the fluids that are contained in the semen, giving semen its whitish color. The urethra, through which semen and urine pass, runs through the prostate, and any disease affecting the prostate can affect the urethra.

Checking the prostate

As a man ages, his prostate gland commonly becomes enlarged and causes him to urinate more frequently. This problem, called *prostatitis*, is bothersome but not dangerous. However, the prostate also has a nasty habit of becoming cancerous, which can be quite dangerous, though it is easily treated if discovered in time.

The way a doctor checks the prostate for changes that can signify a cancerous growth is simply to palpate, or touch, it. So that his doctor can get to the prostate, a man has to bend over and allow the doctor to stick his or her fingers in the man's rectum while, at the same time, the doctor presses outside the rectum. This way, the doctor can actually feel the prostate gland.

Although I don't necessarily blame any man for not wanting to rush off to the doctor to be examined in this manner, a prostate examination is no worse than the gynecological visits we women have to go through regularly, so I won't accept any excuses for not doing it. Now, if you're really interested, you can speak to your doctor about a blood test that may reduce the odds of your having to undergo the actual physical exam. But because regular prostate exams can save your life, I absolutely recommend that you not put them off.

Treating the prostate

Doctors have various treatments for prostate conditions, some of which have side effects that impair sexual functioning. Some medications used to treat either an enlarged or a cancerous prostate can reduce sexual desire. Surgical removal of part or all of the prostate is another measure that can be taken, which also has potential side effects.

The most common form of surgery for an enlarged prostate is called a *transurethral resection of the prostate* (TURP). Approximately five to ten percent of men who are operated on experience impotence following the surgery, and 80 to 100 percent experience something called *retrograde ejaculation*. This means that, during ejaculation, the semen flows backwards into the bladder instead of out of the penis. This condition does not affect a man's ability to have an orgasm, so some men find that retrograde ejaculation does not bother them; others report sex to be less pleasant because of the lack of fluid. Retrograde ejaculation definitely poses a problem if the man is trying to impregnate a woman; in that case, artificial insemination may be necessary.

Because the various treatments for prostate problems, particularly surgery, can leave a man with *erectile dysfunction* (inability to have an erection), many men avoid going to the doctor when they first sense that something may be wrong. Of course the condition will only worsen, and by the time they do go for treatment, it may be too late. Luckily, thanks to the drug Viagra, men who have prostate problems may be able to regain their ability to have erections even after surgery. I discuss Viagra in Chapter 20. While I certainly applaud this breakthrough in terms of sexual functioning, it would please me even more if it meant that more men would go to the doctor earlier so that they could undergo successful treatment.

Chapter 3

Demystifying the Female Parts

- -

In This Chapter

▶ Taking a tour of the female anatomy

▶ Understanding the "men" words

▶ Promoting good breast health

- -

*O*n the subject of our genitals, we women face a conundrum (no, that is not a new sexual term; it just means a puzzle). On the one hand, because our reproductive organs are for the most part hidden away, women in general don't have the same type of familiar relationship that a man has with his apparatus. Some women even try their best to ignore their genitals. They touch themselves as little as possible and never really look between their legs.

On the other hand, these hidden organs have a way of making themselves known with a certain regularity so that, try as we may, they are impossible to totally ignore. And women have good reasons not to ignore these organs:

✔ One of the ways that a woman's apparatus can suddenly interrupt things is if she becomes pregnant. The fact that more than a million teenage women a year in the United States alone have unintended pregnancies is proof that too many women still do not know all that they should about how their bodies work.

✔ Another reason for women and men to become better informed about the female anatomy is that understanding our bodies is certainly key to good sexual functioning, which is the primary purpose of this book.

✔ Understanding female anatomy is important for having a healthy outlook toward women. The idea that a woman's genitals are in some foreign, dank place — the black hole of Calcutta is one name used for it — denigrates not only a woman's genitals but her status as a human being as well.

Although these parts are private in our society because they relate to an individual, I can see no need to keep their general nature private as well.

So whether you are a female or a male, I'm going to make sure that you no longer face a mystery when you contemplate a woman's genitals. Instead, I am going to imprint a topographical map in your brain that you will never forget.

If you're a woman reading this, you have a definite advantage because you can examine yourself. Many women never take the time to look closely at their genitals, and I recommend the practice highly. Because your genitals are not as convenient to view as the male apparatus, you'll need a simple tool: a hand mirror. Take off your clothes and seat yourself someplace where you can spread your legs easily. You can use available light, or, if you're in a dark spot, you can use a flashlight to illuminate the area. I suggest you do some exploring on your own, read the next few pages, and then go back and see if you can identify the various places that I mention.

As far as you guys out there, if you have a partner who's willing, sharing in this experience certainly wouldn't do you any harm, although I have a few words of caution:

- ✔ If your partner has never examined herself before, maybe you should give her some time alone to take this little tour first, because your presence will no doubt be a distraction.

- ✔ When your turn to explore comes around, do your utmost to keep the examination nonsexual, even if you do get aroused (which you probably will). If you can keep the moment on an educational plane, then you have a good opportunity to ask her some questions about how she feels about her genitals, as well as what pleases her and what displeases her when you have sex.

If, after the grand tour is over, you're both so aroused that you need to have sex, then be my guest — but only if you promise to put to use what you just learned and not go back to doing the same old thing.

All Those Latin Terms

Certainly my job would be easier if the medical world didn't use so many Latin terms, which I then have to explain to you — especially because I never took Latin. But because those words apply here, I suggest that you look at Figure 3-1 before embarking on this journey into the female anatomy. That way, you'll have a better feel for what I'm describing as we proceed, and you won't get lost on some side road.

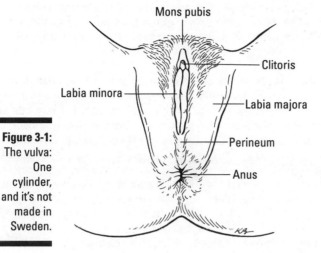

Mons pubis

Clitoris

Labia minora

Labia majora

Perineum

Anus

Figure 3-1:
The vulva:
One
cylinder,
and it's not
made in
Sweden.

The part of the female genitals that you can see is called the *vulva,* which lies between the mons pubis and the anus. The *mons pubis* (also called mons veneris, which in Latin stands for "mound of Venus") is a layer of fatty tissue that lies above the pubic bone, basically acting as a bumper. That part of the female is easily identified because it's covered with pubic hair. The anus is . . . oh, you know what an anus is because, whichever sex you are, you have one.

Viva the vulva

The vulva has large outer lips called the *labia majora* (which is Latin for, you guessed it, large outer lips). Inside these lips are

- the *labia minora* (smaller inner lips)
- the *clitoris* (a woman's most sensitive spot)
- the *urethra* (from which urine is passed)
- and the *vestibule* (not a place to hang your hat and coat)

The vestibule is the actual entrance to the vagina and is covered by a membrane called the *hymen.* When a woman is aroused, the *vestibular bulbs,* which lie underneath, swell with blood and become engorged, somewhat like a penis — which only makes sense, because they are made from the same spongy tissue as the penis.

Whether you're looking at Figure 3-1 or the real thing right now, remember that not all vulvas look alike. In the same way that you'll encounter different models of Volvos, you'll come across many different shaped vulvas as well — but they will all take you where you want to go.

In the early weeks of a baby's formation, when it is still an embryo, the male and female genitals look basically the same because many of the same tissues form both the male and female genitals. For example, the tissues that form the *labia majora* in the female are the same tissues that form the *scrotum* in the male. Upon completion, however, these genitals end up taking different forms. (And a good thing, too.)

The labia majora are made up of two rounded mounds of tissue that form the outer boundaries of the vulva (see Figure 3-2). After puberty, hair grows on them, as well as on the mons pubis. The skin of the labia majora is usually darker than the surrounding skin of the thighs. Within the majora are the smaller *labia minora*. They surround the vestibule and are hairless. The labia minora join at the top to form the *prepuce,* or clitoral hood.

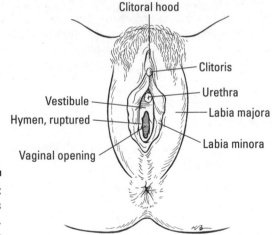

Figure 3-2:
The innards
of the vulva.

Inside the vestibule are the *Bartholin's glands,* whose secretions serve as one of a woman's natural lubricants during intercourse (although the major source of a woman's lubrication comes through the walls of the vagina, as I discuss later in this chapter). These secretions are also an indication that the woman has become aroused, similar to the male's erection. As a woman ages, the glands begin to shrink and secrete less fluid. For this reason, an older woman must often use a lubricant to help keep the area moist during intercourse.

Where the upper ends of the labia minora meet lies the *clitoris,* the principal organ of female sexual pleasure. Pea sized, the clitoris develops from the same tissue as does the penis. Also like the penis, the clitoris has a shaft and a head (glans) and gets engorged with blood during sexual excitement and grows, though certainly not to the extent that a penis does. The clitoris has many nerve endings and is a very erogenous organ, critical to a woman's attaining an orgasm. (See Chapter 11 for more on attaining orgasms.)

Though a lot smaller in size, the clitoris has about the same number of nerve endings as a penis, which is why many women cannot tolerate direct stimulation of the clitoris but prefer to have the area over the hood and the mons pubis stimulated instead.

The clitoris, like the penis, can accumulate *smegma* — a combination of secretions, skin cells, and bacteria — under the clitoral hood. You should be careful to clean this area thoroughly. If too much smegma accumulates, you may have to ask your gynecologist to do a thorough cleaning.

Below the clitoris is the entrance to the urethra, out of which urine flows. The urethra is totally separate from the vagina, into which the penis is inserted during intercourse. Some men, and possibly even a few women, don't realize that these are two different openings, which is one of the reasons that they get squeamish about this region. But, as the penis is really too big to fit into the urethra, it should not be a source of concern. And, because urine also comes out of the penis, no man should feel that the vagina is any less clean than its male counterpart. But, if you still feel uncomfortable about this region, you have an easy solution.

If you want to be absolutely sure that both your genitals and your partner's are squeaky clean, make a wash-up of both organs a normal part of your sexual routine. After all, nobody ever died from being too clean.

Urinary tract infections are fairly common in women, and one reason for this is that bacteria can be pushed back inside the urethra during intercourse. Always keep this area clean, being very careful to wipe yourself front to back and not the other way around.

The hymen: Symbol of virginity

The hymen, when intact, was once considered the traditional proof of a woman's virginity. Her status as a virgin was verified by the bleeding that often occurs when the hymen is first penetrated.

In olden days, the mother of the bride would actually display the bloody sheets after the wedding night to show how pure her daughter had been before her marriage. And, if by some chance the daughter had been slightly impure, some chicken's blood would do — especially because DNA testing hadn't been invented yet.

Today, however, many women break this membrane accidentally prior to their first attempt at sexual intercourse, either by inserting a tampon or while performing vigorous activities, such as bicycle riding. In the vast majority of cases, even an intact hymen has perforations so that menstrual blood can pass through, but some women are born without these perforations and a doctor must pierce the hymen. (By the way, the fact that a woman has broken her hymen before she's had sexual intercourse doesn't change her status as a virgin. Only through actual intercourse can she change that standing.)

The vagina: The main thoroughfare

What makes women different from men is that much of our sexual apparatus is on the inside — most notably, the *vagina*. The vagina itself is a hollow, muscular tube which extends from the external opening at the vestibule all the way to the cervix, which is the entrance to the uterus.

An adult woman's vagina is about 3 to 4 inches long but also extremely flexible. During intercourse, the vagina stretches to accommodate the penis. When a woman gives birth, the vagina stretches even more, becoming part of the birth canal through which the baby passes on its way into the world. When a vagina has neither a penis nor a baby in it, it collapses like an empty balloon.

The vagina does not go straight back, but usually angles upward. (Some women have a tipped vagina, which angles downward, but this condition is not common.) Some women, not aware of the angle, have a difficult time inserting a tampon because they think it should go straight back, which it can't.

The walls of the vagina have several layers (see Figure 3-3). The first is the *mucosa,* or vaginal lining. The mucosa is very thick and has many folds. It responds to the woman's hormonal changes by secreting various types of fluids. Under the mucosa are a muscular layer and a layer of connective tissue (the *adventitia*) that are rich in blood.

Beneath the vagina, on the pelvic floor, are other muscles that are responsible for keeping the vagina elevated, tight, and firm. Women can do Kegel exercises, which I talk about in Chapter 11, to help tone these muscles.

Speaking of working out, sometimes when a woman exercises or has intercourse, the action can force air into the vagina. When the woman changes position, the air goes back out, producing a sound as if she were passing gas. This occurrence is common and should not cause any embarrassment.

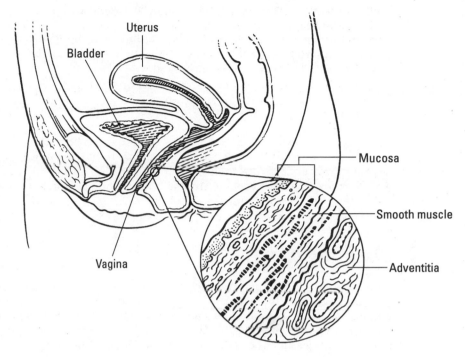

Figure 3-3:
Lubricating
fluids
and an
enveloping
fullness
come from
the vaginal
walls to
enhance
sexual
pleasure.

During sexual excitement, a woman experiences several physical changes:

- ✔ The vaginal lips and clitoris swell.

- ✔ The nipples on her breasts become erect.

- ✔ The vaginal walls fill with blood in a process called *vasocongestion,*
   which is similar to the way blood flows into the penis during erection.

The vagina becomes lubricated by the passage of fluids through the vaginal
walls. This lubrication is not manufactured by a gland, but occurs when fluid
filters into the vagina from blood vessels surrounding it. The vasocongestion
causes increased pressure which, in turn, causes the fluid within the blood
serum to be pushed through the tissues of the vaginal wall.

This fluid has another function besides making it easier for the penis to slide
in and out of the vagina. It also changes the chemical nature of the vagina,
making it more alkaline and less acidic, an environment that proves more
hospitable to sperm.

In most mammals, the female does not provide any lubrication; instead, the
male secretes the lubricant, similar to what the Cowper's gland in human
males produces, but in much greater quantities. Researchers have noted that,
when males of certain species, such as horses, get aroused, a steady stream
of this fluid flows out of the penis.

The vagina goes through several changes in a woman's life.

- Before puberty, the vaginal walls are thinner and the vaginal tube is smaller, which is one reason that so much damage can be done to a young girl who is sexually molested.

- During puberty, the vagina grows, and hormones cause other changes to take place. The vagina becomes elevated, firm, and erect when a woman becomes sexually aroused.

- After menopause (which I explain very soon, so be patient), a woman's hormonal levels go down, and the vaginal tissue becomes more fragile and less elastic. A woman's natural lubrication also declines at this time. Luckily, you have ways to treat all these problems so that they don't affect good sexual functioning.

At your cervix

At the top of the vagina is the *cervix,* which is the entrance to the uterus. The cervix is actually the lower portion of the uterus, and it protrudes approximately one-third of an inch into the vagina. The cervix produces a special mucus that changes according to the woman's *menstrual cycle* — the monthly process of releasing of eggs in preparation for possible pregnancy (see "The 'Men' Words: Menstruation and Menopause," later in this chapter).

- During the first half of the cycle, especially around the time the woman releases the egg (ovulates), her mucus is abundant, clear, and watery. It is quite receptive to sperm penetration and survival, and sperm may live in the mucus for several days.

- After ovulation occurs, the cervical mucus changes dramatically. It becomes thick, cloudy, and sticky, just about impenetrable to sperm trying to pass through the *os,* or opening of the cervix.

Making the cervical mucus impenetrable to sperm is one of the ways that the birth control pill prevents pregnancy. In addition, those practicing natural family planning can test the quality of the mucus as an indicator of fertility (see Chapter 7 for more information on this technique).

The uterus: It stretches, and stretches, and stretches

The *uterus* is about the size of a pear, approximately 3 inches long. A muscular organ, the uterus collapses when empty. Its inner cavity is lined by a tissue called the *endometrium,* which develops and sheds regularly as part of the menstrual cycle. As noted in Chapter 1, menstruation occurs in response to ovarian hormones. The uterus is where the baby develops, and one look at a very pregnant woman tells you that the uterus has the ability to stretch incredibly. Luckily for us women, the uterus also goes back to its regular size after the baby has gone out into the big, wide world — or *we'd* be big and wide forever.

The ovaries and fallopian tubes

Leading into the ovaries are the fallopian tubes, each about 4 inches long (see Figure 3-4). The entrance to these tubes, near the ovary, is fairly large and lined with tiny "fingers," called *fimbria,* which help to guide the eggs released by the ovary down into one of the tubes.

A woman has two ovaries, each about 1½ inches long. The woman's eggs — all 200,000 of them — are stored within the ovaries and then released, usually one at a time, at a signal given by the pituitary gland.

The ovaries also release the female sex hormones, estrogen and progesterone. These hormones act as the triggers for the processes needed to create a baby.

I describe baby-making processes in Chapter 1. If you skipped over that chapter, or maybe even if you didn't, I suggest you go back and read it now. Sex is all about making babies, and that's something you can never know too much about.

Figure 3-4:
The ovaries and fallopian tubes: Where it all starts.

Fallopian tubes

Ovary

Uterus

As far as the role that estrogen and progesterone play in a woman's sexual desire, the evidence seems to tilt away from their having much of a role. Women also produce the male sex hormones, *androgens,* and these may play somewhat of a role, but the evidence is not conclusive.

The "Men" Words: Menstruation and Menopause

I don't know why the two biggest female "problems" start with the prefix "men" — probably a Freudian slip on somebody's part somewhere along the line.

Some women would disagree with my putting the word "problem" in quotes, because they really do think of menstruation and menopause as problems. Because I'm basically an optimist, I refuse to categorize them as such.

Having your period may be inconvenient at times, and some of the aspects of menopause can be annoying, but both processes also have saving graces. I always believe that looking at the glass as half full is better than looking at it as half empty.

Menstruation — Having your period

What can be good about having blood come out of your vagina once a month, you ask?

- ✔ First, because menstruation is part of the process of making babies — and I love babies — the ability to have a child is definitely worth such a small inconvenience.

- ✔ Second, ask any woman who has problems with her menstruation, such as irregular bleeding, and you suddenly discover how nice it is to be able to know approximately when "your friend" will next pay a visit so you can prepare yourself.

- ✔ Third, disruptions in a woman's cycle can serve as an early warning signal of possible health problems, so be aware of your body's regular functioning.

PMS

I suppose that I can't address the topic of menstruation without also addressing premenstrual syndrome (PMS), though I would much prefer not to. Does the onset of menstruation affect women in various physical and psychological ways? I guess that because so many women report that it does, I have to go along with this finding. But it bothers me that some women give in to PMS and use it as an excuse for all sorts of behavior, because men can then use this behavior to justify holding women back.

Now I am not a radical feminist, by any means. I gladly let a man hold a door for me or send me flowers. But I do not endorse any policy that says that a woman can't be given significant responsibilities because of her mood swings. Both sexes have mood swings.

How many men out there have terrible tempers due in part to raging male sex hormones? Do these temper tantrums hold men back? Of course not. So neither should any so-called mood swings hold women back. The only way to make sure that the mood swings don't hold women back is to minimize their effects.

The medical profession has associated more than 150 symptoms with PMS (and you wonder why I think that some exaggerating takes place on this subject!). These include irritation, depression, changes in appetite, abdominal bloating, breast tenderness, poor concentration, insomnia, crying spells, and swelling of the extremities.

PMS occurs during a seven-day period after ovulation and before the menstrual period begins. Some women have only a few symptoms; many may only have these symptoms irregularly, while others get a full-blown PMS attack every month.

No scientific evidence supports any one cause of PMS, although the possible suspected causes include a hormonal deficiency, fluid balance abnormalities, and nutritional deficiencies.

If you suffer from the effects of PMS, I certainly have sympathy for you. But if you use PMS as a reason for not doing your job, you harm all women by making people think that women are not worthy of holding responsibility every day of the month. We certainly need to do more research on this topic, because right now PMS has no proven cause or cure. Until we do learn more and can offer help to those who have PMS, I urge you and every woman to make a strong effort to cope with your symptoms without making life miserable for those around you, especially the men in your life. I believe the time has come for this country to have a woman president, which will never happen if David Letterman and Jay Leno can have a field day poking fun at the candidate's problems with PMS.

Sex and the menses

Now let me come down off my soapbox and talk about sex and menstruation.

I am Jewish, and, for Orthodox Jews, sex is absolutely forbidden while a woman has her period. Many people share this attitude, whether it comes from religious beliefs or just plain squeamishness at the sight of blood.

Ironically, however, many women actually feel more aroused when they have their period, because the pelvic region fills with blood, similar to the flow of blood that occurs in the genitals during sexual arousal.

What if you do feel aroused during your period? No physical reason exists to avoid sex because you're menstruating. You may want to place a towel under you to protect the sheets, and if the man feels strange about having blood on his penis, he can use a condom. But if the urge hits you, you have no reason not to give in to it. Unless your religion forbids it, of course.

Studies show that orgasm can actually relieve some of the discomfort women feel while they are having their period by reducing the feeling of pelvic fullness and cramping.

Although, technically speaking, you should not be able to get pregnant while you're menstruating, Mother Nature sometimes plays tricks on you. You may have some vaginal bleeding that you interpret as the start of your period when it may not be; if you have unprotected intercourse at that time, you may wind up pregnant. If you decide to use natural family planning and rely on your menstrual cycle to plan your sexual activities, then you must keep careful track of your period to avoid making such mistakes.

Now you would think that women feel their sexiest when they are ovulating, because that's when they can become pregnant and hence continue the species. In fact, during ovulation is the only time that females in the rest of the animal kingdom become sexually aroused. Although this heightened arousal may occur in some women, no research has ever found that the condition is widespread, so why this trait has disappeared almost entirely in humans is a mystery.

Menopause — "The change of life"

Menopause is that time in a woman's life when she stops releasing eggs and shedding the lining of her uterus through menstruation. She is no longer fertile and has no more risk of getting pregnant. Although every woman is different, the average American woman hits menopause at 51, so we spend the last third of our lives as postmenopausal women.

Now, if all that happened to women during menopause was that their monthly bout of bleeding stopped, the commercial world would already have made a celebration out of this day, complete with parties and gifts. However, the cessation of ovulation also causes a decrease in the production of the female hormones, estrogen and progesterone, which means menopause has other effects that women sometimes find unsettling.

Easing into menopause

Menopause is not something that occurs suddenly. Usually the changes develop slowly, and the period of change is called the *climacteric.* A woman's period may become irregular and the flow lighter or heavier. The actual length of time for the woman to cease having periods may be one to two years from the start of the climacteric.

However, women may start having hormonal symptoms as many as 10 to 15 years before menopause, and this period of time is known as *perimenopause.* During perimenopause, the egg-producing follicles in a woman's ovaries may become resistant to FSH (follicle stimulating hormone), which is what kicks off ovulation. In an attempt to get those eggs released, the body produces extra FSH, causing a spike in estrogen levels. But because the body produces no normal matching increase in progesterone, rather than a steady decline in hormones, a roller-coaster effect results, which may cause a variety of symptoms including abnormal bleeding, depression, and even *hot flashes* (see later in this section for a further explanation of this symptom).

Abnormal bleeding may cause your gynecologist to order a *D&C (dilation and curettage),* which is an invasive scraping of the uterus. But new techniques using sonograms are now available that can prevent your having to go through a D&C, so talk to your doctor thoroughly before agreeing to any procedure. If your doctor does not have the necessary equipment to perform the new, less invasive procedures, then you may want to find one who does.

Just being aware of perimenopause can bring you great relief, because you'll at least know that you're not going crazy.

A classic symptom of menopause is the *hot flash,* a sudden feeling of heat that takes over the entire body. This can happen at any time of the day or night, and the number of hot flashes and their duration is different for every woman. Because the woman usually also becomes flushed, these hot flashes can be embarrassing, though she certainly has no need to feel embarrassed. Although not every woman experiences hot flashes, the normal duration for this symptom is two years. About 25 percent of women will have hot flashes for a longer period of time if they go untreated. (Skip ahead to the section on hormonal replacement therapy to learn more about the treatment.)

The decrease in hormone production during menopause also causes changes in the vagina and bladder. The vaginal walls thin out, causing vaginal dryness. This dryness, in turn, can cause burning, irritation, and decreased lubrication, which can result in painful intercourse. Similar changes in the bladder can cause a woman to feel the urge to urinate more frequently.

Many women also experience some psychological changes, although these have not been medically proven to be tied to the effects of menopause. They may, in part, be due simply to interruptions in sleeping patterns caused by the hot flashes, or to a woman's reflections on this permanent physical change in her life, which signals the end of youth.

Some harmful side effects of menopause may be *osteoporosis* — a loss of bone strength caused by lower levels of calcium being retained — and possible heart problems.

If you know any families who have two or three children grouped around one age bracket and then another child who arrived ten years later, the odds are that this last child was a "mistake" caused by the onset of menopause. As I said, menopause takes a few years to settle in, and during that time a woman who had regular periods all her life may find that they suddenly become irregular. So if you are of menopausal age and your periods stop for two or three months, don't assume that you won't have any more. You very well may ovulate again, and if you have unprotected sex, then you may find yourself changing diapers at a much later age than you ever intended. Under the medical definition, a woman reaches menopause when she has not had a period for 12 months, so never consider yourself to be into the menopausal years until that period of time has elapsed.

Hormonal replacement therapy

Luckily, medical science has found a way of alleviating many of the symptoms of menopause through estrogen replacement therapy. Studies show that having a woman take estrogen to replace that which she is no longer producing can alleviate many of the symptoms of menopause, as well as protect against certain kinds of cancers, especially cancer of the cervix. But other studies have shown an added risk of breast cancer for some women using hormonal replacement therapy. Any woman beginning menopause should consult her doctor to find out what options are available to her.

Because I'm not a medical doctor, that's all I'm going to say about the physical effects of menopause. (If you're a woman approaching the proper age bracket, I recommend that you go out and buy a book written by a physician solely on this subject or, better yet, ask your gynecologist.) The issue of menopause and sex, however, is a topic that I do cover in Chapter 14. I'll give you a preview of that discussion by saying that my philosophy is a very positive one concerning sex in the later years.

Breasts: Hanging in There

I certainly can't give you a road map to the intimate female anatomy without giving you at least a quick tour of the Alps — or, for some of you, the Appalachians. As you should realize, breast size is of no consequence, except to those men who've spent too much time at Hugh Hefner's knee. Breasts are certainly an erogenous zone, however, and because they do stick out, even while under wraps, they're one part of the body that gets noticed whether you're clothed or not.

Feeding babies

The main purpose of breasts is to feed babies, because after a mother gives birth she *lactates* (that is, makes milk) provided that the baby starts to suck at the nipples. This miraculous process is not only good for the baby's health but also for the mother's, because it gets rid of the excess fat that she accumulated during her pregnancy.

Strangely, for a period of time in the 20th century, Western women gave up the process of feeding their babies from the breast. But more and more women are returning to this method.

If any of you have heard that a mother who is breast-feeding can't get pregnant, think again. Women have a tendency not to ovulate while breast-feeding, but this tendency is not an absolute, as many a woman has discovered too late.

Getting sexual pleasure

The breasts of male and female children are the same. But when a girl reaches puberty, first her nipples and the *aureola,* the darker skin around the nipple, begin to enlarge. As her levels of the hormone progesterone increase, the underlying tissue grows, producing a full breast.

The nipples hold a concentration of nerve endings, and most women's nipples get erect when they become aroused. As an erogenous zone, a woman's breasts serve both the male and the female; men get excited by looking at and fondling breasts, but women also enjoy the sensations.

Many women who masturbate fondle their own breasts and nipples.

Checking for breast cancer

The bulk of the breast is composed of fatty tissue. Because our bodies often store any toxins that we absorb in fatty tissues, the breasts are a common cancer site for women.

One woman in nine will develop breast cancer in the United States. Because of this risk, every woman must examine her breasts once a month. Figure 3-5 shows one technique of checking your breasts for signs of cancer.

Figure 3-5:
Regularly examining your breasts for signs of cancer is an important part of staying healthy.

Remaining consistent about the time of the month you conduct this examination is important because your breasts do change as you go through your menstrual cycle. The most accurate time to check is during or just after your period. By examining your breasts at the same point in your cycle, you can make a more accurate comparison.

When checking your breasts, you are looking for anomalies — things that feel strange — basically a lump of some sort. If you find something, don't panic. Most lumps are not at all dangerous, but you should consult with your physician as soon as possible. And if what you find is an early sign of cancer, be thankful that you did locate it early because, in most cases, it is easily treatable.

You should also have regular breast examinations by a health professional, who may detect something that you would miss, and go for a mammogram whenever your physician instructs you to do so. The older you are, the more important these exams become, and the more regular they should be. After a woman turns 40 she should definitely go once a year (though some say that waiting until you're 50 to begin getting tested is okay), and that rule applies to even younger women if they are in a high risk group. You may be in a high risk group if

✔ you have a family history of breast cancer.

✔ you have never been pregnant.

✔ you had your first child after age 30.

✔ you began menstruating before the age of 12.

✔ you're obese.

✔ you eat a high-fat diet.

✔ you've already had cancer in one breast.

Check with your doctor to determine the best regimen for you.

Be proud of your breasts

Whatever the size of your breasts, they can provide pleasure to both you and your partner. Although small breasts may not get much recognition when you cover them with clothes, after you uncover them in front of a man, he probably won't care about your cup size. So never feel ashamed of your breasts, but flaunt them at the appropriate moment so that they get their due.

Chapter 4

Teenage Sex: What It's All About

● ●

In This Chapter

▶ Coping with changes

▶ Forming friendships and beyond

▶ Discovering your sexual identity

▶ Valuing your family

● ●

1 recently received a letter from a high school senior who was going off to college. He knew that I lectured to college students, and he wanted to know what changes, if any, I'd seen among this group of young people over the years.

My answer to him was that I have seen many changes. Because of AIDS, colleges (and high schools, too) have put a much greater emphasis on teaching their students about human sexuality. Therefore, the questions that I get from students these days are more sophisticated than those I was asked ten years ago. Most college students already know the basics, and they want additional information from me. Nevertheless, the fact that my lectures are usually standing-room-only also shows that young people still have a lot of questions. That's why I continue to go to colleges all across the country, and it's also one of the reasons that I am writing this book.

If you're a teen today, you definitely face a different set of circumstances concerning sex than teens of any preceding generation. The Pill, AIDS, vast numbers of single mothers, gays coming out of the closet — all are factors that just didn't exist not too long ago.

The challenge of being a teenager comes not just in the area of sex, however. Part of the job of each new generation is to climb onto the shoulders of those who have passed before them and take our civilization one step higher. That's called progress.

But to accomplish anything, you first have to learn to become independent from your parents and teachers. And so, as with every generation before you, this search for independence puts you in conflict with the adults of your time. To give you an idea of how long this conflict has been going on, in the fifth century B.C. Socrates wrote "Children today are tyrants. They contradict their parents, gobble their food, and tyrannize their teachers." This attitude is not dissimilar to what some parents have to say about their children today.

These conflicts that you face as a teen don't come only from the struggles with those who are older than you. They also arise directly from the changes that are taking place within you. The process of growing from a child into an adult is never a smooth one. The growth process comes in spurts. Not only are the adults around you confused by the changes that they see taking place in you, but these changes are just as confusing to you and to every other adolescent.

Although the added inches that seem to come out of nowhere are what everybody notices (usually to your embarrassment), the changes taking place inside of you are the most significant ones. Many of these changes come because your hormones, which have been dormant until now, are starting to kick in, bringing with them physical and psychological growth.

Adolescence is a little like the Italian train system — you can never be sure exactly at what time the train is going to leave, nor can you be sure when it's going to arrive at the various stops along the way.

Don't Worry (Much), Be Happy (Lots)

These changes take place in most young people between the ages of 11 and 16. In any particular group of young people, however, you'll find some experiencing changes as early as age nine or ten, and others lagging behind until maybe 16 or 17. To be the first girl to sprout breasts or the first boy to have his upper lip darkened by a light mustache is definitely embarrassing, because everybody is going to notice, you can be sure. But to be the last one in the group, even if nobody seems to notice, can cause even worse worries, because you begin to feel that you'll be flat-chested or hairless forever.

Although the best advice is to enjoy your youth and not worry about such things, I know that doing so is sometimes impossible. These particular changes are too sensational to ignore, particularly when they also affect how you think and feel.

I certainly had my share of problems as a teenager, because I never passed 4 feet 7 inches. As everybody else around me kept growing taller, I stopped. My height did cause me a lot of pain, but after I realized that I was not going to grow anymore, I resolved not to let my height stop me. I think you'll agree that I didn't let my size get in the way. Actually, many short people have succeeded in life because they knew that they had to work harder to get ahead and did just that.

Whatever stage you're in, I give you permission to spend five or maybe ten minutes a day taking stock of yourself and giving in to whatever feelings about yourself you may be harboring. But, after that, you have to pick yourself up and push forward. Your main duty at this time of your life is to do well in school. Luckily, how big or small you are, how developed or undeveloped you are, has no effect on your studies — unless you let it. Just be sure not to let it. Concentrate on your work and getting good grades and, before you know it, your worries about being different from everybody else will take care of themselves.

If you happen to be at either end of the spectrum — an early or late developer — I have two other suggestions:

- ✔ **Look around you at the adult population.** You can quickly see that none of us adults got stuck in childhood. So whether you are waiting for everybody to catch up to you, or if you're the one who needs to do the catching up, keeping one eye on the adults around you will help you to remember that things will all even out eventually.

- ✔ **Learn as much about the growing-up process as possible.** In this book, I give you only the short explanation of the growing-up process, probably no more than what you can find in your health textbook. But you can find plenty of other books meant for teenagers that explain the process in detail. In fact, I even wrote one, *Dr. Ruth Talks To Kids*. I find that if I know about what is going on, even if I can't totally control it, I begin to feel more in control and I make better choices. Really understanding what your body is going through makes distancing yourself from the process a little easier, which can help you to remain a little calmer about it all.

Evolving into Adulthood

At some point during the second decade of your life, your brain begins to stimulate the production of hormones that cause physical changes to take place. We don't know exactly what triggers the brain, though I believe that seeing a few too many episodes of *I Love Lucy* can slow the process down.

The human body produces many different kinds of hormones. When you're about 11 years old, your brain says, "You've had enough playing with toys; now it's time to get serious." Because your brain communicates to you by releasing chemicals, it gets this message across through a series of chemical reactions. For those of you who can sit through the operating sequences on *ER*, here are the gory details:

✔ The pituitary gland releases higher levels of *follicle stimulating hormone* (FSH) and *luteinizing hormone* (LH).

✔ Together, FSH and LH activate the sex organs so that eggs (ova) develop in the female ovaries, and sperm develop in the male testes.

✔ The sex organs then produce their own hormones. Estrogen and progesterone are the two most important female hormones. Testosterone is the principal male hormone.

The physical changes

Here are the general physical changes that take place:

✔ For both sexes height and weight increase, underarm and pubic hair begins to grow, leg and arm hair becomes thicker and more apparent, perspiration increases, and levels of oil in the skin become high (which you can blame for that great bane of all teenagers, acne).

✔ In girls, breasts become larger and more pronounced, nipples stand out more clearly, and the genitals grow and get a little darker and fleshier. On the inside, the uterus and ovaries also grow. At some point during the process, *menarche* (a woman's first menstrual period) begins. It may take up to one and a half years from the first period, however, before her menstrual cycle becomes regular.

✔ In boys, the testicles and penis become larger. At some point, the man gains the capacity to ejaculate sperm. He also begins to have spontaneous erections (usually at the wrong time and place). Most men also experience *nocturnal emissions* (also called "wet dreams"), which are spontaneous ejaculations of semen that occur during sleep.

The psychological changes

As you might expect, going from childhood, where the biggest problem was how many baseball cards or dolls you had in your collection, to adolescence — worrying about how many zits are on your face, when your period will visit you next, what to do with the bedsheets from the wet dream you had last night, or how to get the boy or girl next door to notice you — can be quite traumatic.

Now, just as not every toddler goes through the terrible twos, neither does every teenager grow sullen and moody, as is the reputation. In fact, most people enjoy their teenage years more than any other. Although you may have worries, you also have a lot of thrills. Firsts — be they your first car, first date, first kiss, first act of sexual intercourse, or first orgasm — are very exciting. You'll break away from your parents a little bit more every day, changing schools, learning to drive, developing new friends, staying up later, squeezing pimples . . . okay, forget that last one. But each day brings new challenges, and challenges make you feel more vibrant and alive.

Now, if everything is just ducky, you don't need any help from me. But for those of you who are having problems, let me address some of the most common ones.

Friendships

Adolescence is the term that scientists give to the teen years when a child becomes an adult. It is a time of life when having friends is most important. An adolescent's biggest calamity can be staying home on a Friday or Saturday night. What does happen to some teens is that they go through a period when they don't have as many friends as they would like. Maybe your family moves, or you go away to school, or your best friend with whom you've always hung out starts dating someone seriously, leaving you out in the cold.

What you have to remember in a situation like this is that you can do something about it. The worst thing you can do is simply sit home and mope. You have to go out and make friends. If school is in session, you can

- Bring a fantastic lunch, with plenty of things that you can share, like a bag of potato chips or some cookies, then sit at a table where other kids are eating and offer them what you've brought.
- Join an after-school organization.
- Volunteer to help work on the next dance.
- Bring a Polaroid camera and take pictures of the other students and give them out.

If school is out, try to do things where you can spot other teens and strike up a friendship.

- Go out bike riding or roller blading and try to find some other kids doing the same.
- Grab your basketball, go to the nearest court, and try to get into a game.
- Visit the library, ignore the "Silence" sign, and try to strike up a conversation.

- If a beach or pool is nearby, bring along a Frisbee or a deck of cards and try to get a game going.

- Volunteer your services some place where other teens are likely to be doing the same thing, like at a hospital, nursing home, camp, or zoo.

Don't be afraid to use the rest of your family to help you make friends. Sometimes adults can help match kids together. Instead of making a long face when your Mom suggests meeting somebody, go ahead and meet that person. You really have nothing to lose. If you've got siblings, do things with them, even if they're much younger than you. Maybe they've got friends who have older siblings too.

Sitting home and watching MTV may be easier than getting out and about, but staring at the tube will quickly get boring. The sooner you begin working at making friends, the better off you'll be.

Dating

I could write a whole book on dating for teenagers. If you'd like to read more about dating in general, you may want to pick up a copy of *Dating For Dummies* by Dr. Joy Browne (IDG Books Worldwide, Inc.). For now, I'd like to pass on just a few tips that I think are very important.

- The first is that you should begin by going out in groups. One-on-one dates put a lot of pressure on both parties, pressure that you may not be ready for. Don't let the fact that your best friend has a steady boyfriend or girlfriend influence you. As I've said, teens develop differently, so maybe your friend is ready for a one-on-one relationship and you're not. Then again, your friend may be in over his or her head as well.

Teens who start going steady too early often wind up in trouble. They spend too much time with each other so that they can't concentrate on their school work. They tend to isolate themselves from their other friends, which increases the intensity of their relationship, which can cause them to go too far too soon. Studies have shown that the earlier teens start dating, the earlier they will have sex. And if they break up, they're left feeling even more alone.

If you meet someone who becomes really special to you, then you will naturally want to see a lot of each other. But going out on dates just because some of your other friends are doing it is not a good idea.

- When you do start dating, don't pretend that suddenly your heart has taken complete control over your head. Just because you like someone doesn't mean that you have to take risks in order to see them.

If someone is abusive, if they overindulge in alcohol or use drugs, if they drive dangerously, or if they ask you to go to an unsupervised party or a deserted place or anywhere that you think is trouble, get yourself out of there as quickly as possible.

✔ Always make sure that others — ideally your parents, but at least some friends — know where you are.

Many of you will have a conflict with your parents as to when is the right age to start dating. Because you are their "baby," parents feel they have a right to put on the brakes. You will think that they are being totally unfair. At each step in the dating process you feel a certain amount of magic. You'll feel extremely nervous on your first date, but the experience will also be very special, and the same will hold true for the first time you hold hands, kiss, and have sex. The longer you stretch out this process, the more this magical effect will last. And I believe that most adults looking back would agree that it is better to wait. A carefree feeling that you'll never get back exists before you start interacting with the opposite sex. You will have many, many years of dealing with the opposite sex, so the more you string out the years where this area is not of concern, the better off you'll be. So, while right now you may envy someone who has dated many different people at a young age, if you ask that person a decade from now whether it was the right thing to do, I bet he or she will say that it wasn't.

Sex and Marriage

It's hard to believe that the factors that affect such a vital part of our lives — sex — could change so radically in a short period of time, but they definitely have. Not so long ago, young people could not make any of their own choices about sex. Their parents would decide whom they were going to marry and make all the arrangements — end of discussion. Sure, some people engaged in premarital or extramarital sex, but not without considerable risks. An unmarried pregnant woman couldn't get an abortion, and, in most instances, both her family and society would reject her. With such dire consequences hanging over their heads, most women chose to accept the status quo and not have sex until they got married.

As society began to see women less as chattel, the age for marriage receded more and more. Now people commonly wait until their twenties or thirties before getting married. This longer period of being single, along with other factors, began to affect people's decisions about when to have sex.

Wait for marriage?

Sex before marriage is commonplace in today's world. Consequently, far too many young women are becoming single mothers, a difficult and expensive life for both mother and child.

Part of the reason for the number of unintended pregnancies among teenagers is that girls are getting their menarche earlier and earlier. At the turn of the twentieth century, many girls weren't capable of having children at age 16; now many 12-year-olds are not only physically ready to have babies, but are actually having them.

So now a major dilemma has developed — girls can have babies at a younger age, but society asks people to wait until a later age to get married. If all young people listened to their elders, the period of abstinence — the time during which they're capable of having sex but are waiting until they get married — would just about double. Throw into this mix the fact that the birth control pill allows sexual intercourse without pregnancy, and you have a very anxious and confusing situation for young people.

Whether or not young people get married, they do pair off in great numbers as they get older. In fact, our society encourages them to do so all the time. Certainly just about every young person on TV has a boyfriend or girlfriend or is desperately seeking one. Even at home, aunts and uncles and grandmas always ask even little children whether they have a boyfriend or girlfriend. Under these circumstances, is expecting our young people to put off having sex realistic?

As is often the case, the answer is neither black nor white, but somewhere in between.

What is sex?

Oddly enough, I have to interrupt this fascinating discussion to pose what may seem like a ridiculous question to some: What is sex? I get many letters — from teens especially — asking me to answer this question. Basically what they want to know is whether having outercourse or oral sex is having sex. One thing that outercourse, oral sex, and intercourse all share is that they involve two people giving each other the pleasure that comes from having an orgasm. Because this is a very intimate act, it should be done only by two people who are in a relationship.

So what are the differences among these three?

- ✔ Outercourse — by which I mean two people either masturbating each other or rubbing against each other with at least some clothes on — carries no risk of pregnancy and only a negligible risk of disease.
- ✔ Oral sex carries the risk of transmitting disease but not the risk of pregnancy.
- ✔ Intercourse carries the risk of both transmitting a disease and leading to an unintended pregnancy.

I can see a certain logic to concluding that the stronger the relationship, the more risk it can withstand. In other words, the longer two people are together, the more confidence they can have that neither one is carrying a disease. And if they're really close, and they do cause an unintended pregnancy (because remember, no method of birth control is 100 percent safe), they will have an easier time weathering that storm.

As to the term "virgin," technically speaking you are a virgin if you've never had sexual intercourse. But from a historical point of view, the term virgin meant more than just not having intercourse. It also meant that you had never been intimate with someone of the opposite sex. But you certainly can't say that two people who have spent time together with their pants down giving each other orgasms haven't been intimate. In fact, many people who have intercourse together still find oral sex too intimate.

I know, I haven't really answered the question, "What is sex?" But the fact that one hard and fast meaning for such terms as sex and virgin no longer exists *is* the answer. You're standing on shifting ground, and so you must decide what you want those words to mean. Just make sure that when you do make those decisions, you have all the information you need to make the right ones.

Is there a magic age?

Teens and their parents often ask me what's the right age to have sexual intercourse. Although we do have age limits for certain things — like voting, getting a driver's license, and drinking alcohol — no magic age exists for intercourse, or any other type of sex.

When to have sex is not an issue that anybody else can decide for you. Sure, some adults go around saying, "Just say no," but they're not in your shoes.

Don't rush it

The most important thing that I can tell you is not to rush into anything. Think about your decision carefully and weigh the pros and cons.

Remember, you will never forget the first time you have sexual intercourse. So be as certain as you can be that, when you "do it" for the first time, the occasion is one that you'll treasure for the rest of your life — not one that you'll regret forever more.

Don't be pressured

Never, never have sex because somebody pressures you into it.

If you're with somebody who says that he or she will stop seeing you unless you have sex, then you know what the right decision is: First, stop seeing that person, and certainly never have sex with him or her. That person isn't interested in you, but in sex.

If the person you're with says that he or she is "dying" with the need to have sex, remember two things:

- ✔ No one has ever died from not having sex, but you could die if you have sex with a person who gives you AIDS or cervical cancer (which is associated with human papilloma virus, or HPV). See Chapter 19 for more on HPV and other sexually transmitted diseases.

- ✔ Sexual release is possible without intercourse. That person, or you, can masturbate, and if you feel like doing so, you can help that person achieve sexual release by using your hand.

When to have sex is a very difficult decision to make. I wish I could offer you a role model, but no one has ever lived through the particular circumstances that you face today. The world truly is a different place from when I was a teenager. If you have followed your best judgment in making your decision, no one can say whether your decision, whatever it is, was absolutely right or wrong. Only time and your own life's experience will tell.

Because serious consequences follow the decision to have sex, whatever you do, don't make this choice casually. Don't let peer pressure or the person with whom you are thinking about having sex influence you. Just look deep down inside of yourself. If you do that, I believe that you'll make the right decision *for you*.

Masturbation

In the preceding section, I mention masturbation. This activity is quite common among adolescents. *Masturbation* means touching your genitals in a way that you find pleasing to the point of having an orgasm. I talk about this solo play in more detail in Chapter 17. Although many myths surround this activity, masturbation cannot do you any harm unless you overindulge to the point where masturbating affects other areas of your life, like your schoolwork or your social life.

An issue that often accompanies masturbation is privacy, because one of the reasons that teens seek privacy is the need to masturbate. How much privacy you can get at home often depends on how much room your family has. Your parents and siblings should certainly give you as much privacy as possible, but you have to remain conscious of other family members' rights as well. You can't hog the bathroom or come in late at night and make a lot of noise and then expect others to respect your rights. If you want to be treated as an adult, then you have to act like one also.

Now just because many teens do masturbate, you shouldn't feel that something is wrong with you if you don't masturbate. If you feel the need, that's fine, but it's just as fine if you don't feel like doing it. As with all aspects of your sexual life, the decision is yours — you have control.

Sexual Identity

Teenagers don't always know what their sexual identity will be; that is to say, they're not always sure whether they're heterosexual or homosexual. In fact, even though some pre-teens or teens engage in sexual acts with members of their own sex, that doesn't necessarily mean that they're homosexual (see Chapter 16).

The teen years are a time for learning, and some teens take longer to figure out what type of person attracts them. Here again, a time will come when you are sure of your sexual identity, so don't make a big deal out of it if you're not sure at any one point in your adolescence.

All in the Family

As a teenager, you are beginning the process of breaking away from your family. It is absolutely necessary that you do this in order to develop into a mature individual. But breaking away from your family doesn't mean abandoning them. Yes, you want to spend more time with people your own age, particularly with your friends. But you should also spend as much time as you can with your family. You still need them, and they need you.

Sure you have a great time when you're with your friends, but certain tensions also exist. You have an image to keep up. You must contend with a structural hierarchy — maybe one person is the leader, or several of you are vying for the top spot. And then come the sexual tensions. Teens of the opposite sex are around, so you have to worry about whether you look good, whether you smell good, and whether you're wearing the right clothes. You also encounter competition for the attention of those members of the opposite sex.

But, with your family, you can let your hair down. You can act silly, eat your favorite foods (even if they're not the latest fad), watch the TV show you watched as a child, and talk about topics with your family in ways that you can't with your friends. You can reminisce, look at old pictures, and try to recapture the feelings that you had as a child, which you can do with no one else but your family.

Try to get up a little earlier and have breakfast with your mom or dad. As often as you can, share dinner with the rest of your family members. Try to do things together. Maybe you wouldn't want to be caught dead with your parents at the local mall, but spending a vacation in another city together can be a lot of fun, so don't put the idea down. Friends are great, but they may not always stick by you in times of trouble the way family will. Cut the apron strings, definitely, but don't cut yourself off entirely.

Peer Pressure

All humans feel peer pressure to some degree, but most of us feel it the most during the teen years. Both you and your parents must work through these feelings. If you give in totally to peer pressure, you will do things that you will later regret. At the same time, to survive your teenage years, you must give in to some degree or you'll be miserable. Finding that middle ground can be very difficult.

As for peer pressure and sex, the additional factor of exaggeration comes into play. If a friend told you that wearing baggy pants was cool, you could easily determine if that person was telling the truth just by looking around at what everybody else your age was wearing. Just because people around you say they are having sex, however, doesn't mean that they actually are. People brag about "how far" they've gone, and if you believe them, the effects of peer pressure can become that much stronger. So like a sailor on the high seas who has to take account of the wind, you must steer your life while being pushed by the winds of peer pressure; just make sure that you don't oversteer because of pressures that don't really exist.

Cyberporn

Male teens have a natural attraction to erotic images. If they can't have the real thing, then images become a substitute. Until recently, most teens had limited access to these types of erotic images, but with the Internet now so widely available, many more teens can easily see hardcore pornography.

What's the difference between teenagers seeing triple-X-rated material online as compared to looking at the rather tame images of nude women in a magazine like *Playboy?* The discrepancies skew their expectations of what sex is supposed to be like. Instead of sex being part of a loving relationship, it becomes a sport, the goal of which is to imitate what they see on their computer screens. If reality doesn't match up (and it probably won't), then they will likely be disappointed.

When you see the latest action thriller movie, you know that all the explosions and mayhem come from special effects. But you may fail to recognize that other things you see on a movie screen are not true to life. The same idea holds true for teens who look to the Internet for sexual images. You may be disappointed if your girlfriend doesn't have enormous breasts or is unwilling to take part in a lesbian threesome for your visual pleasure. As a result, you may wind up being unhappy with your sex life even though there is nothing wrong with it.

I know that the availability of these images may tempt you to look at them. If you refrain from giving into this temptation, however, you will be doing yourself, and your sex life, a very big favor.

Don't Stop Here

If you're a teen, you may want to read the rest of this book. It covers some issues that you are not facing right now, but you may well run into at some point in your life. Preparing yourself by knowing the facts is always the best course of action.

Whatever you do, treasure your teen years. They're very special, and you won't get a second chance to enjoy them except maybe through your own children. So have fun, stay safe, and keep reading.

Part II
Making Connections

The 5th Wave   By Rich Tennant

"We met on the Internet and I absolutely fell in looove with his syntax."

In this part . . .

There are still some people out there who think that my only role is to tell people to go ahead and do whatever they please. In fact, I was always old-fashioned and a square, and because of AIDS, I've become even more conservative. I am constantly encouraging people to create a relationship with someone before having sex with that person. This part is all about the preliminaries to good sex: building and keeping relationships.

Chapter 5

Courtship, Marriage, and Commitment: Getting to Yes

● ●

In This Chapter

▶ Finding the right partner

▶ Knowing you deserve love

▶ Strengthening your marriage

▶ Communicating lovingly

▶ Sharing time together

● ●

Courtship, marriage, and commitment — three old-fashioned words for you to contemplate. If you were to study the United States from only what you read in the media and what you see on television, you may conclude that these family values were gone forever. While I have to admit that they're, how shall I put it, on the run, they're not totally dead yet and certainly not forgotten, at least not by this grandmother.

One day society may reach a point where all children are "manufactured," that is to say, either cloned from DNA or put together in a petri dish from donated eggs and sperm. In my opinion that situation would be terrible, but it may happen. At that point, the *raison d'être* — the essential reason — for marriage will have changed so much that maybe the concept will die out. But for now, in this scientifically backward era when most people can't even program their VCRs, marriage is still a viable social institution because it provides the best environment in which to raise children.

Yes, I know that plenty of single mothers and fathers do a good job of raising their children, but face it, the toll that this process often takes on both the parents and the children makes it far from an ideal lifestyle. Because women have jumped into the workforce in such great numbers, I'm not sure that even two parents are enough anymore, and so I certainly do not believe that any of you should consciously try to become single parents.

Now if you don't believe in marriage, then I suppose that you can skip this chapter. But before you skip ahead, let me say one thing to you. Right now you may be saying to yourself, and anyone else who will listen, that you never want to marry. You may always have been single, or you may have once (or twice or three times) been married and decided to swear off this rite. That's fine. I respect your opinion as long as you respect mine. But opinions do change, and so, when it comes to marriage, never say never. Leave your options open in case you do one day fall deeply in love with someone, so much so that you'll want to swear to each other that you'll spend the rest of your lives together.

Starting Off with Courtship

A few hundred years ago, dating didn't exist. If you so much as wanted to talk to a girl, you had to first ask her father for her hand in marriage. The concept of spending an evening together, and of possibly having sex together without first taking your vows of holy matrimony, was simply not permitted (not that people didn't try).

Nowadays, most couples start out dating and then, if they happen to fall in love and it lasts a while, they decide to take the plunge. Sometimes they live together; more often than not they have sex together. When, during this process, does courtship begin? Or does it even exist anymore?

Courtship certainly does exist. Here's a case I know of:

Anthony and Rose

Anthony was about ten years older than Rose when they met. He'd been looking for someone who would make a good mother for his children, and as far as he was concerned, Rose was it. Anthony didn't have any doubts, and he was intent on marrying the girl he had his sights on.

Anthony didn't just take Rose on dates. He took her to the fanciest restaurants. And Anthony didn't send flowers only on Valentine's Day. Rose would receive enormous bouquets almost every day at her office.

Rose liked Anthony, but when he started showering her with all this attention, she wasn't quite prepared. She hadn't been thinking of getting married just yet, but it was obvious from the way Anthony was treating her that a wedding was on his mind.

Rose had had boyfriends before, but nobody had ever treated her like Anthony did. She was very flattered by all the attention he showed her, but she also realized that if he asked her to marry him and she said no, he would probably move on. He had fully committed himself to his quest, and he wasn't the type to accept no for an answer and then just hang around.

It wasn't until the moment that Anthony actually popped the question that Rose made up her mind. She knew that Anthony was a one-in-a-million find, and she decided that she'd have a hard time doing better — besides, she found that she loved him — so she said yes. And as far as I know, they've been living happily ever after.

I have to make a confession here. Anthony wasn't American; he had been raised in Italy, so his ideas of how a male should act when courting a woman were different than those of the average American. (His different attitude also holds true on the highway, which Anthony seems to think is actually the autostrada.) American men tend to be cooler about these things. They won't necessarily commit themselves the way Anthony did, which is too bad. Men who won't commit themselves think that, by holding back, they're keeping some of their freedom, but that's not true.

Giving in totally to your emotions, by diving right in without holding anything back, actually makes you feel a lot freer. For example:

- ✔ You don't have to put on a show for your friends, pretending that you don't care all that much.
- ✔ You don't have to tell jokes about your date behind her back, which you later regret when you're actually holding her.
- ✔ You don't have to feel bad because you're going dancing with your girl instead of watching the game with the guys.

She hasn't wrangled you into marrying her. You're the one who made the choice, who made the commitment to marry this woman, and you're happy to live by it. Being able to say to somebody, "I love you" — that's real freedom. Only giving a piece of yourself, instead of your whole self, means that you're tied down to a sham, and that's what ends up being a shackle around your ankle.

Remember, you can't be tied down to a marriage with somebody if you're the one who tied the knot.

Finding the Right Partner: Difficult, Yes; Impossible, No

Although I will never say that finding a partner is easy (because I certainly faced my own difficulties as a young woman who was an orphan and only 4 feet 7 inches tall), I will make one assertion — it is not impossible. Believe it or not, that's a very big distinction. Sitting in my office chair, I've heard too many people say that they *can't* find a partner. But that's just not so.

Everyone can find a partner, even a wonderful partner. If you've been unable to find the right partner, you may just be going about it the wrong way.

The dreamers

Here's an example of a search for love that was doomed from the start:

Lonely Lisa

Lisa came to see me because she couldn't find a man. She was desperate and cried throughout half of the first session. Lisa had a nice personality and was attractive, although a little overweight. Not a big problem, but one that did require making some adjustments. But what kind of help did she come to me for? What she most wanted from me was to get her a date with a certain very famous TV star.

Not only do I not know this star, not only would I not do such a thing if I did know him, but where in heaven's name did she get the idea that this star was waiting for her to walk into his life? Taking all the factors into consideration — she didn't know him, he lived thousands of miles away, and he was one of the most sought-after bachelors in Hollywood — the odds of their ever linking up were ridiculously slim. She was setting herself up for her lonely nights by choosing such a totally unrealistic goal.

Whatever you think of Lisa, you have to understand that she is not alone. Oh, not everybody has their eyes set exclusively on one TV or movie star (although certainly millions of people fantasize about stars, and doing so is alright), but many of you may have a certain image of the person you want, oftentimes an unrealistic image, so you wind up just as lonely as Lisa.

Not only is expecting your man to look like Tom Cruise or your woman like Sharon Stone unrealistic, but if you base your selection on only one aspect of a person, such as looks or job title, doing so insures that you miss out on meeting some very nice people who may not fit into the one cubbyhole in which you are looking.

The doormats

Be careful not to become so blinded by looks, money, power, or position that you don't see when someone is using you.

People who let themselves be used tend to fall into the same trap again and again, seemingly unable to learn from their mistakes.

As terrible as the heartache you must endure if this happens is the time that you waste. You meet plenty of people who can be great partners, but you don't recognize them and, so, miss the chance to make these connections. Years go by and, instead of having spent them with someone you care about and who cares about you, you spend them alone, with brief interludes of make-believe happiness dating people who turn out to be in the relationship only for themselves.

Paul's story illustrates how easily you can fall into the trap of being used but not loved:

Heartbroken Paul

When Paul came to see me, he was absolutely heartbroken. He'd been dating this gorgeous woman for the last three months. She had recently moved to New York and wanted to become a model. Paul had a few connections, and he was able to open some doors for her. One evening, he took her to a party that a number of people in the fashion industry attended. They met a top photographer, who immediately took a liking to this woman. Predictably, she dropped Paul flat and left the party with this other man.

This wasn't the first time that Paul had allowed a woman to walk all over him. I told him that unless he changed his ways, it wouldn't be the last time, either.

Paul needed to identify his problem in order to keep himself from repeating it over and over again. To be successful in the dating game, you must analyze your faults and the faults that others may have and come up with a mental image of your ideal partner. I'm not talking about finding perfection. Nobody is perfect — except maybe my grandson. But you do have to figure out how to navigate the dating scene so that you end up forming a relationship with someone who satisfies your needs while you satisfy theirs.

The time-wasters

Let me delve a little bit further into the subject of wasting time and offer some advice to those of you who are always waiting to win the dating lottery — some without even buying tickets.

Time-wasters fall into two basic categories:

✔ The first category includes people who always have a string of excuses for not looking for a mate:

   • I have to lose a few more pounds.

   • I have to redecorate my apartment.

   • I have to look for a new job.

- I have to get my bachelor's degree (and then my master's and then my doctorate).

- I have to wait . . . and wait . . . and wait. . . .

If you're one of these people, you can end up wasting your entire life waiting for the right moment to look for a partner.

✔ The other group consists of people who don't make excuses but who won't lift a finger to help themselves. They think that the way to find a partner is to sit and wait by the phone.

That is nonsense.

If you want something in this world, you have to make an effort to get it, and the more effort you put into the search, the better will be your rewards.

In olden times, when families lived near to one another, a whole network of people was looking to make matches for single people. Nowadays, as people move around so much, those networks have been erased. You have to make up for that loss by putting your own network together, piece by piece. Doing so takes some effort, but that effort will also pay off. At the very least, you can make some new friends. At best, you can find someone you love and who loves you.

If you really want to find a partner, you have to go out there and look for one. Make yourself available. Go to parties. Throw parties! Tell everybody you know that you are looking. Put an ad in the personal listings. Go to a match-maker, if that's what it takes. You have nothing to be ashamed of.

Should you use every avenue, from personal ads in newspapers to meeting people through cyberspace? Absolutely. But you do have to be more careful with these mediums. Even the absolute worst blind date, the one with bottle-thick glasses and buck teeth, comes with a reference — somebody that you know knows who they are and where they live. The people you meet impersonally can easily hide their true identities, and, if they're out to harm you, they can do so with little risk (see Chapter 18).

Now most of the people you meet via personal ads, cyberspace, and so forth are just like you, perfectly nice but a little lonely. But you have to take at least the most obvious precautions:

✔ Make sure that the first time you meet is in a well-lit public place, such as a restaurant or popular bar.

✔ Don't be too quick to give out personal information. It may be best to give only a daytime office number at first.

✔ Take a cab home from that first date — by yourself.

Remember, it's a jungle out there, and you're not Tarzan.

The love-at-first-sight syndrome

Another group of people who can end up being miserable are those who suffer from the love-at-first-sight syndrome. The French call it *le coup de foudre* — the bolt of lightning — and think of how rarely people get hit by lightning (thank heavens!). Undoubtedly, love-at-first-sight does happen: Two people meet at a party, ride off into the sunset (or dawn), and live happily ever after. For those lucky few, the experience is great. But for so many others, waiting for love at first sight brings only misery.

If you find yourself wanting nothing less than an instant attraction, you may just be avoiding the time and work required to build a successful relationship. When you'll accept either love at first sight or nothing, be prepared for some problems:

- ✔ You may stare into the eyes of a million people and never see those sparks fly. Or the two of you may be at the bus stop, see each other, the bus comes, zips you away, and you never see each other again. Every week in New York City's *Village Voice* you can find ads placed by people looking for that special someone of whom they caught only a fleeting glimpse. Some people think these ads are romantic; I think they're sad. People who indulge these kinds of delusions often wind up old and alone.

- ✔ While you're waiting for your Venus or Adonis to appear, you're not giving other people a chance, even though, with time, one of them may turn out to be your one true love.

- ✔ You may find yourself always falling in love with people who don't love you back.

  Puppy love is cute in kids, but when an adult goes around acting like a puppy, the act only turns people off. When you begin to act maturely and hold your emotions in check, not only do you wind up with egg on your face less often but you also give potential partners time to get to know you and then fall in love with you.

For more tips on finding a partner, check out *Dating For Dummies* by Dr. Joy Browne (IDG Books Worldwide, Inc.).

Believing in Yourself

Many of the problems that people have in finding a partner come from low self-esteem. If you don't believe that you are worthy of finding a partner, then making it happen becomes very difficult. You may end up in time-wasting situations as a way to sabotage your chances of finding someone just because you don't really believe that you deserve that someone.

But you *do* deserve that certain someone. And you *can* take control of your life and make the changes necessary within yourself so that you can turn those interpersonal failures into successes. You have to find out how to pull your shoulders back, hold your head high, put a smile on your face, and go out there and conquer the world. You can do it!

Moving On to Commitment

If you've already found the ideal partner, marriage may be in your future. But, some people get married who do not plan on a lifetime commitment. In the movie *Jurassic Park,* Ian Malcolm, the character played by Jeff Goldblum, says, "I'm always looking for the next ex-Mrs. Malcolm." If you approach marriage with that attitude, you just may get your wish. No one is perfect. No two people share identical tastes in every way. Conflict is inevitable in every marriage. The situation would be unnatural if no disagreements pop up; after all, you and your partner are not clones.

Your tolerance for that conflict depends very much on your commitment to the marriage in the first place. If you approach marriage with that proverbial ten-foot pole stuck out in front of you, then any marriage you enter into is destined to fail.

Knowing that love isn't enough

Think of a marriage as a house of cards. If you merely place the cards together, the least little wind can bring them tumbling down. But if you glue the cards together, then they're likely to withstand all but the strongest gale. *Commitment is the glue that holds a marriage together.*

Aha, you thought it was love, right? You thought that, as long as you love each other, you can make it through any storm. You'd be surprised at how many people love each other but can never stay married. Love is not missing in their life together; commitment is.

Maybe she's more committed to her job. Maybe he's unwilling to commit because he wants to have sex with other women. Maybe they're both unwilling to commit in case they meet somebody who may be better for them. A lack of commitment doesn't mean that partners don't love each other.

Handling children and commitment

Having children is supposed to be a sign of commitment, but you can't count on that, at least not anymore. With the example of so many single parents, especially single mothers, raising children on their own, couples just don't look at children as reason enough to stay together any longer. I don't think that having children is right if you don't at least think of yourselves as a committed couple, but, sadly, too many people disagree with me. I say "sadly" not because they disagree with me, but because of what the situation can do to the children.

Children are much better off growing up with two parents living under the same roof. Some people dispute that, but they'll never convince me. Now that doesn't mean that I never advise a man or a woman to split from their spouse when children are involved, because I do. If two people are really incompatible, if they're fighting all the time, and maybe even taking their unhappiness out on the children, then divorce is the best recourse. But divorce is not a win-win situation. The situation may be better for everyone concerned after the divorce, but the end result still can't compare to a whole, functional family.

Never having had a father or a mother around is one thing. But, if a child has two parents who suddenly split up, the separation is bound to affect the child. The children may blame themselves for the divorce. They shouldn't feel guilty, because rarely do the kids cause the split, but no matter how much you tell them that they are not the reason for the breakup, they won't believe it. Even if they accept the fact that they didn't do anything to cause the divorce, they'll still think that they could have done something to stop it.

Putting your marriage first

So if love isn't enough, and kids aren't enough, what is this thing called commitment? Its components will be different for each and every person involved in a marriage, but the basic philosophy is the same. Commitment is a willingness to put the marriage ahead of the individual whenever necessary.

Every marriage undergoes trials of one sort or another. One partner may become sick. Money problems may crop up. Parents can put pressure both on their offspring and their spouses. Just the everyday stress of having kids and jobs creates conflicts. And some unlucky souls will face all of the above.

Some pressures are actually easier to handle as a couple than individually. If a natural disaster strikes, such as a flood or an earthquake, it's obviously better to be two people struggling to go on with your lives rather than one. Even if you've lost all the treasures you've accumulated over the years, at least you still have someone with whom to share the memories of the past.

Other situations can be especially hard on a marriage. If you have a boss who expects you to work late every night, not only do you have to struggle with your own anger, but then you have to go home and get nasty looks from your spouse, who is sick of being alone every night. When one person gets caught in the middle and can't bear the pressure, then one side will have to go. In this particular case, it may be the job, or it may be the marriage.

Recognizing factors that tear at a marriage

Finding this "marriage glue" is especially hard in the present era, which is why the divorce rate stands at 50 percent. What are some of the factors in our society today that tear at marriages?

- ✔ **The two-career family model:** Any type of wound needs time to heal, be it a physical one or a psychological one. Therefore, spending time together is very important for two married people. But when both partners work, and they also have the job of taking care of their home, which often falls most heavily on the woman, even little problems can develop into crushing mountains of anger.

- ✔ **Our mobile society:** If you've always lived in one town, you have a whole support system of family and neighbors and friends. When you move, you can build new networks, but they're never as strong as family ties. Plus, networks take time to establish, so if you move every few years, finding people you can really rely on is almost impossible. Not having people you can turn to for help can make it very difficult to cope, especially if you have children.

- ✔ **The media:** In the past, you may have worried about keeping up with the Joneses, but because the Jones family lived right next door, their house was probably similar to yours, and basically you lived the same lifestyle. But today, instead of living next door, "the Joneses" are on your television screen, in your newspapers and magazines, or on your computer screen. You are deluged with new gadgets to buy, new places to go, new sports to take up. Sitting on a rocking chair on your front porch making small talk is not one of the options being pushed, because no one can make a profit from that. But that kind of communication is exactly what a marriage needs most. Far too many options are available, and the media makes spending quality time with your spouse seem like one of the least worthy.

- ✔ **The divorce model:** Divorce used to be frowned upon by society at large, and so a couple's expectations were different. Divorce wasn't just one of several options but was looked on as a last resort. Peer pressure was a strong force keeping a couple from getting a divorce, and that pressure came from family, neighbors, and people on the job. Now society's attitude has totally reversed. These days, your friends may actually encourage you to get a divorce. Nobody at work cares whether you're divorced or not, and maybe your boss even prefers it, because now you can work later. Your family may still not like the idea, but they may live a thousand miles away.

- ✔ **The sexual revolution:** People have always had affairs, but with the consequence for adultery in Biblical times being stoning, adultery was something that people tried to keep under wraps. Today people are told that everyone cheats and that you're a fool if you stick with the same person. Yes, times have changed, but not so drastically as all that. But all this talk about sex does make it harder to accept a so-so sex life with one mate for a lifetime.

All these things are responsible for the rising number of divorces. But, if you make yourself aware of these things and do all you can to counter their effects, divorce doesn't have to be the final chapter of your marriage.

Strengthening Your Marriage

This section looks into what you can do to keep your marriage, be it an existing one or one that is still in your hope chest, from breaking up on the rocks of the 21st century.

Remembering to communicate

Nothing is more essential in a marriage than talking with each other. Telling each other your problems is a way of keeping them from growing to the point where you can no longer solve them. But, you have to be willing to obey certain rules:

- You have to listen to the other person.
- You have to communicate in such a way that you don't cause a fight, which means no put-downs, no threats, no needling.
- You have to pick the time and place where communications work best. Don't start talking about a problem when you're running out the door, late for work. All you will accomplish is a screaming match.

Here are some other hints for keeping the discussion flowing freely and keeping your marriage healthy and happy:

- **Keep problems outside the bedroom.** Don't bring up problems about sex while you're having sex; always bring up sexual problems outside the bedroom. Emotions are at a fever pitch when you're making love, and if you add the wrong catalyst you can get an explosion.

- **Don't argue about kids in front of them.** Never argue about something having to do with the children in front of them. Doing so will give your children the wrong message and, if they choose sides, distort the final outcome. You should always present a united front when you do talk to your children, even if you haven't settled the disagreement. If you give children mixed messages, you can wind up with mixed results.

- ✔ **Think before you speak.** Think before you say something — if what you say will hurt the other person's feelings, maybe you shouldn't say it.

- ✔ **Don't be stingy with compliments.** Everybody likes to hear good news, so pass it on. This idea is especially important if the other person has invested a lot of time and energy into a project, be it cooking a meal or washing the car.

- ✔ **Make a date to talk.** If you're not finding enough time to communicate without planning for it, then make a date to talk. Certainly, if something pressing is on your mind, then you have to find time to talk it out. But even if you don't have a particular problem to discuss, remember that, to keep those lines of communication open, you have to use them on a regular basis.

  Try to pick a time for conversation when the clock isn't ticking. In other words, if your husband gets up early, don't plan on talking to him when you get into bed because he'll worry that it's cutting into his sleep. On the other hand, if you really need to say something, and he has to take a shower, jump right in there with him. You are married, after all.

- ✔ **Bring up pleasant memories.** Going over the good times you shared together can be a soothing balm and help with the healing process of problems you are currently experiencing. Don't hide that wedding album in the back of a closet; instead, keep it out where it can serve as a reminder of one of the happiest days of your life.

Check out *Making Marriage Work For Dummies* by Steven and Sue Klavans Simring (IDG Books Worldwide, Inc.) for more information about communicating effectively with your spouse.

Doing things together

Communication is easier if you and your spouse have things to talk about. If you share a hobby, you will always have a topic of conversation that you're mutually interested in. That hobby can be as simple as reading the same book or something more complicated, such as sharing in the running of a small business.

Here are some other ideas for sharing time with your partner.

- ✔ **Go for walks:** There's no better time to discuss something than when you go for a stroll.

  - You have privacy because only the two of you are there.

  - You have few distractions — and if you have a cellular phone, don't take it (unless a real emergency is pending).

- • By walking, you'll be expending energy — energy that may otherwise be used in fighting. You'll find that, if you discuss issues while being active instead of passive, you'll be much less likely to squabble over the little things.

✔ **Go out on dates:** I know that, with children, finding the time and the money to go on dates can be hard, but having some large periods of time that you can devote to each other is really important. If you don't have any grandparents around, try to find another couple with whom you can exchange baby-sitting duties. If you can't afford a fancy restaurant, go to McDonald's, order your Big Mac to go, and park somewhere quiet for an hour or so.

✔ **Get a lock for your bedroom door:** I'm always surprised to find couples who don't have this little necessity. Your kids need to know that sometimes Mommy and Daddy want to be alone — just to talk or for other, more private reasons. A hook-and-eye type lock costs only about a dollar, and it can be the best investment you ever make.

✔ **Turn down the volume:** Some people seem to always need background noise, be it the TV or radio or a CD playing. Even if the noise is not loud enough to stop conversation, it is still a distraction to conversation. Because time for communication is already short, both of you have to give each other your full attention if you want to really impart information. And, when you get in your car together, don't automatically switch on the radio. Drive time can be great conversation time, unless some DJ drowns it out.

✔ **Organize and prioritize:** With busy schedules, not getting scattered is hard. You keep saying "We'll talk soon," and even though you share the same living space, soon becomes later and later becomes never. Yes, you have things that you must do, but are they all more important than talking to each other? Make a list of what you have to do (dress the kids, walk the dog) and put conversation with your spouse as close to the top as you can.

✔ **Let the machine pick it up or take the telephone off the hook:** Now I love telephones, and I'm on them for hours each day, but just because the telephone emits a loud ring doesn't mean that it always gets first crack at your attention. Sometimes you just have to decide that you won't let the phone interrupt. If the two of you have finally found time to sit down and have a conversation, interrupting those precious moments to talk to somebody else makes no sense. There's nobody more important to you than your spouse, right?

Keeping together when you're apart

In the days when the only way to communicate over long distances was with pen and ink, people actually wrote to each other. Now that the typewriter is already passé, and we have computers and e-mail to make writing easier, people do it less and less.

> ✔ If you have half an hour, and your spouse isn't around, write him or her a letter. Explain how you feel so that you can get a jump start when you do get the chance to talk. How your letter gets there — via post office or e-mail — is up to you.
>
> ✔ You can also jot down brief messages on sticky notes and leave them someplace where your spouse is sure to see them. Just make sure that those short notes aren't always passing on a chore, or your spouse will dread seeing them rather than view them as something to look forward to.

Writing yourself notes about what you need to communicate to your partner is a good idea. How many times have you said to your spouse, "I had something to tell you, but I've forgotten it"? If you'd written it down, you wouldn't have that problem. So next time, do just that.

Letting communication between you and your spouse drift away into nothingness is very easy. Communication is something that you have to work at, and both of you have to put it near the top of your list of priorities to be successful.

Sex and Marriage

Surveys of people with happy marriages have all shown that sex is an important ingredient. It's not the most important ingredient, and most people find that their sex lives do decrease as the years go by, but you cannot let your sex life degenerate into oblivion. Sex is an important way of communicating your love, and, like the other ways of communicating, it takes some effort on your part to make certain that you have enough of it to keep your marriage together.

Obviously, if either partner is sexually frustrated, that frustration will not be good for a marriage. Even if you do not state the word *orgasm* in your marriage vows, being able to derive sexual satisfaction with your spouse is certainly implied. But the sexual union between husband and wife brings more to a marriage than just the easing of sexual tensions. It also brings intimacy, which is another important component to the glue that holds the two of you together.

I regularly receive letters from women who will not let their husbands see them naked because they are ashamed of the way they look. Some of these women have satisfying sex lives, so the problem is not that they're not having sex, but they do keep this particular barrier up. This situation always causes me concern, in part because of the low self-esteem that these women have for themselves, but also because their actions show a lack of intimacy.

A marriage needs intimacy because it shows the world, and the couple themselves, that they really have a special bond between them. That doesn't mean you can't set any boundaries, but the fewer you have, the more intimate you will be. And I'm not only talking about physical intimacy. Being naked together is certainly a good feeling, but you also have to let your partner see into your psyche. If you hide your hopes, your dreams, and your desires from your spouse, then you become strangers in some very basic areas, which is not good for a marriage.

You can also carry intimacy too far and think nothing of, say, burping loudly in front of your spouse as if he or she weren't there. That is not intimacy; it's just gross. No matter how intimate you are, you should never lose respect for your partner. Now, if your intimacy stretches into the bathroom, then there's certainly nothing wrong with exercising any bodily function in front of each other, but that notion doesn't give you license to turn the rest of the house into a toilet.

Finding the ultimate intimacy

The ultimate intimacy has nothing to do with sex and is usually done with your clothes on. It's not complicated or difficult, and it can be done over and over, yet it is very, very rare.

The ultimate intimacy is to totally give yourself to your partner.

Everyone holds things back from the rest of the world, including our spouses. Some of these things aren't important to anyone else and should be held back. If you've got an itch behind your left ear, you have no reason to announce it to the world before you scratch it. That's trivial.

But what if you have an itch in your psyche? What if you were a six-foot-tall, beefy truck driver who always wanted to write poetry but were afraid people would laugh at you? Would you reveal that side of yourself to your wife? And if not, why not? Would you be afraid of seeming weak to her? Do you think you have to keep up a certain image for her to love you?

Every time you hide behind a screen of some sort, you decrease the intimacy you have with your spouse and build walls between you instead of bridges.

You may think that allowing somebody to peer inside you to your very core weakens you. That idea may be true if you let just anyone in, but I'm talking about your husband or wife. And if they love you as much as you love them, sharing this kind of intimacy will strengthen both of you as well as your marriage.

Don't play games with each other

What ruins the intimacy between a husband and wife is when they play games with each other, which means when they keep score.

✔ He did that, so I won't do this.

✔ She didn't let me do this, so I won't let her do that.

✔ Last year we didn't go to the dance, so I won't go to his family picnic.

Every time you look up at that scoreboard, you destroy a piece of your marriage. You are not supposed to be on different teams; you're supposed to be on the same team.

Now, even teammates squabble. Perfect marriages do not exist; things will go wrong, and you'll have your ups and downs. But if your goal is to be perfectly intimate, to be as close to each other as possible, then you'll work those problems out and continue to make progress. If you stop thinking that way — if you start believing that your relationship is a competition — then very soon it will become one, and it will cease to be a marriage.

You can find no better feeling in the world than being one with the person you love. During sex, the intensity of that oneness can be terrific, but that feeling is also a source of strength and comfort 24 hours a day. Work toward having the kind of marriage where you really do feel that you're in this life together. Put in the effort it requires. Break a sweat once in a while. You won't regret it, I promise you.

Chapter 6

Know Your Partner: Asking about STDs

As soon as my little radio show became a national phenomenon in the early '80s and people recognized me, I was constantly being stopped and asked questions about sexual functioning. That hasn't stopped, and so at lectures, in letters, on the street, and even in ladies' rooms, people are always asking me questions. In the beginning — at least for the most part — the questions were pretty much the same, dealing with people wanting to know how to improve their sex lives. Certainly some questions come out of left field, such as the phone call I received on the air about onion rings. (If you haven't heard that story yet, think of the game of horseshoes and let your imagination run wild.) But, by and large, the problems that people came to me with were universal. Then AIDS came along, and people had a new and deadly reason to question sexual practices.

Since the onset of AIDS, I now receive a whole new subset of questions involving that dreaded disease. Some are practical questions about condoms and the like, which I address in Chapter 19. The question that really leaves people confused, however, is how to bring up the subject of AIDS testing with a partner.

I don't want to minimize the risks of other sexually transmitted diseases (STDs). Some STDs have no cure. Some have no outward symptoms but can leave a woman sterile. Several seem to be spreading like the proverbial wild-fire, and all are quite embarrassing to talk about. Left untreated, other STDs besides AIDS could even lead to death (see Chapter 19 for a detailed discussion). But while talking about other STDs with a potential new sexual partner is certainly a good idea, I don't know if such conversations would take place if not for AIDS. Sadly, people have waited for the ultimate risk of death to talk openly about the subject of STDs. Even with that looming threat, I still know that far too many people close their eyes to the potential consequences of having sex.

Talking about STDs, Especially AIDS

In our culture, we don't talk about sex as much as we engage in sexual activities. That's not a good thing, and I have been doing my part to get couples to communicate better about their sexual likes and dislikes. But, because not everybody waits to form a strong relationship before having sex, the issue of AIDS testing can come up before the two people involved are really a couple. They may have to ask some very intimate and personal questions of each other before they really know each other all that well.

Now you can say that, if a couple is ready to *have* sex, then they should be ready to at least talk about it. But that's one of the issues that causes difficulties. Just because one party is ready to have sex doesn't mean that the other one is also. In the old days, pre-AIDS that is, generally the man fumbled and groped his way around, and the woman communicated to him with either a stop or go signal. It wasn't the greatest system — a few men got slapped, and a few women cried — but for the most part it worked. Well, it doesn't work any longer.

In the third millennium, people need to institute a new intermediate step: the AIDS discussion. If both parties clearly want to go to bed together and really look for a simple assurance of probable good health, then this conversation may be no more than a speed bump on the way to the bedroom. But if one person is not confident of the other person's desire to have sex, how should the discussion of AIDS and other STDs be handled?

Let me give you some possible scenarios.

Paul and Juliette

Paul and Juliette have had five dates, and they haven't had sex yet. Their last date was with another couple. They'd gone out dancing, and, during the last few slow dances, Paul had held Juliette very close. He'd had an erection, and rather than pull away from him, Juliette had pushed her pelvis into his. To Paul, it was a clear sign that Juliette was ready to go to bed with him, but because their friends were driving, Paul had to content himself with a goodnight kiss when they dropped Juliette off at her place.

During the week, he called Juliette and asked her to dinner. He picked a place that was about six blocks from where she lived. When he arrived, he parked his car and suggested they walk. After a little bit of banter, he sucked in his breath and asked her: "Do you think it's too early in our relationship to be talking about AIDS testing?" She answered, "No, Paul I don't," and the discussion that needed to take place, did.

By posing the question this way, Paul didn't presume that they were going to have sex. He left it to Juliette to decide. If she'd wanted to wait longer, she could easily have told him so. But, because she was ready to have sex with him, the discussion was able to proceed smoothly. They were both interested in the same goal.

Fran and Tony

Fran met Tony the day after he moved into her apartment complex. She saw him again later at the grocery store, where he was stocking up on supplies. She ended up cooking him dinner that night. He was very busy those first few weeks setting up his apartment and starting a new job, but they did get together for a drink a few times and once for a quick dinner at a local Mexican place.

Tony finally had a weekend off. This time he offered to take her to this fancy French restaurant that Fran really loved. They had a great meal and shared a bottle of champagne that went to Fran's head a little bit. When they got back to the apartment complex, instead of heading their separate ways, as they'd done previously, Tony invited Fran inside and she accepted. They had some brandy while sitting on his new sofa, and soon Fran found herself wrapped in his arms. Her clothes started coming off, and not too much later he was leading her to the bedroom, their clothes scattered over the living room floor.

As they lay down on the bed, Fran asked Tony: "You don't have any . . . uh . . . diseases, do you?"

"No way," he said, "I'm not one of those guys who'll sleep with just anybody." A little voice inside of Fran did start to whisper something, but at that point she was somewhat tipsy, very aroused, and totally naked, and so she didn't bother listening.

What that little voice inside of Fran was trying to tell her was that, although Tony was saying that he wasn't that kind of guy, here he was going to bed with someone he barely knew. Was that really the first time he'd done that?

Most people in Fran's position would have done exactly what she did — given in to the moment. That's why you must have the AIDS discussion long before that moment arrives. Don't wait until you're in a situation where it would not only be embarrassing to suddenly pull back, but also almost emotionally impossible to resist going ahead. Especially exhibit caution when drugs or alcohol are involved. You have to be realistic about sex and know that your ability to resist temptation is not infinite. You have to protect yourself in many ways, not just with a piece of rubber.

Speaking of rubber, what if Tony had added, "and anyway, I'm using a condom"? Would that have made it okay?

Not necessarily, because condoms can break or fall off or leak. Relying on condoms can be enough of a safeguard against AIDS, but only if you really know the person with whom you're about to have sex. In this case, Fran knew next to nothing about Tony, because he'd just moved to town. She certainly had no way of knowing for certain whether he was telling her the truth. He could have been lying, or he may have had diseases and not known it. Even if a condom stays on in one piece, a condom still may not be enough to protect you from other STDs. For example, if someone has herpes and can pass on the disease (sometimes herpes is dormant and other times it is highly contagious), a condom may not fully protect you. If vaginal secretions containing the herpes virus leak onto the man, he can catch herpes.

Whether or not you listen to my advice about forming a relationship before jumping into bed, definitely never put yourself in the type of situation that Fran did. How do you avoid that? Simple . . .

Make yourself a resolution that you will never get undressed until you're sure that doing so is safe. If he starts to unbutton your blouse or she grabs hold of your zipper, tell your partner to stop and explain why. Tell him or her that your reluctance is not because you don't want to become intimate — assuming that you do — but because you need to talk about safer sex first.

After having this conversation, you may both decide to renew your activities, possibly stopping at a prearranged point or maybe going all the way, depending on what you said. Whatever the final outcome, at least you'll know that the decision was calculated and not left to chance.

Steve and Betsy

Steve and Betsy were in college. They started going out in September, and by October they were in love. They would often wind up in each other's rooms for the night and would masturbate each other to orgasm, but Betsy wouldn't let Steve penetrate her with his penis. Steve, who wasn't a virgin, wasn't sure exactly what was going on, and then it hit him: Betsy knew about Steve's sexual relationships with other girls and was worried about AIDS.

One night, after they had dinner together in the cafeteria, he took her for a walk to a quiet part of the campus. They sat down on a bench and Steve sprung his surprise. "I've made an appointment to be tested for AIDS tomorrow." Betsy looked at him for a few moments, not saying anything.

> Finally she said, "Steve, I hope you're not doing this for me. I love you, I really do, but I'm not going to have intercourse with you, or anybody, until I get married."

Steve's brilliant piece of deduction had been dead wrong. Betsy wasn't worried about AIDS. She simply intended to keep her virginity until she found the man with whom she was going to spend the rest of her life. In this case, Steve needed to have a different sort of conversation with Betsy before bringing up diseases — one about their relationship. Betsy hadn't said anything about her commitment to wait because she'd been a little afraid that Steve might leave her over it. She was willing to offer him sexual release and was happy with the orgasms he gave her, but that was as far as she was willing to go.

Betsy should be applauded for wanting to wait. But maybe, because she was the one putting on the brakes, she should have brought the subject up earlier and saved Steve the embarrassment he felt that night on the bench.

Again, you can never assume that the other party wants to have intercourse with you. That's why raising the subject of testing can be so embarrassing in the first place. But, if you use the approach that Paul did (in the first scenario), putting the question within a context from which the other person can gracefully back out, you'll find that you are less likely to stumble the way Steve did.

Facing the STD Stigma

Although AIDS is uppermost in everyone's minds these days, herpes is an STD that was scaring people just before the AIDS crisis broke, and it is still rampant now. If you know that you have herpes, which can break out at any moment, then you have a duty to warn your potential partner so that he or she can decide whether or not to proceed. As I mention earlier in this chapter, a condom does not offer complete protection against herpes, particularly for the male partner. Consider this example.

Iris and Patrick

Iris had recently been dumped by her boyfriend and was still quite upset. When she met Patrick at a bar and he started flirting with her, she decided what she needed to restore her spirits was a night with a good looking man. Both Iris and her former boyfriend had herpes, so it wasn't something she thought much about passing on, and because she really didn't want to scare Patrick off, she opted not to tell him of the risks, particularly because she wasn't aware of having any symptoms. She did insist that he use a condom, which he probably thought was to protect her.

Iris and Patrick continued to see each other, and as Iris became more attached to him, she grew more afraid to tell Patrick the truth. After a month had passed, Patrick came down with herpes himself. He was furious at Iris and immediately broke off their relationship.

Some people believe that you can catch herpes only when the affected partner has a visible outbreak. In fact, a few days before the outbreak becomes visible, the herpes virus is present and can be transmitted to someone else. Therefore, even if you have outbreaks that are very far apart, never assume that you can't pass the disease on to a partner.

You can treat many STDs other than AIDS with penicillin or some other drug (see Chapter 19), which should be your first line of defense for you and your partners. But if you haven't gone for treatment, or if the treatment is still continuing, then you must let your partner know.

The benefits of better communication

Although having the "STD Talk" is not necessarily pleasant, you can derive other benefits from it besides limiting your risk of catching a disease. People tend to shy away from talking about sex — even the good parts. So, after you've broached the subject of sex through the conversation about STDs, don't give it the hot potato treatment and drop it right away. Try using the discussion as a stepping stone so that you can bring up other topics that you also need to address.

One topic that flows naturally from the STD discussion is contraception.

- ✔ Certainly, you should discuss the subject of condom use. Some men absolutely refuse to use them, and the woman should find this fact out ahead of time so that she can decide whether or not to go any further with him.

- ✔ If the woman intends to rely on the Pill for birth control and hasn't started taking it yet, she should tell the man that he has to wait, testing or no, until the gynecologist says it's okay to begin having sex.

The next transition is one that I realize not many people will be able to make, which is to go from talking about STDs to telling your potential new partner the best way to give you an orgasm. It's too bad that this discussion seldom takes place, because anyone who communicates that well ranks among the absolute best of lovers. Even without going that far, however, you can still initiate some communication along those lines.

For example, if you're talking about previous partners, you can use that opening as an opportunity to make a particular point. "A few years ago I dated this guy, Jack. What first attracted me to him was that he was such a gentleman. But when we started having sex, he ended up being too much of a gentleman, too squeamish to do anything but straight sex. You know what I mean?"

Even if your new partner doesn't know exactly what you mean, your partner should get the idea not to be afraid of trying some different things.

Remember that if you do bring up past partners, you don't want to do it in a way that is threatening or that causes performance anxieties. On the other hand, bringing up past partners can be a good way of introducing a subject, so use your past effectively, yet carefully.

Key points to discuss

And don't be afraid to prepare for that moment when the lines of communication are open. If you want to get a particular message across, try to plan some things that you may say. Even if you don't follow the script to the letter, writing some ideas down ahead of time makes the discussion easier.

Because I don't know exactly what your desires may be, I can't give you the exact words you need, but I think some of the following phrases will give you some guidelines for how to work your needs into the conversation:

- ✔ "I'm glad you weren't afraid to bring up the subject of STDs. I'm sure that means that you won't be afraid to tell me if you know of something you'd like for me to do that gives you special pleasure."

- ✔ "I really appreciate that you brought up the topic of STDs. I always feel so tongue-tied when the subject of sex comes up, but I really want to communicate my feelings to you."

- ✔ "Now that I've opened my big mouth about STDs, I guess it won't surprise you that I like to be verbal in bed. I know it bothers some people, and if you tell me to stop, I'll do my best."

- ✔ "STDs aren't the only thing I'm afraid of when it comes to sex. I really dislike it when a guy tries to get me to do certain things."

I think you get the idea. If you want to get across a point that is especially important to you, use the opportunity of the STD conversation to at least give your partner a hint. Later, when you get more intimate, you can work up the courage to say more about it.

How to Get Tested

Simply agreeing that you're going to be tested for STDs isn't enough. Then you have to actually go for the test, and I want to make sure you know what that test involves. Chapter 19 gives some more details, but this section discusses some matters of sexual etiquette that still need addressing.

You can get tested for STDs by your family physician, at a clinic, or at a Planned Parenthood center. A technician draws your blood and sends it to be analyzed. Depending on the procedures used by the place where you take the test, you'll get the results in two to four weeks.

Whether you can trust the test results with regard to AIDS depends very much on the length of time since you, or your partner, has had sex with someone else. Laboratories detect AIDS by checking for the presence of antibodies for the HIV virus in the blood. These antibodies take a certain amount of time to appear in your bloodstream after your first contact with the virus. How long? The Centers for Disease Control in Atlanta recommends waiting six months to get tested. HIV antibodies can be detected anywhere from two to six months after first contact with the virus; the longer you wait to take the test, the more certain the results.

Of course, the matter of trust plays a role too:

 ✔ First, you must be able to rely on whatever your partner has told you about past partners and his or her last sexual encounters with any of them.

 ✔ Then, for the test to mean anything, you and your potential partner can't have sex with anyone else while waiting for those results, or they'll be meaningless.

While on the subject of trust, I know that many of you may not insist on having a new partner undergo any tests. You may decide to put your faith in the reported behavior pattern of this person — relatively few other sexual partners, 100 percent use of condoms — and have sex with him or her, protecting yourself with condoms. As I said before, condoms do not offer 100 percent protection, but only you can decide what to do. I understand that waiting six months for the results of a test is a burden, but I've also seen friends of mine die of AIDS and the consequences of catching some other STDs aren't pleasant either. In my opinion, you should be as careful as you possibly can be.

I certainly suggest that you read Chapter 19 carefully so you can make the decision about how best to protect yourself with as much information guiding you as possible.

The psychological issues

If you feel nervous about talking to a partner about AIDS, STDs, and the issue of testing, I have to warn you that you will feel even more nervous actually going for the test. You may think that you've been careful, or that you've slept with only a few people, but you won't really know that you're HIV-negative until you get the results back. Faced with the reality that you may get back a result that shows that you have been exposed to this deadly virus, you may have a lot of trouble going for the test. And then you face a terrible waiting period until the results come back.

Organizations do exist to help you deal with these psychological issues, and I suggest that you seek one out where you live (see Appendix B). The lab where you get tested may be able to suggest such an organization.

Another reason that you may want to look into these organizations is that, as many precautions as you think you've taken, you may be surprised to find yourself infected with HIV or another STD. If that happens, you're going to go on an emotional roller coaster, and you need to get help dealing with it. The same organization that can help to ease your fears about going for testing can also help you through the crisis of getting a positive result. Being prepared in advance is always best, especially if you're distraught.

Confidentiality versus anonymity

Even if you're a virgin, even if you've slept with only one partner in your life, if you ever need to buy life insurance, you will have to get an AIDS test. Now, as you know, the problem with testing is that sometimes doctors give you the wrong results. I was once diagnosed with having an incurable cancer, and, as it turned out, someone had misread an X-ray and thought my liver was a tumor, so I know that mistakes can happen. Because of the stigma attached to having AIDS, you don't want that information to get out, especially if a further test may come back negative.

Clinics claim that all tests are confidential. Because of the way so many computers are connected to each other, however, I don't know how much value to put in that term. Some tests are *anonymous,* which means that the blood goes to the lab with only a number attached so that only you know the final result. Before you go for the AIDS test, find out if you can have your tests done anonymously. At least that will alleviate one worry — keeping the results to yourself.

Sex without Intercourse

Some people think that the only way that they can get AIDS or other STDs is through vaginal or anal intercourse. They believe that other forms of sex are perfectly safe. Mutual masturbation is safe, providing that you don't have any open cuts on your hand. If a man puts his penis between the woman's thighs or breasts, that can also be presumed as a form of safer sex, provided that he doesn't get some of his semen on his hands and then pass it on to the woman by inserting his fingers into her vagina.

Oral sex is another story. Doctors think that saliva does kill HIV, and so oral sex is safer than vaginal or anal sex. But, even if oral sex is 20 times safer, it is not 100 percent safe. Let me say this again, *you can get AIDS and other STDs through oral sex.* You can perform oral sex on a man *(fellatio)* while he's wearing a condom, and, provided that you're careful not to bite through the latex, that should be a safer form of sex. You can also buy *dental dams,* small rubber sheets that are supposed to make *cunnilingus* (oral sex on a woman) safer. I have to tell you that I have my doubts that someone can perform oral sex on a writhing woman while keeping this dental dam in place. Oral sex is certainly safer than intercourse, but I wouldn't call it safe.

What to Do If Your Partner's Results Are Positive

What if you are confronted with a situation where your partner, or potential partner, has AIDS or some other STD? Perhaps this partner told you, or you both found out when the test results came back. What do you do then?

This question is very personal. First of all, the outcome depends on how well you know the other person. If you and this person hardly know each other, then making the decision to avoid all risks and move on is much simpler than if you've fallen in love. But even if you are head over heels in love, if the test reveals that this person has AIDS, you are certainly free to decide to pull away. After all, you must protect your life, and so far, you have no cure to look forward to.

The next step you must take is to speak to a doctor and do some research. You have to know the risk of your catching whatever disease the test found. If you partner has AIDS, then you must do some very serious thinking. Consider not only that you may become infected, but also that this person will likely get full-blown AIDS and eventually die. If you are not married, you are free, both legally and morally, to move on. Your love or your conscience may tell you to stay, but whatever your ultimate decision, don't make it without carefully weighing all the factors. Don't hesitate to seek professional guidance from a religious leader or a therapist. Few people have to face such difficult decisions, so your decision to seek counseling is not a sign of weakness, but one of good judgement.

What to Do If You Get Surprise Results

You can be infected with the HIV virus for a very long time before you show any outward signs. And many of the other STDs exhibit no symptoms, or do not reveal themselves for years or even decades. This means that you may be on the receiving end of quite a nasty surprise when you get your test results, discovering that at sometime in your past, you were infected by an STD.

If the STD you have is easily cured, then you should go straight to your doctor and do whatever is required. But what if no cure exists, as with herpes? Or what if you have HIV? Do you simply panic? Or go into a deep depression and hide under the covers? You know I'm not going to tell you to do either of those things. What you should do, what you must do, is go for some professional help. Handling a situation like this will not be easy, but it can be made easier. Professionals who counsel people with AIDS, herpes, and other STDs have the knowledge and experience to make the process more bearable for you. They can guide you through the early stages of such a crisis until you get your bearings.

Being diagnosed with AIDS is not the immediate death sentence it once was. By taking a mixture of drugs, called *cocktails,* people infected with HIV can lead fully productive lives for years and years. But it is a complicated process that takes dedication to carry out. You have to maintain that head on your shoulders, so don't waste time panicking — seek out the professional guidance you need right away and start taking an active role in maintaining your health.

AIDS has certainly changed the way people interact sexually. I do all that I can to raise money to fight this dreadful disease, and I hope that one day our scientists discover either a cure or a vaccine. Until then, however, you have to be very careful.

Too many young people think that their youth immunizes them from any form of danger — AIDS, driving too fast, skiing recklessly, drinking excessively — and that's just not true. Some older people believe that AIDS hasn't invaded their segment of the population yet, and that's not true either.

So, as they used to say after the shift briefings on the TV show *Hill Street Blues* — be careful out there.

Chapter 7

Think Safe with Sex: Reducing Your Risks

. . . .

In This Chapter

▶ Using contraception

▶ Understanding your options

▶ Previewing potential new methods

▶ Dispelling common birth control myths

. . . .

As I point out on more than one occasion in this book, the main evolutionary purpose of sex isn't to allow us to have pleasurable orgasms. Sexual intercourse is the way that our species, Homo sapiens, reproduces itself. The pleasurable aspects of sex provide an inducement to do our reproductive duty.

Now I haven't changed my mind on that. But, while for most of mankind's history sexual pleasure and reproduction were basically inseparable, in the latter half of the 20th century and the early part of the 21st century, that has all changed.

Now we can have our cake and eat it too, so to speak, because we can have great sex and terrific orgasms without much risk of making a baby when we're not ready for one. And then, when we are ready to have a family, we can decide how large the family is going to be and pretty much pick the timing of when each child will come into the world.

Not everyone thinks that this freedom is a sign of progress. Many religious leaders decry the concept of recreational sex (sex intended only to provide pleasure). And, because I'm old fashioned and a square, I too say repeatedly that one-night stands are not a good idea, even though you can possibly have sex with hundreds of people and never once make a baby.

The purpose of this book isn't to debate the moral consequences of the sexual revolution, however. Maybe one day you'll be able to buy *Morality For Dummies,* but until then, you're going to have to look elsewhere for a full discussion on the subject.

The only thing that I will state, one more time, is that sex between two people who are part of a committed relationship is much better than sex between people who are basically strangers. I say this not to attach any moral stigma to other types of behavior, but simply because I truly believe that if you follow this advice, your sex life will improve.

Where I do put my foot down, however, is when people have unintended pregnancies because they do not take the proper precautions. Although I am in favor of women having the right to an abortion, I would much prefer to see a world where people would not have unintended pregnancies, thereby wiping out abortion. We do not have the perfect contraceptive, so eliminating abortion altogether is not yet possible. But, if everybody not ready to have a baby used at least one of the methods of contraception that I describe in this chapter, society would be heading in the right direction.

Society has made a lot of progress since I first broke new ground in 1980 by telling people on my radio show, over and over again, that they must use contraception. According to the Alan Guttmacher Institute (a well-known research institute of family planning and sexual health), only 56 percent of women aged 15–44 used contraception in 1982; by 1995, that number rose to 64 percent. Despite that increase, more than 3 million unintended pregnancies still occur every year in the United States. And, according to the institute, the 3 million sexually active women of child-bearing age who don't use contraceptives account for almost half of those unintended pregnancies (47 percent), while the 39 million women who do use birth control account for 53 percent.

Because of these facts, I am still waging the same crusade. In fact, one of the primary reasons I agreed to write this book is to stress birth control. If I can prevent even one unintended pregnancy among the readers of this book, I feel I will have done an important job. So pay close attention to the material covered in this chapter, because what happens to you in the months and years ahead will not affect only you but will also reflect on my reputation!

The Four Basic Types of Contraception

Four basic types of contraception exist:

- Sterilization
- Hormonal methods

✔ Barrier methods

✔ Natural family planning

According to 1995 statistics from the Alan Guttmacher Institute, 61 percent of reproductive age women who use birth control use reversible contraceptive methods like the condom or the Pill. The remaining 39 percent rely on more permanent methods: 28 percent undergo a tubal sterilization procedure, and 11 percent are with partners who have had vasectomies. Female sterilization is the most commonly used birth control method for women over the age of 34. Women in their 20s prefer the Pill, and one-third of sexually active teenage women use the condom as their primary method of contraception.

As a consequence of the AIDS epidemic, a greater proportion of women use condoms. According to the Alan Guttmacher Institute, from 1988 to 1995, the overall proportion of women relying on condoms increased from 15 percent to 20 percent. That number rose from 20 percent to 30 percent among never-married women and from 33 percent to 37 percent among adolescents. During that same period of time, use of the Pill declined from 31 percent to 27 percent, and use of the diaphragm declined from 6 percent to 2 percent.

Remember, only one of these methods of birth control, the condom, significantly reduces your risk of catching a sexually transmitted disease. The condom is not the most effective method of birth control (although it is certainly better than nothing), but it is a vital piece of equipment in the war against AIDS and other STDs. So if you're not with one steady partner, or if your one partner has more partners than just you, you should always have some condoms on hand — and use them!

Sterilization

Sterilization methods come in two basic types: one for women (*tubal sterilization*) and one for men (the *vasectomy*).

Both the female and male methods of sterilization have certain advantages over other kinds of birth control:

✔ They are one-time operations.

✔ They are very effective.

✔ They don't have side effects.

✔ They don't affect sexual functioning.

✔ They eliminate worries about pregnancy.

A brief history of contraception

People have been trying to make the separation between sex and pregnancy for a long time. As far back as 1850 B.C., ancient Egyptians tried many different ingredients to kill sperm (act as *spermicides*), including honey, carbonate of soda, and crocodile dung. (And you complain about inserting a diaphragm or putting on a condom?)

Eventually, the Egyptian version of Planned Parenthood technicians progressed to something a bit less, shall we say, exotic. By 1550 B.C., Egyptian women were using cotton-lint tampons soaked in fermented acacia plants instead. Okay, so it's not less exotic, but it sure sounds better than crocodile dung.

In case you're curious as to how we know all this, the Egyptians used to bury recipes for these methods of contraception along with the women's bodies so that they wouldn't become pregnant in the afterlife. (I wonder if the condom concession at Forest Lawn is still available?)

Various people at various times in history came up with other items for women to insert in their vaginas to try to prevent pregnancy, including discs made of melted beeswax, oiled paper, and seaweed. In the 18th century, the noted Casanova seemed to find some success by placing the hollowed halves of lemons over the cervix of a woman — a precursor to the diaphragm used today, only a little more sour.

These various inserts were called *pessaries,* and British medical researchers cataloged more than 120 different types of vaginal barriers being used in England and in its various colonies during the 1800s. Even though the sun never set on the whole British Empire at one time, apparently considerable hanky-panky went on after dark wherever the sun had set.

You have to go back to the desert for a moment to trace the history of the first nonbarrier method of birth control for women, the *intrauterine device* (IUD). Supposedly, camel drivers used to place pebbles in the uteri of their beasts to keep the camels from getting pregnant while crossing the Sahara, and some British inventors refined that technique to create the IUD at the end of the 19th century.

And then, in 1959, the oral contraceptive pill was given its first approval by the United States Food and Drug Administration, an event that signified the beginning of the sexual revolution. For the first time, a woman could control her reproductive ability (and her menstrual cycle) with a single pill each day, eliminating fears of an unintended pregnancy.

Don't forget the male half of the population, whose principal method of contraception is the condom. That device is said to have been named by a Doctor Condom, who was supposedly a court physician to Charles II of England in the 17th century. His condom was made out of sheep's intestines scented with perfume. Actually, the Italian anatomist Fallopius (identifier and namesake of the fallopian tubes) had created the first condom 100 years earlier. His main goal was not so much to protect against pregnancy as to prevent venereal disease, which the condom did very efficiently, according to his research. The condom is still used today for its ability to protect against most sexually transmitted diseases.

The main disadvantage of sterilization is that it is permanent. If you later change your mind and want to make a baby, it is difficult — and in many cases impossible — to do so.

Many people are surprised that sterilization is the most popular method of birth control. I rarely recommend sterilization because of the permanency. That very permanency, coupled with the security of knowing that the risk of getting pregnant is extremely small, leads so many people to choose this method — especially those who have reached an age when they think they don't want children anymore. But, sterilization can have certain complications as well, including problems stemming from the anesthetic used, bleeding, infection, injury to other organs, and the possibility of failure.

Tying the tubes

A common name for the female method of sterilization is *tubal ligation,* although tubal sterilization can actually be performed in a variety of ways, not all of which call for tying the tubes.

The tubes in this case are the fallopian tubes, in which the egg is fertilized by the first sperm that finds it (see Chapter 1). If these two tubes are cut and tied, the eggs and sperm should never be able to come together (see Figure 7-1). In rare instances, the tubes grow back, and a woman can become pregnant, but this only happens in about 12 out of 1,000 cases.

Figure 7-1:
Tubal ligation gives "tying the knot" a whole new meaning.

As you may guess, tubal ligation requires a surgical procedure, but most women can undergo it on an outpatient basis (either in a hospital or clinic), under local anesthesia, and in under 30 minutes. The cost can be as high as $2,500, but this is a one-time charge as opposed to other methods that involve a cost for every use, such as the condom or birth control pill.

Complications with the procedure are possible, including bleeding, infection, or a negative reaction to the anesthetic. In most cases, however, these complications are rare, and you can easily deal with them.

Women have a number of kinds of tubal sterilization from which to choose, and usually the method a woman chooses depends on other medical factors.

- ✔ One of the two most common types of tubal ligation is called an operative *laparoscopy.*

  - First, the abdomen is inflated with an injection of harmless gas (carbon dioxide), which allows the surgeon to see the organs more clearly.

  - The surgeon then inserts a rod-like instrument, called a *laparoscope,* through a small incision. The laparoscope has a "camera" and light to help locate the tubes.

  - Finally, either with the same instrument or another, the operation to cut and tie the tubes is performed. Complications are rare.

- ✔ A *mini-laparotomy* is the other popular method. It is similar to the laparoscopy, but it does not require a viewing instrument. It is done within 48 hours of giving birth, when the abdomen is still enlarged and viewing is easier for the surgeon.

- ✔ More rarely performed is a *full laparotomy.* This is a major surgery, requiring a much larger incision, full anesthesia, and hospitalization for five to seven days, followed by several weeks of further recovery.

- ✔ *Vaginal procedures* are another option, but they are rarely performed because of the higher risk of infection.

- ✔ Last is the *hysterectomy,* which is the surgical removal of the uterus. This, too, is major surgery, and it is rarely used merely as a method of sterilization. Instead, a hysterectomy may be performed to correct another medical problem, with sterilization occurring as a side effect. With a hysterectomy, the tubes may not actually be involved, but without a uterus, pregnancy is impossible.

With any of the tubal methods of sterilization, the woman's organs function normally so that she still ovulates, has her full set of female hormones, and has her monthly period. The eggs, which continue to be released monthly, simply dissolve the way any unused cells do. (Remember, the egg is microscopic in size, so it really can't do any damage floating inside of you for a while.)

After sterilization, sexual functioning also remains the same, or is sometimes improved because the woman no longer has to concern herself about becoming pregnant. But remember, if you undergo one of these procedures, you have to assume that you will never have children again. I am one of those who doesn't like to say never, but with so many women opting for sterilization, I guess I'm in the minority.

Vasectomy

The male version of sterilization, the *vasectomy,* is also a surgical procedure that is performed on an outpatient basis. In a vasectomy, the tubes that carry the sperm (the *vas deferens*) are cut and tied (see Figure 7-2). Only very rarely do the tubes grow back together, so that only 2 out of 1,000 men who are sterilized cause a pregnancy in the first year after the operation.

Vas deferens

Vas deferens tied and cut

Figure 7-2:
A vasectomy is the male equivalent of tubal ligation.

One difference between the male and female sterilization is that some sperm remain in the man's system after the operation, so you must use another method of contraception for at least the first 20 to 30 ejaculations. You can be certain that all the sperm have passed from his system by getting a simple lab test done on the semen. Ask your doctor for more details.

Some men worry that undergoing a vasectomy will in some way reduce their sexual prowess, but this fear is ungrounded. A man feels no difference in sexual performance after a vasectomy because he can still have erections and ejaculate.

The only change after a vasectomy is that, after the system has been cleaned out, the semen no longer contains any sperm. Because sperm make up only 5 to 10 percent of the volume of the ejaculate, a man who undergoes this procedure will not be able to tell any difference, nor will his hormones be affected in any way. The testes continue to manufacture sperm, but instead of being ejaculated, the body absorbs the sperm.

Vasectomies are much less expensive than tubal sterilizations, ranging in price from $250 to $500. Trying to reverse the procedure, however, costs much more than having the procedure done in the first place. Reversing the procedure requires microsurgery, and very often such surgery is not effective. Therefore, vasectomies are considered permanent.

Attempts have been made to create a reversible vasectomy by installing a valve instead of cutting the vas deferens, but these efforts have not been effective. The sperm, those little devils, have managed to find ways of getting through.

Researchers continue to study vasectomies and their effects. Be sure to ask your doctor for all the latest information before you agree to the procedure.

Hormonal methods

The ancient Greeks had this weird idea that our temperaments and bodily functions were controlled by what they called *the four humors:* blood, mucus, yellow bile, and black bile. Because my television producer and good friend is Greek, I know how some Greeks tend to believe that they discovered everything. In this case, they were right, although they got the details slightly wrong.

The human body secretes close to 50 different hormones in the endocrine system. These *hormones* are chemical substances that go directly into the bloodstream to our various organs and control how they work. The hormones that affect the sex and reproductive systems are absolutely vital to their functioning, and, conversely, by controlling these hormones, we can now affect the functioning of our reproduction with great accuracy. The contraceptive pill works exactly like that, inhibiting pregnancy through the use of hormones.

The Pill

The Pill is a very effective method of birth control — almost as effective as sterilization, in fact — assuming full compliance (that is, assuming that the woman takes the Pill regularly and without fail). Because the Pill made having sex almost risk free, it is credited with starting the sexual revolution in the 1960s, when the use of oral contraceptives became widespread.

The Pill has undergone many transformations since those early days. Although the active ingredients in the Pill are basically the same hormones that a woman's body creates to regulate her menstrual cycle — estrogen and progestin — the high doses used when the Pill first came out caused many side effects. Today's lower dosages greatly reduce these side effects.

These days, the Pill comes in two types:

- *Combination pills,* which contain both estrogen and progestin, keep the ovaries from releasing eggs.
- The so-called *mini-pills* contain only progestin.

The Pill can prevent ovulation, but the primary way it prevents conception is by thickening the cervical mucus so that the sperm cannot penetrate it. The Pill also makes the uterine lining less receptive to implantation of sperm.

If you use the Pill, you must remember to take it every day, and preferably at the same time of the day — say, every morning — for the hormones to work best. (When using the combination pill, the woman goes off the hormones for seven days to allow for withdrawal bleeding, which simulates normal menstrual flow. In most cases, however, she continues to take placebo pills during this time to enforce the habit.)

The failure rate of the Pill relates closely to compliance, so if you are on the Pill and don't want to become pregnant, make sure that you follow to the letter the directions that your doctor gives you.

Besides preventing pregnancy, the Pill has several advantages, including

- ✔ More regular periods
- ✔ Less menstrual flow
- ✔ Less menstrual cramping
- ✔ Less iron deficiency anemia
- ✔ Fewer *ectopic pregnancies* (pregnancies that occur outside the uterus)
- ✔ Less pelvic inflammatory disease
- ✔ Less acne
- ✔ Less premenstrual tension
- ✔ Less rheumatoid arthritis
- ✔ Less ovarian cyst formation
- ✔ Protection against endometrial and ovarian cancer, two of the most common types of cancer in women

When you start taking the Pill, you may experience a little bleeding between periods, which is usually a temporary phenomenon.

Some women fear that the Pill may cause cancer of the breast or uterus because the hormones used have been linked to these cancers in animal studies. Whether or not such a risk once existed, no scientific evidence indicates that this is the case at the doses presently prescribed. In fact, the Pill has been shown to reduce the risk of cancer of the ovary or endometrium.

Just about every woman of child-bearing age can take the Pill, except those women who are smokers over the age of 35. These women should refrain from taking the Pill because it can cause some risks to the cardiovascular system, to which older women and women who smoke are more susceptible. Very recent studies have found this increased risk to the cardiovascular system to be somewhat higher than previously believed, though exactly what those risks involve remains unclear. Some other physical conditions, such as diabetes or a history of blood clots, can make the Pill unsuitable for a woman.

Because of these risks, a physician must prescribe the Pill for you. Because the medical world seems to release a new study every day, keeping up with all the latest information is difficult. So, if you're considering using the Pill, definitely have a talk with your gynecologist so you can be confident that your choice is the right one.

The initial doctor's visit usually costs between $35 and $125, though the cost can be less if you visit a clinic. The pills themselves cost between $15 and $25 per month, though again the cost may be lower at a clinic or through Planned Parenthood.

Do not try to save yourself the cost of a doctor's visit by using someone else's prescription — that's a prescription for trouble.

And I must repeat the warning concerning STDs. The Pill offers absolutely no protection against AIDS or any other sexually transmitted disease, and you must use the Pill in conjunction with a condom if any risk exists that you may catch a disease from your partner.

If you use other drugs — including antibiotics — while you're on the Pill, check with your doctor to make sure that these medications won't interfere with your method of birth control. In many cases, your doctor will advise you to use an additional form of protection at this time.

Norplant

The main problem with the Pill is compliance. Some women forget to take their daily pill and wind up pregnant. *Norplant* was created as an alternative to the Pill for women who worry about this problem.

Norplant uses a slightly different hormone, called *levonorgestrel,* which keeps the ovaries from releasing eggs and thickens the cervical mucus. The drug comes in the form of six soft capsules, about the size of a matchstick, which are inserted under the skin of the upper arm and continually release the hormone.

After a physician inserts the Norplant capsules, they protect a woman against pregnancy for five years. But the use of Norplant is reversible, so any time a woman wants to end her use of Norplant, she can have a physician trained in the process remove the capsules.

Norplant costs about $500 to $750 to be implanted; removal costs from $100 to $200. Some family-planning clinics may provide financing.

The side effects of Norplant, both positive and negative, are about the same as side effects for the Pill, although some women who are candidates for Norplant cannot take the Pill. The most common side effect of Norplant is irregular bleeding. Although this irregularity usually diminishes after about nine months, a small number of women may find that it continues up to five years. Some women have also run into problems when having the Norplant capsules removed, encountering complications during what is usually an easy procedure.

Because of the problems with Norplant removal, new implant systems are being tested. One called *Implanon* is manufactured in the Netherlands. Norplant-II is also in the works. I'll be waiting along with the rest of you to see how the testing goes.

Depo-Provera

Another alternative to the Pill is *Depo-Provera*. Like the preceding methods, Depo-Provera involves a hormone, but instead of taking a daily pill or having rods inserted into your arm, with Depo-Provera you get a shot every 12 weeks.

Certainly, a woman who doesn't like injections won't choose this product. And, although its side effects are the same as the Pill's, if you don't like them, you can't simply stop taking Depo-Provera (like you can the Pill) or have the rods removed (like you can with Norplant). Instead, you must wait until the full 12 weeks have passed for the effects of the shot to go away. That also holds true if you want to get pregnant, though most people aren't in such a rush to have a baby that they can't wait such a short time.

The costs of the injection range from $30 to $75. But, again, a clinic may charge less.

The intrauterine device (IUD)

The IUD is the modern outgrowth of the pebbles that camel herders would put inside their animals to prevent pregnancy (see the sidebar on the history of contraception earlier in this chapter). Perhaps pebbles would also work on women, but I don't suggest you try it — they haven't been approved by the FDA. The IUD, which is approved, is a small plastic device containing either a hormone or copper that is inserted into a woman's uterus. IUDs work either by preventing the fertilization of the egg or by preventing implantation of a fertilized egg in the uterine wall.

The IUD has faced a lot of controversy, so much so that many women no longer consider it an option. One brand of IUD, the Dalkon Shield, did have problems and has been removed from the market. Some other manufacturers then pulled their brands out of the American market in fear of potential lawsuits. However, the World Health Organization and the American Medical Association rate the IUD as one of the safest and most effective temporary methods of birth control for women.

Because of this controversy and because IUDs are of two basic types — ones that contain hormones and ones that contain copper — definitely speak with a doctor or clinician before making up your mind about whether to use them.

Inserted into the uterus through the cervix during menstruation, the IUD can be left in place for up to ten years (some must be replaced every year, some after two years). Exactly how this device prevents pregnancy depends on the type of IUD that you use.

A critical component of the IUD is the string that hangs down from the end and protrudes through the cervix into the vagina. The IUD is very good at protecting against pregnancy — if it is in place. Occasionally, the IUD can slip out, and you may not realize that it's gone. If that happens, you are no longer protected against pregnancy. Therefore, you should regularly check to make sure that the string is in place.

The advantage of the IUD is that — apart from checking for the string — you don't have to worry about it. And the IUD does not change either the hormone levels or the copper levels in a woman's body.

You may have some cramping when the IUD is first inserted, and some women have heavier bleeding for the first few months; a few women may develop a pelvic infection. Even rarer are problems with the IUD being pushed up into the uterus and causing other types of complications. But, all in all, compared to other forms of birth control, and especially compared to using no birth control at all, the IUD is safer than most methods. (But remember that if you are not in a monogamous relationship you still need to protect yourself from STDs.)

The cost of an exam and insertion ranges from $150 to $300.

On the horizon

If I ever find Aladdin's magic lamp and the genie grants me three wishes, I definitely know what at least one of those wishes will be — the perfect method of birth control. Each method that is available currently has drawbacks of one sort or another.

But because I don't believe in genies — or even dream of Jeannies — I would like to see a lot more money invested into this area of research. Some money is being spent, however, and some new developments have come of it.

The vaginal ring

A new method of hormonal control of pregnancy is on the horizon The *vaginal ring* is inserted like the diaphragm (see "The barrier methods" section later in this chapter). It stays in place for three weeks of the month and is removed for one week during menstruation. The ring does not act as a barrier, like the diaphragm; instead, it releases the same types of hormones you find in the Pill. Each ring contains enough hormones for three cycles, so you must get a new one every three months.

Although the ring can cause some of the same side effects as the Pill, these effects should be milder because a woman places the vaginal ring right next to the cervix, so she receives an even lower dosage of hormones than she would if she were taking the low-dose contraceptive pill. Yet she still receives all the same benefits of the hormones in the Pill.

The vaginal ring is still being studied. If this form of contraceptive interests you, check with your doctor every now and then to see if the ring has been approved.

The male pill

A male version of the contraceptive pill is currently under study. Like the Pill for women, this male contraceptive involves adding hormones. In this case, the Pill adds a synthetic version of the male hormone, testosterone, which causes sperm production to shut down for about a week. But, because taking this hormone orally can cause liver damage, the male version of the Pill will never be an actual pill; it will have to be an injection. This contraceptive is still undergoing tests and probably won't be ready for many years.

The barrier methods

The aim of the barrier methods is to block the sperm from getting at the egg. Applying military tactics to this job, the logical place to begin is at the narrowest opening: the cervix. Casanova first tried a barrier method using hollowed-out halves of lemons at the cervix, but these days latex has pretty much taken over for the citrus family.

The diaphragm and cervical cap

The *diaphragm* is a shallow, dome-shaped cup. It has a flexible rim to allow for insertion, because it needs to be folded to be placed into the vagina (see Figure 7-3). The diaphragm is made to block the whole rear part of the vagina, including the cervix, protecting that entranceway from invasion by any attacking sperm.

Because sperm don't give up all that easily, the diaphragm works best in conjunction with a spermicidal cream or jelly. You must leave the diaphragm in place for at least eight hours after sexual intercourse to give the spermicide sufficient time to kill all the sperm. You can leave it in the vagina for up to 24 hours.

The *cervical cap* works the same way as the diaphragm, the difference being one of shape: The cap is smaller and fits more tightly over the cervix. Doctors usually recommend the cap for women whose pelvic muscles are not strong enough to hold a diaphragm in place. Because of the tighter fit, however, some women complain about difficulties in removing the cervical cap.

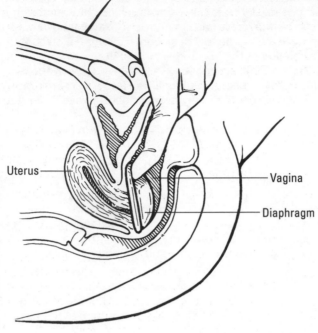

Figure 7-3:
One of
the main
reasons dia-
phragms are
sometimes
ineffective
is because
of improper
insertion.

Uterus — Vagina

Diaphragm

Although neither the diaphragm nor the cervical cap has any side effects, they are not the easiest methods of birth control to use.

✔ The diaphragm or the cap can be cumbersome to insert because you not only have to put cream or jelly on it and then place it in the vagina, you have to insert it carefully enough that you are sure that it is seated properly.

✔ Even though you can insert the diaphragm or cap up to six hours before intercourse — so that you can plan ahead of time and not have to inter-rupt a hot date to put in your diaphragm — if another episode of sexual intercourse is going to take place after the first, you must add more spermicide.

You cannot use either the diaphragm or the cervical cap during menstruation.

The diaphragm does not come close to offering as much protection against pregnancy as some of the other methods of birth control that I cover. In fact, with normal use, 18 out of 100 women who use the diaphragm become preg-nant during the first year. Even among the women who learn to use the diaphragm perfectly, 6 out of 100 become pregnant. On the other hand, if you're not happy messing with your hormones, or if your body won't let you, then the diaphragm is a good alternative.

The spermicides used with the diaphragm do offer some protection against AIDS and other sexually transmitted diseases, but not enough to really count on. If you're at all worried about being at risk, make sure that you also use a condom.

Because both the diaphragm and cervical cap must be fitted, you must visit a physician to get this type of birth control. That visit may cost anywhere from $50 to $125, while the devices themselves cost between $13 and $25.

Both the diaphragm and the cap should last for several years, but you should hold them up to the light regularly to check them for wear, primarily holes. And, if you undergo a physical change, such as a pregnancy or significant weight loss or gain, you should go for another fitting before using the device again.

The sponge

The sponge is just that, a sponge that contains a spermicide that blocks the opening to the cervix. You don't need a doctor's prescription because you can get the sponge over the counter. Because using the sponge came with a risk of toxic shock syndrome, I was never a fan of this particular method of contraception, and because of manufacturing difficulties, the sponge was eventually pulled from the American market. Plans are afoot to bring it back, however. I urge any women interested in the sponge to be cautious and read all the fine print before you decide on using this device.

The condom

When the Pill first came out, people suddenly relegated the lowly condom to the back of the shelf. But then along came AIDS, and the condom's ability to protect its user from transmitting diseases pushed it again to the forefront.

Romancing the diaphragm

If you didn't plan on having sex and so didn't put your diaphragm in place ahead of time, that doesn't mean that the act of putting in the diaphragm has to break up that romantic moment. Instead, try integrating the insertion of your diaphragm into foreplay.

If you're turning your nose up at this suggestion, that's probably because you're a bit squeamish about placing your diaphragm into your vagina when you're alone, not to mention with an audience, albeit of one.

But what you have to remember is that men are visual creatures. The more up close and personal they get with what are normally your private parts, the more excited they become. So, although the thought of putting in your diaphragm in front of your man may turn you off, I guarantee that it will turn him on.

If you don't believe me, try it out. And if it turns out to make you more excited as well, you may find the extra lubrication useful in the insertion process.

I doubt that anyone over the age of 12 doesn't know exactly what a condom is, but, to be thorough, I'll now launch into a description of this rising media star.

The condom is a sheath that fits over the penis, blocking the sperm from being released into the vagina. Most condoms are made of latex, although some are made out of animal tissue (usually lambskin), and now you can get condoms made of polyurethane. Although the latter are more expensive, they're thinner and stronger than latex condoms, nonporous and nonpermeable to all viruses (including HIV), hypoallergenic, safe to use with oil-based products, and heat conductive, which is supposed to make them transmit sensations between partners better.

Lambskin condoms have microscopic holes that, while small enough to stop the sperm in midbackstroke, are big enough to allow viruses safe passage into the vagina. These condoms, therefore, do not offer adequate protection against HIV.

Condoms are widely available at drugstores, at some supermarkets and convenience stores, and in dispensers in many public restrooms. When you purchase a condom, it comes rolled up in a package. You place the condom on the erect penis and roll it down along the shaft, leaving a small pocket at the top to collect the semen. (For you graphically inclined readers, see Figure 7-4.) Be sure to smooth out any air bubbles.

Figure 7-4:
Although how to use a condom may seem obvious, many people wind up paying a high price for not knowing as much as they thought they did.

Leave space at tip

Roll it completely down the shaft

The days of the boring condoms are over. Now you can buy them in various colors, different sizes, and with unique packaging. You can also purchase dry or lubricated condoms (even flavored ones!). Some lubricated condoms include a spermicide for added protection.

Speaking of sizes, condoms for most men are like socks in that they are pretty much a one-size-fits-all piece of equipment. But for men built a lot larger or smaller than average, it is important to look for a condom with a different fit. Men with smaller penises may have a problem with some condoms slipping off during intercourse. They should purchase condoms with a "snugger fit." Among the brands that make this type are Lifestyle and Exotica. Men who are more amply endowed risk splitting a regular condom, but a brand called Maxxum aims at this market. If you have problems finding these condoms in your area, I suggest calling Condomania at 1-800-9-CONDOM and ordering some by mail.

If you use a dry condom and decide to add a lubricant, make sure that the lubricant is a water-based one, like KY Jelly. Oil-based lubricants, like Vaseline, or other products made from mineral or vegetable oils, including Reddi Whip, can break down the latex and make the condom porous. This breakdown can happen very quickly, so do not use any of these products with a condom.

Removal is tricky

The trickiest part of using a condom can be removing it. Always be very careful to make sure that the condom doesn't leak because, if the sperm escape from their little rubber prison, they can make their way up into the vagina and pull off the escapade that you are trying to prevent.

- ✔ Either the man or the woman should hold onto the base of the condom to keep it on the shaft of the penis while the man pulls his penis from the vagina.

- ✔ To minimize the risk of leakage, you should remove the condom before the man loses his erection entirely.

Condoms aren't perfect

Although the condom is relatively risk free to the man (unless he happens to be allergic to latex), it is not the best of methods as far as offering protection from pregnancy. Of 100 women whose partners use condoms, approximately 12 will become pregnant during a year of typical use, because condoms can break during use or semen can spill from them during the removal process. Obviously, the more careful you are using a condom, the more protection it offers. The biggest reason for condom failure, however, is failure to use it in the first place. In other words, a couple may say that their method of birth control is the condom, but they only occasionally use condoms.

If you rely on condoms to protect against pregnancy or STDs, you must use them all the time.

Condoms and the pleasure principle

Although many women applaud the condom because it forces men to take responsibility for something that has long been left to women, men often complain that wearing a condom during sex diminishes their sensations.

Now, for some men who have problems with premature ejaculation, reducing their sensations can be a good thing. But I understand that, for the rest of the men reading this book, reduced sensations are a drawback.

If I could snap my fingers and make AIDS and all the other STDs out there disappear, I would be doing my best imitation of a Flamenco dancer all day long, I assure you. However, the sad truth remains that we do not have either a cure or a vaccine against AIDS, so you really have no choice but to use a condom when having sex that has any risk of passing along a disease. I know that using condoms when the woman is also using a method of birth control only adds to the man's frustration. In such a situation, however, if you stay in the relationship long enough, you may be able to throw those condoms away one day.

Condoms don't last forever

Speaking of throwing away condoms reminds me of something. Some men carry condoms in their wallets on the off chance that they'll get lucky, which is okay as long as you think of that condom the way you think of the oil in your car — you need to change it every 3,000 miles.

I don't want to put a time limit on how long a condom can stay in a wallet before you need to declare it damaged goods. That decision depends on a lot of factors, including how hot it is outside and how big a tush you have. But I will say that a year is way too long, even if you're a skinny guy living in Alaska.

By the way, this advice doesn't apply only to wallets. A man has a number of places where he may keep a "safety," including the glove compartment or trunk of his or his parents' car, his lunch box, his tool kit, or his kilt. Whatever that place is, if it is subject to extremes of cold or heat, assume that, after a while, the condom will no longer be reliably "safe."

The female condom

Because too many men have been giving women flak for forcing them to wear condoms, a female condom has been developed that allows women to protect themselves against sexually transmitted diseases. The female condom is a loose-fitting pouch with a closed end that you insert deep inside your vagina. Like a diaphragm, you can insert the female condom ahead of time or right before intercourse. The closed end must be lubricated first. The open end is left outside the vagina, and the male inserts his penis into it when entering the vagina for intercourse.

Some of the problems that couples have encountered using the female condom include

> ✔ Vaginal irritation.
>
> ✔ The outer ring irritating the vulva or possibly slipping into the vagina during intercourse.
>
> ✔ The inner ring possibly irritating the penis.

Some couples have also complained that the condom reduces their feeling and that it is noisy.

Although condoms for men can cost as little as 25 cents, the female condom costs $2.50. Because it offers women the freedom of self-reliance when it comes to protecting themselves against AIDS, I believe this is a small price to pay.

Foams, creams, and gels

Available over the counter are many contraceptive foams, creams, and gels. They do not require a prescription, and apart from possible temporary allergic reactions to the chemicals of which they are made — which may affect the woman, the man, or both — they have relatively few side effects. They also are relatively ineffective when used by themselves.

Of 100 women who use a contraceptive foam, cream, jelly, or suppository, 21 will become pregnant during the first year of typical use, although if perfectly used, that number drops to three.

The spermicides in these products do offer some protection against HIV and other STDs, but I don't recommend that you rely solely on these products to remain disease free.

Most of these products come with applicators to place them inside the vagina. You use each product a little differently, but in general you should put it in place at least ten minutes before intercourse (though this process can be integrated into part of foreplay). You must add spermicide each time you intend to repeat sexual intercourse.

The Vaginal Contraceptive Film

Another way of applying a spermicide is the Vaginal Contraceptive Film (VCF), a two inch by two inch paper-thin sheet that contains *nonoxynol-9* (a chemical that kills sperm). You place it on or near the cervix, where it dissolves in seconds, releasing the spermicide. Like other spermicides, when used perfectly only six percent of women using VCF become pregnant. Under normal use, however, the number jumps to 25 percent.

These products are easy to buy and easy to use, but they're much more effective when used in conjunction with either a diaphragm, cervical cap, or condom.

Natural family planning

Certainly the best way to avoid becoming pregnant is *abstinence,* or never having sexual intercourse.

Another way is to be abstinent during the time of month when the woman is fertile and can become pregnant (see Chapter 1 for a discussion of these times). This reliance on the time of the month that a woman is fertile is called *natural family planning* (or periodic abstinence, or fertility awareness method, or the calendar or rhythm method).

Natural family planning is based on the regular patterns of fertility that most women have. Right away, you can see the number-one drawback these methods share. Many women are not all that regular, and even those who are regular sometimes have irregular months. When that happens, an unintended pregnancy can result.

To use any of these methods, you must first try to predict when you will next ovulate. Unless you already know that you're "regular," meaning that your period always comes at the same time in your cycle, your first step is to determine what pattern you follow. If your pattern tends to be very irregular, natural family planning carries more risk of pregnancy for you.

Calendar method

Your fertile period is not just the day that you ovulate. The egg lives for one to three days, but sperm can live inside the vagina from two to seven days. This means that, if you have had sexual intercourse before the time that you ovulate, any of those sperm may still be hanging around the fallopian tubes when the egg comes along, ready to ambush the egg and impregnate the woman.

To be safe from pregnancy, you should think of a nine-day period as being risky — five days before you ovulate, the day of ovulation, and three days after that. During that fertile period, you should either abstain from sexual intercourse or use a barrier method.

The other 19 days that comprise the cycle are considered to be "safe," and — theoretically — you can have sexual intercourse during those days without using any other method of birth control and not become pregnant. But nothing is ever certain when those sneaky eggs and sperm are involved, so be aware of the risks.

By now this should be a reflex, but I will give you this warning once again. Even if you are presumably safe from becoming pregnant, that doesn't mean that you are safe from getting a sexually transmitted disease. Unless you are certain that your partner is 100 percent safe, you should make sure that a condom is in place before attempting intercourse.

Basal body temperature

You can use other indications of when you are fertile in conjunction with the calendar method. One is *the basal body temperature method.*

A woman's temperature rises slightly (between 0.4 and 0.8 degrees) when she ovulates. If you take your temperature every morning before you get out of bed using a special high-resolution thermometer, and if you discover a rise one day (and you're sure that you don't have an infection of some sort to account for the rise), then you can presume that you have ovulated and should refrain from unprotected sex.

Of course, any sperm deposited ahead of time can still impregnate you. Therefore, this method only serves as a proof that the calendar method is working.

If you want to get pregnant, the basal body temperature is a good predictor of when you should be having intercourse to make a baby.

Cervical mucus

Another way of checking whether or not you are ovulating is to examine your cervical mucus, which thins out when you are ovulating to allow the sperm to pass through. By continually checking the cervical mucus, you can notice when it begins to thin out, indicating that you have ovulated. Interpreting your mucus is tough without training, so I recommend that you take a class — offered by some hospitals — on how to identify the changes in your mucus if you plan to try this technique.

As with the basal body temperature method, this is a reliable method of telling when a woman has ovulated, which is useful information if you are trying to become pregnant. By itself, however, examining the cervical mucus does not let you know when you are about to ovulate. Therefore, any sperm already deposited in your vagina can impregnate you.

One more way that you can tell if you have ovulated is by recognizing the actual sensations of ovulation, called *mittelschmerz.* Usually, only one of the two ovaries releases an egg. Some women can sense when this happens by a slight pain in their lower abdomen, on either the right or left side. Not every woman has these sensations or recognizes them, so the phenomenon is not commonly discussed.

The sympto-thermal method

When you combine these three methods — the calendar method, the basal body temperature method, and the cervical mucus method — the conglomerate method is called the *sympto-thermal method.* This method can serve as a relatively accurate guide for deciding when to abstain from sex or use a barrier method.

Under normal usage, of 100 women using the periodic abstinence method — meaning they refrain from having intercourse during what they believe is their fertile period — 20 will become pregnant. However, if perfect use can be obtained, the number drops to three.

Because outside factors can play havoc with natural family planning, perfect use is rare.

- A lack of sleep can cause a woman's temperature to vary.

- The consistency of a woman's cervical mucus can change if she has a vaginal infection, of which she may not be aware.

- Either one of a woman's ovaries may decide to evict an egg for nonpayment of rent at any old time.

For more about natural family planning, see Appendix B.

Facts about Birth Control Myths

Okay, so your head is filled with all the facts about birth control. What worries me now is that you may still have some other "facts" floating around up there, which are really myths that can get you into big trouble.

To make sure that you can truly distinguish between fact and myth, I'm going to spell out the myths to you and then dispel them just as quickly.

Douching does not prevent pregnancy

The first myth concerns douching, which is useless both for hygiene and birth control purposes.

The concept of washing out the sperm before they can make their way up into the uterus dates back to at least the time of ancient Egypt (so you see that this falsehood can truly be said to be of mythical proportions). The ingredients used in these douches have changed over the years. When I was young, vinegar was supposed to do the trick; more recently I've heard that Coca-Cola is a douche of choice.

The fact is that, by the time you finish with intercourse and douche, many sperm have already begun their trip toward the egg and are beyond your ability to flush them out.

Although the advertisers on Madison Avenue may not try to convince you to use douching as a contraceptive, they do try to sell the concept of douching as a way of maintaining personal hygiene. Some experts think that women should avoid these products because they kill helpful bacteria, and they certainly don't do any good. If you have nothing better to do with your money, I suggest you give it to the charity of your choice rather than buy these commercial douches.

One time is all it takes

Like the wives' tale about douching, another myth that has gotten a lot of women in trouble is that a woman cannot get pregnant from her first attempt at sexual intercourse.

If her hymen is intact, a virgin may bleed, and she may also suffer a little discomfort. However, these factors are irrelevant to the joining of sperm and egg, so first-timers have to take the same precautions as everyone else.

You can get pregnant without orgasms

Some people believe that if the woman doesn't have an orgasm then she can't become pregnant.

It is true that the vaginal contractions of orgasm cause the cervix to dip into the pool of sperm-laden semen at the bottom of her vagina and can help foster pregnancy. Nevertheless, some of the sperm are going to make their way up the cervix whether the woman has multiple orgasms or none at all.

My advice is to go ahead and have those orgasms . . . after you've taken care of birth control.

Stand-ups don't stop sperm

Some people think that sperm cannot defy gravity, so that, if the couple has sex standing up, she won't get pregnant.

Wrong again, folks. Those sperm are strong swimmers and can go upstream as well as down.

Pregnancy and periods can mix

Some people trust that if a woman is menstruating, then she can't become pregnant.

Although menstruation does limit the odds of becoming pregnant, it is not a 100-percent, sure-fire way to prevent pregnancy. Some women have irregular bleeding, which is not true menstruation. Misinterpreting this bleeding can throw off your strategy for preventing pregnancy.

Pulling out is no protection

And now I come to the most dangerous of myths, which has caused more pregnancies than any other: the epic tale of the withdrawal method.

Through the ages, men have sworn to probably millions of women that they have great control over their ejaculations and that, as soon as they feel their orgasm coming, they will remove the penis from the vagina so she won't get pregnant.

This theory has a lot of holes in it:

✔ In the first place, a lot of men who think they have matters under control, don't. They wind up ejaculating before they can pull out.

✔ Some men, in the heat of excitement, forget their promise and don't pull out.

✔ Even if the man does pull out before he ejaculates, it's already too late. The pre-ejaculatory fluid produced by the Cowper's gland is filled with sperm, and those sperm are already making their way up into the uterus long before their brethren are being expelled onto milady's stomach or thighs.

So, although *coitus interruptus* — the fancy Latin name for this not-so-fancy method of birth control — may be better than nothing, it's not much better. And, of course, it offers little protection against the spread of sexually transmitted diseases.

If Your Method Fails

If a man and a woman want to have a baby together, then finding out that the woman is pregnant can be one of the happiest moments of their lives. On the other hand, finding out about an unintended pregnancy can be one of the loneliest and scariest moments of an unmarried woman's life.

I certainly can't tell any woman what she should do under those circumstances, but I can let you know what your options are.

Keeping the baby

One option is to carry the baby to term and keep it. More and more single women are certainly doing this. Some of these young mothers feel that having a baby is a rite of passage to adulthood, many actually following in their mother's footsteps.

I strongly disagree with this attitude, because a baby brought up in a household without a father is usually missing both the male half of the child's upbringing and often the financial support, too. (Remember, however, that whether you are married to the father of your baby or not, he has a legal obligation to help you take care of that baby financially, and you should stick up for those rights.) These women are better off preparing themselves for adulthood by finishing their education rather than trying to rush into it by having a child.

Some women who have the financial means to bring up a child by themselves decide to become single parents because they can't find an acceptable husband, but they don't want to miss out on the joys of motherhood. Thanks to Dan Quayle, the TV character of Murphy Brown became the epitome of this type of woman.

To some degree, I agree with the then–vice president's criticism, because the "Murphy Browns" of the world are really the exception rather than the rule. As a successful newswoman, she definitely had the financial wherewithal to raise a child on her own. This is not the case with most single mothers, and I believe a danger exists in glamorizing single motherhood on TV. Doing so may lure some women into following in Murphy's footsteps even though they do not have anything approaching her finances.

One thing is for certain: With so many single women having babies, the stigma that was once attached to the status of unwed mother has all but vanished. People may still raise their eyebrows, but they certainly won't stone you.

If you choose to keep your baby, I wish you the best of luck. I went through it with my first child, and I certainly enjoyed motherhood to no end. But, though I know you will have many moments of joy through the years, you will also face many difficulties that mothers with husbands do not.

Of course, you can also marry the father of your child. But I urge you to do this only if the two of you love each other and want to raise a family together. The unintended conception of a baby has created many loving couples, but it's not the best way to start a marriage.

Putting the baby up for adoption

Another option is to have the baby and give it up for adoption. Many couples who can't have children would make wonderful parents for your child. The social worker at any major hospital should be able to guide you into finding a qualified adoption agency.

Giving up a baby for adoption isn't as easy as it may seem. As the baby grows inside of you, you will not be able to keep yourself from growing attached to it, and after you actually see it, the task of giving it up will be heart-wrenching. The emotions that giving a baby up for adoption entail are one of the big reasons I say over and over again how important it is to do everything you can to avoid an unintended pregnancy.

Another thing to consider is that, before you can give a baby up for adoption, the father must also agree. If the father isn't available, later complications can arise if he decides that he wants to raise the baby.

Although in some cases adoptions have been reversed, be very certain that you want to give up the child before you actually do so. Every child deserves a secure set of parents.

Ending the pregnancy early

Some women may choose abortion. An *abortion* is the termination of a pregnancy by the loss or destruction of the fetus before it has reached *viability* — the ability to sustain itself outside the womb.

Some abortions are spontaneous, meaning the woman's body rejects the baby for some reason. This is called a *miscarriage*. Although doctors don't always know what causes a miscarriage, they very often discover that something was seriously wrong with the fetus.

Abortions can also be artificially induced, usually by a physician. Ninety percent of all abortions performed in this country are done in the first 12 weeks of pregnancy, when the embryo or fetus is barely visible or quite small. The usual method of an early abortion is *vacuum aspiration*. The cervix is numbed and the embryo or fetus is removed with vacuum suction through a narrow tube that is inserted through the cervix. Normally, the procedure takes about five minutes, is done on an outpatient basis, and has few complications.

If you wait longer than 12 weeks, everything gets a lot more complicated because the fetus has grown in size so that it can no longer simply be aspirated. The types of procedures range from *dilation and curettage* (D&C), which involves a scraping of the uterine lining, to *dilation and evacuation,* which involves a scraping and aspiration, to the *saline abortion,* in which a saline solution is injected into the uterine cavity. All these procedures are more difficult to perform than simple vacuum aspiration and involve added risks to the woman.

Emergency contraception

Sometimes a doctor can administer a large dose of estrogen and progestogen, something like the early pill, to induce what would normally be termed a miscarriage; that is, the uterus expels the embryo. This dosage of hormones has been nicknamed the *morning-after pill,* but it can be taken up to 72 hours after sexual intercourse. You can find a number of different brands of the morning-after pill, including Alesse, Ovral, Lo-Ovral, Nordette, Levlen, and Tri-Levlen. Each brand requires various amounts of pills and has differing side effects. Only a clinician can administer these drugs, so I advise you to ask your doctor for a recommendation on which brand to use. If you don't have a gynecologist and want to find the address of a clinic near you, call 1-888-NOT-2-LATE.

A pill that has the same effect as the morning-after pill but uses a different combination of drugs is called RU 486 (mifepristone). Developed in France, RU 486 can be used whether the woman is certain that she is pregnant or not, which is especially useful in cases of contraceptive failure (a condom breaking, for example) or rape.

RU 486 works by blocking the effects of progesterone, which is key to establishing pregnancy. Two days after taking the RU 486 pill, the woman is given a dose of prostaglandin; after that, most women experience bleeding and the passage of tissue within four hours. RU 486 can be effective at preventing pregnancy up to ten days after a woman has missed her period.

After many years of being approved for use in Europe, mifepristone was approved by the FDA for sale in the United States in September of 2000.

A woman's right

Abortion is a very controversial topic because many people, either for religious or moral reasons, believe that the embryo or fetus is no different than a baby and should not be destroyed. The Supreme Court has ruled, in the landmark decision of *Roe v. Wade,* that a woman's right to privacy overrides the state's ability to control what she does to her own body, effectively legalizing abortions. Although that decision took care of the legal issues, it did not change the minds of those people who are against abortion, and so the controversy continues to rage.

Abortions really upset me, but what used to happen before abortions were legalized is even more odious to me. At that time, safe abortions, either done in other countries where they are legal or done by real doctors in the United States surreptitiously, were available only to the rich, which forced poor women or women of only modest means to seek out unsafe, illegal abortions that often left them seriously injured or dead.

 Abortion, legal or not, should never be used as a form of birth control. The methods of birth control that exist may not be perfect, but they are quite effective and much better alternatives to abortion. But, no matter how conscientious a women is, contraceptive failures do occur, as do rapes. Because of those circumstances beyond the control of women, I believe that society must retain the right to have an abortion when needed.

Making your decision

Outlining these choices was a lot easier for me than selecting one of them will be for you if you are faced with an unintended pregnancy. This is even truer if you are alone, without the assistance and guidance of the father of the child.

My advice is not to try to make the decision alone. Seek out guidance or counseling from someone, preferably someone who has helped others who've faced the same problems; family members may love you, but their own emotions may supersede your needs.

 Planned Parenthood, where I used to work, is a nationwide agency that specializes in this field. Their counselors are usually well trained and very good at helping women go through the decision-making process.

 Other agencies and clinics also advertise that they are capable of guiding you, but be wary because some of these places are not impartial. Some have a greater interest in getting you to say yes to undergoing a procedure from which they make money than in offering you objective advice. Others may indicate that they give free advice, but the only advice that they give is not to have an abortion.

I often recommend that people consult with their religious leaders on many issues, but, on the issue of abortion, a religious leader may have a point of view that does not allow him or her to be objective regarding your particular circumstances or needs.

So do seek out the guidance of whomever you feel can help you, but remember that the final decision rests with you.

Part III
Doing It

The 5th Wave   By Rich Tennant

"It's an agreement Arthur and I made—he agrees to stay home from the gym 2 nights a week, and I guarantee that he'll still burn over 300 calories each night."

In this part . . .

If you want to be a rock 'n' roll star, first you have to learn to play the guitar. If you want to be a computer whiz, first you have to learn to point and click. And if you want to become a great lover, you have to develop certain skills that you'll read about in these chapters. By the way, you mustn't stop reading until the end, because what goes on after you "do it" is just as important as all the rest of "doing it."

Chapter 8

The First Time

*O*ne of the great things about sex is that, after you do it, after you experience that great feeling that only sex can bring, you get to do it over and over again, literally thousands of times during a lifetime. Talk about a gift that keeps on giving . . . and it doesn't even need batteries!

To the extent that, when you have sex, you will probably wind up with an orgasm or two, similarities exist among all sexual episodes. But you can also find that each time you have sex is very different. At times when passions run high, your orgasm will feel like an explosion. Other times, sex has a more gentle quality but is still very satisfying. However, the one time that is like no other — because it can only happen once — is your first time.

Virginity Is Not a Renewable Resource

Many people have the wrong attitude about the first time. They look at it as a barrier to reaching adulthood, one that they must cross as soon as possible. Or else they feel that virginity is a sign of weakness, as if everybody walking down the street knows that they're a virgin and laughs behind their backs. Whatever your own feelings about being a virgin, society then reinforces that image through peer pressure and the storylines of movies and television shows in which the hero is a macho guy who always gets the girl — and always gets her into bed.

Even your own family can pressure you. Great aunts are forever asking young-sters why they don't have boyfriends or girlfriends yet. Some mothers take their teenage daughters to the gynecologist to be fitted for a diaphragm or get a prescription for the Pill even though the daughters don't have boyfriends and aren't ready for what, to them, is a very embarrassing step. And then even some fathers, when their sons reach a certain age, march them off to visit a prostitute to prove their manhood.

What's the rush?

I say, what's the rush?

Yes, the sooner you start having sex, the more sex you can have had over the course of a lifetime. But if you're not ready for sex, or if you have sex with the wrong people, you can end up a lousy lover, and never have great sex. And then some people start off so quickly that they burn out and give up on sex altogether.

Having your first sexual encounter at an early age does not guarantee that you won't regret it later on. Therefore, I believe that you shouldn't jump into bed with someone just to get the deed over with, though I know that many people still do exactly that.

A few men lose their virginity to prostitutes; many men go only one level up: a local girl who is known to "put out." This girl is usually someone who des-perately craves attention, especially from men. Maybe she is overweight and thinks she can't find someone who'll have sex with her because he loves her, or maybe she was sexually molested as a child and has a very low sense of self-esteem, but the one thing that every guy in the neighborhood knows about her is that she never says no. An older brother or another of the guys who have used her "services" may bring the young man to this girl.

Many young people of both sexes, in America at least, lose their virginity in the back seat of a car. They can barely get their clothes off, they're worried that someone will see them, they're in cramped quarters that make every move uncomfortable, and their goal is to get it over with as quickly as possible.

Treasured memories

To me, all the previous scenarios are sad. Unless you were drunk out of your mind (another sad scene), you will never forget when, where, and with whom you lost your virginity. That memory can be a cold one — with someone you barely knew — or it can be a warm, loving memory — with a man or woman you really cared for, and who cared for you. The fact that you may no longer be together doesn't matter; what really matters is that, at the time, all the vibrations were good ones.

Although I don't necessarily expect you to wait until you are married to have sex for the first time, I do caution you not to throw the moment away, but to treasure it and respect it. Make it special, and you can enjoy replaying the moment over and over again in your head. Make it sordid, and whenever the memory crops up, you'll want to push it out of your mind. Isn't it obvious which is the better set of memories?

First Time's No Charm

Let me admit something here, something that I say in other parts of this book as well — your first time may not be your greatest experience from purely a sexual point of view. Most women do not have an orgasm their first time. And for very many men, the first time is over so quickly that they aren't even sure that it really happened at all. Then why, you may ask, if people don't have such great sex their first time around, do I put so much emphasis on making it special? See the next section for some answers to that question.

Making it special

Sex is not just having an orgasm. Sex is a form of communicating with your partner, sharing a gamut of sensations from the touch of your skin together to kissing, caressing, and then, finally, orgasm. When two people are really in love, they don't just want an orgasm, they want to melt into each other and become one. You certainly wouldn't want to become one with a promiscuous person or a prostitute.

You may not be able to have great sex the first time, but that doesn't mean that the entire experience can't be a great one. You should make the first time special for several reasons:

✔ Your first sexual experience can affect your view of sex for the rest of your life. You can have a wonderful, pleasurable, and loving experience (even if it's not one for the highlight films) if the person with whom you share that first time is important to you, and if you both do it out of love for each other and not just to relieve your sexual frustrations.

✔ Another reason not to share your first time with a stranger or casual acquaintance is that, whether or not you have great sex, at the very least you don't want the first time to be an embarrassing moment, which it certainly can be.

Most people fumble around a bit their first time. Some women experience a bit of pain when a man penetrates their hymen. Some men have difficulties figuring out exactly how to put their penis into the woman's vagina. Isn't it better to know that the person you are with cares about you and will try to protect your feelings? If the most vivid memory you have of your first time is of being highly embarrassed, of someone maybe even laughing at you, what kind of a souvenir is that?

✔ Of course, you also have to think about those sexually transmitted diseases, such as AIDS. Promiscuous people, a category that includes prostitutes and the "easy lay," are much more likely to be infected with diseases.

You're not the last virgin in the world

"But Dr. Ruth," I hear you cry plaintively, "I'm the only one of my friends left who is still a virgin. I can't go on like this. I have to get laid!"

If virginity is really your only problem, then I suggest a little white lie.

The next time your friends kid you about being a virgin, tell them that you're not one anymore. You don't have to say more than that, except maybe to give them a wink. Because a good number of them probably exaggerate their sexual prowess also, I don't think that they'll question you too much.

I am tempted to write that it is amazing how times have changed, so that something that was once a virtue to be honored — that is, virginity — is now a badge of dishonor. I say "tempted" because, although virginity may appear passé, in fact it's not. Certainly most men today would still prefer that the woman they marry be a virgin — at least they say they do. And, in this day and age of rampant diseases, I believe that most women would jump at the chance to get their hands on a virgin for a husband.

So you see, virginity is still treasured — it just seems as if it isn't.

The truth is that the majority of people do not wait until they get married to have sex. The main reasons so many people have sex before they get married these days are the widespread availability of contraceptives to prevent unintended pregnancies and the fact that people delay getting married until they are older.

But having sex before you get married is quite a different thing than having sex with just anybody. You may not end up marrying the boyfriend or girlfriend you have in your college years. But, if you spend two or three years constantly in each other's company, if you say that you love each other and show it in a hundred ways, then you certainly have a relationship in which sex can blossom. Such a union is much closer to marriage than a one-night stand. Thousands of miles closer.

The dangers of demon rum

I have one more point to make before I get off my soapbox on this issue and get to the nuts and bolts — so to speak — of your first time, and that has to do with liquor (and, I suppose, other drugs as well). A lot of people have lost their virginity unwittingly because they were too high to know what was happening to them.

The binge drinking that goes on at college campuses has definitely gotten out of hand. I don't object to drinking per se, but the bingeing that takes place arises mostly from peer pressure, and I do object whenever anybody does anything for the wrong reasons.

So, if you want to get falling-down drunk from time to time because doing so gives you pleasure, be my guest. But I ask you not to do it in situations where you may wind up getting hurt. Obviously, driving when you drink is out of the question. But also, particularly if you are a woman, don't imbibe great quantities of alcohol if you know you may wind up someplace private with a lot of drunken people of the opposite sex.

In other words, if you're a woman at a fraternity party and you have consumed more than you can handle, you have problems. I have heard from too many young women that they've lost their virginity at such affairs, and hearing those stories makes me sad. So don't do it.

Giving the Green Light

The first step in losing your virginity is to let the other person know that you are ready. Even for two people who have been married for 20 years, giving the go-ahead signal can sometimes be a problem. (She's trying on some new clothes in front of him, getting dressed and undressed; he gets turned on, but she's not even close to being in the mood because the red dress she thought would go perfectly with her new bag is the wrong shade and clashes. . . .)

If you've been telling a boyfriend or girlfriend "no" over and over again for quite some time, you can't expect him or her to guess when you're finally ready. And, in any case, having sex for the first time will take a little preparation on both your parts, so it isn't something you want to spring on your partner at the last minute.

Using protection

In Chapter 6, I discuss in great detail AIDS testing and how to bring up that subject, so I won't get into it here. But testing for AIDS is something that you need to do ahead of time, as is choosing a method of contraception. Because you will be nervous the first time, no matter what, you have no point adding to your sense of unease by having doubts as to whether you're protected against an unintended pregnancy or from getting an STD.

Don't fall for the myth that you can't get pregnant your first time, because you most certainly can. (I debunk this and other myths about getting pregnant in Chapter 1.)

- ✔ If you're on the Pill, don't forget that it does not protect you against sexually transmitted diseases. You may want to use a condom as well, so you have to plan for that possibility by making your purchase ahead of time. (You don't want to use the one your boyfriend's been carrying around in his wallet for the last six months, even if he did write your name on it in Magic Marker after you found it in there!)

- ✔ If you've decided on another method, such as the diaphragm, you have to go to your gynecologist or to a clinic to have it fitted.

Because condoms are widely available, men don't have such a problem with getting protection, unless they're too embarrassed to buy them. I sometimes wonder whether men object to using condoms mostly because of the way the condoms feel or because they usually have the responsibility of buying them. However, I know that, as a reader of this book, you won't have that problem because you realize how important being protected is.

Setting the stage

Exactly how you tell your partner that you're ready to have sex depends on several factors:

- ✔ Is your partner a virgin, somewhat experienced, or very experienced? A very experienced partner can provide more support, but you may actually be less nervous with an inexperienced person, because he or she will be less likely to notice if you make any "mistakes."

- ✔ How far have the two of you already gone? If you're already into heavy petting — or even oral sex — you may be much less inhibited.

- ✔ Do you have a place where you already go to kiss and hug and maybe pet? Having privacy is particularly important your first time, because you don't need to be made any more nervous than you'll already be.

Giving notice

Assuming that you've already taken care of the AIDS testing matter and the use of contraceptives, should you tell your partner ahead of time that tonight's the night, or should you wait until you're actually snuggling up? I know that many people, when they are nervous about something, don't like to think about it ahead of time but prefer to just take the plunge — no pun intended. Sometimes I do agree with that philosophy, but not when it comes to sex.

If your first sexual experience has some negative sides to it, it will affect the next time you try. Although you certainly cannot guarantee perfection, you do want to be mentally prepared, and your partner should be as well. If you and your partner are half naked and caressing each other — something that you've done before — and suddenly you give the green light to go all the way, your partner's already turned on and his or her first reaction will be, "Hooray, let's go for it."

That response is only normal. You, on the other hand, may want to go slowly, gently. Therefore, telling your partner ahead of time, before you get to that place where you're going to have sex, is better. Let him or her know that you are ready, say that you're nervous, and ask to take things slowly. If your partner approaches the situation with the mind-set to tread lightly, then you're both likely to do so, and you'll be more likely to enjoy it.

The First Time for Women

Although I certainly hope that all goes well for any of you women having intercourse for the first time, you should be aware of two possible stumbling blocks: breaking the hymen and the possibility of vaginismus.

Breaking the hymen

The *hymen* is a piece of tissue that covers the entrance to the vagina (see Chapter 3). Not every virgin has an intact hymen. Many women break their hymens either when playing sports (particularly bicycling or horseback riding) or by using tampons. If your hymen is already broken, then having sex for the first time probably won't cause you any pain or bleeding. If your hymen is not broken, then you may feel some pain, and you will bleed a little. The pain, however, is very brief and most probably, in the heat of the moment, you can quickly forget it.

If you're concerned about bleeding the first time you have sex, just make sure that you put a towel underneath you.

If you're too tight

Vaginismus is an involuntary tightening of the vaginal muscles that prevents penetration or causes intercourse to be painful. It usually occurs if the woman is nervous. Because you will probably be nervous the first time, vaginismus can happen to you. I'm not saying it will happen, so don't get too worked up over the possibility, or you may actually cause yourself to tighten up. Just be aware that it does sometimes happen and don't think that the condition is permanent.

Some women write to me and complain that they are just built too small to have sex. Many of these women are just experiencing vaginismus and don't realize it. The vagina is made to expand — after all, a baby can come out of there — so it certainly has enough room for a penis.

How can you tell if your partner's difficulty with penetrating your vagina is caused by vaginismus or just lousy aim? First of all, you can probably feel that your vaginal muscles are tighter than normal. But a simple check with your own finger will also give you an answer. Even if you've never tried to put your fingers in your vagina before, just know that slipping them in should be very easy; if you can't easily get your fingers in, then you are experiencing vaginismus.

What should you do if you experience vaginismus?

✔ Engage in plenty of foreplay with your partner (read the next chapter to find out more about foreplay). If you're excited, then vaginismus is less likely to be a problem. So, if your partner didn't give you enough fore-play, go back and start again.

Being excited will also mean that you are lubricating. If you can't get your juices flowing but still want to go ahead with trying to have inter-course, you can use a lubricant.

Be aware that Vaseline and other oil-based products can cause the latex in a condom to deteriorate very quickly. If your partner uses a latex condom, and you don't produce enough lubrication or don't have a water-based lubricant such as KY Jelly on hand, you have to stop short of intercourse.

✔ Relax. The one thing you should not do is try too hard. Just because you can't have sexual intercourse one day doesn't mean that you won't be able to do it the next. Very few women have vaginismus so severe that they require treatment. Just give it a little time, and I'm sure you'll be fine.

✔ Another tip I can pass on to make your first time easier is to put a pillow under your behind. Changing the angle of entry may make it easier for the man to penetrate your vagina, making the whole process easier for you as well.

✔ I have heard from women who have a sort of permanent vaginismus, so that the entrance to their vagina is always tight. They have reported that by using a series of larger and larger expanding *speculums* (the instru-ment used by your gynecologist to examine your vagina), they have been able to expand their muscles to permit intercourse, which was very painful to them before. This condition rarely happens, but it's good to know that there is hope if you run into this problem.

Occasionally, the cause of vaginismus is much more serious than nervousness. If a woman was sexually abused or has a fear of intercourse for another reason, she must first recognize the underlying cause of the problem before she can overcome it. In these situations, it's best to seek the help of a professional counselor.

What to expect

As far as the pleasure you will derive from this first time, you should keep one thing in mind: The majority of women cannot reach an orgasm through intercourse alone. Some women eventually do learn how; others never do. Whichever group you turn out to be in, do not expect to have an orgasm through intercourse your very first time. Now that doesn't mean that you can't have an orgasm at all. Your partner can give you an orgasm using his fingers or tongue or big toe, but he probably won't be able to do it with just his penis inside your vagina.

The First Time for Men

A man may face many hidden traps during his first time having sex; for the vast majority of men, even if they do have problems, they will overcome them eventually.

Controlling your erection

Being nervous can wreak havoc with your ability to have an erection — and who wouldn't be nervous at a time like this? Some men can't get an erection before things get started. Others have an erection, but, when they have difficulties trying to slip their penis into the woman, they quickly develop a case of the nerves, and there goes Mr. Happy. Even if your erection doesn't disappear altogether, if your penis gets a little soft, then you will definitely have problems putting it where you want it to go.

If any of these problems happens, hopefully you have taken my advice and your partner is someone who cares for you. You can take a minute or two to calm your nerves and then have her help you to get a new erection by rubbing or sucking on your penis. Then you can try intercourse again.

Your partner can also help by parting the lips of her vagina with her fingers to make it easier for you to enter. If she's not excited and lubricating, you can use a lubricant. Remember, don't use an oil-based lubricant if you're using a latex condom; if you have one handy, use a condom that's already lubricated.

Premature ejaculation

The problem more likely to cause trouble your first time is *premature ejaculation*. Now I'm not talking about the standard form of premature ejaculation in which a man ejaculates faster than he wants to after he is inside the woman. In that scenario, after you're inside, you've at least reached your initial goal: the loss of your virginity. But some men get so excited by the thought of what they are about to do that they have their orgasm before they penetrate, which is immediately followed by a loss of their erection and the impossibility of intercourse.

Is this situation embarrassing? You bet. Is it the end of the world? Definitely not.

Even if you have problems with premature ejaculation (which you can learn how to treat in Chapter 20), a man can usually keep his erection at least through the process of penetration, so you will probably be successful the next time you try. If you are really such a jackrabbit that, after a half dozen times, you haven't managed to keep yourself from ejaculating before you penetrate your partner, then you should definitely try the exercises that I recommend in Chapter 20; if they don't work, then go to see a sex therapist. (I give you tips for choosing a sex therapist in Appendix A.)

Working through the problem

For the most part, the problems men encounter — either not having an erection or not being able to control their ability to ejaculate — are mental problems rather than physical ones. Physical causes of impotence are difficult to treat, but you can usually correct the mental problems, so don't give up hope.

The most important thing for both men and women to remember is that the first time is only the first step on the road to sexual fulfillment. As long as you make sure that you are sexually literate (which means that you read this book very carefully and pay attention to the advice you find on these pages), I have no doubt that you can become a great lover in no time at all.

The First Time All Over Again

As much sexual experience as you may have, a certain tension always arises when you have sex with a new partner for the first time. Some people get practically addicted to that tension, which is the reason that they keep jumping from bed to bed. But for many people, that tension causes the same types of problems that can be encountered during the very first time, and even some new ones.

A virgin has the advantage of a clean slate. A virgin usually has no extra baggage caused by bad experiences. And a virgin hasn't developed a set of sexual habits yet. For the inexperienced person, everything is possible.

The longer your previous relationship lasted, the harder having sex with a new person for the first time will be. You may not only be nervous about your own performance, but you will have an almost irresistible urge to compare this new person with your former partner.

Try as hard as you can not to give into the urge to compare partners. No two people are alike, so sex with each new person will be different. Because the old person is now out of your life, what good can comparing do? If this new person is a lousy lover, but you like the person enough for other reasons to stay together, then make a point of teaching him or her how to become a better lover. You can't teach a new sex partner how to make love to you the identical way your old lover did — and you'd be better off not dredging up those old memories anyway. Instead, you have to help each new partner become the best lover he or she can possibly be.

Another stumbling block to having sex with a new partner can be the negative baggage that you may bring with you. If you're coming out of a rotten relationship, especially one in which you were abused in some way, then you will be gun-shy; that reaction's only natural. You have to let the new person know that you're extra sensitive so that he or she can proceed carefully. It can take longer to heal an emotional wound than a physical one, but the right person can help speed up the healing process immensely.

If you're coming out of a very long-term relationship, perhaps one that has lasted a decade or two, then another factor that will make adapting to this new person in your life more difficult is that you and your body are now a good deal older. Unless you're Jane Fonda or Dick Clark, your body is no longer what it was, and you're going to be a bit self-conscious about that change. My advice to you is to try to get over that hump as quickly as possible.

Your new partner wouldn't be going to bed with you if he or she didn't find you attractive. So resist the temptation of trying to hide your body. Adopt the philosophy of the nudists, which is that you can actually feel freer naked than with clothes on because you no longer have to worry about hiding your body. Don't slip quickly under the covers, but flaunt your body. If the other person gets turned off, then you're just facilitating the inevitable, but I almost guarantee you that that won't happen.

Hopefully, during your past relationships, you at least discovered how your body responds, and that piece of information is very important. Don't be shy about telling this new person what pleases you. This knowledge may be all that you've been able to bring out of your past relationship, and letting it go to waste would be a shame.

Chapter 9

Foreplay: Stoking the Fire

Foreplay is probably one of the most misunderstood words in the sexual vocabulary. In fact, when some men hear the word *foreplay,* they still think of golf instead of sex. But slowly and surely, the male population is learning that foreplay is as important to good sex as using a nine iron is to good golf.

In its simplest form, foreplay means the touching and caressing that goes on between two people just prior to intercourse. Foreplay helps both partners experience the physical manifestations of arousal necessary for sexual satisfaction.

Foreplay for Life

According to my philosophy, not only must you extend foreplay as long as possible when the two of you get into bed, but you should begin foreplay for your next sexual experience as early as the *afterplay* — the caressing that goes on after sexual intercourse — of the previous sexual encounter.

In other words, I believe that you can consider afterplay part of the foreplay for the next love-making session, whether your next lovemaking takes place the same night or a week later.

If you're interested in becoming the best lover you can be, foreplay should be something you take into consideration with each interaction that the two of you have.

Right now, some of you are probably saying, "Hold it, Dr. Ruth, you mean to say when I ask my wife to pass the salt at dinner, that should be part of foreplay?"

My response is — absolutely. Don't simply say "Pass the salt," but add a term of endearment, such as "Honey," "Love," or even just her name. You see, the better you treat her, and the better she treats you, the better your sex life will be.

If you're still having trouble buying this idea, consider the opposite tack:

- How sexy is it when someone calls you a jerk?
- If someone is rude to you, does it get your testosterone flowing or your adrenaline?

Of course such behavior is not sexy, especially if it takes place regularly. But, in the same way that rude behavior kindles the flames of anger, kind behavior kindles the sparks of love.

If you are kind and loving even during the most mundane moments, you are setting yourself up for terrific sex when the time for lovemaking does come around.

Linking the Emotional to the Physical

To be clearer about the difference between what's considered standard foreplay and my Dr. Ruth version, I'd like to separate, for a moment, the physical effects from the emotional effects of foreplay, especially regarding the role they play in the arousal levels of women.

People usually think of foreplay as a simple cause-and-effect mechanism, setting the stage for intercourse to take place from the physical point of view:

- For sexual intercourse to take place, the man's penis must be erect.
- It helps sexual intercourse if the woman's vagina is lubricating.

Exciting both partners so that these physical manifestations of sexual arousal take place is the minimal role of foreplay.

Because a young man can get an erection simply by thinking about the lovemaking that is going to take place, his version of foreplay can be just walking into the bedroom. That will change as he gets older, but because most young men don't know what the future holds for their ability to become aroused (and in the heat of passion don't much care either), many of them grow impatient and try to make foreplay last as short a time as possible.

You may have heard that women don't reach their sexual peak until they're in their thirties. No physical reason exists to support this notion, and in many women the idea is completely false. Some women do find that sex gets better as they get older, however, and I believe that one of the reasons has nothing to do with women but instead has to do with their men.

Some men only begin to appreciate the effects of foreplay when they are out of their twenties. Consequently, only then do their women begin to get enough foreplay to fully appreciate sex themselves. And after women begin enjoying sex more, they begin wanting to have sex more often.

The Sexual Response Cycle

The reason that sex therapists such as myself exist is due in great part to Dr. William Masters and Dr. Virginia Johnson, who studied the sexual response cycle in the late 1950s and early 1960s.

How did they study the sexual response cycle? They observed more than 10,000 sexual acts in their laboratories. Because even the most serious voyeur would probably have had enough after about the first 1,000, you can appreciate that they were really very dedicated scientists.

And scientists they were, because when I say *observe,* I don't just mean watch. The people who took part in these studies were wired up so that Masters and Johnson could tell exactly what was going on, including how much lubrication the woman was making and the quantity of ejaculate the man released.

As a result of these studies, Masters and Johnson came up with four distinct phases for human sexual response. Later, Dr. Helen Singer Kaplan, under whom I trained, created her own model, which included elements of Masters and Johnson's as well as one of her own.

Examining an individual's *sexual response cycle* is integral to the diagnosis that sex therapists make of anyone who comes to them with a sexual problem. Understanding the various categories of the sexual response cycle can also help you to become the best possible lover, so read the following definitions very carefully.

> ✔ **Sexual Desire Phase:** The Sexual Desire Phase, sometimes called the *libido,* precedes actual physical or psychological stimulation. This is the part of the model that is Dr. Kaplan's alone. Dr. Kaplan believes that certain chemicals in the body (primarily *testosterone* — the male sex hormone, which is also present in females) trigger these inner sexual feelings. Sexual excitement builds upon these feelings.
>
> Dr. Kaplan examined and labeled this phase because of her work in sexual therapy, where she noted that some people's desire for sex was so low that they rarely or never reached the other phases of the cycle. Only by studying what was going on in this earlier stage could she discover what was causing their difficulties.

✔ **Excitement Phase:** The Excitement Phase arises when the genitals experience *vasocongestion*, which is a swelling caused by an increase in blood filling the tissues.

In men, this excitement leads to an erection. In women, this excitement leads to a swelling of the clitoris and vaginal lips, increased vaginal lubrication, increased breast size, and erection of the nipples. Other physical signs of this phase include increased heartbeat, breathing rate, and blood pressure. Arm and leg muscles may begin to tense; some people experience a "sex flush" on the upper abdomen that may spread to the chest area.

This phase is usually generated by one or a combination of several physical, visual, or psychological stimuli, which can be caused either by oneself or a partner.

✔ **Plateau Phase:** In the Plateau Phase, certain aspects of the Excitement Phase reach a slightly higher level, with tensions building.

According to Masters and Johnson, men exhibit two physical signs during this period:

- First, a few droplets of fluid are released at the head of the penis to act as a lubricant for the sperm. (These droplets also contain sperm, which is what makes the withdrawal method so risky. Chapter 7 gives more information on the pitfalls of the so-called pull-out method of birth control.)

- Also, the man's testes enlarge and are pulled closer to the body.

Dr. Kaplan incorporates all these reactions of the Plateau Phase as an extension of the Excitement Phase because the individual does not sense any difference between the excitement and plateau stages, making these subtle differences of no value to her in treating a sexual dysfunction.

✔ **Orgasm Phase:** During the Orgasm Phase, in both men and women, your body goes through a whole series of muscular contractions and spasms, including facial contortions, an increased respiratory rate and heartbeat, and a further increase in blood pressure. Your genitals also experience strong contractions.

The man undergoes the further contraction of ejaculation, which occurs in two stages: the moment of inevitability, characterized by sensations that mark the so-called point of no return (which I talk more about in Chapter 20), followed immediately by ejaculation.

✔ **Resolution Phase:** In this last phase (which only Masters and Johnson include), the body slowly returns to normal — the physical conditions that existed before the Excitement Stage began. This Resolution Phase is much longer for women than for men, making it the basis for afterplay.

In addition, men have the *refractory period,* which is the time needed after orgasm before the man can respond to more sexual stimulation and have another erection and orgasm. In young men, this period can be as short as a few minutes; the length of the refractory period grows as a man ages.

The man reaches the Excitement Phase much more quickly than the woman, and the woman has a much longer Resolution Phase. I suggest extending the concept of foreplay as much as possible to help compensate for this difference.

Flowers as Foreplay

Have you men ever thought of offering flowers as an act of foreplay?

You certainly consider flowers as part of courtship, as well as a sign of love. But such gifts are also part of foreplay. When a woman receives a bouquet of flowers from her loved one, chances are good that she will feel sexually excited as a result. She may even start lubricating a little.

Because women do take longer to get fully aroused, the earlier you send her these flowers, the more time she will have to reap a positive effect from them. My advice is not to bring flowers home with you, but rather to send them ahead of time. With any luck, by the time you walk through the door, the woman you love will already be well on her way to the Excitement Phase of sexual arousal.

Although I am all in favor of variety and spontaneity — so that it is quite all right to occasionally use that excitation that she is feeling and jump right into bed before going out on that date — the longer you can extend foreplay, the better the end result will usually be.

Thinking ahead

Foreplay isn't just an art to practice on your partner; it can also be a method of visualization for yourself so that, when the time comes to make love, you're absolutely ready. For this kind of foreplay to work best, you need to have a particular time planned for the love-making session.

If you're not living with your partner, and you have a date on Saturday night, then you can take a quick break during the day to visualize some of what will be going on as the evening progresses. If you do have a live-in partner, then from time to time make plans in advance to have sex so that you can luxuriate in brief fantasies during the course of the day to prepare.

Dressing for success

You can give your loved one many signals to indicate that sex is on the agenda, and how you dress is certainly one of them. Say, for example, as you're getting ready for work in the morning, you put on your sexiest pair of underwear and make sure that he sees you. He'll get the message, and you'll both be thinking about what's in store for later that night all throughout the day.

You can also create special signals that aren't as blatant as see-through lingerie. For example, say that for your anniversary, you buy him a special tie. If you go to his tie rack and say, "Why don't you wear this one today," he won't need any other clues to know that love is in the air. Or he may say to you, "Why don't you wear that red sweater that I got for you on Valentine's Day?" If you agree, then you'll both know what that means.

By the way, clothing can also have the opposite effect. If you're in the mood for sex but pile on several layers of flannel before you crawl into the sack, you're going to give your partner the wrong message. And, if you're one of those people who is constantly chilly, I suggest you get yourself an electric blanket so that the winter months don't become a period of enforced celibacy.

Dinner for two

One way to prolong foreplay is to have a romantic dinner. Now, a romantic dinner doesn't have to be an expensive dinner. Sure, a beautiful restaurant with attentive waiters and wonderful food helps set the mood, but so does Chinese take-out eaten on the floor, so long as the two of you devote your attention to each other.

Paying total attention to one another is very important. I've heard of many fights that have occurred among couples as a result of a meal out at a restaurant. Maybe she got so picky about the food that it made him upset, or he started ogling a beautiful woman, making his partner angry. And too much food or drink can certainly put both parties down for the count, as far as a later sexual episode is concerned.

A romantic meal is not romantic only because of the setting or the food but also because of the intimacy of spending an hour or so together *focused only on each other*. That means that the communication between the two people — which includes talking, touching, and staring into each other's eyes — is the key ingredient.

For that reason, you can have a very romantic evening at home, because your home may have fewer distractions. On the other hand, if your little dear ones are at home feeding their spinach puree to the dog, or if only one partner always assumes the duties of cooking and cleaning for such an evening, then romance may not come about so easily, and you're better off going to a restaurant, even an inexpensive one.

Using your lips

In my book, *The Art of Arousal*, I chose a painting by the Italian Renaissance painter Correggio as the artwork for the cover. The picture depicts the god, Jupiter, transformed into a cloud, kissing Io. To me, that image illustrates one of the great ways to kiss: so lightly, so softly, with the lips barely touching, so that it seems as if you are kissing a cloud. But you have so many ways to kiss — passionately or lightly, with mouths open or closed, with tongues probing or not — that kissing is truly a gift of the gods.

Most of us think of lovers kissing as automatic, and for most people it is. But not for everyone. I regularly get letters — mostly from women — who complain that their husbands don't kiss them enough. Some of these men do kiss, but only perfunctorily. Others don't kiss at all.

My first piece of advice for people who feel that their lovers aren't kissing them enough is to check their breath. I'm not saying that bad breath is usually at fault, but because you can easily cure it, you should make it your first line of attack. (Because you can't check your breath yourself, you'll have to ask your partner to do it, or, if that embarrasses you too much, maybe your dentist or a good friend can help.)

If your partner, not you, has the problem with frequent bad breath, I suggest you come right out and say so — though not necessarily in the middle of an embrace. Make sure that you have some mouthwash in the medicine chest and then let them know, gently, that they tend to have a problem with bad breath. Show your partner how much you prefer the minty flavor of mouthwash by rewarding him or her with a big kiss.

Another problem with kissing is *French,* or deep-tongue, *kissing.* Some people adore this form of play, while others hate it. Because so many people are orally oriented — witness how much eating and gum-chewing we do — those people who really want to engage in deep kissing have a problem if their mates don't. Because I don't believe in forcing anybody to do anything, the best advice I can give to people who like their kisses to be deep and long is to find out before you get married if you're going to have a problem. Sometimes these problems crop up later in life, but at least you will have tried to head them off at the pass.

Here again, some people avoid French kissing for a reason: They have problems breathing through their noses. If you really love this art form, and your partner can't satisfy you because of a breathing problem, have your partner go see a doctor, as help may be available.

Kissing isn't limited to mouths. You can kiss each other all over your bodies, and both the kisser and kissee should thoroughly enjoy the experience. If you don't want to have oral sex because you are squeamish about the messy results, you can still cover your lover's genitals with light kisses, because doing so is rarely sufficient stimulation to induce orgasm. A few gentle kisses now and then on your partner's genitals will at least let your partner know that, even though you don't want to give him or her an orgasm that way, you are not repulsed by this part of the anatomy — you just prefer to have sex in other ways.

The art of massage

In an earlier section of this chapter, "Dinner for two," I recommend that you and your partner touch each other as one type of communication you can use at a restaurant. But in a public place, this touching can go only so far — holding hands, maybe playing footsie.

I know that some people use the cover of a tablecloth to go further, but I don't recommend that. You may get so lost in the moment that you forget that other people are around, and when they notice what you're up to — and they will, because people-watching is part of what going to a restaurant is all about — you're both going to be embarrassed.

When you're back at your home, however, you can do all the touching that you want. Now what often happens is that the touching people do as they remove their clothes leads right to sex. But if you're in the mood for stretching things out — and this is not something that has to happen every time — then giving each other a massage is a sensual and relaxing way to begin.

Make the moment as sensuous as you can.

- ✔ Dim the lights or use candles.

- ✔ Use some massage oils.

- ✔ Whatever you do, don't rush the massage; try to really feel each other as much as possible.

- ✔ Alternate between strong rubs and gentle caresses. Let the sensitive nerve-endings in your fingertips help you get to know your partner in a new way.

Another sensuous way of prolonging foreplay is to play in some water. Climbing into a hot tub or Jacuzzi together is a great way to unwind, especially at night with only the soft lights glowing from underneath the water.

Hot tubs are a great place to have foreplay, but they can be a dangerous place to have sex. The soothing effects from the elevated water temperature can cause physical problems, especially if your blood pressure and heartbeat are on the rise from sexual excitement. I'm not saying never have sex in your hot tub — the temptation is certainly going to be irresistible at times — but this chapter is about foreplay, and that's what I recommend you use the tub for.

If you don't have a hot tub, you can substitute a bathtub or shower. Washing is a way of gently exploring each other's bodies while rendering a service at the same time.

Some people will not engage in sex with their partners because they are not sure how clean their genitals are. Well, if a woman is washing a man's penis, for example, she can be absolutely sure that it is clean. You may well laugh at this piece of advice, but I have recommended it to many couples where squeamishness or body odors were a problem, and it usually works.

Body mapping

Although you certainly touch your partner's body all over during massage, the goal then is to create sensations, not discover which parts of your partner's body are the most sensitive. With *body mapping,* on the other hand, you aim to discover all of the most sensitive parts of one another's bodies: the breasts, the wrists, the thighs. . . .

The art of body mapping is not only something you do to another person; it is also something that you can do to yourself. Sometimes it is not just where you are touched that creates the best sensations, but how you are touched. Because only you can feel which ways of touching — gentle, rough, continuous, feathery — bring you the most pleasure, you may have to experiment on yourself as well as on your partner.

Body mapping is one of those gifts that keeps on giving because, after you and your partner have explored your bodies and discovered the most sensuous places and what feels best on them, you can use those techniques again and again throughout your love life. So, body mapping is far from just a way to extend foreplay; it is an exercise that each couple should engage in at least once to build a data bank of information for future lovemaking.

You have now entered . . . the erogenous zone

Erogenous zones are the parts of your body that, due to the concentration of nerve endings, are more sensitive to stimulation than the other parts.

Now some erogenous zones are pretty universal. Most women enjoy having a man pay attention to their breasts — and most men don't mind obliging them in this way. But, guys, don't forget what you learned about body mapping. If she likes a soft touch rather than a rough one, or vice versa, then that's what you should do.

Remember that, in foreplay, you're trying to arouse each other, so you have to do what is going to help *your partner* become the most aroused. That's not to say that, if you really enjoy kissing her nipples but that's not number one on her list, you can't do some nipple kissing. You can, and you should. But if she really likes to have her nipples softly feathered with the tip of your finger, then you should also do some of that as well.

Erogenous zones can be anywhere on your body, but here are some of the more popular ones:

- The buttocks
- The perineum (that little line between the anus and the genitals)
- Behind the knees
- The nape of the neck
- And, of course, the genitals

What if you or you partner has an erogenous zone on a body part that's not popular? The answer is, go for it. If your partner loves to have his or her ear-lobes sucked, then that's what you should spend some time doing. Just the way every individual has a unique set of fingerprints, we all have unique erogenous zones as well. Nothing is "wrong" with favoring one body part or another, and the whole point of body mapping is to discover places on your partner's body to touch that you may never have imagined could turn them on.

Following the map

Having a map doesn't do any good if you don't use it. Therefore, after you've discovered which parts of the body your lover likes to have caressed, kissed, licked, sucked, nibbled, tickled, massaged, kneaded, stroked, nuzzled, probed, cupped, pinched, rubbed, blown on, gently bitten, or oiled, go ahead and do exactly that. And I also give you permission to use any potential sex toys that may enhance the sensations you're trying to cause. Among the toys people find erotic are long feathers, vibrators, and dildos, but feel free to improvise or take the non-traditional route. A brush handle can serve as a dildo, long hair can take the place of a feather, but I wouldn't sanction substituting your power screwdriver for a vibrator.

Warning: Ticklish zone

On any given day, a body part that had been an erogenous zone can reverse its magnetic pole and become a ticklish zone. I don't know what causes this phenomenon, but it happens to most people at one time or another. Unless your partner is always ticklish, don't worry if on a particular day you're told not to touch them "there." The warning is not personal and probably won't happen the next time.

Switching Gears: Engaging the Genitals

No matter how long you extend the more languorous, romantic aspects of foreplay, eventually you reach the point of engaging in traditional foreplay involving the genitals. Remember that the ultimate goal of foreplay is to get both partners ready to have an orgasm. Also keep in mind that a young man does not need very much preparation, but a woman almost always does. The reasons are both physical and psychological.

Looking under the hood — Foreplay for her

The physical reason that women usually need more time to have an orgasm is that the main source of a woman's orgasm is her clitoris.

Most women need direct physical contact on their clitorises to have an orgasm. For the average woman, sexual intercourse alone does not give the clitoris sufficient stimulation for her to have an orgasm because the penis does not come into direct contact with the clitoris during sex. One way to solve this problem is for the man to stimulate the woman's clitoris before sexual intercourse, and that is a primary function of foreplay.

Some women can get sufficiently aroused during foreplay that they can then have an orgasm during intercourse without further direct stimulation to the clitoris. Others need that direct stimulation and so may have their orgasms either before or after intercourse, or will use a position for intercourse that enables direct clitoral stimulation. I get to sexual positions in Chapter 10. For now, just concentrate on foreplay's role in giving a woman an orgasm.

Stimulating the clitoris

In dealing with the clitoris, you'll encounter a small Catch-22.

The clitoris is very sensitive, which is why it can produce an orgasm when stimulated. But, because of that sensitivity, stimulating the clitoris can also be painful. The solution to this problem is good communication between the man and the woman — and a soft touch.

Every woman's clitoris is different, and only she knows what kind of stimulation she likes.

If you're a woman, you must tell your partner what method works best for you. You don't have to do this in words. If you are uncomfortable talking about it, you can guide his hand with yours. Let him know how hard he should rub, whether he should touch the clitoris itself or just the area around the clitoris, what rhythms to use — fast or slow — and when to change those rhythms, if necessary.

After a while, if the man is paying attention, he'll get the hang of it and be able to give you an orgasm without any further instruction.

Using more than just fingers

You may have heard me say that a man can use his finger or his tongue or his big toe to stimulate the clitoris. That's true, although I don't think that the big toe method has broken into the mainstream quite yet. From what people report to me, fingers are the number-one choice, the tongue is number two, and in third place is something that doesn't grow on people: *vibrators*.

Many people think of vibrators as good only for self-pleasuring. If a woman needs really strong stimulation, however, or if the man is of an advanced age or incapacitated in some way so that this aspect of foreplay is too tiresome or impossible, then he should feel free to use a vibrator to perform this task. (You need to take some precautions when using a vibrator, and I go into those in Chapter 17.) But in most cases you don't need a mechanical device, and fingers serve quite nicely.

One cautionary note is that fingers are tipped by nails, which can be quite sharp. Most men don't have long nails, so that usually isn't a problem, but if you notice any sharp edges, file them off beforehand.

A nice addition to the finger is lubrication to minimize the friction on the clitoris. In most cases, the woman's own lubrication will do fine, and the man can dip his finger into the woman's vagina occasionally to make sure that the area around the clitoris stays moist. You can also use saliva as a lubricant. You can find plenty of products sold for this purpose, as well, if the woman's own natural lubricants have dried up due to age or if she has a problem lubricating.

All lubricants are not the same. You can purchase a small variety of these products in any drug store, such as KY Jelly (which, although absolutely functional, doesn't have a lot of pizzazz). But, if you make your purchase at either an adult store or through a catalog, you can choose from a large selection of lubricants, some of which come in various flavors and colors.

No matter how excited a woman gets and how much lubrication she makes, the supply is often exhaustible. Sometimes she can run out of lubrication, which can make foreplay, or later intercourse, painful. Both partners must be aware of how moist the area is and make any necessary adjustments.

The man shouldn't limit his attention to just the clitoris. The whole vulva is quite sensitive (see Chapter 3), and the woman may also like having one or more fingers placed inside of her vagina. For this technique, the man may want to try a two-hand approach.

If a man lets his fingers do the walking and explores all around a woman's genitals, he may run into the anus, just down the road from the vagina. Although the anus is also a sensitive area, a lot of germs are likely to be lurking there, unless it's just been cleaned. These germs do not belong inside the vagina, where they can multiply and cause infections. So the man needs to take every precaution to keep his fingers away from the source of germs if he is then going to put them into the woman's vagina.

The tongue: Master of foreplay

The tongue seems to have been perfectly constructed for the art of foreplay, and not just for kissing.

- ✔ Tongues provide their own lubrication in the form of saliva.
- ✔ Tongues are softer than fingertips and have no sharp instruments, such as nails attached to them.
- ✔ Tongues can also be manipulated in many different types of strokes, from the long lap to the short dart.

No wonder that many women consider a man who has perfected the art of *cunnilingus* (oral sex upon a woman) to be a great lover.

Not all women enjoy oral sex. For a variety of reasons, some women do not like to have cunnilingus performed on them.

- ✔ Some women may prefer to have their lover's face next to theirs.
- ✔ Some women may object because of religious beliefs.
- ✔ Some women may feel guilty, thinking that they may have to return the favor, which is something that they are not willing to do.

Whatever the woman's reason, the man needs to respect her wishes. If the woman you are with does not want to engage in oral sex, just put it aside, at least for the time being.

Checking the dipstick — Foreplay for him

As a man gets older, he is less easily able to get an erection.

In adolescent males, erections occur at any time, sometimes even at quite embarrassing times, such as when the teacher calls them up to the blackboard. (I'm not saying that blackboards, per se, are arousing, but if a guy has been sitting a long time and suddenly gets up, blood flow will increase. Some of that blood is likely to go to his penis, particularly if he was just thinking about the cute girl sitting in front of him.)

As a man gets older, he can still have *psychogenic erections* (erections that pop up by themselves), but eventually he loses even that ability and will not be able to have an erection without physical stimulation (I discuss this change in Chapter 20). That stimulation, whether a necessity or not, is part of foreplay.

In many cases, your partner can easily figure out which caresses work best to get a rise out of you. Some men, however, especially those who have masturbated a lot, have developed a specific pattern to getting their erections which only they can produce. In such a case, a man will have to start the process of foreplay on himself. After he is erect, the woman can take over.

Fellatio

Oral sex on a man, called *fellatio,* can be performed to various degrees.

One thing that the woman should know is that the most sensitive area of the penis is usually on the underside, just below the head, so you don't need to "deep throat" a man to give him intense pleasure.

A woman can simply lick the penis, without actually putting the whole organ in her mouth, and still provide the man with a lot of pleasure. When women tell me that they have a problem with fellatio, I often tell them to think of the penis as an ice cream cone and pretend that they are licking it.

When a woman performs oral sex as a part of foreplay, she needn't be concerned about the man ejaculating, although she may well encounter some Cowper's fluid (pre-ejaculatory secretions). If she wants to make sure that she doesn't go too far in pleasing him, she should stop every once in a while and ask him what stage of arousal he is in. If he indicates that orgasm is close, and if oral foreplay is all she wants to do, she should stop.

Actually, the preceding tip goes for any part of foreplay, especially if the man has any problems with premature ejaculation. As I explain in Chapter 20, learning to sense the *premonitory sensation* (the point of no return) is relatively simple for men. All men should learn to recognize the premonitory sensation so that they don't ejaculate before they want to, either in foreplay or during intercourse.

Good communications, whether verbal or just via actions, are an integral part to all aspects of sex, and no one should hesitate to tell the other to stop doing something — either because it's uncomfortable or because it feels too good.

Other zones

The penis isn't the only part of the man that you can use to arouse him. Here are a few, but not all, the parts of a man's body that can also be integrated into foreplay:

✔ The testicles definitely are an erogenous zone (though one that should be handled rather gently, because the wrong move can put a quick end to all the work you've put into foreplay).

✔ Many men enjoy having their nipples either stroked or sucked.

✔ Also on this list of erogenous zones is the anus. Again, be careful not to spread germs from the anus to other parts of the genitals.

Variety Is the Spice of Foreplay

In general, boredom can prove dangerous to good sex, but some people still develop certain set patterns that they require to become fully aroused. For example, say that she needs five minutes of constant licking of her clitoris to become aroused enough to have an orgasm, and nothing else will do the trick. In order to prevent your entire foreplay routine from following the same script every time, make sure you take a different road to get to that required point. Try to avoid turning the entire routine of foreplay into a one-act play — unless, of course, you both decide that you like one-act plays. If you both find comfort in a familiar routine and require that level of familiarity to have the best possible sex, then go for it. Rarely, however, do both partners want to follow an exact routine, so don't be lazy about foreplay. Instead, create different scenarios to keep the boredom at bay.

When to End Foreplay

How can you tell when the two of you have had enough foreplay? You can't. Again, that's why communication is so vital to good sex. Assuming the main point of extended foreplay is to get the woman ready to have an orgasm, she has to let her partner know when she's ready. Ready for what? That's a very good question.

If the woman can get sufficiently aroused to have an orgasm during intercourse, then the answer is that she should tell her partner, either verbally or by touching him in some way, that he should now put his penis into her vagina. But, if she cannot have an orgasm this way, she may want him to continue to stimulate her clitoris up until the point where she does have an orgasm.

I can't give you a right or wrong answer here. The couple must concentrate on what works best so that, in the end, both partners feel satisfied. Every couple is different and so must write their own ending. As long as both partners are working toward the same goal, then the good guys (and that means both of you) will always win.

Chapter 10

Variations on a Theme

● ●

In This Chapter

▶ The missionary position

▶ Female-superior positions

▶ Different breeds of doggy style

▶ Oral and anal sex

▶ Outercourse

▶ Self masturbation — together

▶ Sex during pregnancy

● ●

Foreplay, I think most people can agree, is an erotic activity that has, as its goal, the arousal of both partners. This chapter advances from foreplay to "doing it" — another politely ambiguous term.

What, exactly, is "it"? Is "it" only sexual intercourse? Now, my edition of Webster's dictionary defines sexual intercourse as "genital contact, usually between humans, especially the insertion of the penis into the vagina followed by ejaculation."

But that definition leaves out a lot of what happens between two people when they "do it." What happened to oral sex, anal sex, and mutual masturbation? Aren't people having sex when they do those things? And because women can't ejaculate, and so many women cannot have an orgasm from intercourse alone, aren't they entitled to some pleasure from "it"?

Semantics was never my strong point, so let me just give you a brief description of what this chapter is about: any activity between two consenting adults, who are not virgins, which produces orgasms (I tell you all about orgasms in the next chapter).

Why am I excluding virgins? If two teenagers have oral sex, but not intercourse, are they still virgins? Because no chance of a pregnancy exists, I suppose you have to say that yes they are. But if two people who have had intercourse decide on a particular evening to pick from the sexual menu only oral sex, and could in mid-course decide to change their minds and have intercourse, then I think a distinction exists. It's not a big difference, but I have to draw the line somewhere.

So whether I call it "doing it," "going all the way," "having sex," or "playing hide the salami," basically this chapter covers different ways two people can help each other to experience one or more orgasms.

Getting There Is Half the Fun

Although orgasm is certainly one of the goals of intercourse for both partners, how you reach that goal is where the fun comes in.

Now this book is not the *Kama Sutra,* so I am not going to give you every possible position, especially because I don't suppose that many of you are acrobats. (My lawyer suggested I put several paragraphs at this point stating that I am not responsible for any injuries that may occur as a result of lovemaking using any of these positions. In this case, I'll take his advice up to a point and say that you should always use caution, particularly if you know that you have a particular weakness such as a bad back. On the other hand, one of the reasons I always tell couples to lock the door when they are having sex is to keep children and lawyers out of the bedroom.)

What I do give you in this chapter are the basics, along with the advantages of each position. Don't look for any preaching here, because I don't believe that any one position is more moral or normal than another is. Certainly, some positions are more popular than others, but good reasons exist for that.

A risk comes with reading this chapter — you may get sexually aroused. Don't be alarmed if reading this chapter turns you on. In fact, maybe you should become alarmed if you don't feel certain sensations "down there".

The Good Old Missionary Position

The missionary position (see Figure 10-1) is no more than the male-superior position; that is, the man on top, woman on the bottom, and peanut butter in between. (Scratch that last part. You'd end up sticking to each other and have to call 911.)

Because humans have probably been using the male-superior position since the time of the cave man, you may wonder why it is called the missionary position. According to Polish anthropologist Bronislaw Malinowski, the indigenous people of the South Pacific gave this position its nickname. The South Pacific folks didn't limit themselves to only one position. This "sinful behavior" shocked the newly arrived missionaries who, along with teaching the natives about Christianity, advocated the use of the male-superior position. Hence the name.

Figure 10-1:
The
missionary
position.

If you've ever seen other animals mating, you know that this position is pretty much unique to humans. This is partially because, for many other species, the male-superior position would be impossible (think of turtles, for example) or at best awkward (giraffes).

Now one reason we humans may have made the missionary position so popular is that it differentiates us from animals, but it also has several physical drawbacks. (See the upcoming section "Recognizing drawbacks" for details.) But I don't think that only practical considerations popularized this position, or that men want to show that they are not animals, or even that men want to be the aggressors and get on top. (Certainly when a big male lion grabs his mate's neck in his jaws as he mounts her from behind, he's not being wimpy.)

Face-to-face wins out

I believe most researchers agree that, because we humans communicate so much with each other, either through speech or touch or looks, a position that puts us face-to-face during sex is the one that most people will choose. Of course, I suppose we shouldn't negate as a factor for this position's popularity that it conveniently allows both partners to remain under the covers during the chilly months.

The missionary position is not entirely static, because variations do exist. Although the woman has to spread her legs to allow the man entry, she doesn't just have to lie flat on her back. Most women bend their knees somewhat, but they can actually put their knees in a whole range of positions, including wrapped around the man's back.

In the missionary position, the man doesn't have quite the same range of motion that the woman has, but he can try to ride higher — that is, in a more upright position — which may allow his pubic bone to rub against the clitoris, giving it more stimulation.

Recognizing drawbacks

As popular as the missionary position may be, it does have some drawbacks.

- The most obvious drawback of the missionary position is that the penis thrusting in and out of the vagina does not provide sufficient stimulation to the clitoris for many women to reach orgasm.

  Nor can the man reach the clitoris with his fingers because he is resting on his arms; therefore, the clitoral stimulation necessary for a woman's orgasm is not often present.

- The woman's range of motion is quite limited in the missionary position, other than to thrust upwards in time with her partner.

- If the act of intercourse goes on too long, or if the man is tired or weak for some other reason, the missionary position can be uncomfortable.

- Research has shown that, if a man is tensing his muscles, as he must do to hold himself up, it affects his ability to control ejaculation, so the missionary position can aggravate problems of premature ejaculation.

Some men ask me why women don't just stimulate themselves, because they can usually reach their own clitoris in the missionary position. Although I can't give them an exact answer, I believe that the reason lies in the same psychological factors that keep many women from masturbating. To some degree, this comes from a society that tells women it's not nice to touch down there (though, of course, society has said the same thing to young men, and it doesn't keep more than a small fraction of them from doing it).

Women do seem to prefer to be stimulated rather than to stimulate themselves, however, which is really all you need to know. So, whether you like it or not, and I think most men like it, the power of the female orgasm during sex is in men's hands . . . or tongues, or big toes.

Orgasmic variation

A variation of the missionary position is to have the woman lie back on the edge of the bed or table or boat deck (see, I never want you to become predictable) while the man keeps his feet on the ground, assuming this platform is the right height to allow penetration comfortably for both. Because his weight is no longer on his arms, the man can now use his hands to touch the woman's clitoris and stimulate her to orgasm. In my book, *Dr. Ruth's Pregnancy Guide for Couples,* my co-author and I named a variation of this position after ourselves — the Dr. Ruth and Dr. Amos Position. (Hey, if astronauts can name stars, why shouldn't we name a position?) In our position, the woman, who is lying back on the bed, places one or both of her feet on a chair(s.) This position gives the woman more freedom to move around and takes the man's weight off her belly.

This variation is one of several positions that allows the man to reach a woman's clitoris. These positions are why I say that women can have orgasms during intercourse. Often the key is to use a position other than the missionary position.

These other positions also can make a simultaneous orgasm more feasible, though achieving it is still a tricky operation. Because the woman usually takes longer, the man has to keep his level of arousal sufficiently high to remain erect but not so high as to have an orgasm. At the same time, he must keep in close contact with his lover to try to gauge when she is going to be ready to have her orgasm and, at that point, try to get into higher gear. The problem comes from that little devil of a psychological factor, *spectatoring* — becoming too involved in the process to relax and enjoy it.

The Female-Superior Position

Now that our society is approaching equality of the sexes, there's no excuse for men to always take the superior position. Actually, none of these positions is new, although they do go in and out of fashion. We do know that more women are going on top of their men than did a decade or two ago.

The fact that the female-superior position (see Figure 10-2) isn't more popular is kind of surprising, actually, because the female-superior position offers several major advantages:

- ✔ The most important advantage of the female-superior position is that the man can caress the woman's clitoris with his fingers.

- ✔ The man can both see and fondle the woman's breasts — a double turn-on for men, who are more visually oriented when it comes to sex.

- ✔ Men also report being able to "last" longer in the female-superior position.

- ✔ From the woman's point of view, she can control the depth of penetration and speed of thrust (which sound more like the controls on a Boeing 747 than sexual descriptions). Because every woman develops her own unique pattern that suits her best, this kind of control can be very helpful in bringing her to a fulfilling orgasm.

Figure 10-2:
The female-
superior
position.

The female-superior position can be more tiring to the woman, especially if it takes her a while to have her orgasm. If she suddenly starts wondering why things are taking so long because she's losing strength, then the spectatoring reflex may set in (see previous section), which makes having an orgasm even more difficult. Although some women find being on top a bit too athletic for their enjoyment, you may want to attempt the position at least once in a while.

In case you assume that the woman always has to face the man's head when she goes on top, that is not the case. She can also turn around so that she faces his feet. In fact, in the same love-making session she can turn both ways (or spin like a top, if she's so inclined). One advantage of having her face away from his head is that she can then pay some added attention to his genitals. Most men like having their testicles stroked during intercourse. Do be careful not to be too rough, however, as the testicles are sensitive and a stab of pain can put a quick end to his erection.

For the female-superior position to work best, the man needs to have a very strong erection. If this position doesn't work for you at night, try it in the morning, when a man's erections are usually the hardest ones of the day.

Taking Her from Behind

The taking-her-from-behind position (see Figure 10-3) is not anal sex but vaginal sex, where the man enters the woman from behind, the way most animals do. Penetration can be a little trickier this way, but most couples can figure out a way to make this position work for them.

Figure 10-3:
Doggy style.

Doggy style, as many people call this position, allows the man to reach around and stimulate the woman's clitoris and also gives him an exciting rear view that many men like. This position can be a little hard on the woman's knees, but that is basically its only drawback. One reason this position is not more popular is probably that the woman's view isn't very scenic — unless she has a nice Cezanne landscape in front of her, or a mirror.

In any rear-entry position, the man can thrust deeper into the woman, and can possibly hit an ovary or other organ. This can be as painful to her as hitting a testicle is to him, so I advise caution.

Some people enjoy having their anuses penetrated by a finger as they're about to reach orgasm. This is certainly a possibility for the man to do to the woman in any of the rear-entry positions. After the finger has gone into the anus, be very careful not to then put that finger into the vagina so as not to give the woman a vaginal infection.

The standing canine

Depending on the height of the two partners, rear entry can sometimes be accomplished while both partners have their feet on the ground, with the woman bending over, probably holding onto a chair or some other sturdy object (see Figure 10-4).

This is one of those semi-acrobatic positions good for adding variety and keeping boredom out of the bedroom, but not always satisfactory to either partner because the couple has to concentrate on their sexual arousal while also trying to keep their balance.

Figure 10-4:
The
standing
canine.

One hint I can offer for making this position work for you, at least in a trial run, is to pay attention to your respective heights and make alterations if necessary. Because I am only 4-feet 7-inches tall, I can't reach the microphone or be seen over the podium when giving a lecture, so I ask for a box to be placed behind the podium. (You didn't think I was going to talk about how I manage these sexual positions, did you?)

If a big height disparity exists between the partners, the woman or man can stand on an object, such as a phone book, so that the man can place his penis inside her without either partner having to do a deep knee bend, a position which is hard to hold while trying to enjoy sex.

Splitting the difference

Another position, called the *cuissade* (see Figure 10-5), is half-missionary and half-rear-entry (and maybe half-baked, too, but I don't want any of you to accuse me of having left out your favorite position).

Figure 10-5:
The
cuissade.

✔ The woman lies on her back but turns halfway and puts her leg up into the air (she gets extra points from the judges if she keeps her toes pointed North).

✔ The man straddles the leg on the bed and enters her, while holding himself up with his arms.

This position will definitely cause some heavy breathing, but whether or not any orgasms result will depend mostly on your physical stamina.

Spooning

Another variation of the doggy style, and a much more relaxing one, is the spoon position (see Figure 10-6). Here, the man still enters the woman's vagina from the back but, instead of the woman being on her knees, she's lying down on her side. Many couples are familiar with this position because it's only a short thrust away from a position in which they sometimes sleep.

Figure 10-6:
Spooning.

East Side, West Side, Side by Side

In the side-by-side position, also called the *scissors position* (see Figure 10-7), the woman lies on her back and the man lies next to her; he swivels his hips, interlaces his legs with hers, and enters her vagina from the side. If you're not very good at tying knots, then you may have some initial difficulties getting into this position, but it is a very good one, so don't give up. (If you really have difficulties, contact your nearest sailor.)

In this position, again, the man can easily stimulate the woman's clitoris while thrusting inside her, as well as touch her breasts (and she can touch his). Each partner can see the other's face and, if the temperature is low (or modesty is high), everyone can stay snugly under the covers. It makes you wonder why you'd even bother with the missionary position (unless you have some missionaries visiting you from the South Pacific).

Figure 10-7:
The scissors
position.

Lap Dancing

Lap dancing (see Figure 10-8) is a popular position in certain strip clubs (at least that's what I hear). The way it's practiced in the clubs, however, the man keeps his clothes on, making certain aspects of the act more difficult.

The basic idea, when not done in public, is for the man to sit down and the woman to then sit on top of him so that his penis slips into her vagina. If the woman is sitting so that she is facing him, she doesn't have the control over thrusting that she does in the female-superior position, and, with a woman sitting on top of him, the man can't do very much thrusting either. But, if the woman sits on his penis with her back to him, then she can keep her feet on the floor and go up and down as she would in the female-superior position.

Figure 10-8:
Lap
dancing.

The Oceanic Position

What positions did the natives in the South Pacific favor before those missionaries got there? One, which has been nicknamed *the oceanic position* (see Figure 10-9), is probably just about impossible for most Westerners of today. Because the natives didn't have chairs, they spent a lot time squatting, which they then adapted to sex. In this position, the woman lies down and spreads her legs and the man then squats over her and inserts his penis into her. Supposedly, this gave the man the ability to prolong intercourse for long periods of time. But, unless they happen to be catchers on a baseball team, I doubt that most men can last very long at all in this position.

Standing Up

Unless your bodies match up perfectly well in terms of height and shape, the standing-up position (see Figure 10-10) winds up being a difficult one to achieve. If the man is strong enough, he can pick the woman up so that they can fit, but the exertion is likely to lessen his enjoyment, to say the least.

Figure 10-9:
The oceanic
position.

Figure 10-10:
Standing up.

Personally, I think that the standing-up position appears a lot more frequently in porno movies than in people's bedrooms. But, because I'm not invited into most bedrooms, maybe more sexual athletes are out there than I realize.

The standing-up position is sometimes depicted with both partners in the shower. It looks very romantic, but, as you may know, more accidents occur in the bath and shower than anywhere else, including our nation's highways. Throw some acrobatic sex into this mixture, and the likelihood of injuring yourself approaches that of speeding along at 100 mph on a side street.

Adding a chair into the mix may make the standing-up position more feasible. The chair can be used for balance and to give added height so that the partners' genitals match up without the need for any heavy-duty hoisting on the man's part.

I am all for experimentation and making sex fun, but sex isn't an athletic event, nor are any Olympic medals given out for degrees of sexual difficulty. Orgasms by themselves are a great reward, and, if you can have them without risking life and limb, then why go the extreme route? On the other hand, while I like to ski down a mountain, other people like to hotdog it, so if you can experiment safely and it gives you an extra kick, be my guest.

Oral Sex: Using Your Mouth

Chapter 9 covers cunnilingus and fellatio as forms of foreplay, but obviously either or both partners can continue to excite the other's sex organ with their mouths and tongues until their partner has an orgasm. Of course, a man's ejaculate does bother some women.

A woman can, however, engage in fellatio without necessarily having the man ejaculate into her mouth.

- The best way to avoid the ejaculate is if the man helps her out by letting her know when he is close to having his orgasm. That way, she can put her mouth out of range while continuing to help him climax with her hands and fingers.

- After a while, a woman may be able to sense certain signs, such as a strengthening of the erection, which indicate an approaching orgasm, and duck out of the way without forcing the man to spoil his concentration.

- She can also keep a towel or tissue close by so that, if the man does ejaculate into her mouth, she can easily spit it out without swallowing it. On the other hand, if she does swallow it, not much harm can come of it. Some women even like the taste.

I haven't yet touched upon the positions that you can use for oral sex. Certainly no right or wrong way exists; whatever suits you is best. But one way does have a name of its own — "69," which refers to mutual oral sex. The name comes from the shape of the two bodies as they lie against each other, upside down to one another. Although it really doesn't matter which partner is on top, the man usually is the one to assume this role because he is likely to have to strain his neck more if he is on the bottom. (Sometimes a pillow under his neck can help.) This position may be most comfortable for both partners if both lie on their sides.

The man must remember that oral sex doesn't have to be strictly oral. Because most women like the sensation of having something in their vaginas when they are sexually aroused, the man can insert one or two fingers while performing oral sex to imitate the thrusting of a penis. This feeling of having her clitoris stimulated at the same time as she feels her vagina stretched is what makes some women like oral sex so much.

Anal Sex: Handle with Care

The anus does have a lot of nerve endings, so anal sex can be pleasurable to both the man and the woman, though of course the woman will not have an orgasm from anal sex alone.

Anal sex has certain guidelines that you must follow if you're going to perform it safely.

- ✔ The first guideline has to do with cleanliness. The basic purpose of the anus is to keep fecal matter, which is full of germs, inside the colon until the time arrives to release it. Obviously, merely wiping the area with some tissue isn't going to remove all the germs, so you must wash the area thoroughly.

- ✔ Many folds exist on the inside of the anus, so even an enema won't necessarily remove all germs; therefore, you must definitely use a condom during anal sex.

- ✔ Because the anus was not designed to be penetrated from the outside, you need to use a lubricant to help keep the anal tissue from ripping.

- ✔ Of course, you must never insert the penis into the vagina following anal sex without first removing (or switching) the condom.

If the male half of a heterosexual couple wants to try out the sensations of being anally penetrated, the woman can either use her fingers or try a small dildo (companies make some especially for this purpose) or a small vibrator (see Chapter 17).

Simplifying sexual slang

Because I'm always telling you not to be boring, I thought I'd help you out by including some other phrases you can use when talking about the activities described in this chapter.

Cunnilingus: canyon yodeling, carpet munching, dining at the Y, eating hair pie, egg McMuff, going down, going way down south in Dixie, making mouth music, muff diving, scarfing down, sipping at the fuzzy cup, sitting on one's face.

Fellatio: blowing, deep throating, frenching, getting a facial, giving head, giving lip service, hoovering, putting lipstick on one's dipstick, senor-eata, soiling one's knees, sucking off, talking into the mike, worshipping at the altar.

Intercourse: afternoon delight, balling, boinking, bonking, burying the weenie, dancing the mattress jig, doing the nasty, dorking, feeding the pussy, going star-gazing on one's back, hiding the salami, horizontalizing, meat injection, rumbusticating, shtupping, spearing the bearded clam, testing the mattress.

Outercourse: Heavy Petting Revisited

In the old days, people used to call outercourse *heavy petting* — a phrase that has pretty much gone out of style, as have the reasons behind it. In past generations, few couples would engage in premarital sexual intercourse. Because their sexual tensions weren't any lower than those of today, however, they would mutually release each other from these tensions.

Some of today's young people may not have the same moral or religious reasons for refraining from sexual intercourse, but because of the fear of AIDS, many are reverting to their parents' method and just giving it a new name — outercourse.

Who's on third?

In deciding how far a couple would go, young people used to use baseball terminology. If he got his arm around her at the movies, he was at first base; if he touched her breast, he had reached second; and so on. Home base was intercourse, which left third base for everything in between.

Today's name for third base is *outercourse*, which can range from each partner remaining dressed and rubbing up against the other, to some fumbling around through clothes to touch each other's genitals, to full nudity and a combination of rubbing and touching.

Remember, some STDs such as herpes and genital warts can be passed from one partner to another without penetration. If you engage in full body contact in the nude, you should be aware that you're at risk of contracting or spreading a venereal disease. (Chapter 19 deals with STDs and how to reduce your risk of getting them.)

Avoiding date rape

Another reason that performing outercourse in the nude can be somewhat dangerous is that sometimes matters can get out of hand, and outercourse can become intercourse. Sometimes, this is mutually consented upon, and sometimes it is not. When it's not, it's often called *date rape,* a situation that I have some reservations about.

I am certainly against rape of any sort, and if two people are having outercourse with their clothes on and the man forces himself on the woman, then I believe that is rape. But if a woman allows herself to get into bed with a naked man without any of her clothes on, then, to my way of thinking, she shares some of the responsibility if something happens that she doesn't want to have happen. I'm not excusing the man; I'm just saying that the woman has allowed things to go too far if she is really sure that she does not want to have intercourse.

Certainly, if the couple has gone out for a long time and has a relationship, the woman should be able to have more confidence in such a situation. But if the couple is really only on a date — even if it is the third or fourth or fifth date — she is playing with fire with such behavior. Sorry to say, some women are being burned.

Safe Sex: Playing Alone Together

I generally do not use the term safe sex, because safety from sexually transmitted diseases in most sexual scenarios is not 100 percent. Condoms do break, some viruses can penetrate condoms, and oral sex is not 100-percent safe either.

The one form of sex that is absolutely safe is self-masturbation.

Now you can masturbate alone or with a partner who is also self-masturbating. As long as neither of you touches the other, so that no bodily fluids are exchanged in any way, this sex is absolutely safe sex. You cannot give yourself a sexually transmitted disease, nor can you give a sexually transmitted disease to someone with whom you don't have direct contact.

At one time, self-masturbation with a partner would probably have been considered kinky. I still don't believe that many couples practice self-masturbation, but I'm sure that some do. It's certainly not as satisfying as the other methods, even if you do hold each other before and afterward. But self-masturbation does serve a purpose, and it is worth considering if you are both very concerned about STDs and want something more than self-masturbation while alone.

Sex during Pregnancy

Because reproduction is the evolutionary reason that sex exists in the first place, now and again a woman will find herself pregnant as a result of having had sex. If her pregnancy was unintended, then the fact that she's reading this book is a good thing, so that such a situation doesn't have to happen again. But just because a woman is pregnant, her sex life doesn't have to take a nine-month hiatus.

Orgasms are okay, with changes

Some women feel even more aroused while pregnant than when they're not pregnant, because the added blood flow in the area mimics the *vasocongestion* (when her genital area fills with extra blood) that occurs during sexual excitation. Although sex can continue unabated during pregnancy, she will need to make some changes and take some precautions.

A question that many pregnant women have is whether or not it is dangerous to the fetus if the woman has an orgasm. The answer is no.

Although an orgasm will trigger contractions in both pregnant and nonpregnant women, including contractions in the uterus, these contractions are not the same type of contractions associated with labor. Nor will they trigger labor contractions. Therefore, pregnant women can have all the orgasms they want up until the moment of giving birth. Some obstetricians even suggest to an overdue woman that she have sex because it will relax her and possibly facilitate the birth.

Change positions

Although you can safely have orgasms during pregnancy, you will have to make changes in the ways that you get those orgasms. As your belly gets bigger, certain positions become less comfortable and possibly even dangerous. You can cut off some blood vessels if you lie on your back too long, especially if you have a man on top of you, so the missionary position is one that you should drop when you reach your fourth month of pregnancy.

But that restriction shouldn't prevent any couple from enjoying sex, because the other positions already described work quite well. These include any of the positions in which the woman is either on top or lying on her side.

Some women feel self-conscious about their bellies and thus refrain from using the female-superior position because their bellies show so prominently. It's easy for me to say that a woman shouldn't be ashamed of something that she and her partner created. If she is self-conscious and ashamed, maybe she can overcome that negative view. Certainly the father should do all he can to reassure her that he's not turned off; in truth, many men do enjoy the added voluptuousness that a pregnant woman displays. So, speak up guys and let her know that she's attractive to you.

But if the woman really dislikes the fact that she has a lot of stretch marks, for example (and many women do feel that way), then she certainly shouldn't be forced to show them off while having sex. If she wants to continue using the female-superior position, wearing a light nightgown would be one solution.

Condom usage

Some physicians recommend the use of condoms for vaginal sex during pregnancy because of hormone-like substances in semen that can trigger uterine contractions and because of a possible risk of infection. Your doctor will let you know if your situation requires condom use.

Sex without intercourse

Some couples worry about sexual intercourse during pregnancy, fearing that the thrusting of the penis can damage the baby. In most cases, sexual intercourse cannot do any damage, but certain conditions may prevent a couple from having intercourse. Only about three out of 100 women will have such a problem, and a woman's obstetrician will warn her if she is one of them after seeing the results of her *sonogram* — a picture made by sound waves, which is now a routine part of pregnancy care. Obviously, if after intercourse she notices any spotting or pain, then she should not have intercourse again until she's consulted her doctor. If she does have reason to avoid intercourse, that limitation should not stop her from enjoying sex and from seeking satisfaction, but only cause her to limit the ways in which she does this.

If the man uses his finger to masturbate his partner, or if she masturbates herself, more care must be taken than when doing this during normal times. Because her vaginal area has more blood flowing to it than normal, it will be more sensitive and so more prone to scratches and irritations caused by fingernails or calluses. If a woman does find that she experiences these types of irritations, be sure to use plenty of lubricant the next time you have sex.

Fathers may not know best

Some couples think that anal intercourse is safer for the baby than vaginal sex, but that is not true. In fact, during anal sex the rectum is pushed up against the vagina, increasing the chances of germs entering the vagina and causing an infection. Therefore, sticking with vaginal sex is best.

The man often initiates this switch to anal sex, because he may feel that his penis can do some sort of damage to the baby. This idea is part of a general concern a father can have that sometimes puts a damper on sex: He begins to treat the pregnant woman as a mother instead of a wife and suddenly stops wanting to have sex. This notion is not only unnecessary, it can be counterproductive because it may make the new mother feel unwanted or unloved. So, although both partners have to be more careful and more sensitive during this time, the one thing they do not have to become is asexual.

What about the baby? Will it bother him or her if the couple has sex? Sexual activity may wake the baby and cause him or her to move around, which is a good sign, because it shows that the baby's alert. The baby may react in some other physical ways, such as increased heartbeat, but the parents' having sex will in no way harm the baby. So you don't need to have any concern on his or her behalf.

Be prepared for physical changes

Both husband and wife should be aware of another physical change that takes place in a pregnant woman — what happens to her breasts and nipples. As the pregnancy progresses, the breasts become enlarged, as do the nipples, with the *aureola* (the circle around the nipple itself) growing rounder and darker. The nipple may well protrude more and become darker in color. Just as with the enlargement of her belly, the couple should not feel awkward about these changes. But, as with the belly, the couple may need to change their sexual routine involving her breasts.

When stimulated, the nipples of a pregnant woman release a hormone that can cause uterine contractions. Although scientists have found no proof that this hormone can trigger actual labor, most doctors advise that breast stimulation be kept to a minimum.

One more change of which the couple should be aware is the smell of the woman's vagina. During pregnancy, the vagina produces additional "good" bacteria called *lactobacillus*. These bacteria help to protect the baby, and, while doing their work, they make the vagina more acidic, thus changing its odor. This is certainly not a problem and shouldn't cause the man any concern when performing oral sex.

Speaking of oral sex, some people believe that if a pregnant woman performs oral sex on a man and swallows his semen, it can cause her to have contractions. Just ignore this old myth.

If oral sex is part of the couple's repertoire, including swallowing the semen, the woman can continue doing this during her pregnancy. In fact, because a doctor may discourage vaginal sex for some couples, oral sex is a great substitute.

Oral sex is a good way for the man to give a pregnant woman an orgasm, but he must never blow into the vagina. The forced air can make its way into her blood vessels, which are dilated during pregnancy, and that condition can be fatal to the woman.

Postpartum sex

Even after a birth with absolutely no complications for the woman, the couple cannot have sexual intercourse for about four to six weeks.

Even after the doctor has given the okay, the woman may not yet be ready. Part of the reason may be physical; having a new baby who gets up several times during the night is rather tiring, and the sudden decrease of hormones caused by giving birth can result in a case of "the blues." Psychological factors having to do with becoming a mother may also play into this condition, especially if this is the woman's first child.

This can be a frustrating time for the father, but he has to learn patience. Keeping the lines of communication open is important so that the new mother can let him know how she feels and when she may be ready to try to resume having sex. Certainly he should feel free to masturbate to relieve his sexual tensions.

While I can't give you a set time that the two partners should aim for as far as renewing their sex lives, you should not let your relationship slip too deeply into becoming an asexual one. If you need to make special arrangements, such as hiring a baby-sitter and going to a motel to get reacquainted, you should do so.

Some couples actually split up because they never resume their sex life after having a baby, so make sure that this never happens to you.

Chapter 11

The Big O

Unfortunately, some people adopt a take-it-or-leave-it attitude toward orgasms. But, without orgasms, probably none of us would be here. After all, people have managed to hang onto this planet by reproducing themselves over the millennia just because men and women seek this intense instant of pleasure. Therefore, don't take your orgasms for granted — you have a lot to thank them for.

What Is an Orgasm, Anyway?

Understanding orgasms is important because some women come to me wondering if they've ever experienced one. For those of you who have experienced intense orgasms, this question may seem ridiculous. Many women, however, have never shared in this experience at all. Other women experience what is called a *missed orgasm,* in which the body goes through all the physical manifestations of an orgasm but the woman doesn't really feel it (I go into missed orgasms in Chapter 21). So whether they've just missed a passing orgasm or never even come close, millions of women (and a few men) don't even know what an orgasm is.

An *orgasm* is an intense feeling of physical pleasure that we human beings experience as the culmination of sexual stimulation. When you experience an orgasm, your breathing becomes fast and heavy, your pulse races, the deep muscles in the genital area contract, and your toes may even curl up. In men, orgasm is almost always accompanied by *ejaculation,* the forceful ejection of semen from the penis, necessary for procreation. Women also feel orgasms, although their orgasms are not needed for procreation.

As with every other bodily process, what's going on inside your body during an orgasm is a lot more technical than what you're feeling.

✔ In a man, first the prostate, seminal vesicles, and upper portion of the vas deferens, called the *ampulla,* contract, which forces out the secretions that form the *ejaculate;* then the muscles that surround the penis do their part to actually eject the ejaculate in what is called the Expulsion Phase. The first two or three of these contractions are quite strong, and they're followed by some diminishing spurts.

✔ For women, the uterus and the first third of the vagina, controlled by the underlying muscles, called the *puboccocygeus* (PC) muscle, incur the most contractions during orgasm.

But, as I am fond of saying, your main sex organ is located not "down there" but "up here" — in your brain. So the real importance of all that heavy breathing, those strong contractions, and those ejaculating spurts is the pleasure that you register from the overall feeling, and *that* I can't describe for you; you'll just have to experience it for yourself.

Kegelling is not a new dance

The same muscles that contract in a woman during orgasm can sometimes be weakened from the stretching that occurs during childbirth.

You can strengthen these muscles again by doing the *Kegel exercises,* named after the doctor who developed them. Dr. Kegel's primary purpose was to help women regain control of urination after childbirth, but, when strengthened, these muscles have also been found to increase the pleasurable sensation during intercourse.

Here's how you do these exercises:

1. **First locate the muscles surrounding your vagina.**

   The best way of doing this is to feel which muscles you use when you try to stop the flow of urine. These are the PC muscles.

2. **Practice squeezing these muscles.**

   Inserting your finger into your vagina and then squeezing down upon it may help.

3. **Gradually build up the number of repetitions and the length of each squeeze.**

   Just as with any exercise, increasing your effort will strengthen your PC muscles. Try to build up so you can do three to five sets of ten each day.

You can do these exercises at any time, even while talking on the phone to your boss. After about six weeks of doing the Kegel exercises, you should begin to gain control over these muscles so that you can flex them while you are having sex, adding to the pleasure felt by both you and your partner.

Men, you also have a set of PC muscles, and by doing the same exercises I describe in this section, you too can develop your muscles. Doing this can give you some added control over your ejaculations.

The rocky relationship between women and orgasms

As with the male orgasm, the female orgasm is strongly linked to her own genitals, although many women also report a more diffused sensation that takes place all over their bodies. Female orgasms tend to come in more varieties than male orgasms. Because of that, women's orgasms have been an issue of contention ever since the days of Sigmund Freud in the early 1900s.

This section summarizes a little of the history of this controversy for you, but if you really want to keep up to date, you probably should consult your daily newspaper. New discoveries on this subject crop up nearly every week — or, at least, people claim them as new discoveries.

Freud's "contribution"

The Austrian psychiatrist Sigmund Freud believed that two kinds of orgasms existed — the *immature orgasm,* which a woman reached through clitoral stimulation only, and the *mature* or *vaginal orgasm,* which he believed was more intense. His theory had the effect of making women seek orgasm through intercourse alone — which, for most women, is impossible.

Ernest Hemingway, although not a sex researcher, added to the problem by writing about a sexual episode in his novel *For Whom The Bell Tolls,* in which "the earth moved" for a woman during sex. Suddenly, not only were women not supposed to rely on their clitoral feelings, but they had to have special effects at the same time. And you men think you have it tough!

In the 1960s, Masters and Johnson, the experts who observed more than 10,000 episodes of intercourse (see Chapter 9) did a lot of research and decided that all female orgasms came — so to speak — as a result of clitoral stimulation, either direct or indirect. So the pressure was off, and women could enjoy their orgasms any way they wanted to. This attitude didn't last long, however.

The "gushing" phenomenon

I've received enough anecdotal information through letters and e-mail regarding women who gush out a quantity of liquid when they have an orgasm to believe that the "female ejaculation" aspect of the G-spot actually does exist. I am not going to speculate why it happens or what this liquid is composed of. The simple response for any woman who experiences this phenomenon regularly is to place a towel under her so that any unexpected flood will be absorbed. I mention this only because I don't want anyone to whom this happens to feel particularly embarrassed by it. You are not alone; it happens to many women, so don't allow it to interfere with your enjoyment of sex.

The G-spot — Myth or fact?

Forty years ago, a gynecologist named Ernest Grafenberg claimed to have found a spot in the vagina that seemingly could give women orgasms without clitoral stimulation. In 1982, three researchers wrote a book about this spot, calling it the Grafenberg Spot, or G-spot. Ever since that book's publication, I am constantly being asked questions by women who are desperately seeking their own G-spots.

One reason these women are so concerned is that a G-spot orgasm is supposed to be much stronger than a mere clitoral orgasm; it may even include a supposed female ejaculation. To some degree, the G-spot orgasm relates back to Freud's "mature" orgasm, because people claim that the G-spot is located within the vagina, which would allow a woman to have a G-spot orgasm during intercourse.

The fact that such a wonderful sexual stimulator as the G-spot wasn't better known before the last few years seems odd to me. I've spoken to many gynecologists, and none has provided any hard evidence for the existence of the G-spot. Other people have performed research, but I still haven't seen anything to convince me that this G-spot definitely exists.

Don't get me wrong, I'm not against the G-spot. After all, if some special place exists within the vagina that gives women fabulous orgasms, who am I to complain? My problem with the G-spot lies in the fact that no scientifically validated proof has demonstrated its existence. Yet thousands, and for all I know, millions of women are now looking for their G-spots.

Actually, because of where the G-spot is said to be located, on the interior wall of the vagina, a woman would have a very hard time finding it by herself. Instead, she has to send her partner on a Lewis and Clark expedition up her vagina. When their partners don't find this pot of gold, some women blame them for being inadequate explorers, the two of them end up having a fight over it, and their entire sex life goes down the tubes.

I'm not a big believer in lotteries, but every once in a while, when the jackpot gets really big, I go out and spend a couple of bucks on a ticket. The odds are long, but so what, how much have I wasted? That's my philosophy about the G-spot. If a couple wants to look for the woman's G-spot, go to it — as long as they don't invest too much in this search. If they find a place in her vagina that gives her a lot of pleasure, great. If they don't, they should just forget about it.

Climaxing during Intercourse

The G-spot isn't the only elusive object of desire in the world of sex. Another is for the woman to have her orgasm during sexual intercourse, as opposed to before or after intercourse. Again, the statistics show that most women have difficulties attaining this goal because the penis doesn't provide sufficient stimulation to the clitoris during intercourse.

Because the missionary, or male-superior, position is the one least likely to generate this phenomenon, in Chapter 10 I suggest some other positions that couples can try if they want the woman to reach orgasm during sexual intercourse. By using other positions that allow the man to stimulate the woman's clitoris with his fingers during intercourse, many women can have an orgasm.

The simultaneous orgasm

The other Holy Grail of sex is the simultaneous orgasm, when both partners have their orgasms at about the same time. I can understand the desire for simultaneous orgasms, because sex is something that you do together, like sharing a meal. If the waiter screws up and brings one person's dish first, it's always an embarrassing moment. The person who hasn't been served says, "Go ahead and eat," and the other person is left with a choice of either eating while filled with guilt, or waiting and having a cold meal.

Although sharing the orgasmic moment would be great, doing so is just not always possible. And striving for that achievement can lead to a lessening of the enjoyment of sex. If the man has to repeatedly ask, "Are you ready, are you close?" it disturbs the woman's concentration and can put her orgasm further away. Eventually, the man begins to lose interest. So, because of their search for terrific sex, a couple may wind up with lousy sex.

Having sex with someone is not like being a trapeze artist, where the timing has to be just right or else one of you falls to the ground. If you can have simultaneous orgasms, even once in a while, great, but don't make a big deal out of it if you can't. You're more likely to ruin your sex lives than to perfect them.

Multiple orgasms

Are two orgasms better than one? How about three, four, five, or six?

The obvious answer isn't necessarily the right one here. I believe that it depends somewhat on what you think an orgasm is. If your definition of an orgasm is a very strong, intense feeling that leaves you satisfied afterwards, then you really only need one. Returning to the food comparison, if you've had a full meal and someone put down your favorite dish in front of you, would it appeal to you? Probably not.

On the other hand, the craze a few years back was for restaurants to offer *grazing menus* where, instead of one big dish, they'd bring you many little dishes with different foods. That's a little what multiple orgasms are like: Each orgasm is nice, but it doesn't leave you satisfied, and you wind up needing another, and maybe another, until you finally do get that feeling of satisfaction. Is this better than having one big orgasm? Only the individual can answer that question.

You may have noticed that the last few paragraphs were gender neutral. Although most people who are multiorgasmic are women, some people tout the male multiple orgasm. They teach a method of delaying orgasm, including doing the exercises to strengthen the PC muscles, which is basically an extension of the method used to teach men how not to ejaculate prematurely (see Chapter 20). The man practices the method until he gets so good at it that he can not only delay his orgasms indefinitely, but he can actually have an orgasm without ejaculating. I've never met anybody who can do this, so I don't really know how effective this method is or even how pleasurable, but supposedly it can be done.

An alternative method of having an orgasm, practiced by some religious men in India, is considered a sexual dysfunction in the Western world. In this method, called *retrograde ejaculation,* the semen goes into the bladder and is later excreted with the urine, instead of going out of the penis at the time of ejaculation. Ironically, those Indian men teach themselves this technique because they believe they are saving their sperm, which supposedly gives them extra strength. Actually, all they are doing is delaying its loss.

Although all orgasms are pleasurable, they are not all identical. As the years pass, they often become less intense, especially in men. I say more about this in Chapter 14.

Don't try — Let it come

When it comes to sex, if we humans become too aware of what we are doing, our sexual powers go haywire. Any time we become overly conscious of the sexual process, we begin to lose our ability to perform. This particularly holds true for men who have difficulties having an erection: If they enter a sexual situation expecting to fail, they almost certainly will. The principle holds true for a woman who has difficulty attaining an orgasm. If she tries too hard to climax, the effort only makes climaxing even more difficult.

This effect is called *spectatoring*. In this respect, sex resembles many sports where, if a player tries too hard to hit the ball or to get the ball into the basket, it just won't work. The idea is to let your body take control while your mind relaxes. Under normal conditions, this method works fine, and both partners can have orgasms. But as soon as they are forced to become aware of the timing of their orgasms so that they can reach them together, the couple becomes too conscious of the process and actually loses the control they may otherwise have, which is what makes simultaneous orgasms so elusive.

If you're lucky, an experience like the simultaneous orgasm will happen by itself once in a while and provide some extra enjoyment. But if you try too hard, the odds are against it happening at all.

Chapter 12

Afterplay: Embracing the Moment

●●

In This Chapter

▶ Cuddling to create closeness

▶ Helping the woman wind down

▶ Telling your partner about your needs

▶ Letting afterplay lead to more foreplay lead to more sex

●●

Afterplay is so simple to do that you really have no excuse for not doing it. The only reason that afterplay doesn't conclude many couples' love-making is ignorance, and not just on the part of men. Women may sense the need but don't know enough about their own bodies to ask for the afterplay they crave. So, in this chapter, I explain to both men and women how after-play can enhance their sexual experience.

Uncover Those Ears

All too often, after a man has his orgasm, he doesn't care what happens to his partner, physiologically speaking, when she's had hers. These men cover their ears when they hear a woman ask to be cuddled. The reaction is similar to when their wives mention taking down the storm windows in spring — they head for the attic to hide.

If you want to become a terrific lover, especially in showing your partner that you really love her, then knowledge of afterplay is vital. So I want you to pay close attention.

The simplest of techniques

In terms of technique, there's not really much to afterplay. We're not talking rocket science here. We're not even talking paper airplane making.

Afterplay simply requires that the man take a little bit of time to hold and caress his partner, both physically and verbally, after she has had her orgasm.

Does that sound complicated? Or strenuous? Of course not. Nevertheless, afterplay remains the most neglected part of good sexual functioning.

Although the male half of the couple is usually the main obstacle to engaging in afterplay, women need to read this chapter just as much as men do. Many of us women don't know enough about afterplay either. And if you don't ask for afterplay, you will certainly never receive it.

Stay in bed

To fully appreciate the need for afterplay, look at sexuality researchers Masters and Johnson and their study of 10,000 episodes of sexual inter-course. As I mention in Chapter 9, Masters and Johnson didn't just watch their subjects; they had them wired up to all types of machines that mea-sured their various physical responses during an episode of sex. They mea-sured each person's heart rate; they measured their blood pressure; they measured how much sweat people gave off. And one of the things they noticed was that women take a longer time to come down from the high that they get during sex than men do.

After a man has an orgasm, his penis is not the only thing that shrinks; all other physical manifestations, such as heartbeat and excitation, also come down rapidly. But, just as a woman usually needs a longer time than a man to get sexually excited, she also needs more time to descend from that luscious plateau of sexual excitement.

So, if the man ends the sexual experience by rolling over and going to sleep, the woman is left to come down on her own, which is a lot less satisfying to her than doing it in the arms of a conscious partner. And men don't just side-step the issue of afterplay by choosing the arms of Morpheus, the god of sleep; some men get up to have a snack or to watch television. Other men head right for the showers — a habit probably picked up from sports that leaves the woman not only feeling unfulfilled but wondering if she somehow made the man feel unclean by having sex with him.

Some men not only leave the bed; they leave the house or apartment alto-gether. Even if they don't live there, they shouldn't rush to put on their clothes and bolt for the door as soon as they finish with the sex act. (Unless, that is, the man is having an affair with a married woman, and he hears the husband's car turning into the driveway.)

Both partners must recognize that a woman needs to bathe in the afterglow of her orgasm for a little while for the sex act to be complete for her. How long is a little while? For some women the time can be as short as a minute or two. Others need a little longer than that. I'm certainly not suggesting that the man has to spend as much time in afterplay as in foreplay or sex. He just needs to recognize that afterplay is a woman's legitimate need, and he should lovingly address that need with her.

Staying Awake

Now, I know what a lot of you men are saying right about now: "But Dr. Ruth, I'm not insensitive, I just can't help falling asleep." And you know what my answer is to that? Nonsense.

Of course you can stop yourself from falling asleep after sex if you put a little effort into staying awake. Sex does use up a certain amount of energy, but do you rush home and go to sleep after you come off the court from a tough game of basketball? More likely you go with the guys to a local tavern and unwind over a couple of beers. And that's all that afterplay is, unwinding after a sexual episode.

"But Dr. Ruth," you say, "after that game, I'm not lying in a warm, comfortable bed, and I didn't just have an orgasm, which leaves me totally relaxed, not just physically tired."

Okay, that's true, and I'm not telling you that you can't go to sleep. Sex does often take place in bed at night, close to the time when you would normally go to sleep. But I'm not asking you to pull an all-nighter. Just take a few moments to hold your partner and show her how much she means to you.

Pleading special circumstances

If your lover wants to stay up talking for another hour or two, that's not after-play, that's a gabfest, and you have a right to put an end to it. I'll even agree that in certain circumstances falling right asleep after sex is fine, too. If you have an early morning meeting the next day, or if you have to get up early to go run the marathon, it's perfectly okay to say to your partner, "Excuse me, honey, but I really have to go to sleep now." If you normally "give good after-play," then she'll no doubt give you a pass. It's the men who fall asleep every time with whom I have a bone to pick.

I once received a letter from a man who told me that he owned his own business, which caused him a lot of stress. Because of the stress, he had a hard time falling asleep at night during the week. The one exception was after he had sex with his wife. Then he'd fall right to sleep; instead of getting two or three hours of sleep that night, he'd get the eight hours he needed. Because I wouldn't want to be accused of causing a man to have sleepless nights, I gave him an official Dr. Ruth dispensation from afterplay during weeknights, but only if he promised to make an extra special effort to cuddle and caress his wife after having sex on the weekends.

No hard and fast rules exist concerning afterplay except that you need to recognize this need in a woman and make as strong an effort as you can to meet this need as often as possible.

Communicating the need

Now, if you are a woman whose man is from the roll-over-and-start-snoring-as-soon-as-it's-over school of sex, then you have to speak up. But never speak up about this during lovemaking. All that will probably do is lead to a fight that will ruin whatever pleasure you did get, and his as well.

Always try to communicate sexual matters during a quiet time, when you're likely to have enough time to talk without being interrupted and when you have the privacy you need to speak openly about sexual functioning. A stroll around the neighborhood after a good dinner would do nicely. Explain to your partner that you really would appreciate it if he wouldn't go right to sleep after having sex. Tell him why, let him know how good his staying awake will make you feel (and how good you want to make him feel), and also tell him that he doesn't have to engage in afterplay every time you have sex.

Knowing your limits

Some women who feel that they don't get enough cuddling and face time with their partners on a regular basis may try to stretch afterplay out beyond their actual post-orgasmic needs.

While I am sympathetic to your yearnings, I must caution you about using afterplay to fulfill other desires. If your partner feels afterplay is taking too long, he will look for ways to avoid it. So, after he willingly offers afterplay, don't try to take advantage of his consideration for your needs, unless he really doesn't mind.

Afterplay Creates Foreplay

Men who take time for afterplay will be rewarded not only with more satisfied, and hence happier, wives or lovers, but also with better sex lives. You see, I look at afterplay as really the beginning of foreplay for the next sexual episode. Throughout this book I tell you that the more you stretch out foreplay, the better sex will be the next time. So if you can start foreplay with afterplay right after you have sex, you won't be wasting a single second.

Chapter 13

Spicing Up Your Sex Life

● ●

● ●

*T*om Ewel and Marilyn Monroe starred in a wonderful film called *The Seven Year Itch*. The premise of the movie was that after a certain period of time, presumably seven years, a man would begin to get tired of his wife and go outside of his marriage to find some excitement. People considered the film risqué when it was released in 1955, but an awful lot has happened to relationships since then.

First, the divorce rate started to rise dramatically — people didn't even wait seven years anymore. It didn't take very much to cause a couple to break up, and even children, who were often the glue that held a couple together, weren't holding things together like they used to. I would see many couples who were having problems, and, with all the temptations that seemed to abound, I wasn't always successful at patching things between them.

And then came a new era, the era of AIDS. Suddenly all that green grass on the other side of the fence looked kind of brownish. Today, couples who are having problems that may have caused them to split up ten years ago are now more willing to try to work things out, and not just for the sake of the kids. People today are scared of starting a new relationship, so they're willing to put in the effort to try to save the one they're in.

Therefore your job, if you're married, is to rev up that sex life of yours so that neither partner has any regrets about sticking the marriage out to the not-so-bitter end.

Use Variety to Spice Up Your Sex Life

Variety can heat up your sex life in many ways. If you always go to the same restaurant when you go out to dinner, that repetition can get boring, and boredom doesn't help keep those romantic fires burning. By trying a new place, you get to sample new foods and a new atmosphere. The experience will give you new things to talk about, even if the new restaurant isn't as good as your regular haunt.

The need for variety also holds true in the bedroom. If you always make love exactly the same way, the routine can become boring. A woman may actually come to dread the way a man always touches her in the exact same way. His touch doesn't make her feel special or wanted; it makes her feel like an old shoe.

Make some new moves

Now many men are now saying, "But I like my old shoes best." That may be true, but if Cindy Crawford were coming over to your house, would you put on your old shoes? I don't think so. And if Cindy Crawford were going to go to bed with you, would you use your old moves? Of course not. You'd try every trick in the book to make her feel great, and you should do the same thing for your partner. She may not be Cindy Crawford (or whomever you fantasize about taking to that deserted island), but if you treat her as though she is, you'll both wind up profiting from the experience.

I'm not saying that you have to go to Fantasy Island every time you make love. Often times you both have just enough energy to want to have sex, but you don't have the added energy needed to be creative. Even if you make love the same way nine out of ten times, at least that tenth time, try something a little different. You can use the memories of those more creative times to add sparkle to all your other sexual episodes. On the other hand, if you stay in the same rut, you will only get more and more entrenched in your ways, and then you'll never be able to get out.

Variety can mean making love someplace you've never done it, such as the kitchen floor or on the dining-room table (just make sure that the legs are darn sturdy). You can add variety by making love at a different time of the day, such as early in the morning or in the middle of the afternoon. You can make love with most of your clothes on — or with only one of you naked and the other one fully clothed. Let your imagination fly and see where it takes you.

The one thing I must caution you about, however, is never to pressure your partner into doing something that he or she doesn't want to do. Being creative is fine, but you have to create something you can both enjoy.

Dressing it up

This really did happen to me, and I think it will help elucidate creativity in lovemaking. I was doing my radio show when I received a phone call from a man who said that he'd been living with his girlfriend for several years, and they always had great sex. (He also made sure to tell me that they used contraceptives.) He said that they were getting married in a few weeks, and he needed an idea to make the wedding night special.

I thought about it for an instant and then told him that, after his new wife came out of the bathroom, he should go in and take off all of his clothes, except for a top hat. I thought that was pretty clever, but he one-upped me. He asked me where he should wear the top hat!

Take creativity one step further

Doing "it" on the kitchen counter is different, but you may want to go a little farther than just a stroll down the hall and take your beloved on a romantic vacation. A change of scenery can help not only your sex life, but your intellectual and romantic life as well. A new environment can perk up all your senses, as long as you don't spend all your time in the hotel room. You know I want you to have lots of good sex, but if the two of you are so hot for each other that you can't find time to explore your new surroundings, then you probably didn't need to travel in the first place.

Tradition dictates that a "sexy" vacation involves going to some warm clime, and sitting on a beach wearing next to nothing while sipping strong rum drinks can truly do wonders for your sex life. However, I also believe that a vacation that offers intellectual stimulation, such as going to the Louvre in Paris, the Vatican Museum in Rome, the religious sites of Jerusalem, the theater of New York, or the pyramids of Egypt can also be very sexy. After a couple of days on a beach you can get bored. However, if you're exploring some new city (not just climbing aboard a tour bus but really getting to know it, block by block), some of the atmosphere will seep into your own pores, and you'll start to change into a different, more interesting, and more sexy individual. If you're in a stimulating environment, you and your partner can discover new sides to your personalities, and this type of exploration can be very sexy. If you vacation in a cold climate, ripping off the additional clothing that you'll have to wear may take a little more time when you get back to the hotel, but I assure you the overall experience will be well worth it.

Of course you don't have to blow your life's savings to go on a sexy vacation. Even staying at the motel down the block can add some spice to your sex life. You will have different surroundings, the phone won't ring, and you won't worry so much about the wet spot on the sheets. Or you can rent a cabin in some nearby woods for a weekend. Or go camping. Or even dress up for dinner at home (or have dinner in your birthday suits). As long as you interrupt your daily routine, you'll be breaking away from the monotony of everyday life, which is an important ingredient to creating a more vibrant sex life. For more suggestions on what spices to add to the mix, I suggest you read *Rekindling Romance For Dummies* (IDG Books Worldwide, Inc.).

Don't be a lazy lover

You know that you only get negative results from being lazy at school or at work, so why do you think that you can be lazy when having sex? A lazy lover is a lousy lover. The more energy you put into your lovemaking, the better a lover you'll be.

Now, by energy, I don't necessarily mean more *physical* energy, although it's worth trying if the two of you tend to be passive. The energy I'm talking about is spirit. The more of yourself you put into your lovemaking, the more you can get out of it. Remaining passive is easy for a woman and, although that's okay from time to time, if you always remain passive, you let yourself fall into a dangerous trap. When one partner always initiates sex and the other partner doesn't actively participate, the sex won't be as good for either partner, and problems are likely to occur after a time.

Take charge of your sex life, and you can achieve tremendous results.

Create an Adventure

In addition to using variety, being a little daring is also important. Take a risk on a new position (see Chapter 10 for a selection). What's the worst that can happen? Now when I say don't be afraid to take risks, I'm not suggesting that you do anything really dangerous, especially concerning unsafe sex. But, within reason, the sex act has many variations that don't involve any real harm beyond the risk that one or both of you won't be able to sustain the position or have an orgasm. So you miss one orgasm, no big deal. On the other hand, if you decide that you like a new position, it can bring you many, many orgasms over the course of a lifetime.

Visit a sex shop

Many people wouldn't be caught dead in a sex shop, and my question to them is: Why not? When you're hungry, you go to the supermarket. When you need clothes, you go to a department store. So, if you need a little more variety in your sex life, what's wrong with going to a sex shop?

The number one excuse is "What if the neighbors see me?" If the neighbors are in the sex shop, then they probably couldn't care less. If someone does say something, claim that you're buying a present for a bachelor or bachelorette party. The simplest solution, of course, is to go to a sex shop away from where you live. After all, I'm not telling you to go to a sex shop once a week. Once in a lifetime may be enough, but you should at least go that one time, even if you don't buy anything.

What can you find in one of these stores? Many different varieties of sex stores exist. Some feature mostly X-rated movies. Others have a large selection of so-called *marital aids,* such as vibrators and dildos. Some have sexy lingerie, while others have a great number of leather products. Sex stores often cater to a particular audience, so that one store may have a lot of whips and chains, and another won't have any.

Whatever you do, don't go into a sex store with a serious attitude, or you may wind up being disappointed. Sex is supposed to be fun, and the gadgets and gizmos featured in these stores are supposed to add to the fun of lovemaking. If you're not comfortable using any of these products, then simply browse.

Use a mail-order catalog or the Internet

If you don't dare go into a sex store, or if you don't have one near you, the next best thing is to get a catalog or click your way through a Web site of one of these shops. That way, you can do your browsing without fear of the neighbors peeking in. Companies that sell so-called adult merchandise know that their customers want privacy, so they send their catalogs and merchandise in plain wrappers — even your mail carrier won't suspect a thing.

You can find different catalogs for different tastes. Some catalogs, such as *Adam & Eve,* are erotic in and of themselves — with lots of pictures taken from the X-rated videos they sell, featuring men and women in all sorts of poses, along with pictures of half-naked men and women wearing some of the exotic outfits. These catalogs sell many different types of dildos, vibrators, oils, and games, and the wording leans toward things like "hot," "steamy," and "banned."

Let me warn you right now, however, that these erotic catalogs may offend many women (and maybe a few men). Because these catalogs feature photos of half-naked women with great bodies, many women feel intimidated by them. To these women, such catalogs are more of a turn-off than a turn-on.

On the other hand, most men find these catalogs exciting in and of themselves, so looking at them will probably get their batteries started up. So if you can at least tolerate thumbing through the pages (and the guys in the catalogs aren't half bad looking, in any case), then one of these catalogs can spice up your love life, even if you don't order anything from it.

You can also find catalogs that take a more, shall I say, intellectual approach. Catalogs mailed out by places such as The Townsend Institute, for example, feature how-to videos which, while they are certainly also X-rated, are instructional in nature rather than just fictional stories featuring sex. Catalogs like this also show books and creams and vibrators, but in a much more subdued context and without any nudity.

For the purchase of vibrators and other sex toys, I've long recommended the classy catalog of *Eve's Garden*. The people at *Good Vibrations* also put out a nice, calm catalog, and their operators can answer any questions you have about their products. See Appendix B for how to contact these and other companies.

The variety of Web site catalogs, which includes the ones I mentioned in the previous paragraph, is even broader (see Appendix B for these companies' Web site addresses). If you and your partner plan on doing your browsing together, a catalogue is more conducive to snuggling than a computer monitor (all that typing and clicking means that at least one of you has to keep your hands off the other). But if the urge strikes you to go looking at adult material, the computerized versions offer the advantage of being instantly accessible. The one potential negative is that some catalog Web sites are connected to X-rated sites, and the banner ads may show more explicit images than you want to see.

Watch X-rated videos

The VCR has certainly changed things in the X-rated video market. Such movies, which were once hard to come by, are now readily available. You can watch them by the dozen in the privacy of your own home. I get a lot of questions concerning these videos, so I know that they raise several issues that many couples face.

Because men get more turned on by visual stimuli, manufacturers aim these videos primarily at the male market, which is good for a man looking to find some erotic material to masturbate to, but not so good for couples. Many women find such movies abhorrent. Some dislike them because they depict sex so explicitly. Other women don't mind the sex but feel threatened by the gorgeous bodies of the women featured in these films. And then some women just dislike the sex, the women, the men . . . basically every aspect of these X-rated videos.

Certainly nobody should force another person to watch anything that they don't like, but people shouldn't take these movies all that seriously either. After all, many blockbuster films feature violence and bodies flying all over the place, and, to my mind, that is much worse than showing people having sex.

Some X-rated films supposedly have more of a plot and are more sensitive to a female audience. I don't believe that the difference is enough to convince a woman who hates this variety of film to watch one all the way through, but these films do offer a compromise. However, because the filmmakers know that the market for X-rated films is still mostly male, they have to make the sex quotient sufficiently strong to appeal to that half of the audience.

People often ask me for my recommendations, and, although I'd like to oblige, doing so would necessitate my becoming an X-rated movie reviewer. I don't mind watching these films, but their overall quality is such that I couldn't stand to see dozens of them, much less hundreds. If you order a film from a catalogue like the one put out by Good Vibrations, they're more selective and will give you some guidelines.

Another source for sexual videos is the Internet. Whether or not this medium works for you may depend on the speed of your connection. If you use a 56K modem, then downloading a video may take so long that you'll both be fast asleep before you can see it. Having a faster connection can improve the experience, though the average computer monitor is not very big and generally not situated in front of a couch or bed, which would allow for some physical contact between the two of you.

Whatever video source you use, don't just sit passively and watch. If you see a couple on screen engaging in an activity that you want to try, then hit the stop button, and give it a whirl. The point of watching these movies together isn't to follow the plot, limited as it may be. You do this exercise to add some variety, and being a couch potato isn't very imaginative.

You can use the videos, and television programs, to inspire your love life in other ways too. For example, why not spend an hour pretending you're somebody else, in particular some couple you've watched in a movie or show? If you want to play it for laughs, you can be Lucy and Desi. If you're into classic films, you can pretend to be Bogart and Bacall or Tracy and Hepburn (or the more modern Tom Cruise and Nicole Kidman). Or you can play male and female detectives on *NYPD Blue* who flirt with each other (as they all seem to do on that show eventually). You may already know the ending of these scenarios — that you're going to wind up in the sack — but the intellectual stimulation of figuring out how you're going to get there can make this type of play-acting extrasensory.

Take Charge of Your Sex Life

The success of your sex life is not something that you should leave to chance. Work on it on a regular basis, and you can definitely reap rewards that are worth the effort you put in.

The other side of that coin is that, if you ignore your sex life, if you allow it to slowly peter out (so to speak), getting those fires burning again will be much more difficult. So take my advice and start right now.

Part IV
Different Strokes

The 5th Wave   By Rich Tennant

"IF WE ARE GOING TO DO THIS, CAN I ASK THAT WE NOT DO IT IN THE ROOM WHERE YOU KEEP YOUR PIRANHA COLLECTION?"

In this part . . .

You know the old saying, variety is the spice of life. So, in this part, I'm going to give you lots and lots of variety.

Now, some of this variety won't be right for you, and that's okay. The only way for variety to exist is if we don't all want the same exact thing. But don't be closed-minded. What you don't find to your liking today may become your favorite part of sex someday in the future.

Chapter 14

Sex after 60

• •

In This Chapter

▶ Identifying changes for the woman

▶ Recognizing differences for the man

▶ Knowing the good stuff everyone can anticipate

• •

People have a funny way of trying to paint something that is basically negative so it appears really positive. For example, you've heard people say that stepping in you-know-what or having it rain on your wedding day brings good luck. Although I'm an optimist, I recognize that these sayings are just ways of making people feel good when something not-so-good happens to them.

Some people may say that the phrase "sex in the golden years" fits into the category of simply putting a positive spin on a mostly negative issue. Others may even say that the phrase is an oxymoron, because they think that as soon as people get their first Social Security check, sex goes out the window.

I must be honest with you and tell you that you will experience negative aspects to growing older as far as sex is concerned. After all, so many other physical attributes begin to grow dimmer, why should a person's sexual apparatus remain perfectly fit? And, in fact, it doesn't. But not all the aging factors that relate to sex are negative. And let me make one thing absolutely clear: People can continue having sex right up into their 90s.

Female Changes

Menopause is a fact of life for every woman, although each woman goes through the process at a different age and with different levels of symptoms (see Chapter 3). The end result, however, is the same for all. Every woman who reaches menopause experiences the following changes:

✔ She stops having a menstrual cycle.

✔ She becomes incapable of getting pregnant.

✔ She drastically lowers her production of the sex hormones, estrogen and progesterone.

These changes have several physical effects on sexual functioning. Vaginal lubrication lessens or stops altogether, and the vagina itself becomes drier and less flexible. Intercourse is often painful. Sounds pretty bad, right? Painful intercourse can certainly put a complete halt to your sex life. But you have a simple and very effective solution: Use a lubricant.

By replacing the natural lubricants that diminish as you age with artificial ones, you can maintain your usual sexual functioning. An older woman's clitoris is still sensitive, she can still have orgasms, and she can have comfortable intercourse.

I am not a medical doctor, so I won't go into any detail, but just as a lubricant can solve the problem of vaginal dryness, some of the other side effects of menopause can be treated with hormonal replacement therapy. This treatment is not necessarily right for every woman, but I recommend that every woman consult a gynecologist about this issue, and maybe even find one who specializes in this area.

So you can take care of the negative side of menopause pretty easily. Now look at the positive aspects:

✔ A post-menopausal woman no longer has periods (although some forms of estrogen replacement therapy will restore the menstrual period of a post-menopausal woman). Sex during one's period is certainly not dangerous, but most couples tend to refrain from "doing it" during those few days, especially if the woman has cramps or headaches. With menstruation gone forever, you no longer have good days and bad days, so every day of the month is good for sex.

✔ With the end of menstruation comes the impossibility of becoming pregnant. For many women, whether they use one or more methods of contraception, the risk of an unintended pregnancy does put somewhat of a damper on their enjoyment of sex. They may not realize it when they are young enough to bear children, but after the risk disappears, they suddenly blossom sexually. I've known many, many women who found sex to be much more enjoyable after menopause just because they didn't have this particular worry.

Male Changes

The changes that men undergo vary more from person to person than do the changes women go through, though testosterone levels generally begin to decline in men starting in their 40s. Every woman goes through menopause and, although every man does go through certain changes, the results are not always the same. Some men merely have a decrease in their sexual prowess, which I get into in a moment, while others become impotent. Obviously, the latter result is a serious problem, but even impotence does not have to spell the end of a sexual relationship.

You know you're getting older when. . . .

Let me begin with the early symptoms of a man's aging in regards to sex. A younger man can have an erection merely by thinking about something that turns him on. That is called a *psychogenic erection* (see Chapter 20). He sees an erotic photograph or thinks of the last time he and his wife made love and, voilá, his penis becomes hard and erect.

As a man grows older, his psychogenic erections are not quite as strong. Eventually, a time may come when he can no longer have an erection merely by thinking about something sexy. Now this change does not happen overnight. He still has psychogenic erections for a time, but they become fewer and fewer and need more and more stimulation to take effect. Then, at some point, they stop altogether.

Does this spell the end of his sex life? Absolutely not! Unless, of course, he doesn't realize what has occurred.

Howard and Sarah

Howard and Sarah had been married for 25 years. Howard was usually the one to initiate sex, but Sarah had always been a willing partner. Sarah loved Howard very much and was sure that he had never cheated on her.

As they both approached age 50, they began to have sex less frequently, but when they did engage in it, sex was still very satisfying to Sarah. As the frequency declined, Sarah began to feel sexually frustrated, and so she decided to try to get things going.

She had a few sheer nightgowns in the bottom of her drawer. In the past, whenever she put one of these on before going to bed, she could be sure that Howard would get excited, and they would end up making love. She tried this approach a couple of times, and nothing happened. One time she even reached over to touch his penis, and it was totally limp.

Sarah didn't know what was happening. She exercised regularly, but she had put on a little weight, so she thought that maybe Howard didn't find her attractive anymore. Then she became suspicious. Maybe Howard was "giving at the office" and had nothing left to give her. She became more and more irritated with Howard, and six months went by without them having sex. At that point, Sarah came to see me.

Had Howard been cheating on Sarah? Absolutely not. What he told me when I interviewed him was that his penis had abandoned him. He would look at his wife in her sexy negligee and want to have an erection, but nothing would happen. He was so ashamed of this problem that he wouldn't admit it to his wife. Because neither of them would talk about it, and because neither of them suspected the real cause, what should have been a simple matter developed into a major storm.

Curing Howard

What Howard needed was very simple: physical stimulation. He needed to have his penis touched to get an erection. He had discovered this himself because he, too, had grown sexually frustrated from not having sex with his wife and had begun to masturbate. But because he hadn't wanted to touch himself in front of her to get an erection, he hadn't used this knowledge to get their sex life going.

Howard and Sarah did have a period of awkwardness to get over because they had to develop a new set of signals. In the past, they hadn't usually verbalized their desire for sex. Howard would initiate some sort of sexual contact. If Sarah was interested in having sex, she'd confirm his desire for sex by reaching over and touching his already erect penis, and they'd be off to the races. Other times Sarah would get things going by putting on one of her sheer nightgowns. But Sarah had never had to "give" Howard an erection because he'd always arrived in bed, shall we say, prepared. Howard felt strange asking Sarah to fondle his penis to get an erection, and Sarah didn't feel comfortable reaching over to touch his penis, not knowing whether he wanted to have an erection or not.

Now the lack of an erection didn't mean that Howard didn't want to make love. He just had to figure out how to tell Sarah, verbally, that he was interested. After she knew for sure that he was interested, and if she shared that interest, she would use her hands to give him an erection.

Fellatio and the older couple

As in Howard's case, as a man gets older, he may require greater amounts of stimulation to get an erection. Some men find that oral sex works better than the use of hands. If the wife has always been willing to perform fellatio, then the couple has no problems. If she has never performed fellatio, however, then problems can occur. Not only may she have always felt disgusted by the idea, but if she feels that she is being forced into performing oral sex, she will be even more resentful about having to start.

I get many letters from widows who face this problem. A woman's sex life with her husband may have dwindled slowly over the years, and both partners had become used to it. But then, after her husband passes away, she meets a man who isn't interested only in companionship — he wants to have sex with her. The problem is that he cannot have an erection all that easily and requests oral sex. The woman is in a quandary. At her age, men may be hard to find, so she doesn't want to lose his companionship over the sexual issue. And, because she knows that so many other widows would be happy to do whatever a man who was interested in them wanted done, she feels she doesn't have a lot of leverage in this area. So she writes to me and asks what she should do.

This question is tough for me to answer. On the one hand, I do not believe that anyone should do anything under pressure. But if the alternative is to lose the man and be lonely, that option's no good either. I usually suggest a compromise, which is to have the woman try oral sex. Maybe she won't find fellatio so horrible after she gets used to it. She may even learn to like it. Don't be surprised by that, because I do get women who report exactly that turn of events to me. Or maybe she'll hate fellatio and have to give up on this man. If fellatio is really the only way that he can have an erection, then you really can't blame him for insisting on it.

An end to premature ejaculation: An aging plus

I'm not finished dealing with the negative effects of aging and men, but I didn't want to continue a list of negative items without mentioning a silver lining.

Many men who suffer from premature ejaculation when they're younger find that, as they age, that particular problem often goes away. As their capacity for sex diminishes, men gain lasting power. If their wives really enjoy intercourse, this can signal the start of a whole new phase of their sex lives.

Impotency

Just the way that a man's inability to have a psychogenic erection comes on slowly, so does the onset of impotency. An impotent man first finds that his erections become softer and don't last as long. At some point, he cannot have an erection at all.

Remember: Not all men become impotent. In many cases, impotency is a side effect of another disease or the drugs used to treat another problem (see Chapter 15). Diabetes can cause impotency. So can some of the medicines used to treat heart problems.

Until quite recently many men were too ashamed to ask their doctors about problems with impotency. They just figured that sex for them was over. But since the arrival of Viagra, that attitude has changed dramatically. Knowing that they only have to ask for some little blue pills has allowed many men to open up to their doctors and make that very request. And luckily for most men, Viagra does solve the problem, though as I note in Chapter 20, the medication brings up other issues about communication with one's spouse.

In any case, you should always check with your physician about impotency, especially if you take any kind of medication. Different medications have different side effects. Sometimes, if you complain to your doctor about problems with impotency, he or she can put you on a different type of drug, and the impotency will go away.

Viagra doesn't work for every impotent man. Some men who are on certain heart medications are not allowed to take Viagra. And others have physical problems too severe for even Viagra to help. But, if a man is just not able to have an erection any longer, that does not mean that he can never perform sexual intercourse again. Viagra is not the only solution to impotency; a variety of implant devices are available to allow a man to have erections whenever he wants them. For more information on this topic, see Chapter 20.

The Psychological Bonuses

If the previous section depressed some of you male readers, let me return to those silver linings. These things are not just of benefit to you men, but to both partners, which makes the silver linings even brighter — don't you agree?

When two people first get married, their libidos are so high that they make time for sex even if time is short. It also helps if no children are in the house, so that sex can occur almost any time and not just after the kids go to bed.

As the years go by, and particularly as children arrive on the scene, finding time for sex can become more difficult. And in these days when both men and women are in the work force, not only is the time often in short supply but also the energy.

In the so-called *golden years,* time suddenly grows in much larger supply. The kids are (hopefully) out of the house, and, even if both partners aren't fully retired, in all likelihood they're not working full time. These changes allow the couple to make love at various hours of the day, and in various places — not just at night in the bedroom with the door locked.

Making love in the morning isn't only advisable because it adds variety. The male sex hormone, testosterone, is at its highest level in the morning; if a man has problems with impotency, they are least likely to show up in the morning. Also, after a good night's rest, energy levels may be higher. If you need to have a cup of coffee, maybe even that morning bowl of bran flakes, that's okay. You won't be in a rush, so you can partake of a leisurely breakfast and then go back to bed.

Just as during any other period in your relationship, the more effort you put into better lovemaking during your golden years, the more you can get out of the experience.

Chapter 15

Sex and Illness or Disability

. . . .

In This Chapter

▶ Sexual relationships for paralysis victims

▶ Sex after a heart attack

▶ Sex and diabetes medications

▶ Sex for the mentally impaired

▶ Sex in institutions

. . . .

*T*he very first person I ever treated after I became a sex therapist was in a wheelchair. One of my dear friends, Dr. Asa Ruskin, who has since passed away, was head of rehabilitative medicine at a New York hospital, and he sent this young man to me. Even though I was new on the job, I was able to help him, which has left a particular soft spot in my heart for people with disabilities.

Later on, I taught a course in human sexuality open only to the disabled at Brooklyn College. This was another wonderful experience. The students were great, and they taught me a great deal. As a result, I vowed that I would never do another class like it again. The lessons that these students had to offer were so important and inspiring that I wanted to see these students integrated into regular classes on human sexuality, rather than kept separate.

I believe very strongly that people with disabilities should be able to exercise all their sexual capacities to the full extent of their abilities. Sadly, they are not always permitted to do so, which is as much the fault of the society in which they live as of their disabilities. This chapter discusses the major medical conditions that can affect your ability to enjoy sex. Chapter 2 covers problems caused by testicular or prostate disease, and Chapter 21 handles problems caused by mastectomy and hysterectomy.

We Are All Sexual Beings

In our society, sexuality is usually not something to be flaunted. Although we may admire a brightly plumed bird — despite the fact that those wildly colored feathers have no other purpose than to attract a mate — our underlying

Puritan ethic causes many of us to look down upon a human being who flaunts his or her sexuality.

I certainly respect everyone's right to consider sex as something that people should only do in private, but I disagree with those people who go too far and claim that anything having to do with sex is dirty and ugly. Considering that every single one of us has sexual urges, and that none of us would be here if not for sex, people who think this way are badly mistaken in their attitudes.

The situation is particularly sad when we then extend this ostrich-with-its-head-in-the-sand attitude toward people with disabilities. Some people in our society prefer not to see those who aren't reasonably fit. They'd prefer that people with disabilities stay in an institution or at least have the "decency" to remain at home. Too many among us tend to look at the disabled as somehow subhuman and want as little to do with them as possible. We forget that inside those bodies that may be crippled or blind are fellow human beings — and any of us can join them in disability at any time.

Now, when you put the two attitudes together — our attitudes about sex and our attitudes about the handicapped — it's no surprise that few people feel comfortable with the idea of a sexually active, handicapped person.

This is ridiculous, of course. Because both our families and our peers pass these attitudes on to us, no one is totally to blame. Instead, everyone shares in the fault. Those of us who are not disabled need to understand that those feelings of discomfort that have been handed down to us are not natural, and we can change them if we try.

Although much of the advice in this chapter is aimed at people who have disabilities, it also holds a message for those of you reading these words who are blessed with all your physical and mental faculties. I hope you learn to appreciate that not only is it okay for people with disabilities to have sexual feelings and to engage in sex, it would be unnatural if they didn't.

Sex and Disabilities

Saying that terrific sex is possible and desirable for people with disabilities isn't the same thing as saying that it is easy to come by.

Perhaps the most difficult part of sexuality for many people with disabilities is finding a partner. Some people, who were once physically fit and had a partner, lose that partner after they become disabled. No one can say whether losing a partner is worse than not having one in the first place; both are very, very difficult circumstances. If the disabled person's partner does leave, adding an emotional loss to the physical one, this combination can prove unbearably painful.

Finding a partner

The most important characteristics for a person with disabilities to have in finding a partner are open-mindedness and persistence. You have to learn to have faith in the fact that some people in this world decide whom they want to have as a partner based on the inner person, not a person's physical attributes or financial well-being. These individuals can look beyond physical problems because they fall in love with others based on who those people are as human beings.

For such a person to discover the inner you, you must allow your inner being to shine through. This isn't easy. Often people with disabilities tend to hide themselves in shame or to cover their weaknesses with anger. Although these two common responses are quite understandable, you must let as many people as possible see the real you, the happy you, the sensitive you, the sexy you. Then, hopefully, you'll find a partner.

Some people who become the partner of a person with disabilities are themselves disabled and may even have the same disability. But, if you act unpleasant and make it especially difficult for someone to love you, then whether the person you meet has a disability or not doesn't really matter. People may be sympathetic to others with disabilities, but that sympathy doesn't make them want to spend time with a self-absorbed grouch.

Most disabled people have to struggle every day just to get by, so I know that you possess plenty of strength and courage. I also know, however, that giving up on something long-term, such as finding a partner, is easy to do when just getting down to the street is an effort. But you can't let yourself give up. You have to persevere, because finding someone to share your life with is a goal worth every ounce of determination you put into realizing it.

One benefit to showing your bright side is that, even if you never find a partner with whom to form a loving and sexual relationship, you will certainly make new friends. People can't help but be attracted to a sunny disposition. If you smile, if you give people compliments, if you tell a funny joke, if you give them a big hello, they will respond positively. On the other hand, if you have a sour face, if you mumble, if you complain, then you will turn people off.

Many of you may be saying, "But I have a disability — I have enough troubles. Why do I have to reach out? Why do I have to be the first one to smile?"

Well, you know what? I give the exact same advice to a physically able person who wants to find a partner. Your disposition does play a role in attracting others, and just because you have a good excuse for feeling rotten doesn't change the fact that negative feelings repel people. That's just the way it is; if you want to attract people, then you just have to act attractive.

Partnering the person with disabilities

Comparing pain is impossible, so I would never make a comparison between the hurt felt by those who become disabled, in whatever way, and the suffering of their partners. Nevertheless, I must acknowledge the partners' pain. Without warning, a marriage that included a long list of activities that both partners enjoyed (such as skiing or tennis or making love on the dining room table) becomes one full of obstacles instead. Yes, the physically fit partners still have their health, but their hopes, dreams, aspirations, and fantasies can be just as damaged as those of their disabled lovers.

Sadly, but often understandably, many of these partners leave the marriage. They refuse to accept the limitations put on their lives by living with a disabled person. Sure, the world would be a great place if everyone could be heroic, but not everybody can. We shouldn't condemn these people, because we don't know for sure what we would do if we were in their shoes.

Keeping the relationship alive

Some couples, when one partner's health first fails, swear that they will stay together and work things out. Keeping that promise is not always possible, however. Sometimes the relationship ends because the healthy partner just can't find the strength any longer to take care of a disabled partner and still manage his or her own life. In other cases it ends because the disabled person places too many demands on the partner with too little consideration.

No matter how difficult having a disability is, a disabled person must be willing to give his or her partner a hand. Yes, you may have lost certain faculties, but you have to be willing to exercise the ones you still have to your fullest.

Because this is a book about sex, let me address that particular subject. If a man has an accident and, as a result, loses his ability to have erections, his wife doesn't have to spend the rest of her life sexually frustrated. If he can still move his fingers, if he can still use his tongue, if he can hold a vibrator, he owes his wife sexual fulfillment. If the man abandons his wife sexually while at the same time asking her for all sorts of other help, then she just may not be able to bear all those burdens. The same holds true for a disabled woman who withholds sexual favors.

If a healthy spouse locked into a marriage with a disabled person who refused to engage in any sex came to me, I wouldn't necessarily advise that person to stay within such a marriage. I may feel bad saying it, but I just might have to say that the healthy person has to think of themselves also.

You should also remember that, besides sex, many other things form the glue that keeps a loving partnership together. You have to tell your partner how much you love him; you have to thank her for putting in the extra effort that your disability may cause; in short, you must nurture your entire relationship if you are going to have a successful marriage.

If you and your partner face a disability, I cannot recommend too strongly that you speak to your doctor about sexual functioning. These days, medical help is available. For a man who cannot have an erection, either Caverject injections or Viagra may be effective (see Chapter 20). In the case of spinal injuries, the man may not feel an orgasm the same way he used to, but he may be able to have an erection, ejaculate, and feel pleasure from the experience. If your doctor does not have the information you require on this subject, be advised that facilities exist which have helped disabled men with their sexual functioning, and make an effort to contact the nearest one to you.

I also recommend that you see a sex therapist or marriage counselor — in particular, one who has experience working with disability issues (see Appendix A). Both of you may have worries and fears that play a role in your sexual functioning — maybe even a bigger role than the actual disability. You both need to talk these problems out, and rarely can a couple accomplish this communication without professional help. The same is true of strains other than sexual ones, which can tear at your relationship. Undergoing such trials is never easy, so don't be ashamed to seek help in overcoming them.

Sex after a Heart Attack

When most people hear the term *disabled* or *physically challenged,* they immediately think of someone with an affliction that you can easily see, such as a person who is in a wheelchair, who uses a cane, or who signs instead of speaks. Not every ailment is visible, however, and one of the most common problems that affects sexual functioning is a heart attack.

Overcoming fear

You may have heard rumors of famous men who died because of a heart attack while in the throes of passion. I can't attest to the truth of any of these stories. But I *can* tell you that, for the average person who suffers a heart attack or undergoes heart surgery or even has angina, problems with sex almost always result. Not that these people don't want to have sex, but they're afraid. They worry that, as a result of engaging in intercourse or having an orgasm, they will trigger another heart attack — this time, a fatal one.

This is not an absolutely foundless fear, but recent studies show that the increased risk is really minimal. For healthy people the risk of having a heart attack after sex is about 2 in a million. For people with heart conditions that figure rises to 20 in a million. Even though the number increases by tenfold, you can see that the risks remain very small.

Certainly, for a time after you've had a heart attack, your doctor will forbid you from having sex. And just because the doctor gives you the green light doesn't mean that you will feel ready. It doesn't take much to make a man lose his ability to have an erection, so you can imagine that the fear of provoking a heart attack can certainly cause impotence. For women, the usual problem is *anorgasmia,* the inability to have an orgasm, and it is equally understandable that a woman for whom sex holds no pleasure may be reluctant to participate in the act.

The best treatment for fear of sex after a heart attack is reassurance from your physician or cardiologist. I believe that this reassurance should take place in the hospital while you are still recuperating. Sexual performance is almost always a concern of someone who has had heart problems, and having your fears alleviated as quickly as possible can help speed up your recovery. If you need further tests to determine what you can and cannot do, then, by all means, you should get them. No doctor should consider the loss of sex as no big deal, because it *is* a big deal — not only for the patient, but also for the patient's partner.

By the way, the patient may not be the only one who suffers from impotence or anorgasmia: The partner, who is just as afraid of causing a crisis with his or her lover's heart, can also suffer. The partner may need just as much reassurance as the patient.

One way to overcome the fears associated with sex is to make masturbation the first step and slowly work your way up to intercourse. You can also perform masturbation on your partner so that he or she doesn't have to be sexually frustrated during your recovery.

An inspiring man

On one of my television programs, I interviewed a man who was quadriplegic, and he was willing to talk on national television about the great sex life he had with his wife. He did the best that he could with what God left to him, and he had a very successful marriage.

He is definitely inspirational, and thankfully he is not alone. Many people with physical disabilities have great sex. Anyone who saw *Coming Home,* a 1978 movie about a soldier who returns from Vietnam in a wheelchair, witnessed a demonstration of how sexual and sexy the relationship of a disabled man and a healthy woman can be. A disability does not have to put an end to a couple's sex life, although it will almost definitely mean that they will have to put more effort into seeing that the fires do keep burning brightly.

It may not all be in your head

Fear isn't the only factor that can cause impotence. Vascular problems usually accompany heart problems, so — because a man's erection results from blood flowing into the penis — sometimes the impotence a man experiences after a heart attack has physical rather than mental causes.

Angina, shortness of breath, and palpitations are problems associated with heart conditions, and, although they may not be deadly, they can certainly put a crimp in your sex life. Very often these symptoms show up after you've had an orgasm, during the period that your heartbeat is on its way down. Now, if you get an angina attack (a sharp pain in the chest area) every time that you orgasm, these attacks will not improve your desire for sex. Here, again, you should consult with your physician or cardiologist. Don't be ashamed to ask specific questions. Your doctor may have suggestions that will help you have a relatively normal sex life, and you have every right to find out.

What can you do?

Here are some specific tips that may help you if you have heart trouble.

✔ If you have a heart condition, don't engage in sexual activity when you're angry or under a lot of stress. At these times, the heart already beats faster, and sex would only tax its abilities even more.

✔ See if your doctor can prescribe one of the new drugs such as calcium channel blockers or beta blockers for you. These drugs can make sex easier on your heart.

✔ Some heart patients decide for themselves to take their heart medication, such as propranolol (Inderal) or nitroglycerin, before having sex, thinking that they can prevent heart troubles. Do not attempt such techniques without first checking with your physician. (Propranolol is used on a schedule, so taking it out of schedule can be risky.) Men suffering from impotence may consider taking Viagra. This can be deadly, however, so do not ask for a prescription from another doctor without first checking with your heart specialist.

The medications that are prescribed for heart conditions, such as beta-blockers, antihypertensives, and diuretics, can cause sexual functioning problems of their own. Sometimes your doctor can prescribe alternative medicines that will still be effective without getting in the way of your sexual functioning, so ask questions of your cardiologist.

I have spoken to many cardiologists on this issue; both the medical profession and the patients share the lack of communication. Some cardiologists gloss over the sexual aspects, but many times the patients are simply too shy to discuss their sexual problems with their cardiologist. This embarrassment especially holds true for older people, who form the biggest proportion of heart patients. They may believe that, at their age, sex isn't important. But sex is important, and it can play an important role in your recovery. Don't ignore sexual problems; speak out.

Drugs that can affect your sex life

Many drugs have side effects that pertain to your sex life. The following is a list of drugs that can affect various sexual functions. Take note: These drugs will not affect everyone the same way, but if you are taking one or more of these drugs and you do notice that it is affecting your sexual functioning, speak to your doctor about it. The doctor may prescribe a different drug, or perhaps a different dosage, which can restore your sexual functioning. Drugs that have been on the market for a long time are more likely to affect your sexual functioning, because when pharmaceutical companies first developed these drugs, their main concern was treating the symptoms involved. Only later, as these companies tinker with the dosages, can they delete some of the negative side effects.

Drugs that can affect sexual desire (names in parentheses are brand names):

antihypertensives, antidepressants, hypnotics, antipsychotic, ulcer medications, and antianxiety drugs such as: atenolol (Tenorim), antihistamines, barbiturates, chlordiazepoxide (Librium), chlor-promazine (Thorazine), cimetidine (Tagamet), clonidine (Catapres), diazepam (Valium), disulfiram (Anabuse), estrogens (used in men to treat prostate cancer), labetalol (Trandate), methyldopa (Aldomet), metoprolol (Lopressor), propranolol (Inderal), reserpine (Serpasil), tricyclic antidepressants (TADs), and birth control pills

Drugs that can affect ejaculation:

anticholinergics, barbiturates, chlorpromazine (Thorazine), clonidine (Catapres), estrogens, guanethidine (Ismelin), methyldopa (Aldomet), monoamine oxidase inhibitors, phenoxybenzamine (Dibenzyline), reserpine (Serpasil), thiazide diuretics, thioridazine (Mellaril), tricyclic antidepressants, and selective serotonin inhibitors (Prozac, Zoloft, Paxil, and Celexa)

Drugs that can affect erections:

anticholinergics, antihistamines, barbiturates, chlordiazepoxide (Librium), chlorpromazine (Thorazine), cimetidine (Tagamet), clonidine (Catapres), diazepam (Valium), digitalis, diltiazem (Cardizem, Dilacor), disulfiram (Antabuse); estrogens, ethionamide (Trecator-SC), guanethidine (Imelin), hydroxyprogesterone (for prostate cancer), lithium (Lithonate), methantheline (Banthine), methyldopa (Aldomet), monoamine oxidase inhibitors (MAOs), nifedpine (Procardia, Adalat), reserpine (Serpasil), thioridazine (Mellaril), tricyclic antidepressants, and verapamil (Isoptin, Calan, Verelan)

Drugs that can affect orgasm in women:

anticholinergics, clonidine (Catapres), methyldopa (Aldomet), monoamine oxidase inhibitors, tricyclic antidepressants, and selective serotonin inhibitors (Prozac, Zoloft, Paxil, and Celexa)

I believe that consulting with a sex therapist who is trained in working with people with heart ailments is also a good idea. Sex therapists aren't shy about speaking to you about your sexual functioning, and, if necessary, they can act as an intermediary and speak to your doctor to find out exactly what sexual activities you can perform safely. See Appendix A for more about choosing a sex therapist.

Sex and the Diabetic

One of the side effects of diabetes in men can be impotence. The fact that so many people know about this possibility means that many men who are diabetic suffer needlessly with impotence. In these cases, the impotence is caused not by the disease, but by the anxiety they feel.

If you're a diabetic having problems with your erections (either a softening of the erections or no erections at all), I suggest that you visit a sex therapist for several reasons:

✔ The therapist may be able to help restore some or all your lost functioning, if the cause is not physical.

✔ Even without a firm erection, sexual enjoyment and ejaculation can still be satisfying. A therapist can help you explore these possibilities.

✔ You should visit this sex counselor with your spouse, because she may need reassurance that you are having these problems because of the disease, not because you no longer find her attractive or have taken an outside lover.

✔ You should also consult with your doctor because some products on the market may be able to restore your ability to have an erection, chief among them, Viagra (see Chapter 20 for more about Viagra).

Diabetic women can also suffer from diminished sexual functioning. The intensity of the orgasmic response is sometimes lessened, and she may develop a greater need for increased manual or oral stimulation of the clitoris to have an orgasm. Again, a sex therapist can help you deal with these symptoms.

Sex and the Mentally Impaired

Many people feel that, because mentally impaired people have only the intelligence of a child, they should be treated like children with regard to all their abilities. They believe that the mentally impaired should be "protected" from sex the way we protect children. As a result of such policies — especially if the person lives in a group setting — family or staff make an effort to eliminate any form of sexual interest or expression from these people's lives. They get no privacy and are not even allowed to masturbate.

In many cases, this restrictive attitude toward sex conflicts with reality because, although a person's mental level may be stuck in childhood, physically, he or she goes on to become an adult. The men have erections, nocturnal emissions, and a fully developed *libido* (sex drive) with all the attendant sexual desires. The woman's sex drive also can develop fully, and physically she will have to adapt to having her menstrual periods. Although, for some mentally impaired individuals, sex education can be limited to teaching them not to undress or touch their genitals in public, many others would benefit from learning about safer sex practices and how to handle a relationship.

Because the degree of mental proficiency differs for each individual, how much they should be taught, and how much freedom regarding sex they should get, depends on the individual. Some mentally disabled people marry and have children; for others, such activities are not appropriate.

Anyone — parent, relative, or caretaker — dealing with a mentally disabled person who reaches adolescence cannot ignore sex. As the mentally disabled person grows up physically, his or her hormones kick in, causing a variety of changes, such as the growth of pubic and underarm hair, breasts, and so on. Just as with average teenagers, someone must teach mentally disabled teenagers that these changes are normal. Girls must learn to use a pad or tampon. Boys must be told about wet dreams. Both sexes have to understand the sexual feelings that they are starting to have. Both have to learn about masturbation and that they should do it in private.

Another point to consider is companionship. Everyone needs companionship, and so people pairing off is only natural. Sometimes that companionship develops into a romance, and then a sexual relationship. Some institutions allow this activity to take place, making sure that contraception is used, while others do not. But even keeping men separated from women cannot insure that sexual contact won't take place.

The best approach is to offer all mentally impaired persons sex education so that they can learn to deal with this aspect of their lives. They will benefit from it, and so will those who take care of them. We cannot deny people who have mental impairments the right to fulfill the same needs that the rest of us have, and so we have an obligation to help them learn as much as they can absorb.

Sex and the Institutionalized

Just as people who take care of the mentally disabled must accept the sexuality of those under their care, so must those people who tend to any person who is chronically institutionalized, including those with chronic disabilities and the elderly who are in nursing homes. For the vast majority of these people, whatever disabilities they do have, sexual dysfunction did not place them in the institution.

Institutionalized individuals deserve respect for both their sexuality and their privacy. If they need the door closed to masturbate, caretakers should not disturb them. Many times, people confined to a nursing home form romantic relationships. In these cases, I believe that institutions should designate *dating rooms,* with clear "Do Not Disturb" signs, so that they can enjoy their companionship in whatever way they see fit. Remember, even if a couple does not have intercourse, the pleasure of touching each other, hugging, or kissing is intensified if the couple is permitted to be alone.

In some cases, a couple cannot have sex without assistance. In these instances, I advocate that the staff should be trained to help disabled individuals enjoy the benefits of sex in much the same way that the staff is trained to help these people bathe or use the restroom. Sex is not only for the young and beautiful, but for everybody, and this assistance should be provided in a nonjudgmental way.

What may be the most important element to creating an environment where healthy sexual relationships can flourish in these settings is to make certain that the staff has the necessary counseling to handle such issues just as competently as they give other types of care. Because of the values of our society, helping people to have sex does not always come naturally, but I believe that, given the proper guidance, we can make our institutions a little warmer than they are now by including as much loving as possible.

Uncompromising Compromised Sex

In all probability, sex for a person with disabilities or a medical condition will involve some compromises. Not every position will be possible; maybe even some very basic sex acts, such as intercourse, are impossible. Those limitations do not mean, however, that the two people having sex can't derive a lot of pleasure from their activities. The important thing is not to look at your sex lives as limited, but to try to make the most of the sexual performance that you can have. Discuss your situation with your doctor to find the full range of what is possible for you.

Remember that sex isn't just orgasms. The pleasure that comes from making love (and here, I think, using that term is very important) comes also from touching each other, kissing each other, and caressing each other.

The human body and the human spirit are amazing things. Very often, the body of a disabled person compensates for one loss through the development of other senses. A blind person may find that his or her sense of hearing has improved considerably. A deaf person may develop a keener sense of smell. And so disabled people may well find that the parts of the sex act that are available to them become exquisitely pleasurable.

For this reason, you should never give up. Try to enjoy sex to whatever extent you can and make sure that your partner enjoys it, too. You may find that you gain as much enjoyment as any nondisabled person does and, by fully appreciating the sensations that you do have, maybe even more so.

Chapter 16
Same Sex Relationships

In This Chapter

▶ The roots of homosexuality

▶ Indicators (and nonindicators) of homosexuality

▶ Coming out

▶ Gay sex and marriage

Much of this book deals with heterosexual relationships; that is, relationships between men and women. *Homosexuality* is when men or women are sexually attracted only to others of the same sex as themselves. *(Hetero* means different, and *homo* means the same.) Which one you are — heterosexual or homosexual, that is, straight or gay — is called your *sexual orientation.*

I am often asked why some people prefer to have sexual relations with members of their own sex instead of with the opposite sex. From the letters I get, I know that many people believe that homosexuals choose the homosexual lifestyle over heterosexuality. They think that a gay person makes a conscious choice at some point in his or her life to be gay, and so they also believe that gay people can just as easily change their minds and switch to heterosexuality. Of course, the implication is that they should change back to the more "normal" sexual orientation.

The truth is that we don't know the *etiology* of homosexuality — the reasons that some people are gay while most others are not. In spite of the research done on the subject, scientists have not found any conclusive results. Here are some of the many theories proposed over the years:

✔ Aristotle believed that men who like to be sodomized have an extra nerve running down their spinal cord that ends in the rectum.

✔ Before Aristotle, Persian physicians concluded that the way a boy masturbated, holding the penis either tightly or loosely, would cause him to be either homosexual or heterosexual.

✔ Sigmund Freud thought that homosexuality developed when a boy identified with his mother rather than with his father.

For many years, homosexuality was defined as a mental illness, and treatment was aimed at restoring "normal" sexuality. It wasn't until 1973 that the American Psychiatric Association recognized that homosexuality was not a mental illness.

Here is what modern science has to say about homosexuality:

✔ Research with twins has demonstrated that a genetic component to homosexuality does exist, but genetics is not thought to account for all cases.

✔ Anatomical studies of the brain have shown some apparent structural differences between homosexuals and heterosexuals, but to date this research, while continuing, is still speculative.

Although humans have been studying the issue for thousands of years, we still can come to no conclusion about what determines sexual orientation. All we do know is that homosexuality among men and women has existed for as long as history has been recorded, that homosexual lifestyles are no more likely to disappear than heterosexual ones, and, as far as I am concerned, that homosexuals should be treated with the same respect as every other human being.

The Right to Be Gay

Is knowing why some people live a different lifestyle important? In a perfectly open society that attached no consequences to one's sexual orientation, knowing what caused different sexual orientations may not be important. But, because some people in our society publicly advocate that homosexual men and lesbians be prevented from — or even punished for — living their lifestyles, I do think that understanding the reasons behind homosexuality is relevant.

You see, if gay people do have a choice in their lifestyles, then some can perhaps legitimately argue that society should try to control how they live. (Some lesbians say that they did choose lesbianism for political reasons, but that subject is beyond the scope of this book.) Society singles out a number of different modes of behavior to restrict. Some think that because we ban things such as prostitution and sex with minors, we could also ban homosexuality in our society. (I'm not saying I advocate this, because I don't.) Sodomy was certainly illegal all across the country for many years and is still outlawed in some states (see Chapter 22).

But what if sexual orientation is beyond our choice? What if we are born with our sexual orientation and cannot change it? Can you really fault homosexuals then? Should society pass laws forbidding gays from having sex if that is the only way that sex is pleasing to them?

Now, as a Jew, I know that the Bible specifically bans homosexual acts, and therefore many believers in the Bible consider homosexuals to be sinners. The problem with relying on the Bible is that so much of what it says is open to interpretation, and — of necessity — some of that interpretation may be more human than divine. (For example, just a few pages from where the Bible bans homosexual acts, it admonishes us not to wear clothes made from different types of cloth. How many of us follow that regulation?) Some religious denominations, such as the Episcopalians, voice support for homosexual priests despite these Biblical injunctions. Many Christians also support our armed forces despite the fact that one of the Ten Commandments says "Thou shalt not kill" and Jesus instructed his followers to turn the other cheek. The only thing we know for certain is that we are all here on this Earth together.

Separation of church and state

In America, we believe in the separation between church and state. Believers in the Bible are certainly free to stop themselves from committing certain sexual acts, but, under the U.S. Constitution, their beliefs do not confer on them the right to force others to believe or behave as they do.

Sexual practices between gay men and women, when done safely, do no one any harm. Although gay sexuality may not fit the mold used by most people, I believe that we shouldn't criticize gays for behavior over which they may really have no control, and which doesn't harm anyone anyway. Nobody forces anyone to be gay, and neither should anyone force someone not to be gay.

As fellow humans, we in the majority heterosexual population must learn to be more open-minded and not condemn those gay men and women who live among us. Rather, we should treat them as we would any other of our brothers and sisters on this planet.

No carte blanche

What two consenting adults, whatever their sexual orientation, do in the privacy of their home is their own business. Now this doesn't mean that I give blanket absolution to every form of homosexual behavior. For example, I believe that some of the activities that take place in public areas, like at gay bars and bathhouses, go too far — especially in this era of AIDS.

Homosexuals are as capable of responsible sex as are heterosexuals — and they're just as capable of irresponsible sex as well. Considering that heterosexuals have a 50 percent divorce rate and often have multiple sexual partners over time, expecting homosexuals to be any different by picking one partner and staying with him or her for a lifetime is unreasonable.

A person in either lifestyle should make a serious effort to form a relationship before having sex. And all sexually active people — gay and straight — should employ safer sex practices.

Determining Your Orientation without a Compass

I am sure that many heterosexuals are reading this chapter out of curiosity, and that's great. Some straight readers may even get turned on by reading about gay sex, which may confuse them. They may suddenly start to wonder whether or not they themselves are gay. So, before getting to the sexual part of this discussion, I'd like to familiarize you with the very beginning of the process — uncovering your sexual orientation.

What turns you on

Getting excited by reading about gay sex, or even having fantasies about engaging in sexual relations with a member of your own sex, does not mean that you are gay. A gay person definitely knows whether he or she is gay, and that identification does not come because of an occasional gay fantasy.

In addition to gay fantasies, a common occurrence among young teen males is to do some sexual experimenting with another male. This experimentation may take the form of masturbating together, or actually masturbating each other. This type of behavior doesn't usually go any further than that; it stops on its own. Again, sexual experimentation among teenagers is pretty common and does not indicate any homosexual tendencies.

What does indicate that a young person is actually a homosexual?

The best indicator of homosexuality is if you can get sexually excited *only* by thinking about having sex with someone of your own sex (even if you have sex only with members of the opposite sex).

Living in the closet

Saying that someone is "in the closet" has a range of meanings. Basically, the phrase refers to someone who does not openly admit that he or she is gay. Some people who get married, have children, and spend an entire lifetime living with and regularly having sex with a member of the opposite sex are really not heterosexual at all. To get excited, these people have to fantasize about having sex with a member of their own sex.

People who appear to be openly heterosexual may actually lead clandestine gay sex lives in several different ways:

✔ Some people visit gay bars when the opportunity presents itself, go to areas where gay prostitutes are known to hang out, or merely masturbate while looking at gay magazines.

✔ Some people lead a gay lifestyle only when in the presence of other gays, but put on a front of being heterosexual in other settings, such as at work or school.

✔ Some people may never actually engage in any form of gay sex, but, nevertheless, deep down inside, are gay.

Many of these people, especially in today's more liberal atmosphere, do end up "coming out of the closet" at some point in their lives. Others box themselves in so tightly that they just don't feel that they can survive the revelation, and so they hide their gayness for their entire lives.

Coming Out

Prior to 1969, few gays would consider publicly revealing their sexual orientation (also called *coming out),* but a riot in New York — caused by a police raid of a gay bar called The Stonewall — politicized many gays and started what was called the Gay Liberation Movement. This movement insists that society treats the homosexual lifestyle the same as the heterosexual one, and that people give gays rights equal to those of everyone else. Since then, the U.S. government has passed many laws that give gays much more freedom than they once had to practice their lifestyles. Nevertheless, many members of our society still frown on gays — oftentimes, including the people who are closest to gays: their families.

Coming out to family and friends

The adolescent years are never easy for anyone, but they are certainly a lot more difficult for gay young people. Not only do gay teens have to confront their own emerging sexuality, which is different from that of most of their peers, but they must then face the rebuke that their sexuality often brings from their immediate families. Revealing one's homosexuality is never easy — for young or old — but the process can be particularly difficult for teens, who are dependent on their families and have not yet established their own private lives with their own place to live and a job to provide financial support. In fact, the rates of suicide for young homosexuals are much higher than for heterosexuals of the same age, in great part because many cannot cope when faced with rejection from their families.

No two families react the same way when a son or a daughter comes out of the closet. Some parents may have suspected for a while and learned to accept it, so they have a general sense of relief that the subject is out in the open. Other parents react very negatively, upset that many of their expectations for their child — the traditional heterosexual marriage followed by a number of grandchildren — have suddenly disappeared. They may also react negatively, in part because they feel that their child's homosexuality reflects badly on them (and the way they raised that child) in the eyes of the rest of the family as well as friends and neighbors. In some families, the reaction is split, with one parent accepting the son or daughter's announcement and the other going so far as to cut off all contact.

Parenthood is never easy, but, because the expectations of most parents are turned topsy-turvy by the announcement that their child is gay, having some mixed emotions in the beginning is normal. Getting past those feelings and rebuilding your family's unity is the key, and I don't believe that you can help do that without some preparation. If you are forewarned about how your family may react, and have been told ways to handle these reactions, you are much more likely to end up being accepted by your family.

Until recently, the decision of whether or not to tell your family that you are gay was entirely up to you. Sadly, that has not been the case for many homosexual men who contracted AIDS. Testing HIV-positive has pushed too many men in the last decade to tell their families about their sexual orientation. I want all of you — gay and straight — to think of that sad scene the next time you consider practicing unsafe sex.

The most important advice I can give to those of you who are gay and who have not revealed your sexual identity to your family is to immediately find a counselor who has worked with other gay people facing this problem to give you guidance (see Appendix B). The counselor's experience in this area can be invaluable to you in obtaining the best possible results from your circumstances.

Coming out to the world

Most gay people come out to a potential sex partner first. That experience itself can be very scary. What if that person turns out to be straight? Rejection is always traumatic, but especially if the other person is actually repulsed by the offer, as a straight person approached sexually by someone of their own sex often is.

Eventually, most gay people do meet other people who share their lifestyle, and the support that they get from others helps them to then declare their sexual orientation to their families and friends. One new way of discussing the topic that is helping many teens come out is computer bulletin boards (see Chapter 18). Using this method of communication, teens can find out about the gay lifestyle without having to reveal their own identity until they are ready to do so.

Coming out in your profession or on the job can be much more risky. Openness about one's sexual orientation doesn't always translate well in the business world. Because of this, many gay people who do not hide their status at home are very careful about whom they tell at the office. Some companies will not hire a homosexual simply because of the strain that an HIV-positive person may put on their health benefits program. In other cases, some employers are becoming less tolerant of their homosexual employees, either because of their own fear of AIDS or because of a concern that their other employees may react negatively.

This on-the-job discrimination against homosexuals can backfire in the battle against AIDS. For appearance's sake, a gay employee may avoid forming a relationship, which forces him or her into the dangerous world of anonymous sex, where the risk of getting and spreading AIDS is so much higher.

Not so long ago, more and more gay people were revealing their secret. Since the advent of AIDS, however, many gay men have decided to keep their sexual orientation private once again.

Because a gay person can never know exactly what the outcome of his or her coming out will be, the decision is always a heavy burden. If everything goes right, gay men and women may feel as though a tremendous weight has been lifted from their shoulders because they no longer have to lead dual lives. On the other hand, if they end up losing contact with certain family members and friends, many people may find the loss a heavy price to pay for admitting their true identity.

Coming out when you're married, with children

The gay man or woman who marries someone of the opposite sex and also has children faces a double burden if he or she decides to later reveal a different sexual identity. In addition to his or her own suffering, his or her partner and children undoubtedly suffer tremendously.

Although the gay person certainly feels a sense of loss at leaving the spouse and children, the gay person will likely eventually blossom within the gay community. However, for the partner who is left behind, the grieving process can be worse than that caused by the death of a spouse. That person now has not only lost a spouse, but has also had his or her own sexual worth badly damaged. The partner whom they loved, and whom they thought found them sexually attractive, may have never actually felt that way. This realization comes as a crushing blow. Although the newly identified gay person will find acceptance in the gay community, his or her former spouse often finds no comparative support. Because this phenomenon has spread in the last decade, support groups are now forming in various places to help such abandoned spouses. Still, many of these people end up facing their loss alone.

These negative consequences do not result from the gay people making a bad decision by coming out. Rather, I believe that these gay people made a bad decision when they got married in the first place. By allowing society to pressure them into leading a lifestyle that did not suit them, they end up causing many other people a lot of pain and suffering later on — in addition to the suffering they endured themselves while leading a life not truly their own.

Outing

Some people within the gay community believe that all gay people should reveal their homosexuality. These people sometimes act on this belief and reveal the secretly gay person's sexual orientation to the world at large in a process called *outing*.

As you may expect, I am totally against outing. I have seen the pain and suffering that gay people go through when they freely decide to reveal their true selves, and nobody has the right to force someone else to undergo that process.

Finding support

Not long ago, left-handed children were forced to learn to write with their right hands. Society has since learned to accept lefties, and in some endeavors, such as sports, many lefties actually have an advantage.

I hope one day we will feel the same way about gay people that we feel about lefties. The pressures that our society puts on gays to keep their sexuality hidden causes untold damage. And the guilt for this lies not on gay people, but on all of us for trying to force them into adopting a false sexual identity.

Gary

I had a young man come to see me who was very distressed. He'd known he was gay since he was about 14. He was a "Navy brat" and desperately wanted to please his father and also join the Navy, but he knew he couldn't do that as a homosexual. Therefore, he hid his sexual orientation. Because he needed sexual release, he would go into gay bars for impersonal sex, but never allowed himself to become emotionally involved with any gay man. Hiding a full-blown relationship, he reasoned, would be much harder than keeping his sexual encounters a secret.

Gary did not join the Navy, but he still feared his parents discovering his homosexuality. The reason that Gary came to see me was because, for the first time, he had developed a crush on another man — a coworker. They'd had sex, but Gary didn't know how to handle the situation. He asked me to help him forget this man, but, of course, what he needed was instruction on how to tell his family who he really was so that he could fully develop as a human being.

Although everyone focuses on the AIDS crisis among homosexuals — and the disease certainly has had a horrible effect on this population — at the same time, gays have been building networks to help each other live more satisfying lives. They've organized politically, with groups such as the National Gay and Lesbian Task Force, so that in major cities with large gay communities, homosexuals have gained many, if not most, of the same civil rights as heterosexuals. Gay resorts have sprung up where homosexuals can gather without feeling different. And *The Gay, Lesbian, and Bisexual Students' Guide* (NYU Press) lists all the colleges in America and rates them as far as the hospitality they provide to gays.

All these changes have made life a lot more pleasant for homosexuals since the Stonewall incident (see "Coming Out" earlier in this chapter), but far too many people still remain ignorant and discriminate against others because of their sexual orientation.

Homosexual Sex between Men

Homosexual men practice a wide array of male-to-male sexual activities — many of them identical to heterosexual activities. And, in a gay relationship, the feelings of love and caring can be as strong as in any heterosexual relationship.

Because of the traumatic effect that AIDS has had on the gay community, I am listing gay sexual practices in order of their safety — a major concern for both gays and straights. I particularly want young homosexual males to hear this message about safer sex. Although the older gay population, which has seen so many of its members suffer and die, has adopted safer sex practices, reports indicate that young gay men are still flirting with danger.

- At the safest end of the spectrum is *voyeurism;* that is, watching other people have sex. This activity may be compared to straight men going to topless clubs; although, because of the atmosphere of the gay bar and bath scene, masturbation more likely accompanies voyeurism among homosexuals.

- Group masturbation is another common practice in certain homosexual communities. This may either be solo masturbation done in the presence of others, or mutual masturbation, which is sometimes done in *circle jerks* where one man masturbates the next, who masturbates the next, and so on. Because of the dangers of AIDS, most major cities have developed *J/O Clubs* (the J/O stands for "jerk off" or "jack off"), which are places where gay men may masturbate together. These clubs usually have strict rules against other, dangerous forms of sex.

- Kissing is something that appeals to some gay men, though not all. For some gay men, kissing is the primary or only form of physical contact they have with other men.

- *Frontage* is the term applied to the practice of two men rubbing their bodies against each other, usually until climax. This is considered a safe form of sexual activity.

- *Fellatio,* oral-penile sex, is considered to be the most common form of sex between men.

Because the risks of transmitting an STD are greater if one person ejaculates into the mouth of the other, ejaculating in the mouth is often avoided. Because of the leak of Cowper's fluid, however, such oral sex still has some danger to it unless the person on whom fellatio is being performed wears a condom. Kissing other bodily parts includes little risk, except for anal kissing, or *rimming,* from which many STDs can be passed on.

✔ The most risky form of gay male sex is *penile-anal sex*. This is when one man inserts his penis into the anus of his partner and thrusts until he achieves orgasm. The person whose anus is being penetrated, the *bottom,* may also find pleasure from having his prostate and rectum stimulated in this manner. The transmission of STDs is at its highest during anal sex because the ejaculate can contain the viruses. Because the rectal lining is often torn or abraded during this sexual practice, the viruses then gain easy access to the bloodstream.

The use of condoms is a must for safer penile-anal sex; although, because of the amount of physical activity, condoms are more likely to break during anal sex than during vaginal sex. So, even with a condom, anal sex remains a risky activity.

The relationships between homosexual men have undergone several transformations since the Gay Liberation Movement began. Many gay men, especially in bigger cities with large gay populations, at first became ultra-promiscuous. They had sex with literally hundreds of other men, even if they also formed a relationship with one other man.

With the arrival of the AIDS epidemic, however, many homosexuals chose to have sex only with one partner. Sadly, many gay men made this decision too late — they had already contracted the disease. Today, some younger homosexuals are returning to unsafe sexual practices. I can only hope that they use safer sex before it is too late.

Lesbian Sex

Much of what is considered to be lesbian sex resembles what heterosexuals consider to be foreplay (see Chapter 9), because intercourse between two women is not possible. These activities include touching, kissing, licking, and sucking over the entire body.

✔ Because, in a lesbian couple, both partners have breasts — which, in women, are especially strong erogenous zones — these are usually a central part of sexual activity, including the rubbing of both sets of breasts up against each other as well as much nipple play.

✔ Body-to-body rubbing is another important method of sexual activity. When two women lie face-to-face, one on top of the other, pressing their genitals together and grinding them one against the other, this is called *tribadism*. In the 19th century, lesbians were sometimes referred to as *tribades* because of this practice. One reason that lesbians use this technique is that it allows the hands and mouth to be free to stimulate other parts of the body.

- Because the clitoris is the most sensitive part of a woman and, through its stimulation, she achieves orgasm, it plays a central role in lesbian sexual activity. Most lesbians enjoy touching and rubbing the clitoris, as well as the entire genital area, using fingers and sometimes vibrators.

- Oral sex is also popular. The use of the "69" position, during which both partners can perform cunnilingus on each other at the same time, is common to some lesbians. Others avoid it, however, because they find that simultaneous sex is too distracting. Those women prefer to take turns.

- Vaginal penetration by a partner's finger or tongue is common, as is the insertion of foreign objects. Some lesbians use dildos to replace the sensations that accompany having sex with a man. But, because many dildos are shaped like a penis, some controversy exists in the lesbian community as to their use. Many lesbians reject dildos because they are male-defined, which clashes with the strong political beliefs of some lesbians. (Chapter 17 covers dildos.)

- Other lesbian sexual practices include stimulation of the anus, including *rimming* (moving the tongue around the edge of the anus) and penetration of the anus with a finger or dildo.

Although orgasm is certainly a goal of lesbian sex, many members of the lesbian community believe that all sex play is valid and that the goal should be pleasure, whether that leads to orgasm or not. However, some studies have reported that the frequency of orgasm for lesbians who have partners is higher than that of heterosexual women. Researchers have speculated that lesbians tend to arouse each other more slowly and communicate more during the sex act, telling each other more explicitly what is sexually pleasing.

The relationships of lesbian women have tended to be more couple-oriented than the relationships of homosexual men, both from an emotional and a physical point of view. Lesbians seem more interested in intimacy, and less demanding sexually.

Gay Marriage

Although our society condemns gay people for being promiscuous, it also puts roadblocks in front of gays who want to make a commitment to each other. Many people want to limit the concept of marriage to the union of a man and a woman. Nevertheless, the obstacles against gay marriages are slowly being eroded. For example, some religious denominations now perform gay marriages, and such unions are even gaining legal status in some states, such as Vermont. (See Chapter 22 for more on gay marriage.) Because I want to wish a healthy life to all human beings, I believe we must encourage all people, including gays, to form long-term relationships.

Chapter 17

Solo Play and Fantasy

●●

In This Chapter

▶ Understanding how masturbation got such a bad rap

▶ Knowing when to say when

▶ Discovering who masturbates

▶ Doing it

▶ Pairing masturbation with make-believe

●●

To start off, I have good news and better news. The good news is that I'm going to give you permission to do something that some other people may have told you not to do. The better news is that hair won't grow on your palms if you do it.

The Mythology of Masturbation

For any of you who haven't heard the myth about hairy palms, let me explain. People have long frowned upon masturbation, and in ancient times viable reasons existed for this attitude, besides the fact that no one had yet invented Vaseline.

✔ If people, particularly men, masturbated, then they wouldn't propagate as much. And, in the early days of mankind, when infant mortality was high and life expectancy low, making babies was important for the survival of the species.

✔ The elders of the tribes disapproved of masturbation because they believed that each man was born with only a certain amount of sperm, and if he wasted that sperm masturbating, he'd have none left to impregnate a woman. (I wonder what their attitude would have been if they'd known that a man can make 50,000 sperm a minute. Let the good times roll?)

SEXUAL MYTH
exposé
!?
exposé
exposé

Over the years, society never completely lifted this ban on masturbation. During the Victorian Era in England, for example, the crusade against masturbation grew to a fever pitch; the list of ills that people claimed masturbation caused included insanity, epilepsy, headaches, nosebleeds, asthma, heart murmurs, rashes, and odors.

Worse than the supposed symptoms of the Victorian Era were the weapons that parents used to try to curb their children's masturbatory activities. These methods included restraints of all kinds and medical procedures such as circumcision, *castration* (removal of the testes), and *clitoridectomy* (removal of the clitoris) — a terrible practice that is still widely used throughout Africa and performed on millions of women, not only to curb masturbation, but all sexual pleasure.

But, whether cultural or religious beliefs caused the ban on masturbation, the elders knew (from their own experience, no doubt) that young boys and girls don't always listen to their elders (surprise, surprise). Therefore, they invented some myths about masturbation that would have the persuasive powers that laws wouldn't.

Many of the myths against what people labeled "self-abuse" were based on the notion that the consequences of masturbating included a physical sign that revealed to the world that the individual was a masturbator. This threat of public exposure was supposed to coerce potential "self-abusers" to keep their hands away from their genitals. Among these scare tactics was the myth of the hairy palm, but, because the possibility of having to comb your palm every morning wasn't always scary enough, the elders also threw in things such as going blind or insane.

Neither the bans nor the myths have stopped in the new millennium. Many religions forbid masturbation, and the ad agency for an acne treatment got into the picture and suggested that masturbation causes pimples. ("Oh no, a zit, now everyone at school will know why I close the door in my room!") All these myths are, of course, nonsense.

The story of Onan

The early Jews certainly were against the *spilling of seed* (an old-fashioned term for masturbating). You can read about their concern in the story of Onan in Genesis in the Bible, out of which came the word *onanism* as a synonym for masturbation. Actually, Biblical scholars now believe that, rather than masturbating, Onan practiced *coitus interruptus* (withdrawing before ejaculation) so that he wouldn't impregnate his brother's widow, as customs and religious law dictate he do. If Onan had known what everyone who's reading this book knows about the sperm in pre-ejaculatory fluid, he would have stuck to the original version and masturbated instead.

Too Much of a Good Thing?

Not a whit of scientific evidence shows that an orgasm obtained through masturbation is any different from one obtained during sexual intercourse, or that such an orgasm can cause you any harm. But that doesn't mean that masturbation doesn't have any negative consequences. Masturbation can be abused, as can anything — including the things we need to survive, such as the food we eat (look at how many overweight people are in the world today) and the air we breathe (as in hyperventilation).

As for masturbation, some people overdo a good thing and get hooked on gratifying themselves, sometimes masturbating many times a day. They do it to such an extreme that they don't leave themselves the time or energy for much of anything else, including finding a partner.

Okay, so how much masturbation is too much? People often ask me that question, but I can't answer it directly. You see, you really have to turn this question around to get the right answer. In other words, if you live a satisfying life, if you have friends, do well at work or in school, are in a loving partnership with someone, and you're both satisfied with your sex life together, then how often you masturbate really doesn't matter. On the other hand, if you are lonely and out of sorts, and you rely on masturbation to make yourself feel better instead of going about the business of making your life work the way you want it to, then you may be masturbating too much, no matter how rarely you actually do masturbate.

Masturbation is a good form of sexual release, but sometimes you need that sexual tension to get you going, to give you the incentive to find a partner, seek out new friends, look for a new job, or whatever. So, if you need to get your life in order and do masturbate a lot, I suggest you cut down. You don't have to stop altogether, but, if you can reduce the number of times you do it, you may find that you can begin to add some other positive aspects to your life.

What you're looking for is a happy medium. If you're single and actively seeking a partner, then masturbating to keep yourself from feeling sexually frustrated is fine. Just don't do it so much that you wind up being more attached to your genitals than to the world outside.

If your partner is satisfied with your sex life, and you would like more orgasms than the two of you have together, then masturbating when the mood strikes you is okay. But do make an effort to see if your partner would be willing to engage in sex with you more often. Don't be lazy and rely on masturbation to satisfy all your sexual needs, because a sexless marriage is not fulfilling and will likely not last very long.

Masturbation for Life

Today people know that masturbation is a healthy part of growing up. The practice can start in infancy and continue right through adulthood.

Masturbation in infancy

Going back to the very beginning, did you know that some male babies are born with an erection, and some girl babies are born lubricating? I wouldn't be surprised to find out that some babies massage their genitals while still in the womb.

Many children touch themselves "down there" because doing so feels good, even though they cannot yet derive the full pleasure of masturbation by having an orgasm. Most parents stop their children when they catch them playing with themselves. That reaction's okay, but how the parents put the kibosh on this behavior can be very important to their children's sexual development.

Teaching children that our society frowns on enjoying any form of sexual pleasure in public is fine. But, hopefully, you can pass along this information without giving children the idea that masturbation (or sex) is bad, per se. If you yell at your children when they play with themselves or slap their hands, they're going to get the wrong message: that sexual pleasure, in and of itself, is bad. As a result, when these children become adults, they may not allow themselves to fully enjoy sex.

You can teach children not to pick their noses in front of others without giving them a complex, so you should be able to do the same thing about touching their "private parts." Probably the reason that many parents have difficulties in this particular area is that they were made to feel ashamed when they were little, and they still haven't overcome those feelings themselves. So parents end up passing on these feelings of shame to their children. But if you can make yourself aware of what you're doing, then, hopefully, you can tone down the way you admonish your child in order not to give him or her the same sense of shame that you may have.

What parents must explain to their children is that touching one's own genitals is okay, but only in private. How many parents actually give the first half of the masturbation speech, the part that says the practice is okay? Probably very few. And how many parents actually give their children the privacy to masturbate; in other words, knocking before they walk into their child's room and walking away if asked to do so, without asking all sorts of questions? Also probably very few. And so, in the vast majority of cases, masturbation starts out as something forbidden that a person must do on the sly, and these early experiences shape much of our society's attitudes about sex in general.

Masturbation in adolescence

Although infants are very aware of their sexual organs, as children grow up, they go through what psychiatrist Sigmund Freud termed the *latency stage,* when they pretty much put sex out of their minds. The latency stage is the period of time when boys think that all girls are yucky, and girls think that all boys are even worse.

At some point — and that point is different for every child (it can start as early as the preteens or not begin until the late teens) — the sex hormones kick in and puberty begins. The child starts to develop what are called the *secondary sex characteristics,* which include things such as growing pubic hair and developing breasts. At that point, an interest in sex also starts, and that is the time when masturbation likely begins.

Surveys have shown again and again that boys masturbate more than girls do. By the time most men reach adulthood, more than 90 percent have masturbated to orgasm at least once. For women, the percentage is closer to 60 percent. Some of this difference may be explained by the fact that many women who masturbate report that they do not begin until they are in their 20s or 30s, while men report that they usually begin in their early teens. However, even when adults are asked the question, more males than females report masturbating.

I believe that several reasons exist for this:

- ✔ A boy's genitals are just handier to reach. A boy becomes used to touching himself when he urinates, and so less of a taboo surrounds those parts.
- ✔ Males also become aroused more quickly than females, so they can more easily grasp the opportunity to masturbate.
- ✔ Society is much more strict and repressive with females than with males, making female masturbation less likely.

As more and more women become sexually literate, they give themselves the freedom to explore their own sexuality, so I believe that those percentages will become a lot closer as time passes.

Masturbation in adulthood

This huge misconception exists that, when a person reaches adulthood, masturbation stops. That is certainly not the case for single adults, and it isn't the case for married adults either.

Many married people masturbate. Although some do it for "negative" reasons (that is to say, they do it because they are not satisfied with their sex lives with their spouses), many more do it simply out of enjoyment. Some people find that they derive greater sexual pleasure from masturbation than from sexual intercourse. Others have a higher sex drive than their partners do and require sex more often. Still others integrate masturbation into sex play with their spouses.

These cases illustrate two sides of masturbation:

John and Mary

When John and Mary first got married, they had sex just about every day. After five years and two children, the frequency of sex dropped precipitously to about once a month. Although Mary wasn't looking for sex every day, once a month was too little for her. Though she tried to lure John into having sex more often, it usually didn't work.

One night Mary awoke to find John out of bed. She got up to look for him and was surprised to find him in the study, where he had a porno tape playing and his hand on his penis. Because he hadn't heard her come into the room, she tiptoed back into bed and didn't say anything to him, but that's when she sought my help.

When I finally spoke with John, he admitted that he would masturbate once or twice a week in front of the TV set late at night. The reason he gave me was that he got really turned on by porno films, but Mary wouldn't watch them with him. He started watching them on the sneak, and it developed into a habit that he couldn't seem to break, even though he felt guilty about not having sex with Mary as often as she would like.

I helped them to develop a compromise. Mary agreed to watch a porno film with John once a month, but she got to veto certain subject matters. John agreed to have sex with Mary at least once a week, which was all she really wanted, and then, if he still had the desire to masturbate, he could.

I suppose some wives have always lost out to masturbation, but the temptations that are available these days — pornographic films for playing on a home tape machine, magazines on every newsstand, sex phone lines, cybersex, and everything else — seem to have increased the frequency that people report such problems to me, either privately or in letters. The best solution is a compromise, such as the one Mary and John worked out. Rarely do two people have exactly the same sex drives, so John has no reason not to masturbate, as long as he doesn't take anything away from Mary's enjoyment of sex.

Jim and Jackie

This was a second marriage for both Jim and Jackie. Jim's first wife had died of cancer, and Jackie was divorced. With his first wife, Jim had a fairly sedate marriage. He and his wife had sex about once a week, and both had been satisfied with that. In Jackie, he found just the opposite of his first wife. Jackie seemed to want sex every night, and at first Jim had been thrilled. Although Jim had forced himself to keep up with Jackie during their courtship, six months after the wedding day he was beginning to wear out. He worked long hours and couldn't continue to have sex with Jackie every night, and he started to beg off more and more.

Jackie still felt those strong urges to relieve her sexual tensions, but because she never knew in advance whether or not Jim would agree to have sex with her, she became more and more frustrated.

Although I am normally all for spontaneity, in this case, I decided that what Jackie and Jim's sex life needed was a structure. Jim agreed that he would have sex with Jackie twice a week, and they would pick which days would work best ahead of time. This way, Jim could reserve his energies on those days for sex with Jackie, while Jackie was free to satisfy herself through masturbation on the other days.

Communication is often the key to solving marital problems such as these, and if it takes a therapist of some sort to break the ice, then by all means go ahead and visit one (see Appendix A for help on choosing a sex therapist).

How to Masturbate

Although I'm sure that most of you already know how to masturbate, I don't want it said that I left out such a basic part of good sexual functioning, so here are some instructions.

Before I get into specifics, let me say loud and clear that the best tip that I can give you is to do what feels best to you. There's no right way or wrong way. You can use your left hand or your right hand or both hands. Whatever turns you on, as the saying goes . . . and those words can't be more appropriate than in the case of masturbation.

Male techniques

A common word for masturbation is *a hand job,* and the hand is certainly the most popular instrument used by men for masturbation. What are the alternatives, you ask?

Some boys masturbate by rubbing up against the bedsheets. Some men masturbate by putting their penises inside of a specially made, life-size rubber doll. Sex shops also sell devices that simulate a vagina. Many, though not all, of these devices look like a vagina, and the man can add lubrication to make the rubber *feel* more like one too. I don't know how popular these alternatives are, although my guess is that the vast majority of men rely on their own two hands.

Some men put a lubricant, such as Vaseline, either in their hand or on the shaft of their penis. Some men prefer to masturbate lying down, others standing up, and others don't care what position they're in. Most men enjoy looking at erotica of some sort while they masturbate, so the only kind of atmosphere they require is enough light to see the foldout properly.

Younger men sometimes practice group masturbation, nicknamed a *circle jerk* because the guys involved usually sit in a circle. Although this activity may appear to have homosexual overtones, it really doesn't for most of the males involved (see Chapter 16).

Mutual masturbation between two young men is not all that uncommon either; again, it does not mean that either of the participants is gay. Research shows that about 25 percent of heterosexual males engage in such activities in their early teens, while 90 percent of homosexual teens do.

Female techniques

Although males all tend to masturbate pretty much the same way, females don't. The key, of course, is clitoral stimulation, but the ways women achieve clitoral stimulation vary. Certainly many use their hands, the way men do, but many women who feel the need to masturbate are reluctant to touch themselves. And many women require more stimulation than their hands can provide.

Out of those needs has developed a multimillion-dollar industry in the manufacture and sale of vibrators. Vibrators come in many different types, each with its own pluses and minuses. I wrote some material that accompanies one particular device that oscillates instead of vibrates, called the Eroscillator. The following descriptions will give you a good idea of the choices that are available. (If you want more information, I suggest you call one of the companies listed in Appendix B, and they will gladly send you a catalog.)

I'm all in favor of vibrators if a woman needs the extra sensations on her clitoris to become orgasmic, and I often recommend them to women. The problem that vibrators have is that the sensations they offer can become addictive. In other words, no man, sans vibrator in hand, can achieve the same level of sensation that a vibrator can. If a woman becomes used to having her orgasms via a vibrator, and she then has sex with a man, she may well end up disappointed.

In my opinion, a vibrator is great for learning how to have an orgasm if you can't do it with just your hands. A vibrator is also very good for giving yourself a special treat now and again. But if you plan on having sex with a man sometime in the future, then don't make a habit out of using only a vibrator to have your orgasms. Vary the techniques you use so that, when sex becomes a shared experience with a man, you'll be in peak form.

Plug-in vibrators

Plug-in vibrators are the most powerful ones available; some women find them too powerful. Many plug-in vibrators are marketed as body massagers. Undoubtedly, some people use them only as body massagers, but certainly a great portion of their sales are to women who use them to stimulate the area around the clitoris. Among the brands of plug-in vibrators are the Hitachi Magic Wand (see Figure 17-1), Magic Touch, and the Sunbeam Stick Massager. You can also purchase attachments that can help to pinpoint the vibrations on a particular spot: the clitoris.

Figure 17-1:
The Magic Wand has been called the "Cadillac" of vibrators.

Courtesy of Eve's Garden

The Eroscillator is a plug-in type, but instead of vibrating, it oscillates, up to 3600 times a minute, which provides different and intense sensations that women who've tried it say they prefer. This device has several heads and, because it comes with a step-down transformer, is safe to use around water.

Other plug-ins include the double-headed massagers and the coil-operated vibrators. The double-headed machines multiply the possibilities (such as stimulating the clitoris and anus at the same time), and a man can even place his penis between the two vibrators. The coil-operated vibrators are smaller than the wand-type, a lot quieter, and also more easily carried in a purse. The Prelude 3 was one of the first of this type (see Figure 17-2).

Figure 17-2:
The
Prelude 3
has
attachments
for extra
pleasure.

Courtesy of Eve's Garden

Because the coil-operated vibrators were really developed more for sexual play than for massage, you have a long list of various attachments available to use. These attachments offer different types of stimulation, and I usually suggest to a woman that she try out several different varieties to discover which ones give her the most pleasure.

Battery-operated vibrators

Battery-operated vibrators are less expensive than the plug-in type, they're more easily carried, and they offer more gentle vibrations — which can be a plus or a minus, depending on your particular needs.

Many battery-operated vibrators come in the shape of a penis and are called *phallic-shaped*. Because most women need clitoral stimulation, a penis-shaped vibrator is not a necessity for every woman, although many women certainly enjoy the vibrations inside their vaginas as well. You can also find battery-operated vibrators that are long and smooth but not actually penis-shaped, some of which come in small sizes so that they are both portable and concealable in a purse or luggage.

Some vibrators don't look at all like what they are. The Hitachi Mini Massager is small, square rather than phallic-shaped, and has a cover to hide the head — very discreet in appearance. Also, some are devices meant to be entirely inserted into the vagina; these are nicknamed *vibrating eggs*.

Butterflies are vibrators that come attached to bikini-like straps so that you can wear them, like a bikini bottom, for hands-free vibrating. You can also buy a butterfly pouch, which can hold one of the smaller battery-operated vibrators.

Although I see nothing wrong with walking around in public with a vibrator secretly working its magic on your clitoris (and certainly knowing that nobody knows that you're being stimulated can add to the erotic effect), I must caution anyone who wants to use one of these devices not to do so while driving a car. Remember that we're all after safer sex.

Other equipment

Most vibrators are made for clitoral stimulation, but what if you want or need to feel something inside your vagina while the vibrator is doing its job on the outside? That's where a *dildo* comes in. A dildo is a phallic (penis-shaped) object that you insert into your vagina to simulate the feelings that you would get from a real penis. Dildos have been around a lot longer than vibrators. In olden days, dildos were carved out of wood, ivory, or jade. Nowadays, silicone rubber seems to be the material of choice.

Many dildos look exactly like an erect penis, and they come in all sizes. But because lesbians form a large group of dildo users, and many prefer a dildo that doesn't look like a penis, you can purchase dildos that come in all different shapes — some are simply smooth, and others look like a woman or a fish or a whale (see Figure 17-3). You can even purchase double dildos so that two women can simulate intercourse on each other and harnesses so that a woman can strap on a dildo to use on a partner, but I'm getting away from masturbation here, which is the theme of this chapter.

Figure 17-3:
Dildos come in many shapes.

Courtesy of Eve's Garden

I do what???

If you're still not sure of how to masturbate successfully, then you may be interested in a tape produced by Betty Dodson, Ph.D., who has made a career out of the practice. She gives classes to women on the art of self-pleasuring, but if you can't attend one of her classes, the next best thing is to buy a copy of her video, *Selfloving: Video Portrait of a Women's Sexuality Seminar.*

Betty filmed one of her workshops in which ten women, ages 28 to 60, sit around, nude, and practice what Betty preaches. Nothing is left to the imagination, so be prepared to see it all, knowing that afterward you won't have any questions left about how to use a vibrator and what the results can be. You can purchase the video through Eve's Garden (see Appendix B).

Water works

Another medium that seems to satisfy many women is flowing water. Many women masturbate by running the water in a bathtub, lying down in the tub, and placing their buttocks up against the end of the tub so that the running water lands right on their clitorises. The temperature, strength of the flow, and so on can be adjusted to suit the individual. Women report that this technique gives them a very satisfying orgasm without the need for direct contact using their hands or a piece of equipment.

Hand-held showerheads, particularly the ones with massaging jets, are also very good. And, if you have access to a Jacuzzi, you can use the water jets in those to good effect. With any of these methods, you can not only have a great orgasm, but you'll also be exceptionally clean.

Speaking of clean, if you're ever in Europe where you have access to a bidet, here's a tip: Although the porcelain accessories that sit next to the toilet were developed for hygiene purposes, many women have found them to have other, more exciting uses.

Fantasy

Men are definitely stimulated by visual images, which is why 99 percent of the magazines that show naked people are aimed at men. Although women certainly appreciate a good-looking guy, seeing a close-up glimpse of his genitals will not generally serve as a turn-on. What most women prefer as erotic stimulation is fantasy.

Now men fantasize also, and many men fantasize while masturbating, but the method of choice for men is still visual. Women, on the other hand, usually spend more time masturbating to reach their orgasm, so that they can leisurely construct a nice, long fantasy that will get them in the right mood for an orgasm.

Other people's fantasies

If fantasies interest you, and you want specific ones, I suggest you buy one of Nancy Friday's books. She has assembled several collections of women's and men's fantasies *(My Secret Garden, Women On Top,* and so on) that most definitely make for interesting and highly arousing reading. Although I wouldn't be upset if you became aroused while reading this book, excitement's not my main purpose, so I leave the recounting of other people's fantasies to Nancy Friday and stick to giving you advice — and I do have advice to give you concerning fantasies.

Anything goes

First of all, no fantasy is wrong. In fantasy, you don't have to worry about safer sex, what the neighbors may say, or anything else. If you want to make love to Alexander the Great and his whole army, be my guest. If you want to fantasize about Hannibal and his elephants, go ahead. Literally, whatever turns you on is A-OK.

"But Dr. Ruth," people always ask me, "if I fantasize about someone of the same sex, doesn't that mean that I'm gay?" The answer to that question is no. But it doesn't mean that you're not gay either. Now, if you can only have an orgasm while fantasizing about someone of the same sex, even when you are with a partner of the opposite sex, that's a different story. But if you occasionally fantasize about someone of the same sex, that doesn't mean you're gay. For more about sexual orientation, see Chapter 16.

Sharing your fantasies

Another question people often ask me is "Should I share my fantasies with my spouse or lover?" The word that comes to mind here is *caution.* Some partners don't mind hearing their lovers' fantasies; some even get aroused by them, but some get very jealous. If you feel the need to talk about your fantasies with your partner, do it very carefully. Here are some tips:

- ✔ **Make the first one very tame.** Maybe your favorite fantasy is being a Dallas Cowboys cheerleader caught naked in the locker room with the whole team. That's fine, but tell your partner that your fantasy is him finding you naked in your office after hours. If he reacts positively, then you can work your way up to telling him your real fantasies down the road.

- ✔ **Use common sense.** If your husband is built like Woody Allen, and you tell him you're always fantasizing about Arnold Schwarzenegger, how do you think that information will make him feel?

- ✔ **Remember the Golden Rule.** If you tell your partner about your fantasies, be prepared to hear his or her fantasies back. If you think that you may get jealous, then don't open that Pandora's box in the first place.

A fantasy is a fantasy is a fantasy . . .

I've run into people who were intent on making their fantasy become a reality, and most of the time that does not work. Obviously, if your fantasy is rather simple, such as being covered in whipped cream and having your partner lick it off, then having your dream come true may be possible. (And yes, the pun was intended.) On the other hand, many fantasies can either get you into trouble (the kind that have to do with making love in public places, for example), or make you very disappointed (your Woody Allen may wreck his back carrying you over the threshold).

My last piece of advice regarding fantasies holds true for nonsexual fantasies as well as the sexual ones — remember that they are fantasies. Some people trick themselves into believing that their fantasies are real. If your fantasy lover, for example, is a movie or TV star, that's great. Plenty of people have fantasies about their favorite stars. But if you're single and you go so far as to turn down dates because they're not with that famous movie star, then you're in big trouble. In your fantasies, you can make love to anyone; in real life, you have to find a partner who wants you. Fantasies are wonderful tools; just be careful how you use them.

Chapter 18

Cybersex and Other Variations

● ●

In This Chapter

▶ Sex online

▶ Phone sex — Reach out and touch someone

▶ Sex talk on the air

▶ Sex on TV

▶ Multiple partners

● ●

*W*hen teenagers get their hands on a dictionary, what words do they look up first? And when high schoolers get their biology textbooks on the first day of school, do they hunt right away for the picture of a frog? Of course not. That's why it wouldn't surprise me if some of you have turned to this chapter before reading any of the others.

I'm not going to scold you for doing that, because I never blame anyone for wanting to learn about any aspect of human sexuality. So, if you believe that this chapter is where your knowledge is weakest, then start reading!

I can't deny that I have the same curiosity about sex. When I was a little girl, I made a precarious climb to unlock a cabinet on the top shelf where my parents kept what was called in those days a "marriage manual," which basically taught people about human sexuality. (My parents could have used that book before they were married because, ironically, the only reason that this little contraception-pusher is in the world is that they failed to use any.) By making an artificial mountain out of some chairs, I not only took the risk of getting caught, but I may easily have tumbled down and broken my neck. So I recognize that all people wonder about sexual matters, and the higher that cabinet is — that is to say, the more forbidden it seems — the stronger our interest. That interest is fine, *but*. . . .

Even though reading about kinky sexual acts, looking at pornographic pictures, using those thoughts as part of fantasy, and sometimes even sharing those thoughts with a partner can enhance good sexual functioning, actually engaging in what most of us consider deviant sexual behavior is another story. From my experience as a sex therapist, the end results just don't turn out positively. Although sex can be a wonderful part of the glue that holds a couple together, pushed to its extremes, sex can just as easily be the storm that tears them apart. Even if both partners willingly enter into the world of "extreme" sex, the odds are that they won't exit that world together.

Sex creates very powerful feelings that people need to keep under control. In that respect, sex is very similar to the human appetites for such items as liquor, drugs, or gambling. Some people need only one taste of such things, and they plunge into the abyss called addiction. So, while I support people having a glass or two of wine with dinner, you have to be aware that you may be one of those people who cannot have even one sip of alcohol without setting off a chain reaction that you can't control. I'm even more in favor of people enjoying sex than alcohol, but you must understand that sex, too, can be abused.

The biggest dangers of venturing into the outer fringes of sexual behavior used to be that you may find your relationship left in ruins, or maybe a string of them destroyed. But nowadays the dangers have increased a hundredfold because the risk of catching an incurable, deadly disease lies just around the corner of most of these forms of sex.

My advice is to tread very carefully. Peek through that knothole in the fence if you want, but don't try to climb over it. That fence is there for a reason, and you should heed the warnings to keep out.

Cybersex: Sex and the Computer

I suppose that, because they've computerized everything else, sex wasn't going to escape this "cyber-"revolution. I must admit that even I, a grandmother who doesn't know how to turn on one of those computer contraptions, have moved onto the information superhighway with my own Web site on America Online, www.drruth.com.

When it comes to passing on information about sex via the computer, I say great. When it comes to other forms of what's been dubbed *cybersex,* I say maybe. You're an adult. You can decide for yourself. Just make sure that you protect children from inappropriate material (see Chapter 23).

Computers as sex objects

It shouldn't come as a surprise that one of the few areas where investors have actually made money on the Internet is in the business of sex. Sex sites abound online, making an almost infinite amount of hard core pornography available for people to download right into their computers. I have long said that using *erotica* (literary or artistic works having erotic content) can increase arousal, but the cornucopia of explicit material offered on the Web gives even me reason to pause.

Looking at pornography can become addictive, especially when a person sees such vast quantities of material. Imagine what would happen to alcoholics who found a secret passage into the basement of a liquor store. Could they resist going back for more and more? Of course not, and for similar reasons, many men wander into the world of cyberporn and then can't escape. I hear about some of the married ones, because their wives complain to me, but imagine all the single guys out there who turn to their computers for sexual gratification. If you bring home a porno magazine, you can spend only so much time looking at it before you get bored. But if you have literally millions of images available on the Web, then you can spend all your free time surfing. And now the Web can even compete with the VCR because streaming video technology permits voyeurs to watch XXX-rated footage on their computers. (The most popular example is probably home videos that Pamela Anderson and her former husband, Tommy Lee, made for their private viewing pleasure, which ended up all over the Net.)

You be the director

Not all the sex on the Net has been filmed. You can find sites that offer a live person that only you can see and talk to. You can tell that person exactly what you want him or her to do and then listen to what he or she says. If you want two people to act out your fantasies, these sites can accommodate you as well. Partaking in this activity costs a lot more than simply watching prerecorded material, but some people find directing a fantasy with real people well worth the cost.

All fetishes welcome

The wide variety of material offered on the Net can also lead people to discover sexual appetites that they may never have suspected they had. For example the types of material available on one site fall into categories such as old, ugly, fat, blood, spit, menstrual, medical, zoo, pee, poo, enema, and fart. It doesn't bother me that you can find the Top 100 sites for foot fetishists — www.barefoot.com and www.lustfulltoes.com, to name two. After all, the various types of fetishists (I knew about rubber fetishists, but I only found out about balloon fetishists by looking on the Web) can't help themselves, so why shouldn't companies cater to them as well? But when material of every possible description is labeled "erotic" and placed under the roof of one site, the resulting combination can distort people's views — especially young people who may never have dreamed that such practices existed. Yet young people are precisely the ones who have the most curiosity about sex and are most likely to go nosing around these sites.

Limited access

Many of the really hard-core sites require an age check, or even a credit card because they charge their users. That limitation doesn't seem to deter most young men, however, and other sites offer similar material without these checks. Parents need to consider adding whatever software they see fit to keep teens from exploring such hard-core sites. However, if the parents of only one teen on the block don't add such protection to their computer, you may lose all control over whether or not your child gets a peek at these sites. (See Chapter 23 for more information on children and the Internet.)

While most sites (especially those looking to make money) do force you to register in some way, plenty of sites, often called "amateur" sites, don't require you to do any more than click on the word "Enter." By doing so you "swear" to be over the age of 21. You don't have to bring your wallet or even your ID to surf the wildest waves on the Web.

Finding sexually explicit material on the Net

Some of you who've never tried turning your computer screen into a virtual swingers' club may wonder how you go about locating sexually explicit material on the Web. Actually, tumbling down this particular rabbit hole is very simple, though getting back out is not always as easy — and not just because the pornography is addictive. These sites often link back to each other so that when you open one site, the only other place you can go is another sex-related site. The process is spooky. When you're caught in one of these whirlpools of naked flesh, the only thing you can do is to shut down your Internet connection. Even then, half a dozen screens showing women performing various sex acts may still be decorating your computer's desktop.

If you go to any search engine (like Yahoo! or Excite) and type in the word "sex," your computer screen will soon fill up with very graphic images. If you want some guidance in this area, let me offer you two points from which to start.

- ✔ **Web rings:** These sites all deal with the same topic and are tied together so that you can go from one to the other, either in a direct path, or at random. You begin the process by going to www.webring.com. Go to the ring labeled Sexuality and you're on your way. You get some descriptions of each ring so that will give you a good place to start.

✔ **About.com:** This site offers you a guide to any subject on the Web, including sex. James Martin was a guide I found who gives descriptions and links to hundreds of sites about sex. (At the site, type in his name and hit search.) Even if you don't agree with his tastes all the time, at least you can get a vague idea of what a site contains before you click on it — and that can save you a lot of time. A site such as this one also tells you in advance whether or not a particular site charges a fee or asks for some sort of ID. If you don't want your name linked to any XXX-rated sites, then finding sites that don't require any personal information not only keeps your wallet from becoming anorexic but it also prevents a paper trail for anyone to follow if you decide to run for president.

Not always chaste chatting

While the erotic images on the Web mostly target men (even the pictures of naked men are shown for the gay Net surfer), you can find another entire universe aimed at both women and men — chatting. What is chatting? Basically, chatting is sitting at your computer and sending messages back and forth to someone in real time, unlike e-mail where you have to wait to get a reply. Chatting is very similar to talking on the phone, except that you can't hear each other.

Just as only a fraction of the Web deals with sex, most chatting goes on between people who know each other and has nothing whatsoever to do with sex. Any teens who have access to a computer spend inordinate amounts of time chatting with their friends about anything and everything. Many lonely people, on the other hand, sit at their computers looking to meet someone "special." Sometimes they succeed, and sometimes they merely fall prey to someone whose sole purpose is to deceive.

Anonymity online

Because people use nicknames instead of their real identities when chatting, you can easily remain completely anonymous. That anonymity has good points and bad points. Keeping your privacy is good, but the person with whom you're chatting may turn out to be a serial rapist, which you won't know until you meet face-to-face. Therefore, I advise you to be very, very careful before agreeing to give any personal information to a stranger with whom you chat.

I know that some people have found the man or woman of their dreams on the Web (and that's great), but someone else's good fortune doesn't offer you any protection whatsoever. If you do decide to forge ahead and make direct contact with someone you've only chatted with online, please take every precaution. If you want to give out a phone number, give your work number first, or maybe a cell phone number, so that your home address can't be traced. (You may consider giving your office address when registering a cell phone.) If you decide to meet, do so in a very public place such as a crowded restaurant or busy bar where you can easily get up and leave.

Putting safety first

What really scares me is when I get letters from people who say they're going to meet their cybersex buddy for the first time and they want tips from me about how to make it the greatest sex ever. My reaction is — hold it! You shouldn't even think about having sex with this person until you actually meet and get to know each other. Even if the person tries to be perfectly honest and even if you've had cybersex, you can't know a person well enough to have sex with them just from chatting. We discover so much about each other from body language and voice inflection that thinking you can possibly know someone well enough to have sex with them based strictly on an electronic relationship is ludicrous.

You must also hold yourself back for reasons of safety. If you've agreed to meet and have sex, you may have a very hard time pulling back if you start to get the wrong vibrations from that person. For this reason, you should agree only to meet, and to do so only in a public place where you can quickly and safely exit.

Is chatting cheating?

A very common question that I get these days comes from someone whose spouse has developed a relationship with someone on the Web and who wants to know whether their spouse is cheating. As I say throughout this book, I am in favor of a married person masturbating if that person has a stronger desire for sex than their mate does. As long as the couple is having sex, neither party should be ashamed to masturbate if he or she feels the need when their partner either doesn't want to engage in sexual relations or is not around. But that type of masturbation is a solo activity. If you masturbate while chatting with someone in a very sexual way, and the other person does the same, then you are not acting alone. I consider such an activity to be cheating. You are developing a very close relationship with this other person on the computer, using activities that are very personal and should be shared only with your spouse.

Friends first

What if you have developed an online friendship with someone of the opposite sex but do not engage in cybersex? Is that cheating? I don't think a clear-cut answer to that question exists. Just for a moment, consider a similar scenario not involving the computer. Say that you have lunch with a co-worker of the opposite sex once a week. Is that cheating? Not necessarily.

You can definitely keep such a relationship on a strictly platonic level. What if you have lunch with that person every single day? Now the ground gets a little murkier, and circumstances come into play. If your relationship with your spouse has some small cracks, and if you find the person with whom you're lunching sexually attractive, then you may be flirting with danger.

You must apply the same principles to online chatting. If you rush home every evening and can't wait to log onto the computer to chat with this other person, then you are definitely taking time away from your spouse, and, at the very least, sharing your emotional involvement with this other person. This certainly verges on cheating. On the other hand, if you find someone online with whom you share a common interest, such as a TV show, and you chat every week after watching the latest episode, then I don't *think* that you're cheating.

Only the chatter knows

In reality, only the chatter knows whether or not he or she is cheating. Say, for example, you are friends with the couple who lives across the street. And say that you have sexual fantasies about the person of the opposite sex in that couple. You know the signs — you purposely cross the street and make excuses to talk to that person one on one whenever you can, or you go over just to be "neighborly." If you keep everything out in public, that type of relationship can go on for years and nothing sexual may develop from it. But now put that same relationship inside a computer. Instead of keeping a picket fence between the two of you, you're communicating in a very private way and may be passing on some very private comments.

Chatting in a private way can build an intimacy that definitely falls under the banner of "cheating." So, while I have no precise answers, I will say that if you're honest with yourself, you will know when you're crossing that line. And you should stop right there and then, unless you don't intend for your marriage to last forever.

Exploring other online options

The big advantage offered by computer sex forums is that they are organized according to subject matter, which means that you can quickly find other people who share your tastes and communicate with them, passing on ideas, places to go, and things to do. Because the Internet is without guidelines, when I say that you can chat about any topic, I mean *any* topic. Some of the names of these forums should give you a clue as to what you can find: "Pumps, Leather, S&M," "Water Sports," "Piercing," "Dressing for Pleasure," "Dominance and Submission Only," "Loop and Lash B&D," "Zoo Animal Lovers," "Ten Things Every Lesbian Should Know About Love and Sex," "Penis Names," and "Below the Ankles — Feet." Had enough?

As those names imply, not all chatting is innocent and not everyone wants a long-lasting relationship. Some people go online looking only for cybersex, which may frequently result in masturbation. When that is the main aim of a particular computer forum, it is called a J/O (for *jerk off*) session. The people who inhabit these forums regularly call themselves cybersluts — and who am I to disagree? Such chatting starts with people talking dirty to each other. Eventually the two people may exchange nude pictures of each other. Cybersex is not the same as phone sex between two people who have a relationship — where two people who know each other but can't be together masturbate while on the phone. If you already have a relationship, even if you've never had intercourse, phone sex is much different than having cybersex with someone you have never met. I talk about phone sex more in the "Sex and the Telephone" section later in this chapter.

Adult BBSs

If you're handy with a modem, you can access some of the most popular bulletin board systems (BBSs), which, naturally, focus on sex and adult-oriented materials. Check the back of computer magazines (such as *Boardwatch Magazine*, which lists the Top 100 BBSs yearly), your local newspaper, bulletin board books (*BBSs For Dummies* comes to mind) to get you started. BBSs cover virtually every topic that you can imagine — including personals and "XXX." Many BBSs have chat facilities.

Naughty newsgroups

Think of the Internet's UseNet newsgroups as the largest bulletin board system in the world, with more than 250 newsgroups devoted to sexual issues. You can get pictures, sounds, movies, and text stories. You can also access discussions of fetishes, erotica, gay and lesbian issues, and sex toys, just to name a few. You can find the primary newsgroups in two areas, under *alt. binaries.pictures*, and *alt.sex*. Active discussions also exist in the *alt.personals* area, and in *soc.hierarchy,* particularly *soc.motss* (Members of the Same Sex), *soc.couples,* and *soc.singles*.

E-mail ecstasy

It seems like the entire world has access to e-mail — and love letters have never been the same. Just be careful to whom you send your letters!

E-mail (electronic mail) works among all the major online systems — such as America Online, EarthLink, and AT&T WorldNet — the Internet, many individuals with Internet accounts, and corporations and educational institutions.

And e-mail also allows you to send pictures along with text. Just be careful about what kind of pictures you send where. For example, if you send an e-mail to someone at his or her office, chances are an employer may be able to see your message. Not only can you be embarrassed, but the person on the receiving end can lose his or her job.

More and more stories have shown up in the news about employers who check what is going in and out of their employees' e-mail addresses. The courts have ruled that employers have a right to do this, and so you must expect that such checking may happen. Employers are concerned both with e-mail content and with making sure that their employees aren't wasting too much time surfing the Web instead of working. I believe that most employers would warn an employee about wasting time, but if they catch an employee sending or receiving pornography, that may very well be grounds for immediate dismissal.

Off-line viewing

You don't necessarily need to have your computer connected to the Web to view erotic images. You can get CD-ROMs that contain hundreds of erotic images, from the *Playboy*-type to vintage postcards to . . . whatever. CD-ROMs look like the type of CD you play music on. They have room for lots and lots of information, so they are used to input material into your computer that won't fit on a floppy disc. Some of these CD-ROMs have video games that also appeal to prurient interests. If you're interested in purchasing any of these CD-ROMs, look in just about any computer magazine and you can find plenty being offered.

And newer computers also have *DVD* (digital video disc) players included, so that if you want to spend your next airplane ride looking at an X-rated movie, and no one is sitting in the seat next to you, you can do that too.

Virtual sex

Peering into the future, many people are speculating on what virtual sex (or, as some have called it, *teledildonics*) will be like. *Virtual reality* is a computer-generated way of putting you into another dimension instead of just staring at a screen. You put on a special headset that allows you to see only what the computer wants you to see, and, by moving your head and hands, you can actually manipulate the scenery.

Of course, if that scenery includes a gorgeous woman or a hunk of a man, you will want to manipulate more than the air, which is why futurists envision some further attachments such as a clinging penis holder or vaginal prod so that you can make the realistic effects an all-over-body experience. I don't know how satisfying that type of sex will be compared to the real thing, but it certainly is safe because the viruses of humans and computers aren't interchangeable.

More for women?

Speaking of the future, I want to add one hope regarding computers and sex, and that has to do with women. To a great degree, cybersex has appealed more to men than to women. But now that more women than men log on to the World Wide Web, that situation is certainly going to change somewhat.

What form may material aimed at the female market take? How about some cyber-romance novels? Or a serialized sexy soap opera that has a plot to go along with the nudity?

I'm not an expert in computers, so I can't really say exactly what this female-oriented material should consist of, but whatever the final form, it should be longer on plot, filled with fantasy, and loaded with romance. I hope that somebody makes an effort to produce more material that will make cybersex as much fun for us women as it is for men.

Sex and the Telephone

Because sex is a form of communication, it is only natural for the telephone to play a part in our sexual activity. In fact, the telephone was a forerunner of cybersex. The anonymity of communicating by phone quickly made it the ideal way of asking someone out for a date. On the telephone, the physical reaction of both the person asking and the person being asked can remain secret, which makes the process a little easier on everyone.

That anonymity also encourages many people to flirt over the phone (as they do over computer lines). In most cases, that flirtation never goes any further, especially because a great distance may separate the two people. And, although some people may "give great phone," you may be sorely disappointed in them if you see them in the flesh.

These forms of sexual contact are basically innocent, but Alexander Graham Bell would probably have buried his invention if he'd foreseen some of the other ways that people have transformed his telephone into a sex toy.

Obscene phone calls have long been a problem, although innovations such as Caller ID may soon make them a thing of the past. Some of these calls are merely pranks pulled by rambunctious teens looking more to shock than to actually excite anybody, least of all themselves. However, some people do become addicted to making obscene phone calls. Not so long ago, a college president lost his job because of his habit of making such calls.

Pay to play — 900 or 976 numbers

Recently, people have used the phone lines more and more for conversations that have, as a goal, one or both parties reaching an orgasm. Some people have always "talked dirty" to each other while masturbating. I even recommend such behavior to couples who are separated by long distances and want to keep their sexual relationship going while living apart. But what made the use of such behavior explode in popularity was the commercialism that came after the breakup of the Bell telephone system and the deregulation of the industry.

Nowadays, you can find hundreds of phone numbers that are exclusively used for sex (most are 900 numbers or have 976 exchanges). You can call and speak to someone who will fulfill whatever phone fantasy you may have — talking about sex to a woman or a man, ordering a submissive slave on the other end to obey your every command, or being dominated by a cruel master — all accompanied by the masturbation of the callers, who can make the fantasy last and pay the additional costs, or hang up as soon as they find the relief that they were seeking.

Because we are in need of safer sexual outlets, I suppose that these phone sex companies do fill a need, but they also bring some drawbacks that disturb me:

- ✔ I don't believe that children are adequately protected. In theory, you have to be 21 or older to call, but do they really check? Even if callers are supposed to use a credit card number, what if a child, even a teenage child, uses a parent's number?

- ✔ Another drawback is the cost. Some people have gotten addicted to phone sex and end up with astronomical bills. I have to admit that, if these people are adults, they make these calls of their own free will, but it still bothers me.

I just called to say . . .

How about phone sex between two people in a relationship? If they're in a long-distance relationship, sure. But if they live nearby and they regularly have telephone sex as a means of safer sex, I'm just not sure. How realistic is it that two people who go out and date will continue to have sex only when they have a telephone line between them? Eventually, they will want to get together, so they had better be prepared for that moment and not rely on phone sex to keep them safe. However, I can't really criticize any couple who does have phone sex because, in this day and age of AIDS, no measure that you take to remain healthy can be regarded as extreme.

The phone can be a helpful tool to spice up your sex life, even if you're married. When you talk on the phone, you're speaking right into the other person's ear. Whispering "sweet nothings" — or "hot somethings" — into the phone, so that only your lover and you can hear them, can let you get up close and personal at any time of the day or night. You can use these moments as part of your overall strategy for foreplay. And, if the circumstances are right, once in a while you can even have real phone sex, with one or both of you masturbating, just to throw in some variety.

Sex and the Radio

Here is one area where I can rightfully take my place in history, because I helped to pioneer the concept of *media sexuality education*. My little radio program, "Sexually Speaking," first aired in 1980 in New York on WYNY on Sunday nights from 12:15 to 12:30 a.m. It really amazed — maybe the better word would be shocked — people to hear me talk about penises and vaginas and orgasms on the radio. What made the program acceptable was that I didn't do it to shock people, but rather to inform them. And I believe that my accent, which some people identify with the psychiatrist Sigmund Freud, also helped.

People still talk about the first time they ever heard my show with almost the same awe they have for the first time they ever "did it." Sex still plays a role on radio, but, surprisingly, radio broadcasters still use it mostly to shock. I do regret that less information about sex is broadcast these days on the radio than offensive language.

But radio remains a "cool" medium. By cool I mean that, although you hear certain words more often than you once did, none of the talk is really sexy. I don't believe that listening to any of these radio programs really turns anyone on.

Sex and Television

Being a visual medium, television always had the potential to bring sex directly into people's homes, but in the early days, even married TV couples such as the Petries on *The Dick Van Dyke Show* had to sleep in separate beds. Broadcast television in America stayed fairly tame for many years because, like radio, it was available to everyone, children as well as adults. Nudity appeared on European TV long before it did on the American tube, and, apart from a few shows such as *NYPD Blue,* both naked bodies and certain words have remained taboo on mainstream TV even up until today. But TV soon branched out way beyond network television, which is where sex has played a big role.

Cable took television off the public airwaves and out from under the scrutiny of the government. R-rated movies quickly made their appearance, and certain public access shows, especially in big cities, took advantage of the new freedom and began to air both raunchy talk and naked bodies. But the producers of even these shows were always a little worried that they may go too far; as a result, while the shock value was certainly there, much of the erotic content was missing. As time went on, pay cable networks branched out beyond showing just movies. HBO, for example, developed series with sexual themes, most notably *Sex and The City,* which has gotten much publicity. And The Playboy Channel is, as you would expect, devoted to soft porn and has lots of people who pay money to take a peek. You can now see truly erotic movies on pay cable, but those are still tame compared to the type of materials available on videocassette.

Renting films to view alone or together

Although I would object to some X- or NC-17-rated movies in America because of their violent content, in general, I am in favor of people renting erotic films. For the single person, erotic films provide an outlet for masturbation that, considering the dangers posed by going to a prostitute or having a string of one-night stands, almost makes the availability of these films a public service. And, for couples, viewing such films can provide some added spice and maybe even the knowledge of some new positions or techniques. European films are much more sophisticated in this respect, providing truly artistic treatment of sexual subjects.

Starring in your own sex flick

On the heels of the videocassette player came the video camera, which now enables couples to star in their own versions of *Deep Throat.* Again, if filming your sexual escapades adds a boost to your sex life, then I'm all for it. But I must advise certain precautions:

- ✔ Don't pressure your lover into doing something that he or she doesn't want to. If one partner wants to film lovemaking, and the other objects, that's the end of it — no filming.

- ✔ If you want to keep those tapes, remember that you always have a risk that they'll fall into the wrong hands. My advice is to watch the tapes a few times and then erase them.

Now I know that some people actually take those tapes of themselves and sell them so that others can rent them at their favorite video store. My opinion of that? It's downright stupid. It's almost guaranteed that somebody will show those tapes to the one person who shouldn't see them — possibly your kids, your parents, your boss, or your biggest customer. And it may not happen this year or next year, but five years down the road, and then the consequences may be even worse. You may no longer be with the person in the film, and your new partner may not be so open-minded.

If you really want the extra thrill that comes from knowing that other people are watching you have sex, then videotape your lovemaking while fantasizing that the camera is connected to NBC and is broadcasting to millions of homes. But don't ever actually let such a tape leave the confines of your house.

Pulp nonfiction

I suppose I would be unfair to my friends Hugh Hefner and Christie Hefner (Hugh's daughter and president of *Playboy*) if I failed to mention the grand-daddy medium of porn — print. Despite all the competition from computers and videos, *Playboy, Penthouse, Hustler,* and similar magazines still sell millions of copies every month. The magazines remain popular for several reasons. First, you can't take your VCR into the bathroom with you, so anyone who doesn't have complete privacy in their living environment, be it a teenager living at home or a young adult in a college dorm or shared apartment, will rely on something more portable. Second, the image quality is superior, and you can find articles and jokes, which offer an excuse to buy such publications. I actually like reading *Playboy* from time to time because of the articles, so that is a legitimate excuse.

While magazines that show pictures of naked men have failed to attract a large audience of women, the romance novel is an industry unto itself. These novels fall into several categories, some of which have very little actual sex and others that let off a little cloud of steam every time you turn a page. They all follow a formula, which is why many people turn their noses up at this literary genre, but the formula is the same as what you find in a men's magazine, and no one who buys these novels is looking for great literature anyway. I would like for both sexes not to criticize the other's erotica, but I suppose as long as a battle of the sexes exists, this front won't enjoy any peace either.

Sex with Multiple Partners

Before the printing press existed to print pornographic literature, or the camera to take lewd pictures, or motion picture cameras, phones, computers, or any of the modern gadgets that people now use to take sex where it had never gone before, men and women still found ways to enjoy elicit pleasures. The most common of these was to have more than one sexual partner. Some cultures, such as parts of the Middle East, gave this act official sanction by allowing men to take more than one wife, which probably took half of the fun out of the practice.

To some degree, adultery in ancient times was more forgivable than today. Parents often forced young people to marry a particular person, and, although many of these marriages worked out fine, many did not. If someone got stuck with a sexually incompatible partner or one whom he or she hated — and especially because divorce was almost nonexistent — it's easy to understand why some of these people looked for greener pastures.

The lure of adultery

I've read several different accounts as to the number of people who commit adultery today, and the studies are all contradictory. Some reports say that couples rarely remain faithful throughout a marriage, while others assert the opposite. Because no one can seem to agree on the actual numbers, I won't try to give you any percentages, but you don't need statistics to know about something that takes place under your very noses. Incidences of adultery abound all around us, be they among the rich and famous that we read about in the news, or among our neighbors and coworkers that we hear about through the grapevine.

Cheating comes in all different forms, from the man who goes to a prostitute while on a business trip, to the woman who sees an old boyfriend every Wednesday afternoon, to adulterous couples who see more of each other than they do of their respective spouses. But, whether quickies or lifelong affairs, all cheating affects a marriage in some way or another, because the cheating person usually must lie about what he or she did, which leads to a string of other lies, all of which begin to tear at the bonds of marriage.

One recent development that has impacted this type of behavior is the risk of AIDS and other STDs. (I discuss more about those ramifications in Chapter 6.) Nowadays, I find that more and more people try not to stray. Why? They try to patch up their marriages and work things out simply because they fear the health consequences that fooling around on their spouses can bring.

To the extent that people try to have better sex with their spouses — not to mention build better relationships — I applaud this movement. Nevertheless, I do wish that it had arisen in greater part due to the spread of knowledge about good sexual functioning rather than out of fear of disease.

Wife swapping, swinging, and group sex

Of course, not all sex that married people have outside their marriage involves cheating. Some couples make the conscious decision to have sex with other people.

✔ Some couples bring a third person into their bedroom, be it a man or a woman, which is called a *ménage à trois*.

✔ Sometimes two couples get together and trade partners, which is called *wife swapping*. (I think that the fact that it's not called husband swapping is significant, but more on that in a minute.)

✔ Sometimes a larger group of regulars meets in someone's home to exchange partners, which is called *swinging*.

✔ And sometimes a group of strangers just gets together, usually at a club, and has sex with anyone else who happens to be there, which experts label *group sex* and people used to call an *orgy*.

All these activities grew in popularity in the late 1960s and early 1970s. I believe this practice mostly resulted from the development of the birth control pill, which allowed people to have sex without the risk of pregnancy. But this type of behavior has been going on for a long time (take, for example, the notorious Roman orgies or the scenes depicted on Angkor Wat, the temple in Cambodia), and the behavior will never totally disappear.

Throughout this book I say that sex becomes better as the couple learns to communicate on a higher level and further their relationship. So why do people want to have sex with people they barely know? What's the attraction?

✔ A little bit of exhibitionism and voyeurism lives inside us all. Some people are appalled at those feelings and do the best they can to hide them, while others enjoy giving into them, and you can certainly do that at an orgy.

✔ Another attraction is the promise of strong visual stimulation that comes from watching new partners or other couples engage in a variety of sexual activities.

How fulfilling are these exchanges sexually? For many men, to whom visual stimuli are very strong, these scenes can do a lot for their libidos. On the other hand, many women need to concentrate to have an orgasm, and these situations are not conducive to their sexual functioning. Therein lies the answer as to why the practice is called *wife swapping* — because men usually derive the most pleasure from these situations and push their wives or partners into them.

Although the men are usually the instigators, I've seen situations where they've also been the ones to most regret having started their wives off on this path.

Betty and Phil

Betty and Phil were married for about five years when someone Phil knew at work — I'll call him Gary — invited him to go to a wife-swapping party. Phil was very eager to go, but Betty wasn't. He kept begging and pleading, and eventually she consented, but she kept to herself the real reason that she had said yes. Betty had met Gary at the company Christmas party and found herself attracted to him. She would never have acted upon that attraction, or at least that's what she told me, but when Phil begged her to go, she decided that maybe the chance to be with Gary was an opportunity not worth passing up.

In fact, Gary had caught Betty looking at him, which is why he asked Phil to join the group in the first place. Naturally, when things started getting hot and heavy at the party, Betty and Gary gravitated toward each other and wound up having sex. Phil had sex with someone at the party and then went looking for his wife. When he saw her going at it with Gary, he at first dismissed it, but after a while he started feeling jealous. This jealousy affected his ability to have a second erection, and so he became really upset. On their way home, Phil lashed out at Betty, who fell back on the argument that going to the party had been his idea.

Eventually Phil's jealousy calmed down, and he started fantasizing about the party. When the next one rolled around, he decided that they should go. Betty tried to talk him out of it, but he swore up and down that he wouldn't be jealous, and so they went.

I don't have to tell you the rest of the story, as I'm sure that you can guess the ending. Betty came to me to see whether I could help her repair her marriage, and I did try. But it was really too late. Gary aroused much stronger sexual feelings in her than Phil did, and because she and Phil had no kids, she finally decided that she'd prefer to spend the rest of her life with Gary.

So, while Betty did find the experience of wife swapping pleasurable, her focus all along was really on one man, Gary, and not having sex with a variety of different men. I think that many women who enter into this scene have similar experiences to Betty's. Even if, initially, a woman does have sex with a lot of men, she doesn't necessarily have to be sexually aroused for that to happen. Eventually, however, she fixes her focus on another man, not her husband. And then, when her husband realizes this, the trouble begins.

Of course, couples for whom swinging works out don't go to see a sex therapist such as myself, so perhaps this sort of lifestyle works for more people than I know. But I've seen enough people who've had problems with these situations to know that the risks to a marriage are great. You see, the libido is very strong, but it is also easily satisfied. There's no such release as an orgasm for jealousy. Jealousy is the type of emotion that tends to build and fester over time, and that usually spells trouble. The only advice I can give you now is to keep thoughts about group sex as your fantasy and don't try to live them out.

Part V
Maintaining Healthy Sexuality

The 5th Wave
By Rich Tennant

"Oh, wait a minute Arthur! When I said I'd only have safe sex with you, this isn't what I meant!"

In this part . . .

Sex is a bodily function, which is good. That means that it's a part of our very nature. But, like any other aspect of our humanity, things don't always work out exactly as we would want them to. After too much exercise, your muscles might be sore, and after a great meal, you might have gas.

I may not be able to help you make the earth move every time you make love, but in this part I do offer you practical advice that may help to bring a little more pleasure into your life.

Chapter 19

What You Can Catch and How to Prevent It

In This Chapter

▶ Recognizing a host of sexually transmitted diseases

▶ Evaluating risks for men and women

▶ Fighting the sexual invasion

▶ Maximizing protection

*I*n a perfect sexual world, terrific partners would be easy to find, everyone would have great orgasms easily, and no one could get sick from having sex. Of course, we don't live in a perfect world, sexually or any other way, and so one out of four Americans between the ages of 15 and 55 will catch at least one sexually transmitted disease (STD).

"Did she say *at least* one?" Yes. Because more than 30 sexually transmitted diseases exist, oftentimes the people who engage in the behaviors that lead to getting one disease wind up getting more than one. In case you haven't heard already, the sexual revolution of the previous decades, in which people suddenly felt free to have sex with a number of partners, is over. With so many diseases around, you can say that society is now in the middle of a sexual invasion, with the result that having multiple partners can lead to mucho trouble.

If you have had sex many times with many partners, don't assume that you are disease-free just because you don't have any symptoms:

✔ Many people with STDs, especially women, don't show any symptoms at all.

✔ Other people with STDs have only a slight fever, which they don't connect with an STD, and no more symptoms for years. Although having an open sore certainly means that you are highly contagious, the fact that you have no symptoms at all does not mean that you can't give someone else the disease.

✔ Just because your partner has no outward signs of having a sexually transmitted disease doesn't mean that your partner is disease-free; because your partner may never have had any symptoms, he or she can pass something onto you in all innocence.

Did I say something about the sexual revolution being over? If you want to remain healthy, you must act as though the sexual revolution is dead and buried.

The Sexual Invasion: Repelling STDs

Because the sexual invasion encompasses so many different STDs, it is a complicated battle to fight. Furthermore, since the arrival of AIDS, the consequences of failure are more likely to be deadly. My advice, therefore, is to find yourself one partner, make sure that you are both healthy, use condoms if you have any doubts about your respective health, and practice safer sex.

Because this advice may come too late for some of you, or because accidents happen no matter how hard you try to prevent them, I'm going to give you a list, in alphabetical order, of some of the diseases that you may run across. Although the figures used in this book apply to the United States, which keeps careful statistics, they generally hold true throughout the developed world. Third world countries vary widely in the incidence and prevalence of STDs. As they say, to be forewarned is to be forearmed; read this list carefully so that you can become as familiar as possible with the enemy.

Before I go into the list itself, a few other words of advice.

Because AIDS, which has grabbed all the headlines, hit the gay male population first in the United States, you may think that men are more likely to suffer from STDs. But taking all the STDs together, the consequences of this sexual invasion are worse for women than for men. Here's why:

✔ Women tend to get STDs more easily than men, probably because they receive fluids during intercourse.

✔ Many of these diseases do not show any initial symptoms in women.

✔ Treating a woman who has an STD is often more difficult than treating a man.

✔ More often than not, the woman ultimately suffers the more serious consequences of STDs, such as infertility, ectopic pregnancy (pregnancy that occurs outside the uterus), chronic pelvic pain, and even cancer.

If you do have a sexually transmitted disease or even think that you have one, see a doctor. This advice may sound obvious, but too many people don't seek medical help, probably because of embarrassment. They may be embarrassed because they don't want to reveal their sex life or because they don't want to submit to an exam of their most private parts, or both.

An all-too-common form of treatment adopted by young people is to self-prescribe medication. If a doctor has prescribed a medication for one person, a friend of that person with similar symptoms may use that medicine too. Sharing prescriptions is a bad idea. Even doctors sometimes have difficulties diagnosing which STD is which. By taking the wrong medication, you may make your situation worse.

Candidiasis

Often called a yeast infection, *candidiasis* is actually caused by a fungus, candida, that normally lives in people's mouths and intestines, as well as in the vaginas of many healthy women. When the body's normal acidity doesn't control the growth of this fungus, an overgrowth can occur. Candidiasis is the result. Its symptoms can include a thick, white, cottage cheese-like vaginal discharge; itching or irritation of the vulva, penis, or testicles; a yeasty odor; and, sometimes, a bloated feeling and change in bowel habits.

- ✔ The fungus, candida, can also appear in the mouth, throat, or tongue; when it does, the disease is called thrush.

- ✔ Candida is not usually spread as an STD, but it can be — more likely through oral sex than intercourse.

Among the factors that can lead to abnormal growth of candida are birth control pills, antibiotics, pregnancy, diabetes, HIV infection (or any other immune system dysfunction), douching, a woman's monthly period, and damp underwear.

Prescriptions for antibacterial creams, ointments, or suppositories are the normal cures. Single-dose oral antibiotics have also recently become available and are highly effective.

Some of the medicines used to treat a yeast infection may weaken latex condoms or diaphragms. If you use either of these methods, consult with your pharmacist or provider.

Chancroid

Chancroid is a sexually transmitted disease caused by the bacterium *Haemophylus ducreyi*.

- ✔ Chancroid usually starts as a small pimple on the penis, labia, or cervix.

- ✔ If untreated, the pimple can grow into painful genital ulcers accompanied by swelling of the lymph glands that drain the ulcer.

- ✔ Chancroid is often accompanied by a fever, and the genital swelling can make walking difficult.

Chancroid symptoms are more often painful in men than in women. Chancroid is easily treated with antibiotics; if it's not treated, however, the ulcer can grow to the point where amputation of the penis is necessary.

Chancroid is common in Africa but rarely seen in the United States. Because anyone with the disease is much more susceptible to HIV infection, chancroid can have serious consequences.

Chlamydia

Chlamydia is the most common STD in the United States, affecting three million people every year.

- ✔ Chlamydia often has no symptoms in women; in men, the first symptoms are usually painful urination and pus coming from the urethra.

- ✔ Symptoms may start within a few days after sexual exposure.

- ✔ In women, the disease can cause scarring of the fallopian tubes, sterility, infertility, ectopic pregnancy, or chronic pelvic pain.

- ✔ In men, the organism is thought to be responsible for half the cases of *epididymitis*, an infection of the epididymis (a series of tiny tubes that lie on top of the testicle), which can cause painful swelling of the testicle.

Although doctors can successfully treat chlamydia with tetracycline or other antibiotics (a single-dose version is available), they often have difficulty diagnosing the disease because of the lack of visible symptoms. People who have chlamydia and do not take all the medicine prescribed for the full time that it's prescribed often get the disease again (because they are not fully cured the first time). Because gonorrhea often accompanies chlamydia, doctors usually treat the two together.

Although most people who have chlamydia have no symptoms and thus don't even know they have the disease, they can still suffer the long-range consequences. Because chlamydia is so common, people who have sex with multiple partners, and especially if they don't use a condom, should be tested once a year, even if they feel healthy.

Cytomegalovirus (CMV)

CMV is a rare disease passed during close personal contact, including sexual intercourse, and through blood transfusion and shared needles.

- ✔ Although the man or woman infected with the disease often has no symptoms, CMV can have severe effects on a newborn infant if the mother is infected with the virus during her pregnancy.

- ✔ Not every baby whose mother has CMV will become infected; however, a small number of babies who are infected suffer serious damage to their central nervous systems.

Doctors can diagnose CMV through a blood test, but they have no known treatment or cure.

Genital warts

Approximately five and a half million people are infected in the United States every year with genital warts, which are caused by the *human papilloma virus (HPV)*. HPV has become so common that it is estimated that 80 percent of sexually active people contract it at some point. Among people between the ages of 15 and 49, only one in four Americans has not had a genital HPV infection, though in most cases the virus is harmless and exhibits no symptoms. Genital warts are spread through vaginal, anal, and oral intercourse. They can also be passed on to infants during childbirth.

- ✔ Not always visible, the warts are soft and flat; they grow on the genitals, in the urethra, in the inner vagina, in the anus, or in the throat.

- ✔ The warts often itch and, if allowed to grow, can block openings of the vagina, anus, or throat, causing discomfort.

- ✔ Because genital warts can be microscopic and therefore unseen by the naked eye, they can easily be passed to sexual partners.

High-risk strains of HPV do exist and can cause cervical lesions which, over a period of time, can develop into cervical cancer if untreated. Doctors can detect HPV lesions with annual pap smears, which is why all sexually active women should have yearly pap smears.

The discovery of the link between HPV and cancer is relatively new, and much confusion exists among the general public on this issue. The vast majority of women who are diagnosed with cervical cancer have never even heard of HPV. The virus may also have a link to anal and penile cancer in men, which makes screening for HPV so important.

Doctors can treat genital warts in several ways, including topical medical creams, some of which require a prescription and some of which don't.

Over the counter medications for other types of warts should not be used on the genitals.

In cases of either large or persistent warts, other treatments may include surgical removal, freezing using liquid nitrogen, or cauterization by electric needles. Because doctors have no cure for HPV, genital warts can reoccur, and the virus can remain in the person's cells indefinitely, though often in a *latent* (or not active) state. Most people who do have reoccurring genital warts have only one more episode. Even in rare cases of people with multiple reoccurrences, the body's immune system usually develops an immunity within two years. On the other hand, removing a person's genital warts does not mean that he or she cannot transmit the disease.

Although condoms do offer some protection against the spread of HPV, they provide no guarantee against its transmission because they do not cover the entire genital area.

Gonorrhea

The number of reported cases of gonorrhea has been steadily declining in the United States. In fact, the latest figures show that only 650,000 new cases develop every year. 50 percent of women and 10 percent of men with the disease show no symptoms, so they don't know they have it. When symptoms do occur, women may have a green or yellow-green discharge from the vagina; frequent, often burning urination; pelvic pain; swelling or tenderness of the vulva; and possibly arthritic-like pain in the shoulder. Men may have pain during urination or a pus-like discharge from the urethra.

- ✔ Gonorrhea can be spread through vaginal, anal, or oral intercourse.
- ✔ Gonorrhea can cause sterility, arthritis, heart problems, and disorders of the central nervous system.

> ✔ In women, gonorrhea can cause pelvic inflammatory disease, which can lead to ectopic pregnancies, sterility, or even the formation of abscesses.

Penicillin was the treatment of choice for gonorrhea, but, because more recent strains of the disease have become penicillin-resistant, doctors now use a drug called ceftriaxone. Gonorrhea is often accompanied by chlamydia, and so doctors often treat them together.

Hepatitis B

Hepatitis B is the only sexually transmitted disease for which a preventive vaccine exists. Hepatitis B is very contagious, 100 times more so than HIV. Hepatitis B can be transmitted through intimate contact as well as sexual contact, so that kissing, sharing the same toothbrush, or sharing needles can transmit the disease. Health-care workers are particularly susceptible and almost always get vaccinated.

> ✔ Hepatitis B can cause severe liver disease or death, but the virus often has no symptoms during its most contagious phases.
>
> ✔ While reported cases number about 240,000 a year, estimates show that one American in 20 will get hepatitis B at some point during his or her lifetime, and the disease can remain active throughout that person's life.

No medical treatment exists for hepatitis B, but, in 90 percent of cases, the body's own immunological response causes the disease to fade away. It is particularly important that people with multiple sex partners get vaccinated.

Herpes

Herpes, which is caused by the *Herpes simplex virus* (HSV), is another incurable STD. Herpes actually has two forms: herpes simplex–type 1 (HSV-1) and herpes simplex–type 2 (HSV-2), although 1 is most often associated with cold sores and fever blisters "above the waist." About 80 percent of American adults have oral herpes. Estimates state that 25 percent of adults have genital herpes, though most are not aware of it, and their symptoms are too mild to notice.

The most common symptoms of genital herpes arise from a rash with clusters of white, blistery sores appearing on the vagina, cervix, penis, mouth, anus, or other parts of the body. This rash can cause pain, itching, burning sensations, swollen glands, fever, headache, and a run-down feeling. The first symptoms may be more severe than the symptoms of later outbreaks because the immune system is not as well prepared to fight off the disease the first time around. However, a person may have no symptoms whatsoever, and his or her first outbreak may occur months or even years after exposure. HSV-2 symptoms can occur on the thighs, buttocks, anus, or pubis. People who suffer only mild symptoms may mistake them for some other condition such as insect bites, jock itch, yeast infections, hemorrhoids, or ingrown hair follicles. Some lesions may be so small that they remain invisible to the human eye.

These symptoms may return at regular intervals, sometimes caused by stress, menstrual periods, or other factors that are not well understood. Although these symptoms can lead to discomfort, they are not dangerous, and herpes does not affect the immune system or lead to other health problems.

Most people think that herpes is contagious only when the sores are present, but studies have shown that some people may spread the disease during the few days just before an outbreak called *prodrome,* when they have no sores. An infected person may figure out how to recognize the warning signs that occur during prodrome, which may include itching, tingling, or a painful feeling where the lesions will develop.

- ✔ During pregnancy, herpes may cause miscarriage or stillbirth, and the disease can be passed on to newborns.

- ✔ If the sores are active during childbirth, they pose serious health consequences for the babies. To avoid these consequences, doctors usually perform cesarean sections when active sores are visible during the time of childbirth.

- ✔ If you have herpes, you should always use a condom when having sex, unless your partner already has the disease.

Although you should always use a condom, you should know that condoms can't entirely protect you from herpes. If the man has the disease, and the only sores are on his penis, then a condom can protect the woman. However, because vaginal secretions may leak over the pelvic area not protected by the condom, the condom does not protect men as much.

Herpes can spread beyond genital contact to other parts of the already-infected person's body. If you touch a herpes sore, always wash your hands thoroughly before touching anyone else or any other part of your body.

Be aware that oral herpes can be transmitted by kissing, sharing towels, or drinking from the same glass or cup.

Recent developments in the treatment of herpes include new, more accurate tests, and although doctors still have no cure for herpes, new medications are effective at keeping the virus in check. Acyclovir (Zovirax) has been available for ten years and can now be obtained in generic form. Valacyclovir (Valtrex) and Famciclovir (Famvir) have a more active ingredient and are better absorbed and need to be taken less frequently. See a doctor if you suspect that you have the disease both to make sure that herpes really is the cause of the symptoms and to learn how to live with herpes and not spread it to others. If you're the infected person, the doctor can give you a set of rules to follow to help keep you from contaminating other people or other parts of your body.

Human immunodeficiency virus (HIV) and AIDS

If you've heard of only one sexually transmitted disease, that one is the acquired immunodeficiency syndrome (AIDS), which is linked to infections by the human immunodeficiency virus (HIV). Why is so much more attention given to this disease than to any other STD? The answer is quite simple: AIDS is deadly, and it has no cure and no vaccine.

HIV now infects less than one million people in the United States but close to 34 million people worldwide. Of the nearly 6 million new cases expected this year, about 40,000 will occur in the United States. HIV is most commonly passed on through sexual activity or by shared needles. It can also be passed through transfusions of contaminated blood products (though since 1985 all blood is screened for HIV in the United States), from a woman to her fetus during pregnancy, and through breastfeeding.

Although HIV has been detected in small quantities in body fluids such as saliva, feces, urine, and tears, to date no evidence exists that HIV can spread through these body fluids, despite extensive testing. You can't contract AIDS by touching someone who has the disease, by being coughed or sneezed on by that person, by sharing a glass with that person, or through any other routine contact that may take place.

But if you think that you are safe from AIDS because you are not a homosexual man, you're wrong. Because anal sex — a form of sex most common among homosexual men — is more likely to allow the transmission of the disease, this plague decimated the homosexual community first in the Western world. But in Africa, where AIDS is most common, it is primarily a heterosexual disease. Even in the West, the incidence of AIDS is rising faster among heterosexuals than among homosexuals. A growing number of women are getting the disease as well. AIDS poses a risk to everyone.

- HIV infections weaken the body's ability to fight disease, causing acquired immunodeficiency syndrome (AIDS) and other health problems.

- A person can be infected by HIV and not show any symptoms for up to ten years.

- If AIDS develops, a variety of different ailments may attack the body, leading to death.

Two known human immunodeficiency viruses exist, HIV-1 and HIV-2. They both cause disease by infecting and destroying blood cells called *lymphocytes* that protect the body against infection. HIV-1 is most common in Western countries; HIV-2 occurs most frequently in Africa, where the disease is thought to have originated.

The first case of AIDS in America was reported in 1981. By 1994, more than 300,000 cases of AIDS had appeared in the United States, resulting in more than 200,000 deaths.

Doctors diagnose HIV infection with tests to detect HIV antibodies in the blood (see Chapter 6). These antibodies usually appear in the bloodstream three to eight weeks after infection, though it may take as long as six months for these antibodies to show up. Because of this window of time, a person can have a negative HIV test and still be able to pass the disease to others. In addition, the first 60 days after being infected with the virus is a period of high contagion. For that reason, you should always use a condom; it's impossible to really know whether or not a partner can infect you.

Initial symptoms may resemble those of a common nonsexual disease, mononucleosis: high fevers, swollen glands, and night sweats. Following that you may go through a period, which commonly lasts for years, during which you have no symptoms. Eventually, as the body's immune system weakens from fighting HIV, some *opportunistic microbe* — an organism that the body's immune system would normally dispose of — causes an infection, such as pneumonia, that just won't go away. At this point, a doctor usually discovers that the person is infected with HIV and diagnoses a case of AIDS. In the

United States, the median life expectancy from the time of infection is about 12 years. Life expectancy is shorter for those people infected by transfusions of blood or blood products and for people who do not get good medical care.

Medical science has, as yet, produced no vaccine against AIDS, nor has it found a cure. The medical field has developed many different drugs that can now help prolong the life of a person with HIV and manage the various symptoms. Three basic categories of drugs exist. First are the antiretroviral drugs that inhibit the growth and multiplication of HIV at various steps in its life cycle. Doctors prescribe these drugs in groups known as *cocktails*. Other drugs fight the opportunistic infections that may occur because HIV lowers the immune system's ability to fight them. A third group, which is more experimental and has not proven very successful, helps to boost the immune system.

Molluscum contagiosum

The Molluscum contagiosum virus can cause a small, pinkish-white, waxy-looking, polyp-like growth in the genital area or on the thighs. It is spread by sexual intercourse but can also be spread through other intimate contact. Doctors can usually treat it by removing the growths either with chemicals, electric current, or freezing.

Pelvic inflammatory disease (PID)

Pelvic inflammatory disease, or PID, is the term used for a genital infection in a woman that has spread into the deeper organs of her reproductive system, including the uterus, fallopian tubes, or the structures around the ovaries. PID is not really a sexually transmitted disease, per se, but may be a consequence of an STD, usually either gonorrhea or chlamydia. PID occurs when an infection in the genital tract is not caught and treated and then spreads from the cervix up into the uterus, fallopian tubes, and ovaries. Estimates indicate that a million cases of PID are reported a year in the United States, with another million going unreported because of minimal or no symptoms.

The symptoms of PID can include fever; nausea; chills; vomiting; pain in the lower abdomen; pain during intercourse; spotting and pain between menstrual periods or during urination; heavy bleeding, discharge, or blood clots during menstruation; unusually long or painful periods; and unusual vaginal discharge.

Most cases of PID require a hospital admission and intravenous antibiotics for several days. In addition, you absolutely must refrain from any sexual activities. A person with PID may require surgery to remove abscesses or scar tissue or to repair or remove damaged reproductive organs.

Whether treated or not, PID can lead to sterility, ectopic pregnancy, and chronic pain. The more often PID strikes a woman, the more likely she is to become sterile.

Pubic lice

Pubic lice, also called *crabs* or *cooties,* can be spread not only by sexual contact but also by coming in contact with infected bedding, clothing, and toilet seats. Their bites cause intense itching.

You can treat pubic lice yourself with over-the-counter medications including Kwell, A-200, and RID. In addition, you should thoroughly wash or dry-clean all bedding and clothing that has come into contact with the lice.

Syphilis

Syphilis was first noticed in Europe in the 15th century, coinciding with the return of Christopher Columbus from the New World. No one knows for sure whether the disease came from America or West Africa, but it did cause a tremendous epidemic with a high fatality rate.

Syphilis is caused by a spiral-shaped, snail-like microscopic organism called *Treponema pallidum*. Because syphilis resembles so many other diseases, it is known as "the great imitator." The disease progresses over a long period of years with different stages along the way.

- The primary syphilitic lesion is the *chancre:* a circular, painless, and firm sore that appears at the site of the invasion either on the lips, mouth, tongue, nipples, rectum, or genitals anywhere from 9 to 90 days after infection.

  Six to ten weeks later, the chancre heals by itself, followed by a symptomless time (latent period) of anywhere from six weeks to six months before symptoms of secondary syphilis appear.

- Secondary syphilis is marked by rashes of various types that do not itch and that heal without scars. These rashes indicate that the microbes have traveled through the bloodstream and lymphatic system to every organ and tissue in the body.

  Secondary syphilis is followed by another symptomless period, which can last a lifetime, or the disease can reappear after a number of years.

- Tertiary syphilis attacks the nervous system and can destroy normal skin, bone, and joints as well as interrupt the blood supply to the brain. Syphilis can be deadly in this last phase.

Syphilis is passed from one person to another during vaginal intercourse, anal intercourse, kissing, and oral/genital contact. The disease is especially contagious while the sores are present in the primary stage.

Treatment with long-acting forms of penicillin is effective for primary, secondary, and latent syphilis; however, the damage caused by tertiary syphilis cannot be reversed by penicillin therapy.

The number of syphilis cases in the United States has fallen dramatically. In fact, syphilis is now confined to only 1 percent of U.S. counties and may be entirely eliminated. Sadly, 65 percent of the cases of congenital syphilis occur among African Americans, and this is also believed to be a contributing factor to the spread of HIV among this same group.

Trichomoniasis

Usually called "trich," trichomoniasis is one of the most common vaginal infections, causing about one-fourth of all cases of vaginitis. Many women have no symptoms, and men rarely have symptoms. Symptoms that can appear include a frothy, often musty-smelling discharge and itching in the vaginal area. Sometimes people also experience an increased urge to urinate.

Doctors can treat trichomoniasis with antibiotics, and any sexual partners should be treated as well to prevent reinfection.

Vaginitis

If you experience a vaginal discharge or burning or itching in the vaginal area, you suffer from vaginitis. Vaginitis can be triggered by several different organisms. The disease is not always spread through sexual contact, but, because a man who carries the organisms may not have any symptoms, treating both partners is usually a good idea so that you don't keep passing the infection back and forth. The symptoms include

- A burning or itching of the vulva.
- An abnormal vaginal discharge, sometimes tinged with blood.
- An unpleasant odor.

Most women get some type of vaginitis during their lifetime. Treatment varies according to the cause of the disease.

Let's Get Serious

Doctors have no vaccine against AIDS. They have no cure for herpes. You can get STDs that have no symptoms but can later leave you sterile. Are you scared of catching an STD? If you're not, you should be — scared enough to practice safer sex.

I use only the term *safer* sex. Truly *safe* sex means celibacy. Safe sex *can* also mean monogamous sex with an uninfected partner, but, sorry to say, one mistake by one of you (perhaps even before you met because some of these diseases don't make themselves known for years) can lead to both of you becoming infected, so we're really back to *safer* sex.

Certainly the fewer partners you have, the less risk you have, but catching a disease can happen in only one instance with an infected partner.

Remember, when you go to bed with someone, the germs of every partner that this person ever had climb under those covers with you.

Condoms give good, not great, protection

And what about condoms? Condoms offer protection — that is absolutely true. But condoms do not offer absolute protection against AIDS or the other STDs. Why?

- ✔ Condoms sometimes break.

- ✔ Condoms can break down in the presence of oil-based products.

- ✔ Condoms sometimes leak when you take them off.

- ✔ People sometimes forget to use condoms.

- ✔ Even people who do use condoms for intercourse often don't use them for oral sex, which, while less risky, is not safe.

Some STDs are spread through contact with other parts of the genitals, including any leakage of vaginal fluids.

So the best preventive measure is a combination of responsible sexual behavior and condom use. Adding spermicide to condom use is even better, especially for women.

Have a relationship before you have sex

I know that finding one person to fall in love with when you are young and sticking with that person for the rest of your life is difficult. That situation is ideal — for preventing AIDS and a lot of other social ills — but it's unrealistic to assume that everybody can do that. Most people do have multiple partners, and so most people are at risk.

But just because the vast majority of people have more than one partner is not an excuse for you to have as many partners as you can. I believe it is just terrible that people out there still engage in very risky behaviors, especially among the gay population that has been devastated by AIDS.

I don't like to preach because I know it doesn't do any good, but I can't avoid saying one more time to all of my readers — please be careful, your life is at stake.

Don't Be a Silent Partner

In our society, more people are willing to engage in sexual activity together than to talk about it, and a good deal of the blame for sexually transmitted diseases comes from this failure to communicate.

You all know the Golden Rule about doing unto others as you would have them do unto you. If you planned to have sex with someone, and they had a sexually transmitted disease, wouldn't you want them to tell you in advance? The same applies to you: If you have a sexually transmitted disease, you have to tell any potential partners. Notice that I said potential, because I won't hide the fact that, if you tell somebody that you have an STD, that person may suddenly run in the opposite direction. If you have a disease such as herpes, which never goes away, you will face not only a lifetime of outbreaks, but also difficulty in finding partners. You have to accept that. You cannot go around infecting other people.

By the way, Dr. Ruth isn't the only one saying that you have to warn prospective partners if you have an STD. One U.S. woman was awarded $750,000 in court from her ex-husband because he gave her herpes, and the legal trend is to make people accountable.

But I don't want you to be up front about your disease merely to keep the law away from your bankbook. I want you to do it because you have sex only with people whom you care about, with whom you have a relationship, and to whom you don't want to pass a sexually transmitted disease.

Some of you may want to be honest but are saying to yourselves right now, "How do I do it?"

I say more about this subject in Chapter 6, but in a nutshell, the answer to your question is very simple: You just do it. If you have the gumption to have sex with somebody, then don't tell me that you can't work up the courage to open this subject. I'm not saying doing so is easy. I *am* saying it's not impossible, and that you have to do it.

Minimize Your Risks

After reading this list of sexually transmitted diseases, you've probably had the thought that maybe sex isn't worth the risk. The problem with that reaction is that it will fail you when you most need it.

What do I mean by that? At some point, you'll be with somebody you're very attracted to sexually, and that person is attracted to you. Maybe you'll be in your apartment, or maybe in the other person's. And you'll be kissing, hugging, and stroking each other. Temperatures will start going up. Clothes will start coming off. An erection and a lubricated vagina will be on the loose. A comfortable bed will be nearby. You'll both be absolutely ready to have sex, and you won't have a condom nearby.

In that scenario, will you remember these pages and all these nasty and deadly sexually transmitted diseases? Will you be willing to say no, or to put your clothes back on and go find an all-night drugstore? Or will you say to heck with the risks and jump into bed?

Although some of you may have the fortitude to place caution ahead of passion, many of you won't. For that reason, you have to be prepared ahead of time. Carry a condom in your purse or pocket or glove compartment or bedside table.

You all know my reputation. I don't try to scare people away from having sex. Instead, I want to make sure that you have the best sex possible. But an integral part of great sex is healthy sex, protected sex. Although, in the heat of passion, you may well be willing to take any risk, afterwards, if you catch one of these diseases — especially AIDS — you'll regret that orgasm for the rest of your life.

Have great sex, but be careful. In fact, have terrific sex and be very careful.

Chapter 20

Impotence and Other Male Sexual Problems

1 know that many of you men don't believe that your gender suffers from any sexual dysfunction, even if you yourself may be a prime example. The reason for this idea is that in general, men have a tough-guy image to keep up and so are less likely to seek help for a problem of any sort, especially if it has anything to do with their "John Thomas," or whatever pet name you have for the penis.

But, as reluctant to admit it as you or any man may be, many men do suffer from a sexual problem of one sort or another, at least at certain times in their lives. Sometimes sexual problems can result from disease, such as testicular or prostate cancer. (I discuss these problems in Chapter 2.) But, lucky for you, the most common male sexual problem is not a physical problem at all, but a learning disability.

Premature Ejaculation

The subject that people ask me about most often is premature ejaculation. I get questions from men who suffer from the problem and from their partners, who also suffer as a result of the problem. (I've yet to hear from any family dogs, but I'm sure that even they can suffer from the problem, because ill-tempered masters aren't as generous with their treats.)

First, we have to define *premature ejaculation*. The definition that I use is that a man is a premature ejaculator when he cannot keep himself from ejaculating before he wants to. Notice that I said before *he* wants to, not she. That distinction is important.

Because not every woman can have an orgasm through sexual intercourse, a man can possibly keep his erection all night and still not satisfy the woman he's with, if all the couple does is have intercourse. But, because most women do want to feel the sensations of sexual intercourse, no matter how or if they reach their orgasms during intercourse, most men need to do all they can to figure out the techniques that allow them to last for a certain period of time.

Just how long is the period of time a man needs to last? Now we have to go back to my definition — the time frame depends on the man. If your partner reaches her orgasm after 20 minutes of intercourse, then aiming for that amount of time is good. If she doesn't climax through intercourse at all, then maybe you only want to last for ten minutes. What's important is that you learn how to gain control of when you have your orgasm, so that you can decide when to ejaculate instead of ejaculating due to circumstances beyond your control.

As with many sexual dysfunctions, different degrees of premature ejaculation exist. Some men are so severely afflicted that they cannot last long enough to penetrate a woman for intercourse. Some men even climax in their pants at the very thought that they may have sex with a woman. But even a man who can penetrate his partner and last 15 minutes may fall under the umbrella of premature ejaculator if he wants to last five extra minutes and cannot do so.

Does circumcision make a difference?

The penis of a man who has not been circumcised is often more sensitive than a circumcised man's (see Chapter 2). The reason for this is that the glans, or head, of a circumcised penis gets toughened by coming into contact with the man's underpants all day without the protection of the foreskin.

I don't know of any scientific study on the effect of circumcision, but, for most men who are premature ejaculators, the problem is in their heads — not the heads of their penises. So I do not believe that circumcision makes a significant difference. Most certainly a man who is not circumcised can learn how to prolong his climax just as effectively as a man who is.

The age factor

A young man's *libido* (sexual drive) is stronger than an older man's, and so premature ejaculation is a problem that sometimes disappears, or at least decreases, with age. Mind you, I said sometimes. I've heard from men in their 80s who've suffered from premature ejaculation all their lives. And when I say that the problem lessens, I've also heard from men who were able to last three minutes instead of two, so how much better is that? My advice is not to wait for age to take care of this problem, but rather to act as soon as possible.

Home remedies

You all know men who refuse to stop and ask for directions when they're lost, so it shouldn't come as a surprise that many men decide that they can handle the situation by tinkering with their technique, rather than by seeking professional help. As you may expect, the results are mixed, so, although I don't recommend any of these ideas, here they are:

The "slide" technique

Probably the most common method that men use to control their orgasmic response is to think of something that is not sexy. Woody Allen immortalized this technique in a film where, in the middle of making love, he yelled out "Slide!" He was thinking about Jackie Robinson running the bases, instead of the woman he was with, in an attempt to delay his orgasm. (By the way, the film is *Everything You Wanted to Know About Sex But Were Afraid to Ask*.)

This technique can work to some degree, but it's not a good way of making love. This technique makes a chore out of the sex act, rather than something pleasurable, and your partner may feel that wall you put between you and the act and think that you want to distance yourself from her.

Rubber love

Condoms do cut down on the sensations that a man has, and some men can control their premature ejaculation by using condoms. If one condom doesn't work, they put on two or more.

I certainly recommend that people use condoms — sometimes I sound like a broken record about it — but my goal is to prevent the spread of STDs. Using these same condoms as a crutch, lessening your pleasure, is a shame when you have a better way.

Snake oil

You can find products on the market that supposedly lessen the sensations in the penis so the man can last longer. In the first place, I do not know whether these products really work. But, even if they do work, just as with condoms that lessen sensation, why go for the quick fix when you can have a permanent cure?

Masturbation: Taking matters into your own hands

A method adopted by some young men is to masturbate prior to going out on a date that may lead to sex. The object here is to decrease the intensity of their desire for sex in the hopes of gaining some control.

Although this method sometimes works, it has several drawbacks:

- Masturbation may not always be possible. What if the two of you are living together or married? Or what if the woman pays a surprise visit to your dorm room?

- Another drawback is that of timing. What if you masturbate in anticipation of having sex after the date, but she wants to have sex before you go out, and you can't get an erection?

- And then there's your enjoyment. The second orgasm may not be as pleasurable as the first, and, with all the worrying about when to masturbate, the sensory experience of sexual intercourse ends up being diminished.

When it comes to curing premature ejaculation, my advice is to keep your hands to yourself and practice some self-control.

Different positions

Some men do say that they have more control over their orgasms in one sexual position or another. The missionary position is probably the one in which men have the most problems, but not always. I even had one man write to me saying that he could control his climaxes if he was lying on his right side but not his left.

Some researchers have found that greater muscular tension can increase the tendency toward premature ejaculation, which means that the missionary position, in which the man holds himself up with his arms, may accentuate premature ejaculation. But, because I really believe that this condition is a psychological one rather than a physical one, some psychological factors, different for each individual, may also come into play regarding positions.

If you find that you have more control using some positions than others, then sticking to those positions is a possible solution to the problem — but not the most satisfactory one. If you limit yourself to that one position, sex may become boring. Why not try to discover how to take control of the situation altogether so that you can engage in any sexual position and still have control?

The real cure: Recognizing the premonitory sensation

The real cure for premature ejaculation is for you to learn to recognize the *premonitory sensation*. What is that, you ask? The premonitory sensation is that feeling that a man gets just before he reaches the point of no return, also called the *moment of inevitability*.

Each man has a certain threshold of pleasure; after he crosses it, he cannot stop his orgasm. A fire engine may go through the bedroom, and he would still have an orgasm and ejaculate. But, right before he reaches that point, if he so desires, he can cool the fires and not ejaculate. And if he wants to abandon his status as premature ejaculator, he must learn to identify this sensation.

How do you learn to recognize this premonitory sensation? By treating your orgasm with kid gloves and approaching it very carefully. You cannot imitate the Road Runner, heading for the edge of a cliff at full throttle, and then apply the brakes and stop just before you fall off the edge. With that approach, you're more likely to wind up like Wile E. Coyote, who always chases right after the Road Runner. He can never seem to stop in time and ends up racing over the cliff and plummeting down into the canyon.

The idea, then, is to learn how to slow down the process before you get too close to the edge. Exactly how you do this depends on several factors, the biggest being whether or not you have a cooperative partner, with the accent on *cooperative*. Someone you've had sex with only a few times, and not very satisfactory sex at that, may not be willing to be as supportive as you need. But if you have someone who loves you, and who wants to make your sex life together better, then you're probably well on your way to curing the problem.

Although curing premature ejaculation as a couple may be easier, making progress alone is not impossible. In other words, you can practice recognizing premonitory sensation through masturbation and begin to develop some control. (Not every man can learn this control by himself, because the presence of the woman causes some men to get overexcited in the first place.) Practicing this technique alone probably takes more effort and more self-control, but it is certainly worth your time.

The start-stop technique

In 1955, Dr. James Semans, a urologist at Duke University, developed a simple technique for treating premature ejaculation (which he learned from a prostitute). This treatment was later propagated by the noted sex therapist Dr. Helen Singer Kaplan, under whom I trained at Cornell University–New York Hospital. It's called the start-stop technique and involves learning how to recognize the premonitory sensation and stopping before you get to the point of inevitability. You do this by slowly increasing your level of arousal, stopping, allowing yourself to calm down, and then heading back upwards again. Some people advise assigning a numbered level, from 1 to 10, with 10 being the point of no return. If that numbering system helps you, fine. If it distracts you, then just concentrate on the sensations.

When a couple comes to me looking to solve a case of premature ejaculation, I usually forbid them from having intercourse for a set time, as a way of removing the pressure from the situation. I don't want them to remain sexually frustrated, so I allow them to give each other orgasms after their lessons, but not through intercourse.

During a couple's first lessons, the woman uses her hand to arouse the man and stops the motion when he signals her to. Slowly, he begins to exercise more and more control. Depending on the man, this whole process can take a few weeks or a few months, but the process is almost always successful.

Masters and Johnson squeeze technique

The noted sex researchers Masters and Johnson developed a variation of the start-stop technique, called the *squeeze technique*. With this method, rather than merely stopping stimulation to the penis, the man's partner squeezes the *frenum* of the penis (the strip of skin connecting the glans to the shaft on the underside of the penis) until the man loses his urge to ejaculate. Because the start-stop technique is usually effective, the squeeze technique is not as commonly used.

Another useful aid in controlling premature ejaculation can be the *pubococcygeus (PC) muscle,* which, when squeezed, has a similar effect to the woman squeezing the base of the penis. The first thing you have to do is find this muscle. Put a finger behind your testicles. Pretend that you are going to urinate and then stop yourself. You'll feel a muscle tighten, and that's your PC muscle. If you exercise this muscle regularly, by squeezing it in sets of ten (the Kegel exercise of Chapter 11), it will get stronger, and you can then use it to help control your ejaculations.

Is it really that simple?

When I describe the treatment to some men, they look at me and say, "Is it really that simple?" The answer to their question is yes and no. The technique itself is very simple, but it involves some discipline, and that discipline's not always so simple.

Some men, when they first start doing the exercises, are all gung-ho. They look forward to solving this problem, and, if their partners are equally excited, they apparently make a lot of progress, at least during the initial stage. But then they get impatient. They don't listen to Dr. Ruth, and they decide to try what they've learned before I give them permission. Sometimes it works, and sometimes it doesn't. When the technique doesn't work, they get disappointed, and some men even give up entirely.

Learning to exercise control is not always easy. Look at all the people who cannot stop themselves from overeating or smoking cigarettes. If premature ejaculation is a habit that has become highly ingrained, you cannot assume that you can make it go away without some effort on your part. But, or should I say BUT, if you do put in the necessary time and effort, you *can* gain control over when you ejaculate.

Going for help

This section tells you enough that, if you suffer from premature ejaculation, you can try to cure yourself on your own. As I said, this process works much better if you have a partner who wants to help you. Although trying on your own is okay, that method doesn't work for everyone. Some men need the extra guidance provided by a sex therapist. In that case, my advice to you is to go and find one. For more information on how to go about doing that, see Appendix A.

The Other Extreme: Impotence

On the opposite end of the spectrum from men who get overexcited and can't control their ejaculations lies the next most common male problem: impotence.

By *impotence,* I mean a man's inability to have an erection. This condition is also called *erectile dysfunction* or *ED.* The causes of impotence can be either psychological or physical, while the degree of impotence can vary from a simple loss of rigidity to a total inability to have an erection. Although impotence can strike at any age, it becomes much more common as men grow older. Among men in their late 70s and beyond, some symptoms of impotence are almost universal.

Because I know how much importance you men put into your erections, let me say right away that impotence does not necessarily mean the end of a man's sex life. Depending on the cause of the problem, several possible solutions are usually available, so take heart.

The precursor: Loss of instant erection

I can say a lot on the subject of impotence, but the most important point has to do not with actual impotence, but with its precursor. The reason its precursor is so important is that it affects every man, at least every man who reaches a certain age in life, so pay careful attention to this section.

It sneaks up on you

Young men get erections all the time, often when they least expect to and at embarrassing times. A variety of stimuli can cause these erections — something visual, such as the sight of a pretty girl in a short skirt; a fantasy about that girl in the short skirt; or even just by a whiff of perfume that reminds the young man of that girl in the short skirt. This type of erection is called a *psychogenic erection,* meaning it is stimulated by something that triggers the brain to release hormones that cause an erection.

At a certain age — and that age differs with every man, but ranges from his late 40s to early 60s — a man loses his ability to have a psychogenic erection. That ability usually doesn't disappear all at once; he begins to get fewer psychogenic erections and may not even notice at first. But eventually the decrease becomes apparent to him, and, at some point, his psychogenic erections cease altogether.

This change can be a precursor to impotence, but it is not impotence because the men experiencing this change can still have erections. All that changes, when a man arrives at this stage in life, is that he needs direct physical stimulation to his penis to get an erection. He has to either use his hands or have his partner use her hands or mouth to make his penis erect.

Spreading the word

The loss of psychogenic erections wouldn't prove much of a problem if men expected the change, the way that women expect the hot flashes that accompany the start of menopause. Surprising, at least to me, is that so many people still have no idea that this change is part of the natural progression of growing older. This lack of knowledge causes the real problem.

The reaction of many men, when they can no longer get erections the way they used to, is to think that they must be impotent. Rather than seeking help, they begin avoiding sex. When this happens, wives think that their husbands have either stopped being attracted to them or that they are "giving at the office." Some couples fight over this problem; others withdraw from each other.

This breakdown of a relationship is so sad to me because it's not necessary. All that these couples have to do is include foreplay for the man exactly the way they have used foreplay for the woman's benefit all along. If they do this, then they have no problem.

I think that one of the reasons the loss of psychogenic erections is not so widely known is that the condition doesn't really have a name. One may call it a symptom of so-called *male menopause*, but men don't like that phrase (and I really don't blame them) because it is really not appropriate. We need to coin a catchy phrase for this syndrome; then the media will pick up on it, and a lot of unhappiness can be prevented. I think a good name would be The Male Cooling Off Period. (Why don't you e-mail me at www.drruth.com and tell me of any names that you can think of. Maybe together we can make some real progress toward removing this cause of a lot of unhappiness for some men.)

Impotence in older men

As a man gets older, his erections begin to get weaker and weaker, and he may need more and more stimulation to get an erection. Some older men can get an erection but can't keep it long enough to have intercourse. Sometimes they can get an erection, but the erection is not stiff enough to allow for penetration.

These are all real, physical problems, but they don't necessarily spell the end of a man's sex life. If men understand that age causes these problems, and if they're willing to take appropriate action, many men can continue to have sexual relations through their 90s.

"Mike"

I was holding regular clinics in the department of geriatrics at New York University Hospital in New York, and many of the men who came to see me had problems with impotence. I remember one man in particular, I'll call him "Mike." He was well into his 80s, and he hadn't had sex in about a dozen years. When his erections began to peter out on him, he just gave up.

The only reason this man came to the clinic to see me was that he had started seeing a woman, and she wanted to have sex. When he told her that he couldn't, she told him that he had to at least try, and so, to please her, he sought help from me.

I had him checked out by a urologist and, physically, he was fine. I worked with him for about a month, and one day he came to see me in the clinic, beaming. He and his lady friend had had intercourse the night before, and he couldn't have been happier. I've helped a lot of people over the years, but I have to say that the morning that man reported to me his new-found success made me the happiest of any.

The morning cure

For many men, the best solution to their problem with impotence is just to change their sex habits to suit their age. The easiest suggestion I can offer older men is to have sex in the morning instead of at night. Because you are probably retired and have no children at home, you have no reason to always try to have sex at night, except the force of habit. However, you have good reasons that illustrate how changing your routine can help you to become better lovers:

- Older gentlemen are often tired after a long day. Getting the blood to flow into the penis is what an erection really is, so the more tired you are, the more difficult it is for this process to work correctly. In the morning, you have more energy, and so you can get erections more easily.

- The male sex hormone, testosterone, is at its peak level in the morning and at its weakest at night. Because this hormone is instrumental in effecting erections, trying to get an erection in the morning makes a lot of sense.

Now I don't recommend trying to have sex first thing in the morning. Because you probably don't have to be on a rigid schedule, I suggest waking up, having a light breakfast, and then taking your partner back to bed for a sexual interlude.

Some older men resist this suggestion at first. For some reason, doing all that planning doesn't suit them. But, if they do listen to me, many men find that the fires that had died down start burning once again (see Chapter 14).

The stuff technique

Now, if some men think having sex after breakfast is strange, imagine how hard-headed some men are when it comes to getting them to try to have sex without first having an erection. But sometimes this technique works the best.

The *stuff technique* is just what it sounds like. The man, with the help of his partner, stuffs his nonerect penis into her vagina. Sometimes, after a man begins to thrust, the blood flows into his penis and that elusive erection finally rises to the occasion.

Short-term impotence

Unlike long-term impotence, short-term impotence is almost always psychological in nature. Many, many men, at one time or another, suffer from impotence — meaning that they can't have an erection when they want one. In fact, sometimes because they want an erection so badly these men fail.

Susan and Jimmy

Susan was a transfer student, and Jimmy spotted her the very first day he returned to college in his senior year. She had the type of looks he'd always dreamed of, and, to his amazement, when he struck up a conversation with her, she responded.

Jimmy had slept with a few other girls during his college years, but the thought of actually going to bed with Susan drove him wild. He managed to play it casual for a while, and, after a week went by, he asked her out on a date. She accepted, and they had a great time. They had a few more dates, each one advancing further than the last, so that, on his fifth date with her, Jimmy was pretty sure that they were going to have sex.

The anticipation was almost torture to Jimmy, and he had an erection for much of the day. They went to a dance and, with their bodies clinging to each other during all the slow dances, Jimmy felt that he was as ready for sex as he ever had been.

Jimmy had never had problems getting an erection, but as they were walking back toward his dorm, he started having doubts about his ability to please Susan. He was sure that someone as good-looking as Susan had had sex with all kinds of guys, and he began to question whether or not he could stand up to the test. By the time they got back to his room and took off their clothes, Jimmy was in a state of pure panic, and his penis reacted accordingly by staying limp. Jimmy was more embarrassed than he ever thought possible.

Anticipatory anxiety has caused many a Jimmy to experience similar problems. *Anticipatory anxiety* means the fear or expectation of a possible failure causes an actual failure. If a man starts worrying about his erection, usually doing so is enough to prevent him from having one. And the more he worries, the more likely that he will fail the next time he tries. Many men, because of one failed erection, have suffered through years of misery.

Visit a urologist

In younger men, such as Jimmy, impotence is more often than not psychological rather than physiological, so curing the problem is usually easy with the help of a sex therapist.

If a young man comes to my office with a problem such as this, the first thing I do is send him to visit a *urologist,* which is a medical doctor who specializes in the care of the *genitourinary tract,* the urinary tract in men and women and the male genital tract.

> One reason I send men who experience impotency to a urologist is to make sure that their problem is not physical, which I could not handle because I am not a medical doctor.

✔ The other reason I send them off to have their physical plants checked out is that just getting that clean bill of health is often enough to clear up the problem.

You see, many of these men worry so much about something being wrong with them that just hearing from a doctor that they're A-OK is enough to give their penises the psychological lift they need.

Even if the doctor's visit itself is not sufficient, it is a very good first step.

Build confidence

After sending an impotent client to a urologist, my next job is to build the man's confidence in his penis back up to what it was before he ran into trouble. Sometimes just getting him to masturbate does the trick. Sometimes I have to get him to do certain confidence-building exercises with his partner. These exercises usually involve prohibiting intercourse for a while, but allowing the couple to engage in other sexual activity. The man can usually get an erection when he doesn't have the pressure of needing an erection to penetrate the woman. After he gets his erection back, transferring that confidence to having erections when he plans to have intercourse is usually easy. In the majority of cases, if he's willing to work at it, I can get him back to his old self.

Study sleep habits

If the man is physically sound but doesn't respond to treatment, the next step is to find out if he has erections while he's asleep.

During the course of the night, a healthy man gets several erections during REM or "dream" sleep. He's not necessarily having an erotic dream or any dream at all, but having erections is definitely part of the male sleep pattern. This phenomenon even has its own name, *nocturnal penile tumescence,* and initials, NPT. Having initials means it's really official.

Because a man usually does not have performance anxiety while he's asleep, a man who suffers from impotence during his waking hours but doesn't have a physical problem usually has erections while he sleeps.

The simple, at-home test to find out whether you're having erections during your sleep is to wrap a coil of stamps around the base of your flaccid penis. If you find the circle of stamps broken when you wake up, you probably had an erection. (Once in a while the tooth fairy goes astray, but usually she's too busy checking children's beds.)

If the coil of stamps doesn't work, and I still suspect nighttime erections, a sleep lab is the next step. At a sleep lab, physicians substitute the stamps with plastic strips and Velcro connectors, which — as you may guess if you're as big a fan of the post office as I am — are more reliable indicators than postage stamps. And doctors have even more precise devices, if needed.

If all this testing doesn't turn up any sign of erections, then I have to send the client back to the medical community, because I can't do anything for him. But, for many men, these tests do uncover some erectile functioning, which probably indicates that the problem is psychological in nature. This is not true 100 percent of the time, but it certainly deserves following up. The basic aim is to build back his confidence to the point where he can have erections while he is awake — and even with a woman around.

When Mother Nature needs a boost

If none of the techniques discussed in the previous sections helps you to deal with your impotence, then you may have to help Mother Nature with medical or mechanical assistance. In fact, 80 percent of erectile dysfunction (ED) problems occur as a result of serious medical conditions including diabetes, hypertension, or prostate cancer surgery. These conditions are much more common in older men, though they can happen in men of any age.

Oral medications

The FDA's approval of the drug Viagra in 1998 significantly enhanced the medical world's arsenal of weapons for treating ED. Developed by the drug company Pfizer, this little blue pill is effective in 75 to 80 percent of men who suffer from ED. The biggest exception is men with heart conditions who take nitrates such as nitroglycerin, because the combination of the two drugs can be deadly.

Viagra, the brand name given by Pfizer to the drug Sildenafil, must be taken one to four hours before sexual activity and requires sexual stimulation to take effect. Patients who take Viagra may have some mild side effects, such as headaches or seeing halos around objects, but they seem not to bother most men who take the drug. Viagra has become very popular, and, disturbingly, not only with men who suffer from ED, but also with men who feel it will increase their sexual pleasure even if they can have erections without the drug. The following are some of the reasons taking Viagra may be dangerous for men who can have erections:

- Viagra is a prescription medicine. Men who don't have ED and take it do so without a prescription.

- Viagra has side effects. Men with ED may be willing to endure those side effects as a trade-off for having erections. But, because the FDA hasn't given Pfizer approval to use Viagra on men without ED, it's not yet known what those side effects can do to them over the long-term.

- Some men get *priapism,* a permanent erection (see "Priapism — The Case of the Permanent Erection" later in this chapter), from taking Viagra. Although no concrete studies have been done, men who can normally get erections and still take Viagra may be more prone to this condition than men who can't have erections naturally.

Other pharmaceutical companies are working on different drugs, for example Uprima being developed by TAP, which will have the same effect as Viagra but will use slightly different methods. Pfizer is also working on different methods for delivery of Sildenafil including a slow release pill, a rapid release pill, and a rapid acting nasal spray.

But because Viagra does not work for every man, let me give you some information on all the other options.

Penile implants

Penile implants are either hydraulic or non-hydraulic. The *non-hydraulic prostheses* are basically semi-rigid rods that doctors surgically implant within the erectile chambers. Although they are reliable, they have one major drawback — after the surgery, the penis is always in a rigid state. You can push your penis down when you're not having sex, but the erection may still be visible, which can be embarrassing.

The surgery required for the penile implant does leave soreness in the area, and you can't have sex for several weeks. But most men report very good results and are quite happy. The only men who seem to complain are those whose hopes were too high, and who expected to have erections as strong as the ones they had in their youth. This will not — and cannot — happen because the erection is permanent, and it needs to be at least somewhat concealable.

The *hydraulic prosthesis* has a fluid reservoir and a mechanical pump that a man uses to fill the prosthesis and create an erection when he wants one. Men report liking the system, but it has been prone to mechanical failure. Like the implant, it requires a surgical procedure.

Injection therapy

Another method that was developed in the 1980s is self-injection therapy. The latest product is Caverject. A man injects his penis with a medication that relaxes the muscles, thus allowing the blood to flow into the penis and cause an erection. Although the thought of injecting yourself in that particular spot may not sound appealing, the penis is an area relatively insensitive to pain, so you can barely feel the injections. Most men who use this system have reported good results. Possible side effects include scarring and, rarely, *priapistic erections* — sustained erections that won't go away without medical treatment. (You can flip ahead in this chapter for more on priapism.)

Vacuum constriction

Another method of relief for impotence is the use of *vacuum-constriction devices.* Basically, a man places a vacuum pump over the penis and, as the air is pumped out, blood flows in, creating an erection. He then places a ring at the base of his penis to hold the blood in place.

I do receive letters from men and their wives saying that vacuum pumps work wonders (and at least these devices do not require surgery). But certain side effects have kept vacuum-constriction devices from becoming very popular:

- ✔ The erections these devices produce are not as rigid as those produced with a prosthesis.
- ✔ Sometimes mild bruising occurs as a result of using these devices.
- ✔ Some men have difficulty ejaculating after using these devices.

But vacuum-constriction devices are a possible alternative for someone who doesn't, or can't, undergo surgery or use a drug, and who doesn't care to stick a needle into his penis every time he wants to have sex.

The down side of these "up" therapies

Whether a man takes a pill, injects himself, or uses a vacuum pump to get his erection, the fact that he can have an erection does not necessarily mean that his partner will be ready to have sex. If a man without ED approaches his wife for sex and she turns him down, he may be frustrated but he also knows that he'll have plenty of additional erections, perhaps even during the course of that same day. But a man who pops a pill or injects himself may be a lot more demanding because he has gone to some "lengths" to obtain his erection. If he does not consult with his better half, then she may not enjoy any resulting sexual interplay. So, the decision to use one of these methods is not one that the man should make alone, but rather in conjunction with his partner.

Some couples, the ones who have always had a good sex life and look at ED as a major problem, adapt themselves to Viagra easily. But some women, who have either never enjoyed sex very much or have lost interest in their later years, consider their husband's inability to have sex a godsend. Their attitude may seem wrong, but no one can know what their married life has been like, so one can't jump to conclusions.

For these reasons, I believe that no man should take Viagra, or use one of the other methods for overcoming ED, without first having a long talk with his spouse. Men should decide ahead of time how to deal with the changes that such therapies will bring into their lives. In some cases, men may need to undergo some sort of psychotherapy — sexual or marital — to successfully make this transition. So, while society should praise the development of Viagra, people must exercise some caution as well.

Retarded Ejaculation

Premature ejaculation and impotence are the two main male sexual problems, but some men encounter other, more rare, problems, such as retarded ejaculation. Unlike premature ejaculation, where a man can't stop himself from ejaculating, *retarded ejaculation* means he can't make himself ejaculate.

Now, although being able to last a long time is something our society puts great value on, retarded ejaculation is definitely a case of too much of a good thing, at least for the man . . . even if he brags about his lasting powers to cover up the problem. Obviously, a man who cannot ejaculate will wind up feeling frustrated and angry and may actually begin to turn off to sex.

Sometimes a medical problem causes retarded ejaculation, in which case only a urologist can help. Sometimes the cause is psychological, so that a sex therapist such as myself can treat the problem. One factor in the psychological causes can be a relationship problem, so that the man is unconsciously holding back. In that case, fixing the relationship is key to curing the problem.

Priapism — The Case of the Permanent Erection

Like retarded ejaculation, priapism is another one of those too-much-of-a-good-thing conditions. In *priapism,* a man develops a permanent erection. This erection can result from the man injecting himself with medication because he suffers from impotency, or from some disease that thickens the blood, making it impossible for blood to leave the penis after it has entered. Sickle cell anemia is one such disease.

Although priapism was named after the Greek god of fertility, that fact certainly doesn't make the man afflicted with this problem feel good about his masculinity for very long. Priapism is not only painful, but the man usually ends up in the emergency room. Doctors can now treat priapism without surgery, but the condition still requires medical care.

The Bent Penis

Peyronie's disease inflicts some men with their worst possible nightmare — they go to sleep with a functioning penis and wake up the next morning with a penis that bends so severely when it becomes erect that intercourse becomes impossible (see Figure 20-1).

Figure 20-1:
Peyronie's
disease
throws a
curve in
men's sex
lives.

The cause of Peyronie's disease is unknown; in many instances, it arises as a result of an injury. In early stages of the disease, men usually experience pain associated with having an erection. Sometimes that pain begins before the actual curvature starts, so that it can act as an early indicator.

How bad can Peyronie's disease get? Bad enough for doctors to describe severe cases in which the erect penis looks like a corkscrew. On the other end of the spectrum, the bend may be very slight, not affect the man's ability to have intercourse, and not cause any concern. In mild cases of the disease, if the man has any pain, it usually goes away on its own; all the doctor has to do is reassure the man that in two to three months all will be well.

Sometimes the curve disappears on its own. Because the disease is basically a scarring process, some men have reported positive results from taking vitamin E, although no scientific proof exists that this technique works. Surgery can sometimes remove the scarred tissue, but surgery can also result in a loss of the man's ability to have an erection, so that he would then need to have a prosthetic device implanted.

The best advice I can pass on to any of my readers who have Peyronie's disease is to visit a urologist who can help you. Some men are so embarrassed by their condition that they won't try to get help, but urologists have helped many men with this problem, so you have no reason to be shy.

I've received letters from men or their wives saying that they've lived with Peyronie's disease for years, and some have even consulted physicians. So let me add here that, if the first urologist you consult can't offer you any help, look for another one. Doing so is worth the effort.

Lack of Desire

Another problem I'd like to tackle is lack of sexual desire (which can affect women, too; see Chapter 21). One of the most common causes of this problem these days is stress. You come home late every night from work, or you've lost your job or whatever, and sex becomes the last thing on your mind. If your partner is amorous and then starts to complain about being rejected, you become even tenser and want to have sex even less. A vicious cycle builds up, and the couple's sex life can deteriorate down to nothing.

Can you fix a problem such as this by yourself? Maybe, but it's not easy. One of the components of this problem is usually a lack of communication. And breaking down the barriers that have been set up can be very hard to do. My recommendation is to visit a sex therapist or marriage counselor (see Appendix A).

Some of the causes of loss of sexual desire are not emotional but physical. A good sex therapist always asks that the man see a medical doctor first to rule out any medical problems. (Testicular and prostate cancers, treatment for which can affect the libido, are covered in Chapter 2.)

Show 'em Who's Boss

I hope that, if you have any of the problems mentioned in this chapter, or if you ever develop them, you won't turn your back on them but instead will take some positive action. Many men act as though their genitals are separate from the rest of their bodies and not totally under their control. But, of course, that is ridiculous. So, if something is bothering you, take charge and get the problem fixed.

Chapter 21

Low Libido and Other Female Sexual Problems

Although many men believe that the most common female sexual problem is the headache (as in, "Not tonight, dear, I have a headache"), sexuality in women seems to be a more complex proposition than it is in men.

That Elusive Orgasm

The main female sexual problem, simply stated, is that many women have difficulties achieving an orgasm. The complexity of the situation stems from the broad array of reactions that women have to this problem, ranging from a desperate need to experience orgasms all the way to relief at not having to experience them, with many subcategories of reactions in between.

Banishing the word frigid

I want to start off on this topic by banishing a word you may have heard applied to women who have problems with orgasms — *frigid*. In the first place, the connotations of the word are totally mistaken. Using the term frigid implies that the reason a woman may have problems reaching orgasm is that she has a heart made of stone-cold flint. The truth is that the warmest, most loving woman in the world — a woman with the proverbial heart of gold — can have problems experiencing orgasm.

Secondly, most women who do not have orgasms, or who have difficulties obtaining orgasms, are capable of having orgasms; they just don't know how to jump-start their orgasmic engines. For these reasons, I prefer the term *pre-orgasmic,* because it connotes that these women will one day be orgasmic, as soon as they set their minds to it.

An orgasm waiting to happen

Many reports indicate, and my own practice bears this out, that the number of pre-orgasmic women is high. Now, for a small percentage of these women — about 5 percent of all women — no cure exists. Such women usually have a physical problem, such as diabetes or alcoholism. But the vast majority of women, 95 percent in fact, can have orgasms, as long as they get the right information.

What can cause a woman to be pre-orgasmic? Society at large, for one thing. In the not-too-distant past, society thought that a woman wasn't supposed to enjoy sex. Sex was only for procreation, and, as long as the woman could become pregnant by having sex with her husband, what more did she want out of sex? Pleasure? What an absurd idea — if not a sinful one.

Lucky for us women, this attitude is changing, particularly in Western cultures. But it has not entirely gone away in the United States, and, on a worldwide basis, the idea is far from extinct. Believe it or not, today, even in a new millennium, millions of women, mostly in Africa, are forced to undergo *clitoridectomies* (the removal of their clitorises) so that they cannot enjoy sex. This horrible torture continues, not just because the men in their society impose the practice on these women, but also because so many of the older women who have undergone this "surgery" (which is rarely done by a surgeon) believe that the next generation needs to undergo the same process.

Society probably developed these attitudes long ago because an unintended pregnancy was such a dangerous and unpreventable occurrence, along with the fact that keeping track of people's lineage was important. If women weren't supposed to like sex, and if sex didn't bring them pleasure, then they wouldn't stray and have children who were not their husbands'. Although I don't believe that this excuse was ever valid, certainly no reason exists for such an attitude today. People now have numerous means of preventing pregnancy, and many women do enjoy terrific sex. A woman today can be as sexually adventurous as any man without becoming "with child" (not that I advocate such behavior by either sex, especially because of the risks of sexually transmitted diseases).

In any case, because society has discouraged women from giving full expression to their sexual feelings, and because the orgasmic response is not as "automatic" for women as it is for men, many women end up being pre-orgasmic or, if they are orgasmic, they have difficulties having orgasms regularly.

I have to stop and make an important point here, and that is: A woman should never feel pressured into having an orgasm by society, by the man in her life, or even by reading this book. If I am against one thing, it's pressure — especially because I know that, when it comes to sex, pressure has just the opposite of the intended effect . . . even if the person putting the pressure on you is you, yourself. If you're desperate to have an orgasm, that desperation is only going to make it tougher for you to achieve orgasm. The most important step in becoming orgasmic is learning to relax. And, if you really don't ever want to have an orgasm, then that's okay, too, as long as you are honest with yourself, and you don't just say that because you think that you can't learn.

Helping yourself

Because every woman is different, I can't give you any hard-and-fast rules to becoming orgasmic. Learning what gives you an orgasm, followed by what gives you a fabulous orgasm, is part of the overall procedure of becoming orgasmic. But, if you've been having problems, then I recommend one method that is an integral part of a sex therapist's repertoire — masturbation. (Chapter 17 explores this subject in detail.)

Although almost every adolescent boy masturbates, masturbation is not as prevalent among adolescent girls. I'm not saying that many girls don't do it, just that the practice is not universal the way it is for boys. In fact, the sex researcher Alfred Kinsey reported that, although most males who are going to masturbate during their lifetime will have done so by the time they reach their late teens, fewer than half the females who even try masturbation have done so by that age. You can find some possible reasons for this in Chapter 17.

In the not-so-distant past, marriage was something that was arranged — and often at an early age. If a 16-year-old girl was already married and engaging in intercourse with her husband, then masturbation wasn't such a big issue. But today marriage, if not intercourse, is often delayed, and that fact means that women are more responsible for their own pleasure.

Women usually have several sexual partners over the course of their lives, and, luckily for them, men today are much more likely to concern themselves with the woman's sexual enjoyment than in olden times. But, if a woman wants to be orgasmic, she has to teach those partners what to do to please her, and, for that to happen, she must discover for herself the things that please her.

Now this doesn't mean that a woman can't use the help of a man to discover what things give her pleasure. In the best of worlds, her first lover would be so good that he would explore her body with her, and together they would find the best ways of bringing her to ecstasy. The problem is that, all too often, a woman's first lovers are only worried about their own orgasms. Having sex in the backseat of a car, worried about whether or not a police officer may come by and flash a light on your exposed genitals, is not the best of circumstances for two young lovers. So, although plenty of young women are having sex in their teens, they are not necessarily having orgasms.

Faking it

Are all the young men who have sex with pre-orgasmic women brutes who don't care whether their partners enjoy sex or not? Some certainly are, but most are not, and you really can't fault them. These men think that they're doing a great job as lovers because the women they're with are faking orgasms.

Does faking it really work? Are the men really fooled? If you've seen the film *When Harry Met Sally,* then you know the answer to that one. But for those of you who haven't (and you really should go out and rent it), the answer is yes, a woman can fake it so well that no man will be able to tell that she's not having an orgasm.

Now I wouldn't make not faking it a hard-and-fast rule. You may well have times in your life when your partner really wants to make love to you and really wants you to enjoy it, such as on your wedding anniversary, and you just aren't in the mood. If you tell him that you don't feel like having an orgasm, even if you agree to have intercourse with him so that he gets his pleasure, then he will probably be disappointed. So, if you want to fake it occasionally, then I say go ahead.

But if you fake it all the time, if you never have an orgasm and cover this lack by faking it, then that behavior has to change. I don't mean that you have to stop faking it right away, but I do mean that you should make the effort to find out how to have an orgasm. Then you can stop faking it, because you're really having it.

The most important ingredient in discovering how to have orgasms is a relaxed atmosphere. Having a partner around, even someone you love very much, may not be relaxing enough for you to have an orgasm.

Wendy

Wendy came to see me when she was 28. She'd had several boyfriends and even lived with a man for three years, but she had never had an orgasm. The problem wasn't that the men she'd had sex with hadn't tried. The man she lived with had really given it all he had, showing patience and spending long periods of time trying to make her climax. In the end, he left her because he couldn't provide her with sexual pleasure. Sex became unsatisfying to him as well as to her, so he ended up sleeping with another woman, whom he finally married.

Wendy had tried to masturbate, but it never worked for her. She didn't really like the idea, and, when she tried, she would be all tense. After five minutes of touching her vagina, she would give up.

I told Wendy that she should set aside an hour a night for a week to practice, but that she should not try to have an orgasm. She should touch herself and think pleasant thoughts, but the goal was to find out what made her feel good, not to have an orgasm.

She was an obedient client, and she didn't have an orgasm that first week. But, when she came for her next visit, she told me how excited she had become the night before and that she thought she was ready. I gave her permission and asked her to call me the next day, and was she ever grateful during that phone call.

What Wendy needed was to discover how her body responded without having the pressure to have an orgasm. The world is full of Wendys, and they too need to explore their vaginas and clitorises to see what feels best.

Some women can't stand to have their clitorises touched when they've reached a certain point of excitement. Their clitorises become so sensitive that direct clitoral contact is painful.

Brenda

Brenda was a virgin when she fell in love with Brad. He, on the other hand, had slept with many women and thought of himself as an expert lover. He had discovered how to give these other women orgasms by using his finger and his tongue, and he had no doubt that he could do the same for Brenda.

The first time they had sex, Brad spent half an hour rubbing and licking Brenda's clitoris, and all she felt was a tremendous irritation. For several days, she was really sore. When he started to do it again the next time, rather than endure the pain, she faked an orgasm. That made Brad feel great, but it also meant that Brenda would never have an orgasm as long as she was with Brad, because he was certain that he knew exactly how to bring her to orgasm.

When Brenda practiced masturbation after seeing me, she discovered that what gave her the right sensation was to touch *around* her clitoris, not directly on it. By rubbing around her clitoris, she discovered how to give herself orgasms. Because Brenda was able to teach her next boyfriend exactly what she needed and didn't need, they had a satisfying sex life.

I need more

Some of the women whom I send off to practice masturbation tell me that, no matter what they do, they can't seem to get sufficient stimulation. They report feeling as if they're close to having an orgasm, but they can't get past that point to actually have one.

For women who just can't seem to give themselves orgasms, I usually suggest buying a vibrator. Vibrators can often supply the added stimulation that these women need. Not every woman uses the vibrator directly on her clitoris, because the sensations are too intense; others absolutely need to. Some women who use vibrators also need to have the feeling of something filling their vaginas, and so they may insert a dildo into their vaginas while using the vibrator on their clitorises.

If you want to find out more about vibrators and dildos, or about masturbation, read Chapter 17. After you've discovered how to give yourself an orgasm with a vibrator, you must then transfer that ability to your partner. Hopefully, the added excitement of having sex with a partner will be enough that he can bring you to orgasm without using a vibrator. You can show him what you discovered with the vibrator — how and where you need to be touched — and he can duplicate those movements with his finger or tongue and get the same results. If that process doesn't work, then you may want to have him try with a vibrator.

Because vibrators can provide so much more stimulation for the woman, weaning yourself from it may take a while. But I believe that most couples would prefer not to have to be dependent on a piece of mechanical equipment such as a vibrator. Of course, if you can't discover how to have an orgasm without using a vibrator, then that's not the end of the world. No one would ever put you down for taking a car to get around instead of walking, so I wouldn't make a big deal about having to use a vibrator to have an orgasm.

The flat moment

Some women can bring themselves, or have their partners bring them, very close to an orgasm. They have all the physical signs of being about to reach an orgasm, but all of a sudden they reach a *flat moment*. When this happens, these women think that they're not going to have an orgasm. And, as soon as they think that, it becomes a self-fulfilling prophecy, and they don't.

Pat

When Pat came to see me, she was in tears before she got halfway through her story. She so badly wanted to have an orgasm, but she was sure that she was incapable.

The first thing that I do when a new person comes to my office is to give a sexual status examination, which means I ask every detail imaginable about his or her sex life. When Pat described to me what sex was like with her husband, I immediately sensed that she may be one of those women who have problems getting through the flat moment.

Her husband could bring her to a high state of arousal, but, after a while, she would suddenly go back down. As soon as that happened, she would get frustrated, stop the lovemaking session, and start to cry. Her husband, needless to say, was becoming as frustrated as she was.

I instructed Pat not to stop her husband when she felt that her sexual excitement was going down, but to let him keep doing whatever it was that had been working up until then. She seemed doubtful, but she agreed to give it a try. Sure enough, after a few minutes more of having her clitoris fondled, Pat's arousal level resumed its steady climb, and she had an orgasm.

The key to overcoming the flat moment is to keep at it. Not every woman goes through this flat moment, but enough do to indicate that the problem is a fairly common occurrence. But the flat moment is only a momentary thing. If the stimulation keeps up, then a woman will go back upwards on the arousal curve and have her orgasm. So, as far as the flat moment goes, persistence is everything.

The missed orgasm

If you've ever misplaced something — such as your glasses or the keys to the car — you know how frustrating an experience that can be. Imagine the frustrations of not being able to find your orgasm!

Right about now, those of you not suffering from this condition are probably saying to yourselves, "Dr. Ruth, you're pulling my leg. How can you miss an orgasm?" I know that the partners of women who have missed orgasms don't understand the problem, because they report their concerns to me in their letters or in my office. When a woman tells her spouse or lover that she doesn't know whether she's had an orgasm or not — something that men have absolute certainty about — he just can't believe it.

And the women themselves can't really believe it either. They say to me: "Is it possible? Can I not recognize an orgasm? Isn't it supposed to be a very strong, very intense feeling? How can I not recognize it? How can I miss it?"

Unlike a woman who cannot have an orgasm, a woman who has missed orgasms does have an orgasm, at least physiologically, but the sensations don't register in her brain. What I mean is, her heart rate goes up, her vagina lubricates, she has all the outward physical signs of an orgasm, but none of the pleasure.

Treating women who have this problem can be a bit tricky. They have to be taught to feel the orgasms that their bodies undergo. Knowing that they indeed have orgasms, at least physically, is usually helpful to these women. A sex therapist may use any of several different modalities of treatment.

If you have missed orgasms, I definitely recommend seeing a sex therapist, because you probably won't be able to handle this problem on your own. Appendix A discusses visiting a sex therapist.

I can give myself an orgasm, but he can't

Some women are definitely orgasmic, because they can give themselves orgasms through masturbation anytime they want to, but they can't have orgasms with their partners. A variation of this problem is when a woman is orgasmic with one partner and *anorgasmic* (unable to have an orgasm) with another.

Sometimes the cause of this problem is as simple as not having enough foreplay. Other times, the reason is complex and requires therapy. But, if this problem affects you, before you flip ahead to Appendix A to find out how to locate a sex therapist, you can try a few things on your own.

The key to making progress here is figuring out how to relax with your partner. Because you know that you are orgasmic, that knowledge should give you some of the self-confidence you need to overcome the difficulties you may encounter. In the first place, that knowledge gives you a fallback position. If you don't have an orgasm with your partner, you know that you can satisfy yourself at some later time. Remembering this may be important to developing the relaxed attitude you need to have an orgasm with a man.

What you must do in a situation like this is to become a teacher. Think back to your favorite teacher in school. More than likely, that teacher was able to make you laugh while he or she was teaching you. In the bedroom, as in the classroom, having a sense of humor is very important. If you adopt a positive but lighthearted attitude, you'll be more likely to succeed.

This instruction session can be a highly erotic moment, if you let it. The first thing you should do is let yourself fantasize about the session for a few days before it actually takes place. Think about what you will do with your partner during this show-and-tell session. Maybe you can even masturbate while you think about it. The picture that you have to put into your head is not one full of stress and worry, but instead one that has a warm, loving glow.

You can take two basic approaches to showing your partner what you need to reach a climax, and you can choose either one or combine them.

- One is to show him how you masturbate without allowing him to take part.
- The other is for you to masturbate yourself using his hand.

To combine these approaches, you can start masturbating yourself and then take his hand and guide it through the right movements. Explain to your partner ahead of time that he's not to take any initiative but just do whatever you tell him to, which can simply be to lie back and watch. Maybe "watch" isn't exactly the right word, because he has to pay attention. He has to carefully note what you do to bring yourself to orgasm, and the sequence in which you do it.

Now, when his turn comes, he may not get it right the first time, and that's okay. Remember, you can give yourself an orgasm anytime, so, if you don't have an orgasm during the first couple of sessions with him, don't worry. If I sense my client is very uptight, I order her not to have an orgasm just to take the pressure off. This way, she can show him the motions she likes, and he can try them, but orgasm won't be the goal.

Whether or not you have an orgasm from these sessions, I can assure you that they'll prove highly erotic to your partner. Watching a woman masturbate herself is a fantasy of many men, which is why X-rated movies and girlie magazines often depict it. So, whether or not you get very turned on by this lesson, I can guarantee you that he will, and you shouldn't leave him frustrated. Make sure that he has an orgasm, either by engaging in intercourse, by stimulating him orally or manually, or by letting him stimulate himself; that way, he'll volunteer for as many private lessons as you need.

Ouch! — It's Too Tight in There

Some women get so tense from the thought of having intercourse with a man that their vaginal muscles involuntarily tighten up to the point where penetration by the man's penis is painful or sometimes even impossible. This condition is called *vaginismus*.

If you have this problem the first time you have intercourse, you may believe that it has something to do with the size of your vagina, but that is very, very rarely the case. The cause is almost always that the muscles at the entrance to the vagina have contracted tightly as a result of tension.

Now the first thing that I do when a woman comes to me complaining of painful intercourse is to send her to her gynecologist. Although the size of the vagina is almost never an issue, some women may have a separate medical problem, and sex therapists have to rule that out anytime pain is involved.

Assuming that she gets a clean bill of health, then, once again, the treatment involves getting her to relax. What exactly she must do depends on what the other factors are. If she's also never had an orgasm, then discovering how to give herself an orgasm through masturbation may be step one. If she's already orgasmic, then my instructions have to do with getting her partner more involved in the orgasm-producing process.

Although doctors can usually treat vaginismus itself, when untreated, the condition can be a very serious issue between a couple. This idea is especially true if the woman is a virgin, gets married, and intends to lose her virginity during the honeymoon (see Chapter 8). She and her new husband are both all set to start their sex life, he tries to penetrate her with his penis, and either she feels too much pain to let him continue or he can't get in at all. This situation usually results in bad feelings at best, or very often in a fight, followed by tears. If the couple doesn't go to get help, it may even mean the end of the marriage.

Lack of Desire

One of the major reasons a couple gets married is to have sex. True, they also do it to have a relationship, share companionship, have children, provide financial and emotional support, and many other things, but sex is definitely a major part of the pact.

Now, if you believe almost every comedian that you see on television, all husbands want sex all the time and almost all wives never want sex. Because life is not a sitcom, the truth is not so cut and dried. I hear from many women who want sex more often than their husbands do. But, sadly, many women do have problems with sexual desire.

Some of these women start out with a low sex drive. Others have problems after they have children. Still others don't begin to have such problems until after menopause. A number of women also have low desire after surgery to remove their ovaries, called an *oophorectomy,* or the uterus, a *hysterectomy.*

Low desire needn't mean no sex

For the partner who has a very low or nonexistent desire for sex, be it the woman or the man, the problem is not as acute as it is for the partner who does want to have sex. The person with the higher sex drive may feel constantly frustrated, rely on self-pleasuring, or find another partner. In the first two instances, the marriage often suffers, because the anger from the frustrated partner usually spills over into other areas. The last choice usually spells the end of the marriage.

As you know, I am not in favor of pressuring anybody into having sex. On the other hand, I do take pity on the frustrated partner, so I strongly believe that something needs to be done when one person has a very low desire for sex. Notice I said *very* low. Two people rarely have exactly the same level of desire for sex, so most couples have to compromise somewhat. But "somewhat" cannot equal sex every other month.

You can treat the problem

The cure for such a lack of desire depends on the cause:

- ✔ **Depression:** If a woman suffers from depression, then she probably does not want to have sex. If she gets help for her depression first, then her libido will probably go up by itself. A woman may also suffer depression after a hysterectomy, equating the loss of her uterus with the loss of youth, femininity, and beauty. If the woman also has her ovaries removed, she is thrown in to "early menopause," which brings its own set of problems (see Chapter 3). If you feel low and have recently had a total hysterectomy, speak with your doctor and consider counseling (see Appendix B).

- ✔ **Childbirth:** New moms sometimes get so emotionally tied up with their babies, not to mention so tired from lack of sleep, that they lose interest in sex. The dads, who may have stopped having sex with their wives during the last month or two of their pregnancy, and who gave her the time she needed to recover from the effects of giving birth, begin to get testy after several months have gone by.

  Although these new mothers may have some very good reasons, in my opinion, using them is a mistake. You may have to make a conscious effort to put the spark back into your sex life. Get a grandparent to baby-sit (they'll love it) or hire a baby-sitter and go out with your husband for a romantic evening. If the baby is a light sleeper, or if you have other distractions in the house, rent a motel room. But don't just let sex slide.

- ✔ **Menopause:** The production of a woman's sex hormones declines during menopause, causing certain side effects that can affect a woman's sex life. But menopause does not have to mean an end to sex. In fact, many women find they have a stronger desire for sex after menopause because they no longer have to worry about becoming pregnant. Plus, menopause is a time when women and their husbands have more privacy because their kids have grown up and moved out.

You may have to make some adjustments for menopause, such as using a lubricant, but you can still have a satisfactory sex life. For more suggestions, read Chapter 3 and Chapter 14.

Lately, much talk (not to mention books and magazine articles) has focused on the effects of hormones on women who lose their desire for sex. Some people say to take estrogen, which besides any effect it may have on the libido, can help decrease the thinning of the vagina's walls if applied in cream form. Others suggest that postmenopausal women take testosterone, the male hormone that women do produce in lower quantities during their childbearing years, but the production of which decreases after menopause.

I am not one to jump on bandwagons, particularly if these therapies have side effects that doctors may later find are quite serious. Taking one of these hormones can help the libidos of some women, but the same is true of taking a *placebo* (a sugar pill). At this point no absolute proof exists that taking hormones can safely alleviate lowered sexual desire in postmenopausal women. Medical science makes breakthroughs every day, so you can certainly check with your gynecologist, but make sure that you listen very carefully to the risks when your doctor discusses this subject.

Because plenty of older women enjoy sex a great deal without taking any extra hormones, most older women who suffer from a lack of desire do so, in my opinion, from some psychological reason, which means that a sex therapist can probably help them.

I am most certainly not saying that a woman should expect to have lowered desire or do nothing about the condition if it occurs. You absolutely should speak with your doctor and consult with a sex therapist if you have no medical problem. But women should be aware that if they have the expectation that their desire for sex will go down after menopause then it's likely that they will experience a loss of libido caused by their lowered expectations, not any physical reason. The most important thing you can do is not to accept such a condition without putting up a fight. Take a multilevel approach to finding a remedy, including talking yourself into having sex, seeing your doctor, and, if need be, seeing a sex therapist.

Problems with Body Image

I don't know if most of the fault lies with Madison Avenue (home of the advertising industry), Seventh Avenue (home of the fashion industry), or

Lake Shore Drive (home of *Playboy*), but modern women face a lot of pressure when trying to bridge the gap between their bodies and today's "ideal" body type.

Putting away the scales

A quick glance through the history of art, going back to the very first statues made by cavemen, shows that men have always liked the so-called voluptuous woman. As luck would have it for any voluptuous woman living today, our society now puts a premium on being skinny. Most women may like to lose a few pounds to resemble the women they see on TV and in magazines. But they don't let the fact that their bodies are more suited for Rubens' paintings of voluptuous nudes rather than Hugh Hefner's sleek centerfolds stop them from having sex. Nevertheless, I do get letters from women all the time who say that they're too fat to have sex with their husbands.

Most of these women are not saying that their partners have any problems with their bodies. Yet some of these women won't even take off their clothes in front of their husbands — even though they've been married for 20 years. Now you can't tell me that their husbands would have stuck around so long if they didn't find their wives sexually attractive. After all, not every man wants to lie on top of a woman who is all skin and bones. But these women believe that they are unattractive, and they let that belief spoil their lives in myriad ways.

Women suffering from a body-image problem don't need a sex therapist so much as a counselor who can help them to overcome their low self-esteem (see Appendix B). Sometimes just getting them to believe that their husbands really do find them attractive is all that it takes. For other women, the task is more difficult. At the extreme end of the spectrum are anorexic or bulimic women who still believe that they need to lose weight, even though they are wafer-thin.

Beautiful at any age

Some women begin to have these same feelings of inadequacy as they grow older. As a woman ages, her body starts to change — certain parts sag, wrinkles appear, and she looks less and less like she did in her wedding picture. Has this woman become less attractive to other men? Probably. Has she become less attractive to her mate? That's another story.

The attraction that a woman's partner feels for her does not stem only from looks. A lifetime of shared memories, including experiences, can more than make up for any changes in appearance — especially when he no longer can fit into the tux he wore on his wedding day, either.

None of us is perfect, but that doesn't mean that we can't enjoy sex just as much as those cover girls and guys, and maybe even more so.

Sex after a Mastectomy

One in nine women in America will be diagnosed with breast cancer, and many of those women will undergo a *mastectomy,* the surgical removal of a breast. Naturally, survival is the first concern, but women shouldn't forget their sexual feelings either.

Because the breast is regarded as a symbol of femininity and attractiveness, and is often a source of sexual arousal in the man, a woman who loses one or both breasts often has a strong fear of rejection. Some women choose to have reconstructive surgery. Although the new breast looks good under clothes, the look and feel of the breast changes, and so that fear of rejection still lingers.

Another factor to consider is that many women go for surgery thinking they may only be having a *lumpectomy,* the removal of a lump in the breast, and wake up from surgery having lost their entire breast to a mastectomy. In such cases, postoperative counseling is usually vital. A doctor or social worker can usually recommend a counselor to the woman, and many hospitals have support groups.

What a counselor must do in treating women who've undergone such surgery is regard the return of sexual functioning as matter-of-fact so that the woman receives the message that she won't be rejected.

The husband or sexual partner should be part of the counseling process, and he should provide plenty of reassurance, especially in the physical form of touching, kissing, and hugging. Because of their fear of rejection, most women won't initiate sex after a mastectomy, and the partner may also hold back, because he's not sure whether she's physically ready.

Good communication is necessary after a mastectomy, and a counselor can help establish this. Some counselors believe that the husband should participate in the physical recovery right from the very beginning, assisting in changing the dressing during the hospital stay as a way of letting his wife know that her new appearance is okay with him.

Support groups composed of other women who have undergone mastectomies can be especially helpful to a woman who doesn't have a partner, but they can also help any woman get through the trauma of losing one or both breasts (see Appendix B).

Some women have similar feelings after a hysterectomy. Discuss these feelings with your doctor.

Chapter 22

Sex and the Law

This book is supposed to help you achieve good sexual functioning, right? So why have I included a chapter having to do with sex and the law? One reason may be that more than 400,000 lawyers work in this country, and I want all of them to buy a copy of this book.

But seriously, my reason for including this chapter is that, despite the fact that having sex is one of the most private things people do in life, these private moments are very much under the rule of law; although, over the last few decades, the laws that govern sex have been severely weakened or, in many cases, removed altogether from the books. But these hard-won freedoms will only last so long as people realize that they have them and work together to protect them.

Society in the Bedroom

The laws currently on the books concerning sexual conduct, as well as those all through the ages, are based first on a moral code. People developed these codes over time as they decided what was the right and wrong way to act. Because the human child takes so long to develop to the point where it becomes an adult and can function on its own, people realized that the survival of humanity demanded that children be born into an environment where they could be nurtured for many years. And because society required women to take care of the children at home — whether that home be a cave, tent, castle, or mud hut — men had to take up the duties of hunting for food and protecting the home from predators, both of the four-legged and the two-legged variety.

For a woman to have a child without a man being around probably meant death to both the woman and the child. Societies couldn't allow that. So they developed codes which insisted that, before men and women had sex and produced children, they had to make a commitment to each other. Society at large upheld these commitments, be it through simple tribal justice or the fully developed legal codes of today.

Those codes held up for thousands of years, and they were certainly still in effect while I was growing up. But in the United States and many other Western countries, those thousands of years of tradition have crumbled. Thanks to the invention of the birth control pill and other forms of contraception, sex has been separated from pregnancy, leaving people to make up their own rules. Some of the laws that govern sexual conduct still remain on the books, but most of these go unenforced and are only vestiges of the past.

I do believe that some of the of individual laws are still relevant, and I'd like to examine them because they can teach us some very important lessons when it comes to good sexual functioning.

The Laws against Child Abuse

We may no longer absolutely need both a mother and a father to support a child — witness the millions of children of single parents who manage to survive, if not thrive, in our present day world. Nevertheless, our children still need to be protected from the damage that adults can inflict upon them. You read in the newspapers all the time about children who are hit and burned and neglected in every way, but one of the most common forms of child abuse remains sexual abuse.

As a mother, I cannot fathom why an adult would want to have sex with a child. I can maybe understand the notion a little in the case of an adult and an adolescent. Although the law still considers adolescents to be children, they may, in fact, be very developed from a sexual point of view (such as the fictional Lolita, who exuded such a strong sexual hold over Humbert Humbert, even if she didn't fully understand the consequences of what she was doing).

But even the Lolitas of this world need the protection of the law. And, of course, those even more innocent little ones, whose sexual abuse really sickens me, certainly need protection, right? I mean, that goes without saying because, after all, who would ever question such laws?

The North American Man Boy Love Association (NAMBLA), that's who. This organization advocates the removal of such laws so that men can freely have sex with little boys. NAMBLA says that people consider this sort of behavior wrong because society says such acts are taboo. The group says that the boys themselves like the attention and are not harmed in any way.

To me, this idea is utter nonsense. But I bring up this group for a reason. You'll always find those people around who say that society has too many laws, and that governments should perform only a few limited tasks, such as defending the nation from intruders and maybe building roads. They definitely reject the idea that government has any role to play when it comes to sexual behavior. You may instinctively agree with that, until you think about NAMBLA. More than 99 percent of people believe that these men are sick, yet they do exist. And so society needs laws to protect children even, or maybe especially, from what people do in the privacy of their homes.

The Age of Consent

Statutory rape is defined as an adult having sex with a minor, even if the minor consents.

The *age of consent* — the age at which people may decide on their own to have sex with someone older than they are — has changed over the years. In England, from the 16th to the 18th centuries, the age of consent was only ten. Then it jumped to 16, where it currently sits (except in the case of male to male sex, where the age is 18). In the United States, each individual state sets the age of consent, and it can range from 14 to 18 for heterosexual sex and 16 to illegal for sex between two people of the same gender.

The age of consent does not mean the age when a young person *should* have sex. It only means the age that is legal for that person to have sex with an adult. Considering that young people mostly have sex with people their own age, the actual ages at which people first have sex vary widely.

The Legal Marriage Age

Separate from the age of consent is the age at which a person can get married without parental consent, which, in the United States, is also set by each state. Some countries, especially in Latin America, Africa, and Asia, encourage early marriages for girls, shortly after puberty.

Through most of human history, not the child but the parents chose the spouse, especially in the case of young girls who were married off to older men because of some political or other gain to the parents. Although this custom has been dropped from American society, the practice is still very common around the world. In fact, I know Camelia Sadat, the daughter of the late president of Egypt, Anwar Sadat. Camelia's father married her off to an older man when she was only 13.

Which is worse, the father forcing his 13-year-old daughter to get married, or an adult falling in love with a teenager and running away to have children? I'll let you think about that. But I believe that whatever answer you come up with, you'll find yourself agreeing that society does have a responsibility when it comes to children and sex.

Incest: A Violation of Trust

Another area of the law that also dates back to Biblical times includes laws that forbid incest. *Incest* occurs when two people who are closely related have sexual intercourse. Here again, these laws are based on experience. People noted that, when a pregnancy resulted from close relatives having sex, the offspring often had physical or mental disabilities.

Although many parents fear sexual abuse from those outside their family, most sexual abuse occurs within families, and incest is certainly part of the problem. (Other types of child sexual abuse, such as sodomy or just fondling of the child, would not be considered incest as no pregnancy can result.)

When family members molest children, the consequences are often more serious than if strangers molested them because the natural element of trust between adult protector and child is destroyed. Often other members of the family are either unaware of what behavior is going on, or, at the very least, close their eyes so as not to see, making the child feel even more abandoned.

Adults must take responsibility for the welfare of any child that they know. Sexual abuse always has serious effects upon the child that, if not apparent right away, will appear as he or she grows up. Children must be protected. Many people who practice child abuse were abused as children themselves. Abuse is an evil circle, and all people must share in the responsibility of breaking it.

Sex Education: Spreading the Word

If parents have the right to say whether or not their child can get married, do they also have the right to stop that child from being taught about sex in the schools? While some people (and I'm one of them) rank sex education right up there with the three Rs, others fear that having their children learn about sex will turn them into sex maniacs.

In European countries, such as Sweden, where sex education is mandatory, not only are the children not sex maniacs, but the rates of teenage pregnancy (including illegitimacy and abortion) and sexually transmitted diseases are very much lower than rates in the United States. Sex education policies vary from country to country. In Sweden, sex education begins when school starts, for children at age 7. In the Philippines, sex education is mandatory at the high-school level. Other countries with mandatory sex education include Germany, France, and China.

In most of the United States, if parents really object to having their child taught about sex in school, they can request, usually in writing, that their child be excused. My suspicion is that most of the parents who object to sex education don't ask that their children be excused because, if they did, then they themselves would be faced with the task of educating their children about sex — something that I don't think most of these parents want to think about, much less actually do.

On the other hand, I do agree with the courts in Florida that convicted a couple of "lewdness" for answering their 14-year-old son's question about where babies come from by demonstrating for him the method by which he had been created.

I am also in agreement with one argument used by people who oppose sex education because of their religious beliefs. Many of these people object to sex education, not because they don't want their children to know about the birds and the bees, but because they want to see a moral message imparted at the same time. I also feel strongly about this idea — so strongly that I wrote a whole book on the subject, *Sex and Morality*.

 Because we are not allowed to promote religion in U.S. public schools, most teachers conduct sex education classes in a very straightforward fashion, without talking about right and wrong. I don't think that this approach teaches children all they need to know. Schools force children to understand the basic concepts of arithmetic, even though they can perform all the functions with a calculator. So I think people also need to explain to children how morals fit into good sexual functioning, rather than just give them the mechanics. I believe that schools can impart this general moral message without connecting it to any one religion.

 Children are too impressionable to give them the facts about sex without telling them about the risks of sexual activity and the moral framework they need to make good judgments.

Rape: A Growing Concern

The law defines rape as a man having sexual intercourse with a woman, who is not his wife, without her consent. Rapes are often violent acts, but even if the man uses no force, if the woman consents because she believes that she may be in danger, then she has been raped.

Certainly, rape is and should be illegal, and rapists should be prosecuted to the full extent of the law. On this issue, my feelings are with the majority. But on a subdivision of this issue, I part company with many people, and that subdivision is date rape.

Naturally, I am not in favor of rape of any sort, or even of people pressuring each other to have sex. But, if a woman gets fully undressed and climbs into bed with a man she knows, she has to be aware of the risks. She may only want to go so far, but unless she knows the man very well, and unless she communicates how far she is willing to go quite explicitly beforehand, the chance for a miscommunication is good — especially if both parties have been drinking.

My advice to any young woman who wants to avoid date rape is to watch your step — stay in control. Don't drink and be sure to give clear signals about how far you want to go before you two come to the stopping point. If you get a man too excited, he may not be able to control himself. That has nothing to do with the law, but rather with human nature.

But, even in criminal cases where the rapist and the victim are strangers, legally defining rape has never been easy. For some time the law presumed that if the woman didn't actively fight back against the rapist, she displayed an element of consent. Today, the U.S. legal system recognizes that to fight back can put the woman in even greater danger. So now a man can be convicted of rape even if the woman does not put up a struggle. But this definition of rape can make it easier for a man to be falsely accused.

And, as if this subject wasn't complicated enough, a new twist has recently been added: *marital rape.* Society has always assumed that no such thing as marital rape could exist because marriage was thought of as blanket consent to all sexual intercourse on the part of the woman. But more and more society is coming to realize that, even in marriage, sex requires the active consent of both partners and that, just as spousal abuse exists, so does spousal rape. The laws dealing with spousal rape are different in every state, but society has certainly made tremendous progress in protecting women from abusive husbands.

The Law and Contraception

The reason that I became a sex therapist is that, for a time, I worked for Planned Parenthood. When women starting asking me questions about sex that I didn't know the answers to, I decided that it was time to go and study the subject more in depth. Because of those early years at Planned Parenthood, I have a great respect for the founder of that organization, Margaret Sanger, as well as for all the other people who fought against the laws that made contraceptives illegal in the United States.

That's right. Until 1965, contraceptive devices were illegal in many American states. The Supreme Court, in the case of *Griswold v. Connecticut,* ruled that the Constitution barred states from interfering with a married couple's decisions about childbearing. (Unmarried people were not given the right to get contraceptive services until the Supreme Court's 1972 decision in *Eisenstadt v. Baird.*) Today, you can walk into a drugstore or even some supermarkets and pick a box of condoms or a spermicide right off the shelf (see Chapter 7 for more information about birth control). I consider this tremendous progress, though even today not everyone agrees with me.

Contraception is freely available in most European countries (except for Ireland) and in some third world countries, such as India, though the issue in developing countries is still controversial, and many areas still ban contraceptives and even information about them.

The Law against Spreading Diseases

With so many people coming down with sexually transmitted diseases, and with the consequences being so grave, it was only a matter of time before the courts got involved. I've been telling you in this book to practice safer sex, but from a legal point of view, doing so is no longer enough. The U.S. courts have ruled that if you have an STD, you must inform any potential sex partners so that they can decide for themselves whether or not the risk is worth it. And, in fact, more than half the states have laws that make it a crime for a person with HIV to have sex at all.

In addition to AIDS, herpes has also been a prime instigator of court cases, and some celebrities have settled multimillion-dollar damage cases for having passed on this disease that has no cure. And several states have expanded the scope of their oversight to the passing on of any STD. Not only do such laws open up a person with an STD to civil lawsuits that can cost millions of dollars, but in some states passing on an STD is a felony offense (as opposed to a misdemeanor), so that the carrier may face a long jail sentence. So if you're a carrier of any STD, you must tell the truth, or what you don't say may be held against you.

The best advice I can give you is to be open and honest. You may lose some sexual partners that way, but at least you can keep yourself from paying for past mistakes again and again.

Abortion: A Legal Safeguard

Another issue where people have wide disagreement is abortion. An *abortion* is the artificial ending of a pregnancy before the natural birth of a child. Until the Supreme Court's 1973 decision in *Roe v. Wade*, abortions were illegal in the United States — although that fact didn't stop women from having them. The wealthier women went to have their abortions in other countries where they were legal. Some middle-class women found doctors willing to perform illegal abortions for a price. And the poor women would go to illegal abortionists, most of whom were not doctors. Many of those women died as a result.

Abortions do upset me. As a mother, the idea goes against my instincts; as a religious woman, it also goes against the rules of my faith. But the situation for women before abortions became legal, with so many women dying, is to me even worse. Now if I had only one wish, it would be that no woman would ever want to have an abortion again. But I know that this wish will probably never come true because society is a long way from having the perfect form of contraception, people are even further away from perfectly using the methods of contraception available, and, finally, people may never totally eradicate rape and incest. Because of this imperfect world, I believe that abortion must remain legal.

Having said that, let me tell you a story of what happened on my radio show one night. A woman called me and said that she had already had three abortions. I asked her if she was sexually active, and she said yes. I asked her if she was using a contraceptive of some sort. When she answered no, I hung up on her.

Although I am in favor of having abortion available for cases of contraceptive failure or rape — as I told my radio listeners — I am totally against people using abortion as a method of birth control. Abortion is not something to be taken lightly. Abortion may be a freedom that people should have, but people should definitely not abuse it.

The Law and Homosexuality

The men who make up NAMBLA (the organization which asserts that men should have a right to have sex with boys) are *pederasts,* a variation of homosexuals who enjoy seducing young boys more than adult men. Most homosexuals are not pederasts, yet they all seem to share the blame, even if their sexual behavior is only among consenting adults. Is that fair?

Before all you heterosexuals answer that question, I want you to answer another question. Should you take the blame for all the heterosexual men who seduce young girls? Or what about all the heterosexual fathers, uncles, and brothers who commit incest with young girls in their family? Does that have anything to do with your having sex with a consenting adult heterosexual? No, right? Then why should the state care what two consenting homosexual men or lesbian women do behind closed doors?

Actually, today's laws were written not so much against homosexuals themselves as against their sexual practices. As far as homosexuals are concerned, vaginal intercourse is impossible. The main sexual acts that homosexuals do engage in, oral and anal sex, were labeled *sodomy* and made illegal; although, the way these laws were written, a heterosexual couple partaking of these practices was committing a criminal act just as much as a homosexual couple would be.

But it wasn't the content of the laws that affected homosexuals so much as the way these laws were enforced. If you admitted to being a practicing homosexual, then you were also admitting to breaking the laws against sodomy. And if the police decided to go after you, your bedroom may well prove to be a target for an investigation.

At one point every state had sodomy laws on the books. Thirty-two states have now repealed or struck down those laws, but in *Bowers v. Hardwick,* the U.S. Supreme Court ruled that the Constitution does allow states to pass such laws against sodomy.

Not every culture has condemned homosexuality. Homosexuality was a well-known part of the culture of the ancient Greeks, but many other cultures throughout the world and throughout the ages have also allowed homosexuality to flourish. One can easily say that the United States in the 21st century is one of those cultures. But, historically, being a homosexual has also meant risking death for practicing one's sexual orientation — most notably during the Nazi era in Germany.

Gay Marriage

While many people condemn homosexuals for having anonymous sex in gay bars and bathhouses, others go so far as to say that because of their behavior so many gay men deserve to be afflicted with AIDS. On the other side of that coin, gays are prohibited from officially declaring themselves committed to one partner via the act of marriage.

Apart from wanting to encourage gays not to be promiscuous, gay unions have many other positive consequences. Picture a gay couple, lesbian or homosexual, who have been together for 20 years. Legally each partner can be barred from visiting the other in a hospital, making medical decisions on a partner's behalf in the event of sickness, taking sick leave to care for a partner, choosing a final resting place for a deceased partner, obtaining domestic violence protection orders, getting an equitable division of property in a divorce, or having joint child custody, among many other legal ramifications. Clearly such a couple loves and trusts each other as much as any heterosexual couple, so why should the members of that couple be denied these basic rights? I am talking here about a civil marriage, not a religious one. Most religious groups would maintain their right not to marry gay people, but should the states allow religious beliefs to keep gays from having their basic rights?

While no state allows gay marriages, Vermont permits *civil unions* for same-sex couples. According to the Vermont law, spouses in a civil union enjoy the same state law protections and responsibilities as do heterosexual spouses, so that they can be considered "legal next of kin." Same-sex couples who do not live in Vermont can enter into one of these civil unions, but how this union affects their civil rights in the state in which they live is not clear. As more gay couples enter these civil unions, test cases will certainly surface in other states when such couples try to claim these rights back at home. And the Vermont law also says that to divorce, one of the parties must live in Vermont for a year, so eventually that issue will also raise questions.

Prostitution: The Case for Legalization

Prostitution — sex for money — is known as the world's oldest profession. In ancient times, among the Jews, Greeks, and Romans, prostitution literally was a profession, meaning it was a legal way to earn a living. In some European countries, prostitution still is legal, and approximately two million prostitutes ply their trade illegally in America. In addition, illegal prostitution flourishes in many parts of Asia and Eastern Europe. Given the history and widespread use of prostitution, does continuing to keep it illegal make sense?

In my opinion, prostitution should be made legal everywhere in the United States, not just in Nevada. I held that opinion before the onset of AIDS, and now I believe in it even more.

Prostitutes can be major spreaders of sexually transmitted diseases. In the days when the big worry was syphilis, which was treatable, that was no big deal. But today, because AIDS has no cure, it is a very big deal. Society hasn't been able to put a stop to prostitution yet, so there really doesn't seem to be much hope that people will be able to stop it in the foreseeable future.

So what are the alternatives?

- ✔ Alternative one is to continue the current situation, where prostitution is illegal but continues to flourish and is a major contributor to the spread of AIDS.

- ✔ The other alternative is to legalize prostitution, control it, make sure that the prostitutes are as healthy as possible, try to keep them off drugs where they may share needles, and make sure that they or their partners use condoms.

A good many prostitutes — females and males — enter the field when they are under age. Often they are tricked into becoming prostitutes, and made to become drug addicts as well. I can't say that this particular aspect of prostitution would disappear if prostitution were legalized, but it would certainly be curtailed, and the people regulating the houses of prostitution would ensure that no minors were allowed to work there.

I admit that, even if prostitution is legalized, every prostitute won't be perfectly healthy, and some illegal prostitutes will still ply their trade — in other words, society won't be able to fully stop the spread of AIDS via the prostitute population. Although society won't be able to halt the spread of AIDS passed on by prostitutes, what if legalization cut it in half? Isn't that worth something?

Pornography: Erotic or Obscene

I can't begin to discuss this topic without defining what *pornography* is, and doing so is not easy because, to some degree, pornography is in the eye of the beholder. To get a handle on the word pornography, I need to bring in two other terms so that I can make a comparison. The first of these is *erotic*. To me, any work of art — a book, poem, painting, photograph, film, or video — that contains an element of sexuality is erotic. Now in my book, *The Art of Arousal*, I included some paintings that to me were erotic because of their overall content, but in which all the subjects were fully clothed. So you see, the notion of erotica has a very broad description.

Now some erotic material is stronger than others: It's more frank, with a greater element of sexuality, and it was made with the intention to arouse sexual feelings. That material is what I would call pornography. If that material steps over another boundary line, so that it is bizarre, brutal, and really shocking — and thus against the law — then I consider it obscene.

Obviously, one person will find certain pictures only erotic, another will believe them to be pornographic, and a third will see the pictures as obscene — which is why these terms do not come with hard-and-fast rules. What the U.S. courts have said is that the community must decide, and that decision has proven to be as difficult for the many as for the few.

What I consider obscene, and what governments should put a stop to, is any material in which the sex involves violence or children or animals. But I don't think that the government has any business banning a film because it shows two people having intercourse, oral sex, or anal sex.

Let me quickly add that I am talking about having these materials available for adults, and kept out of the hands of children. I don't like seeing all those magazine covers (that clearly show more than they cover) in a newsstand where children passing by can see them. And, if a video store wants to stock X-rated films, I believe the store should keep them behind a closed door, not just on one shelf where a young person can still see them.

Some people object to such material altogether, because they believe that it drives men to act out the fantasies that seeing these images creates. I disagree. In countries where pornography is legalized, such as Denmark and West Germany, the statistics for rape have not risen — and, because a larger percentage of women began to report rape, its overall occurrence may well have gone down.

Everyone needs a sexual outlet. In an ideal world, that outlet would come in the form of a spouse. But many people, for whatever reason, cannot find a permanent partner or even a series of irregular partners. That they end up taking their sexual frustrations out on others should not come as too big of a surprise. Given outlets for this sexual energy, these people end up having better control over themselves, and erotica assists greatly for one such outlet: masturbation.

Some feminists believe that, because pornography tends to feature women and make them sex objects, pornography is demeaning to women and devalues their worth. Certain images, be they visual or verbal, no doubt do demean women. And I would deem many of those images obscene. But I don't think, as a whole, that pornography hurts women in any significant way. One can certainly make the point that the latter half of the 20th century and beginning of the 21st century has seen both the spread of feminism and the spread of pornography. Although I am not saying that a direct correlation exists, I do believe that if society were to begin repressing one of those freedoms — in this case, the freedom to view pornography — doing so may well portend a return to the suppression of women as well.

Erotica does have its down side, however:

- Some of the women who perform in these films or pose for these pictures are being exploited. Maybe they have a drug habit to support or a child to feed. Although these women may deserve sympathy, I don't know that, if the sex industry were wiped out tomorrow, they would end up being better off.

- Some men become addicted to erotica. They abandon their wives in favor of videos, or they never marry in the first place because they can't tear themselves away from their stack of magazines. The question society has to ask is whether all people should have their rights to view such material squelched to protect the small percentage of people who abuse these materials.

My opinion is that society should not limit the majority, in this case, to "save" the minority. But if you disagree with me, that's fine. That difference of opinion is what makes this such a great country.

Adultery: Cheating the Law

Adultery occurs when at least one of the two people having sex together is married to someone else. Laws have historically banned such practice. In the 19th century, Nathaniel Hawthorne's novel *The Scarlet Letter* featured banishment and the wearing of a red letter "A" on the woman's dress as a punishment for adultery. Even today, some states continue to have laws against adultery. One of the reasons for originally banning adultery was that wealth was mostly passed on from generation to generation; playing around with the gene pool by having sexual relations with outsiders was not looked upon kindly.

Whether or not adultery should be a criminal act today, it certainly can have a negative impact on a marriage. Adultery is probably the single most-cited grounds for divorce. I am not one of those people who says that every marriage has to last forever, but it would be preferable if people would decide to end their marriage *before* having sex with other people. You do, after all, take a vow to be faithful. But I also know that adultery will never go away, whether it is against the law or not. People do fall out of love, for whatever reasons, and cheating is oftentimes easier than separating.

Strange sex laws

As you probably know, many sex laws have been on the books for ages and are never enforced. Nevertheless they are the law of the land, at least in that particular city or state. You should not take these laws seriously, but because they may bring a smile to your face, I thought I'd include a few that I found while surfing the Net.

✔ In Alexandria, Minnesota, no man is allowed to make love to his wife with the smell of garlic, onions, or sardines on his breath.

✔ In Hastings, Nebraska, no couple is allowed to sleep in the nude, and every hotel must supply its guests with clean, pressed nightshirts that must be worn even while having sex.

✔ In Newcastle, Wyoming, an ordinance bans couples from having sex while standing inside a walk-in meat freezer.

✔ In Bozeman, Montana, all sexual activity between members of the opposite sex is banned in the front yard of a home after sundown, if the people are nude.

✔ In Liberty Corner, New Jersey, lovers in a parked car who accidentally sound the horn face a jail term.

✔ In Coeur d'Alene, Idaho, police officers aren't allowed to investigate activities in a parked car until they drive up behind the car, honk the horn three times, and wait approximately three minutes before investigating.

Chapter 23

Keeping Children Safe

● ●

In This Chapter

▶ Playing doctor

▶ Answering questions about sex

▶ Understanding the importance of privacy

▶ Keeping your children safe from strangers

▶ Teaching your teenager about sex

▶ Protecting kids against cyberporn and X-rated videos

● ●

*W*hen I was a teenager living in an orphanage in Switzerland, one of my duties was taking care of the younger children. Later on, I worked as a kindergarten teacher in Paris, where I was surrounded by children all day long.

My doctorate is in the study of the family. I am the mother of two children and the grandmother of three. Needless to say, I love children, and making sure that they remain safe is a high priority of mine.

Although I can certainly give you some good advice on how to teach children to cross the street so as to minimize their danger or how to tie their shoelaces so they won't trip on them, you didn't buy this book for my expertise in those areas, did you? In this chapter, I tell you how to help keep children safe from the risks they face from sex.

Not Everything Is Dangerous

Let me begin with a situation that just about every parent faces (and many find embarrassing) but that poses little or no risk to the child. Even though children are not capable of having sex, their sexual organs are sources of pleasure to them. Some parents think that, if their child touches his or her own genitals or plays doctor with the kids next door, then the child is doing something harmful. This line of thinking couldn't be farther from the truth.

The reason that children touch themselves is simple: It feels good, just the way it feels good when adults touch their own genitals. So the idea that children would be curious about these good sensations and would try to duplicate them is perfectly natural. This process begins in the womb, where boys have erections and girls' vaginas lubricate, which should prove to you that this phenomenon is perfectly natural and can do children no harm. And you certainly can't stop children from doing these things while they are inside their mothers, nor can you say that they are behaving immorally, so you have no reason to stop them after they are born.

Because in our society anything to do with sex is kept private, adults do need to tell children that they shouldn't touch themselves in public. Children can understand this rule, just the way they learn that they are not allowed to pick their noses when they're out in society. But, in the same breath that you tell your children not to touch themselves in public, you have to reassure them that wanting to touch their own bodies is normal. If you overreact and don't reassure them, your children may think that they are doing something bad, and thinking of themselves or their bodies as bad can lead to sexual problems for your children later on. Chapter 17 discusses this subject in greater detail.

You should always call children's body parts by their real names, so that children learn the appropriate terms instead of family names which, though cute, may confuse them later on when other people use different words.

Teaching Proper Functioning as Well as Proper Etiquette

Remember, although keeping your children safe from sex abuse (a topic I get to later in this chapter) is important, you as a parent also must see to it that they function well as sexual beings. If your children get all sorts of hang-ups passed on to them from you, then those ideas will affect their sexual behavior throughout their lives.

If your children are ashamed of their bodies — if they feel guilty when they touch themselves — then those same feelings will not suddenly go away. If you weren't raised openly, then it is understandable that you may have difficulty being open with your children. But do make the effort, because the openness pays off in the long run. You probably have many good traits that you want to pass on to your children, but I hope you agree that making them sexually uptight shouldn't be on that list.

No Prescription Needed to Play Doctor

Although many parents buy children a toy doctor's kit, most don't do so in anticipation of what a doctor's visit really entails. Exposing body parts normally kept clothed and even touching these parts as they play doctor — also known as "I'll show you mine if you show me yours" — are common practices among children.

Basically, most children play doctor because they are naturally curious about each other's bodies. Under normal circumstances, no harm can come to children this way. If you discover children engaging in this activity, you do have to tell them to stop — not because their behavior is inherently bad, but because you don't want the other parents in the neighborhood to think you're running an illegal sex clinic in your basement. But don't tell them to stop in an angry way, as if they had been behaving badly. Just let them know that people have to respect one another's privacy and that they shouldn't engage in that kind of play anymore.

Although it's okay for children to experiment with their bodies through games, I do need to give you a few words of caution:

- ✔ Make sure that an older sibling doesn't take part in this play. That can change the dynamics, especially if the older child is heading toward puberty.

- ✔ Keep an eye out for how often children play these games. In most cases, this behavior is not a regular habit among children, like playing tag. Sometimes, however, one child tends to lead the others in such games again and again.

  Any young child who seems to be obsessed with sexual matters may have a problem. Perhaps some form of sexual abuse is going on in that child's home, or maybe the parents are just overstimulating the child in some way, but you don't want to have it affect your child negatively.

  If you find that the neighborhood children play doctor regularly, and especially if one child seems to be the instigator, find a way of stopping the activity. You may want to talk to the other parents, but certainly try to take your child out of this situation.

- ✔ One consequence of such games, or of little girls seeing their brothers naked, is that the daughter may feel that she is missing something — namely, a penis. Again, don't make a big issue out of this, but simply explain to her that boys and girls are built differently and that she is not missing anything; rather, she is constructed just the way Mommy is and is perfect just the way she is.

Answering Children's Questions

If you're a parent, or if you hang around kids long enough, at some point you will be asked a question pertaining to sex. Many adults panic when confronted with such questions. Right away, they think that they're going to have to explain the whole scenario, and they're just not ready to do that.

My first word of advice is to relax. In all probability, the answer the child is looking for is something very simple. You should answer honestly, but give only one piece of information at a time and see if that satisfies the child. If children are too young, they're not ready to hear the whole explanation of the birds and the bees, so don't rush into it without first ascertaining exactly what kind of answer they want.

Little Jimmy

Little Jimmy was five and had just started school two months ago. One day, he came home and asked his mother this question: "This girl in my class, Kim, said that she was different from me. How is she different from me?"

Jimmy's mom jumped to the conclusion that this was one of those questions that she'd always dreaded. She sat Jimmy down and spent ten minutes telling him the differences between boys and girls. When she finished, she gave a deep sigh, hoping that she had answered his question. She asked him if he wanted to know anything else.

"Yes, Mom. Kim said she was Chinese. What does that mean?"

As you can see, Jimmy's mother could have saved herself having to give that particular lesson if she had asked her son some more questions before starting in. And, although it certainly did Jimmy no harm to hear her explanation of what makes boys different from girls, that wasn't his question. He probably didn't pay all that much attention to what she was saying, because he wasn't hearing the information he was seeking.

One day, the question your child asks will be about sex, and then you have to be prepared to answer it. One recommendation that I can give you to make this situation a little bit easier is to buy a children's book on sexuality ahead of time and get it out when the time comes. Then you can be prepared if your child really does want to know, or need to know, the answers to some questions having to do with sex.

You may be wondering why I said "need to know." I wasn't referring to something actually having to do with sex, at least not yet. Sometimes your child may be hearing things that he or she finds frightening from other, possibly older, children. You have to be ready, in those situations, to give your child a full lesson so that he or she understands that there's nothing to be frightened of.

Having a book to look at together makes teaching your child about sexuality a lot less embarrassing for both of you. You can read the parts that embarrass you, rather than having to stumble around in your own words. And the book will probably have pictures or drawings to help you.

After you've given your lesson, leave the book out so that your child can look at it on his or her own. I wrote a book for 8- to 12-year-olds titled *Dr. Ruth Talks to Kids*. One of the first things I say in that book is that children should be allowed to take the material into their rooms, close their doors, and read it in private. Just the way that adults need privacy when it comes to sexual matters, so do kids. And you have to respect that privacy.

Personal Privacy

Teaching your children about privacy is critical. Make sure that all your children understand that, not only are they allowed to maintain their privacy at home, but they absolutely must maintain it outside the home, especially when around strangers. Now you don't want to frighten your children, but you do have to make sure that they understand that, unless Mommy or Daddy says it's okay (such as when the child goes to the doctor), no one is allowed to touch their private parts. The fact that child molesters are out there is very sad, but they do exist, and you have to teach your children to be extra careful.

Now, if you listen to the media, child molestation seems to be rampant. I've read estimates that say that as many as 40 percent of all children are sexually abused in some way. Let me start on this topic by saying *calm down*. Child molestation certainly exists, and you must do all that you can to protect your children, but common sense and my own experiences as a sex therapist tell me that it does not go on as much as all that.

Because children will try to give answers that they think adults want to hear, I don't know whether we can ever get a scientifically valid survey as to how much child abuse really exists. I do believe that the pendulum has swung too far in the direction of identifying child abuse. These days, things have gone so far that, if a little girl falls down and starts to cry in a playground, the father of another child may hesitate to help the girl because he fears that he may be accused of child abuse. Society has to bring back a little sanity to this situation, because paranoia isn't good for people's mental health either.

Warning Signs of Possible Sexual Abuse

Although I believe that the percentages are much lower than proclaimed, child abuse certainly does exist and, as a parent or guardian, you have a duty to protect your child. A report issued by the Sexuality Information and Education Council of the United States (SIECUS), on whose board I used to sit, gives certain guidelines that I want to pass on to you. You should watch for the following behaviors to see if a child under your care is enduring sexual abuse:

✔ The child focuses on sexuality to a greater extent than on other aspects of his or her environment, and/or has more sexual knowledge than similar-aged children with similar backgrounds who live in the same area. A child's sexual interest should be in balance with his or her curiosity about, and explanation of, other aspects of his or her life.

✔ The child has an ongoing, compulsive interest in sexual or sexually related activities and/or is more interested in engaging in sexual behaviors than in playing with friends, going to school, and doing other developmentally appropriate activities.

✔ The child engages in sexual behaviors with those who are much older or younger. Most school-aged children engage in sexual behaviors with children within a year or so of their age. In general, the wider the age range between children engaging in sexual behavior, the greater the concern.

✔ The child continues to ask unfamiliar children, or children who are uninterested, to engage in sexual activities. Healthy and natural sexual play usually occurs between friends and playmates.

✔ The child, or a group of children, bribes or emotionally and/or physically forces another child/children of any age into sexual behaviors.

✔ The child exhibits confusion or distorted ideas about the rights of others in regard to sexual behaviors. The child may contend: "She wanted it" or "I can touch him if I want to."

✔ The child tries to manipulate children or adults into touching his or her genitals or causes physical harm to his or her own or others' genitals.

✔ Other children repeatedly complain about the child's sexual behaviors — especially when an adult has already spoken to the child.

✔ The child continues to behave in sexual ways in front of adults who say "no," or the child does not seem to comprehend admonitions to curtail overt sexual behaviors in public places.

✔ The child appears anxious, tense, angry, or fearful when sexual topics arise in his or her everyday life.

- The child manifests a number of disturbing behaviors having to do with toilet habits: plays with or smears feces, urinates outside the bathroom, uses excessive amounts of toilet paper, stuffs toilet bowls to overflowing, or sniffs or steals underwear.

- The child's drawings depict genitals as the predominant feature.

- The child manually stimulates or has oral or genital contact with animals.

- The child has painful and/or continuous erections or vaginal discharge.

If you discover that your child is showing any of the above signs, consult a professional — starting with your pediatrician — to find out whether or not a problem exists. Don't try to confront this situation by yourself. Even an expert may have difficulty trying to discover the truth when dealing with a child, and any efforts on your part may only frighten the child so that you will never find out whether anything is wrong.

The Accidental Voyeur

I don't want you to worry about the time your child accidentally catches you making love. This situation happens to plenty of couples, and, if you don't make a big deal of it, the child will probably not realize what was going on, and there will be no consequences whatsoever.

The danger to children comes not from an accident, but from repeatedly seeing material not suited to their age. You certainly know that, if you show a small child a horror movie, that child will have nightmares. Well, if you let children watch shows that have a high sexual content, they may have the equivalent to a nightmare, only, instead of scaring them, it may play havoc with their libidos.

Knowing that Mommy and Daddy love each other is important for children. If you and your spouse kiss and hug in front of your child regularly then, if someday your child does catch you having sex, he or she won't connect it with something terrible — even though the noises adults can make while engaged in sex can frighten a child.

Again, although no great harm can come to a child from catching you "in the act," a very cheap method of protection is available — the eye-and-hook lock. You can purchase such a device for less than a dollar, and, if you remember to lock it when you make love, you can save yourself some embarrassment, if nothing else.

Protecting Your Children from the Media

A report issued by the Sexuality Information and Education Council of the United States noted that professionals, meaning counselors and teachers, find that children demonstrate sexual behavior much more frequently now than they ever did before. The reason for this is simple: Children today see so much more sex in the media.

Although, as an adult, you may welcome the fact that television has become more open about sexual matters and that you can rent R- and X-rated films to watch in the privacy of your home, seeing this type of material will overstimulate your child. Just watching the soap operas with your kids is enough to make them lose the innocence that they deserve. Children do imitate the behavior of adults they see, and, if they see sexual situations, they will try to copy them. Because children do have sexual feelings, some of these behaviors can have direct consequences, so that a child may start to play with his or her genitals on a regular basis because that child has been overstimulated.

By letting children see sexual material regularly, you also put them at risk if they do come in contact with someone who is looking to take advantage of them. If a child sees people on TV having sex — and I don't mean anything more than the type of scenes soaps show all the time — then, if some adult proposes that that child do something similar, he or she will not be frightened but may accept this behavior as normal.

You can do several things to protect your child, although the most important is to keep a careful eye over what your child watches.

- ✔ Keep any tapes that may be inappropriate to children out of their reach. Don't leave these videos out along with the rest of the tapes. Do the same with other erotic material, including magazines and books.

- ✔ When going to the video store to rent movies, be strict about the Motion Picture Association of America (MPAA) ratings. Kids may plead with you, but show them the rating on the box and don't give in, because, after you do, going backwards will prove very hard.

- ✔ Most cable companies offer ways that you can lock out certain channels that carry material not suited to children. Call your cable company and find out what you can do.

- ✔ Children shouldn't watch too much television in the first place, but certainly not late at night when adult programming is on. If you have a child who won't sleep, the last thing you should do is let that child come into your bed and watch TV with you. You'll not only be encouraging your child not to develop proper sleep habits, but you may be overstimulating him or her as well.

✔ Try not to let your children watch the news. Oftentimes the news carries stories inappropriate for children. Because the topics switch rapidly, inappropriate stories may come on before you realize it.

✔ If you use baby-sitters, give them specific instructions concerning what shows your child can and cannot watch. Tell your child these rules, and afterward, ask your child whether he or she watched any forbidden shows. Little children are not likely to lie about such things.

✔ If you have children of a broad age range, make sure that the older children don't watch inappropriate shows around their younger siblings.

I know how easy using the television as a baby-sitter is, especially in this day and age when both parents work. I'm not saying not to do it, but just take every precaution you can. This is even more important if your children fall into the category of "latch-key kids" — that is to say, they are alone from the time they come home from school to when a parent returns home. If inappropriate material is around, the temptation to watch it may be strong. So, if you have such material in your home, make sure that you take the time to remove it or put it under lock and key.

Protecting Your Children from Cyberporn: Good News and Bad News

Kids are certainly smarter than adults are about computers: That's the bad news. The good news is that, recently, all the major commercial online computer services, many adult bulletin board systems, and now even the Internet, started providing tools for parental control. With varying degrees, they let you surf for what you want without worrying too much about whether your kids can also find the material.

Educating your kids

But, as always, common sense prevails: Tell your kids that the same rules they use when walking down a street (see "Giving the Speech about Strangers" later in this chapter) apply when they surf the Net. The National Center for Missing and Exploited Children (1-800-843-5678) has an excellent pamphlet, *Child Safety on the Information Highway,* which lists some good guidelines:

✔ Set guidelines for how your child uses the computer and discuss those guidelines with your child.

✔ Don't let your child give out personal information, such as address, phone number, or school name, online.

✔ Don't let your child arrange for online meetings with a stranger or send his or her photograph.

✔ Tell your children to come to you *immediately* if someone sends them messages that they don't like.

Controlling kids' access

Allowing adults access to a wide range of material while protecting children from it has thankfully become a priority for online companies and users. The commercial online services, as well as the Internet, have several ways of protecting curious young minds from getting inappropriate materials. To get the latest information, I suggest you visit GetNetWise.com. This site is provided as a public service by the Internet industry, both corporations and public interest organizations. The companies involved in this site read like a laundry list of the top Web names, including America Online (AOL), AT&T, Disney, Microsoft, Yahoo!, and so on. On this site you can find search engines for kids that do not bring up unwanted sites, free downloadable filtering software, and information about kid-safe browsers.

Dozens of software filters are now available, and GetNetWise.com can lead you to the one that has the features you want. You can get similar information at www.safekids.com.

No matter how safe you make your home computer, your child may have access to other computers that do not have such filters. While elementary schools may well install these features, public libraries usually do not because they would block adults using them, which raises free speech issues. And, of course, your child's friends' computers may not have the same safeguards as the one in your home does. So be sure to include other accessible computers when setting the rules for your children.

Giving the Speech about Strangers

Parents now have two speeches to give to their children. The first is how to handle strangers and the second is about sex. The tricky part about the first speech is that you want your children to recognize the dangers posed by strangers, without being so scared that they won't leave your side.

I suggest that you give the speech about strangers in pieces and repeat it often. Kids don't really comprehend too much new material at one time, and they usually must hear it more than once for it to sink in. Also, children can grasp more mature concepts as they get older. Although saying "Don't accept candy from a stranger" may be enough for a four- or five-year-old, a slightly older child has to be told that it isn't just candy that he or she should turn down, but also any favor, including money or a ride home from school.

Telling kids to tell an adult

As important as telling children what they shouldn't do is telling them what they *should* do if a stranger approaches them improperly, which is to run away and immediately tell an adult. I think the first part, not doing certain things, is easier for a child than the second part. Why? Because if they experience sexual abuse, kids will often put it out of their minds or, if they sense that they may have done something bad, actually try to hide it from you.

Because you want your children to tell you about *anything,* you must be very careful to let them know that you will not punish them if they report that something occurred. Passing this reassurance along is not easy, and, once again, I think that the best way to do it is to repeat the message several times until you are relatively sure that your child does understand.

If a child does report something out of the ordinary to you, don't overreact. The child will sense that something is wrong, and that may shut off communication at a time when you need your child to tell you as much as he or she can. Try to remain calm and matter-of-fact while you dig for information.

Organizing with other parents

Having a network set up *before* trouble happens rather than waiting until afterward is always better, which is why I recommend that you organize with other parents and nonparents on your block right now. Again, this is not an issue to get hysterical about — a child abuser is not hiding under every rock — but being prepared in case one does show up is certainly a good idea.

The organization you set up can be quite simple. It can consist of one meeting at which everybody agrees to watch out for each other's children, and you put together a list of names and phone numbers. The most important aspect of this organization is that, if any adult on the block sees something going on with your child which he or she thinks may be suspicious, that adult will know, ahead of time, that he or she has your permission to investigate.

That Other Discussion — Sex Ed and the Older Child

Throughout this chapter, I give you some ideas about how to handle the-birds-and-the-bees discussion with little children, but that heart-to-heart talk gets a lot more complicated with older children. Many parents slough it off and hope for the best, but in this era of AIDS, doing so is a risky maneuver. Yes, your child will probably be told some things about AIDS and other sex-related topics at school, but will that information be enough?

In my opinion, sex is a topic that parents and schools should handle together, with active participation by both groups. School teachers are better equipped to actually teach the material, because they are professional educators, and you are probably not, but injecting the moral message, which is an important component, is the parents' responsibility.

I think that schools should notify parents when they teach these particular topics and send home some sort of questionnaire for the parents to fill out, sign, and return to the school. This form would require that the parents ask their children certain questions to make sure that they understood the lesson. Part of the process should include a discussion between the parents and the child, during which the parents can add their moral guidance. Both parents should participate in this discussion, if possible, and they should make a vow ahead of time to keep the tone of the discussion as calm as possible so that tempers don't flare, which can happen with teenagers.

Contrary to what many people believe, recent polls have shown that as a whole parents do want their children to be told explicit information in school. AIDS has worried all parents, and most realize that the best protection they can offer their children is correct information. However, if a particular school system is not doing an adequate job, then parents must take a larger share of the responsibility.

Knowing doesn't equal doing

The biggest worry that some parents have expressed about sex education is that, if they acknowledge to their teens that sex does exist, and if they go over safer sex practices with them, then they will be giving the message that having premarital sex is okay. That fear is groundless if you, as a parent, take charge of the situation. If you tell your teen in no uncertain terms that you do not approve of premarital sex, then your teen will not get mixed signals.

If you don't buy that idea, think of some other examples. How many fathers have taken their sons aside and taught them how to box, throwing punches while protecting themselves with their other hand? When the father does that, does he expect the child to march next door and get into a fight with the kid who lives there? Of course not, he just wants him to be prepared. Or, if a mother gives her daughter ten dollars before she goes out on a date so that she can take a cab home if the boy gets fresh, does she expect that to happen?

I don't believe in giving percentages, so I won't here, but I do know that many teens engage in sex. Therefore, letting your child go out into the world, possibly not sure of what constitutes safer sex, is much riskier than telling that child the facts about sex.

I don't believe in scare tactics, either, because I know that they don't work. During World War II, the army showed recruits films about venereal diseases that should have scared the pants *on* them, but did it work? No. If a soldier had the chance to visit a prostitute, he never gave those films a thought.

The libido is very strong, and, if two young people fall in love, their relationship may lead to sex. You can slow the process down, but, if sex is going to happen, you can't stop it. You can't be there every second. Because of this fact, your job as a parent includes making sure that your child understands safer sex procedures.

To give or not to give condoms

Some parents take their responsibilities so seriously that they make sure that their teens, particularly boys, know where condoms are kept in the house. Because no parent can resist the temptation of counting those condoms from time to time, you must be prepared to accept your child's sexual life if you adopt this policy.

If you know yourself well enough and are sure that you will stick your nose into the situation as soon as those condoms start disappearing, then maybe you'd better not play drugstore. Condoms are easy to buy these days, but your child's trust is not. If your child thinks that the only reason you stored those condoms was to catch him or her using them, then you may seriously damage your relationship with that child.

Other Messages You Don't Want to Send

You communicate to your child in many ways, and that communication always has an effect, even if you don't realize it. So watch what you do and say in front of your children. Let me give you some examples:

Daddy and Debbie

When Debbie was a little girl, she was always sitting on her Daddy's lap, giving him hugs and kisses, and he loved it. Then when she started showing signs of becoming a woman — when her breasts started to develop and the rest of her figure filled out — Daddy withdrew all these physical signs of affection. He decided that they were inappropriate and began treating Debbie as if she were just another woman and not his little girl.

Debbie felt really hurt when that happened. She didn't understand why Daddy was rejecting her. She felt that she had done something wrong and, to make up for that, she looked for someone else who would make her feel good the way Daddy used to — and she quickly found a boy who satisfied those urges.

Some girls react the way Debbie did if their fathers suddenly pull away from them during puberty. Others think of their new bodies as ugly, because Daddy rejected them, and they crawl into a shell. Neither reaction is good, and that's why dads have to be careful how they treat their daughters.

Billy's case shows how some parents may fail to acknowledge their children's individuality.

Dad and Billy

Billy's Dad had never dated much in high school. He ended up marrying the first serious girlfriend he had in college, and she was the only woman he ever had sex with. Although he loved his wife, he often had regrets that he hadn't had more lovers.

Dad and Billy were always close, playing sports together or watching games. When Billy started dating, Dad began to live vicariously through his son. He would admire the girls that Billy brought around, and he would encourage Billy to have sex with them by making various comments like, "Boy, she looks like she's good in bed."

Billy may not have had sex with these early girlfriends, but from the way his father was talking, it appeared as if he was supposed to, and so that's exactly what he did. But he resented his father for it. The closeness that the two shared started to disappear, because Billy didn't want his Dad even to know when he was dating someone, and he especially didn't want to bring those dates around the house.

Parents can make all kinds of mistakes, but they may not realize the seriousness of the mistakes having to do with sex. Try to analyze your behavior around your children from their point of view. If you don't like what you see from their perspective, then try to change your ways. If you have difficulties doing this but suspect that you may be making some mistakes, go out and get some books that cover the areas where you have some concern.

Remember, although sex makes it easy to become parents, it does not make us experts at parenting. But you can discover how to be a better parent, and doing so is definitely worth the effort.

Part VI
The Part of Tens

The 5th Wave   By Rich Tennant

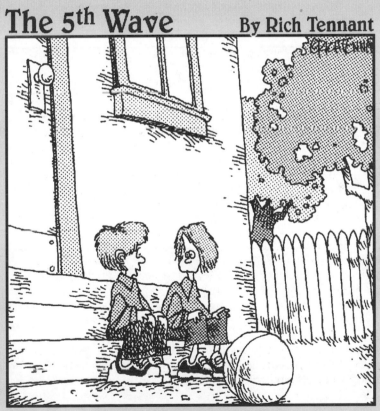

"I KNOW WHAT A ROMANTIC GETAWAY IS. IT'S WHEN MY PARENTS TELL ME TO GET AWAY FROM THE HOUSE FOR A FEW HOURS."

In this part . . .

In the Jewish tradition, the number 18, which stands for life, is considered to be a lucky number. But my good friend John Kilcullen at IDG Books seems to be more attached to the number 10. Maybe it makes him think of Bo Derek. Well, I liked that movie, too, because Dudley Moore is short like me. So you see, it's all in your outlook. And if there's one thing that I hope you've gotten out of this book, it's to look at the bright side of life. *L'chaim*.

Chapter 24

Ten Dumb Things People Believe about Sex

. . . .

In This Chapter

▶ Hanging on to your virginity

▶ Knowing that more isn't always better

▶ Understanding that heterosexuals can get AIDS

▶ Comparing partners

▶ Becoming a better lover

. . . .

The key to good sexual functioning is to be sexually literate, and one important way of earning your master's degree in sexual literacy is to do a little housecleaning upstairs and sweep away any sexual myths that have been hiding in the corners of your brain.

Many people still believe some very dumb things about sex, so don't be surprised if you find some of these damaging concepts lurking about your brain cells. And some of these ideas aren't that easy to get rid of, either. So telling yourself only once not to believe any of these falsehoods isn't enough; you have to maintain a steady vigilance to make sure that they don't come creeping back. You may get used to relying on a crutch belief such as "I can't become a better lover," but you have to develop the reflex of throwing that belief away each and every time it pops back into your brain. Anyone can become a better lover. But you have to work at it.

If I Haven't Had Sex by the Time I'm 18, I'm a Loser

When you're 85 years old and you look back at your life, the age at which you first had sex will be absolutely irrelevant. You won't care, and neither will anybody else. But for many 18-year-olds, or 22-year-olds, or 25-year-olds who are still virgins, the weight of this sexual status seems to grow heavier by the hour. Somehow, they feel that the fact that they've never had sex is written across their foreheads for all to see, and that everyone is laughing at them.

If you're in this category, please don't put any added pressure on yourself. If you feel sexually frustrated, you can masturbate. Be grateful that you can give yourself orgasms rather than resenting the fact that someone else isn't doing it for you.

Now, if you don't have a significant other and you feel lonely, then finding a partner is a goal worth going after. And then, if you do find someone to love, having sex may become a realistic possibility. But you may be just as happy waiting to have sex with that person until you get married. That decision's up to you.

Remember, many people start having sex when they're very young, but because the situation isn't right, they never discover how to become great lovers and never have terrific sex lives. Rather than rushing into sex just because you reach a certain age, find out how to give your feelings time to grow and develop. You're better off if you wait to have sex until the time is right and the person with whom you have sex is right.

The More I Score, the More Pleasure I'll Have

I am not one of those who say that you should absolutely never have a one-night stand. In some instances, the chemistry between two people is very strong, the opportunity is perfect, and passing up such a moment is very hard. If you are very careful about protecting yourself, and if you are fully aware of the risks involved, then a one-night stand may be something that you indulge in once, or maybe twice.

But some people make one-night stands a part of their lifestyles. For these people, variety is the spice of life. They don't want a relationship but prefer a string of sexual partners. To them, quantity, not quality, makes the best sex.

If you're one of those people who think that more sex is better than good sex, all I can say is that this attitude is dumb, dumb, and dumb.

In the new millennium, with AIDS spreading and other sexually transmitted diseases already rampant, if you multiply the risks by multiplying your partners, you are asking for trouble. Safe sex between two people simply doesn't exist — only safer sex. Although you may not catch an STD the first time you have a one-night stand (or maybe not even the second or third time), each time you have one, you increase the odds — in particular, because those people with whom you have these one-night stands are obviously also prone to risky behavior. So if you have one-night stands again and again, at some point, you will come out a loser.

And what if you're a woman and a mistake happens and you wind up pregnant? What kind of support do you think you will get from someone you barely know?

Apart from the risks, one-night stands just do not make for the best sex. What makes having sex with another person better than masturbating is the intimacy, the shared feelings, the romance attached to the moment. None of these circumstances exists during a one-night stand.

And then you have to deal with the next morning. Was it the first of a long string of sexual encounters, or a one-time affair? If you want to see the other party again and they'd rather not, imagine how much worse the feeling of rejection will be than if they'd said no in the first place. And if you're the one doing the rejecting, well, how good an experience can the one-night stand have been if you never want to repeat it?

Putting another notch on your bedpost is not as satisfying as exchanging the full range of emotions that pass between two people who make love.

Being a Heterosexual Makes Me Immune to AIDS

Because, in the United States, the AIDS epidemic struck the gay community first, many straight people refuse to admit that they can catch this deadly disease. They think that they can engage in unprotected sex without suffering any consequences. Well, guess what? That's just not true.

In Africa, where AIDS is the most widespread, the disease primarily affects heterosexuals. And the fastest growing rate of AIDS in Western countries is among heterosexuals, not homosexuals. The pool of heterosexuals who have AIDS grows every day and, therefore, so do the risks to every other heterosexual.

Your sexual preference does not make you immune to this killer disease. At the moment, nothing does. Therefore, you have to protect yourself and always follow safer sex practices. (Chapter 19 discusses sexually transmitted diseases, including AIDS, in detail. If you're guilty of overlooking the threat of AIDS, then I insist you read that chapter!)

Believing that AIDS can happen only to gays is a prejudice that can cost you your life.

The Grass Is Always Greener in the Neighbors' Bedroom

Some people think that they're missing out by staying within the bounds of marriage. When it comes to having an affair, these people believe that the grass is greener in the next pasture. Although sexual boredom is certainly something to watch out for in your own life, maybe you ought to remove those green-colored glasses when looking over the neighbor's fence.

Sex is pervasive in the media these days. On TV and in newspaper and magazine articles, you can discover exactly what's going on under everyone else's covers if you believe all the reports, especially those that draw their conclusions from surveys of one kind or another. And if the activities in your bedroom don't appear to measure up with what you see or hear, then you become dissatisfied with what had been a satisfying sex life.

My advice to you is to take all the information that people throw your way with a grain of salt. When people answer all those questionnaires, do you really believe that they tell the truth? Would you be completely honest, or would you exaggerate a bit?

In my opinion, most people exaggerate. So when you read how often people are having sex, or how many partners they've had, or any of the other statistics that float around, and then look at your own life, yours may seem inadequate. But if those numbers are all inflated, then you're really not losing out, are you?

Stop paying attention to what everybody else is supposedly doing and concentrate on how to make the best of what you already have. Most people can improve their sex lives, and I am certainly an advocate of that. But if you try to make those improvements only because you want to keep up with the Joneses, then you'll only be setting yourself up for disappointment. (Besides, the Joneses may be trying to keep up with YOU!)

Having Sex Will Make Everything All Right

Sex is not a cure for a lousy relationship. That fact may seem obvious to some of you, but many people, particularly women, don't seem to know this. A woman may be in a relationship with someone who mistreats her, and, instead of running for the hills, she agrees to go one step further along and have sex with him. Why? She thinks that, because sex is what he seems to want so badly, he'll change into a pussycat after he's had his way with her. In some cases, both partners get some pleasure out of this sex; in others, only one. But sex is not enough to hold together a relationship, no matter how good it feels.

This idea is a prime example of putting the cart before the horse. You have to work on the relationship — build it up and make it into something worth sharing together — before you add the final ingredient, which is sex.

Sex is like the whipped cream you put on an ice cream sundae. Without the ice cream to hold it up, the whipped cream alone is not satisfying. But mixed in with the rest of the ingredients, that whipped cream tastes absolutely delicious.

Sex by itself cannot make up for all the other inadequacies of a relationship, so before you have sex with someone, build the foundation first.

A Good Lover Must Be an Open Book

When you first meet somebody, you probably try to sweep parts of yourself under the carpet. If you have pimples, you cover them with a cream. If you have bad breath, you suck on a mint. If you're a slob, hopefully you put on some nice clothes.

If the two of you hit it off, slowly but surely you begin to peel away the layers and reveal your true selves. Part of that revelation certainly takes place if you have sex together. Other aspects of your personality that you reveal have nothing to do with sex but are just as important, or more so, as far as letting the other person know who you really are.

This process is wonderful and vital to building a relationship, but you can also take it too far.

- ✔ If you love the other person, but you think that his nose is too big, there's no point in telling him that again and again, or even once.

- ✔ If, when you're making love, you fantasize that you're actually in the arms of Sharon Stone or Harrison Ford, don't tell your partner that, either. The information serves no purpose other than to hurt your partner.

- ✔ And if you've always fancied making love in the center ring of the circus but your partner is a prude, then don't bother revealing this side of yourself. If you do, it can only lead to your partner thinking less of you.

Yes, you should be as honest as you can with your partner, especially if you are married to him or her. But honesty is not the best policy if all that it accomplishes is to cause pain to the one you love.

I Should Always Compare Sexual Partners

I can understand comparing certain things. If you compare two restaurants, for example, and you decide that you like one more than the other, then the next time you go out, you can go back to the one you prefer. The same goes if you visit different places on vacation or decide between two pairs of shoes.

But comparing partners, sexually that is, can be a lose/lose situation. Now I'm not talking about comparing two people from whom you intend to choose. I mean when you have developed a relationship with someone, you enjoy each other's company, and you end up becoming lovers. If, at that point, you begin to compare the way this person makes love to the way your previous partner did it, you're asking for trouble.

Although sexual feelings can be very strong, they are at the same time very fragile. For example, if a man worries about whether or not he can get an erection, he probably won't be able to get one. Or if a woman starts to think, "When is my orgasm going to come?," it probably never will.

You see, although you may think that your sexual feelings happen only between your belly and your knees, in fact, they are right at the top of your body, between your ears. And that means that it's easy to distract your mind from the business at hand.

So if you start the comparison process — even if your new lover comes out on top and proves to be the better lover — the fact that you're busy comparing instead of letting your mind go and partaking of the pleasure of the moment lessens your enjoyment.

So play down those urges to compare lovers and keep your mind focused on what's happening to your body right then and there.

I Can't Become a Better Lover

If you ever read the life story of someone at the top of their field — a professional athlete, a famous actor, a great artist — you always find that those individuals worked very hard to get where they are. Sure, natural talent has something to do with how good you are, but seeking to improve your skills is just as important, because the more effort you put into being good at an art, the better you become.

This idea is just as true with sex. Everyone can become a better lover. Some of the most common difficulties that people experience can be easily alleviated. I get asked two questions more than any others:

✔ Men frequently ask me what to do if they are premature ejaculators. I say, because this condition is only a learning difficulty, any man who puts his mind to it can eradicate the problem. And if he does this in partnership with his significant other, the process will be that much easier. (See Chapter 20 for more on the topic of premature ejaculation.)

✔ Among women, the most common problem I see is the inability to have an orgasm. Here again, the vast majority of women suffering from this problem are really only _pre-orgasmic,_ which means that they definitely can teach themselves how to have orgasms and can then pass on that information to their partners. (See Chapter 21 for more on the topic of being pre-orgasmic.)

The old saying "never say never" applies to sex as well.

Lovers Are Like Siamese Twins

He likes chocolate; she likes vanilla. She loves fish; he adores burgers. She loves the opera; he falls asleep in his seat. Yes, you and your lover probably have some tastes in common, but certainly not in everything. And why should you?

Naturally, this notion goes for sex, too. Although I'm sure that you both enjoy orgasms, how many you need in a particular period may well vary, as well as your likes and dislikes for the methods you use to have those orgasms.

If you accept that you are different, and if you agree to make compromises, then you shouldn't have any problems adapting to each other. One of the skills you may have to learn is how to satisfy your partner when you're not interested in having an orgasm. But learning that skill is not that difficult, and doing so can help make your relationship a lot better.

However, having unrealistic expectations can get you into trouble. So don't expect your partner to be your Siamese twin. You'll be a lot happier for it.

I'm Too Old to Have Sex

Human beings find that many of their faculties grow weaker as they grow older, but none that so many people give up on as easily as sex.

If your eyesight gets weaker, do you give up reading and watching TV, or do you run to the eye doctor to get glasses, or at least a stronger prescription? If your hearing becomes impaired, do you go around saying "What?" all day long, or do you get a hearing aid? If you have trouble walking, you can get your hip replaced, or at least use a cane to get around. So if your sexual apparatus diminishes, why would you give up on it entirely?

That sexual functioning declines with age is a given, but that it disappears altogether is most definitely not. As you grow older, you go through certain stages, which are different for men and women. Men lose their ability to have psychogenic erections and need their partners to stimulate their penises. Some older men lose even that ability, but now with drugs such as Viagra, they have another solution. Women stop producing natural lubricants and have to apply the store-bought variety. (You can find out more about these changes in Chapter 14.)

If wearing glasses doesn't interfere with your enjoyment of reading a book, then adapting to the necessities of age when it comes to sex shouldn't be that big of a deal either, as long as you don't make an issue out of it. And certainly you should never give up on this most enjoyable aspect of life.

Keep having sex as long as you physically can, and sex will help keep your life worth living.

Chapter 25

Ten Tips for Safer Sex

There are no absolute guarantees when it comes to having safe sex between two people, but you can enjoy saf*er* sex if you're careful to follow the guidelines that the experts have developed.

If you can't remember the following ten tips, then write them down with a felt marker on your wrist every time you're in a situation where you may have sex. Do this until the time comes that they're indelibly etched in your brain — right next to the spot where the law of always backing up your computer files sits.

Learn to Say No

No one ever died from sexual frustration, but you can't say the same thing about sexually transmitted diseases.

Just because you haven't had sex in a long time and the opportunity presents itself doesn't mean that you should give in to those urges. The less you know about a person, the greater the likelihood that he or she can infect you with a disease. So learn to say no to casual sex.

Yes, you can try to protect yourself, but you have no 100-percent sure way of doing that. Considering that I'm talking about your life here. Isn't it worth being cautious?

Limit Your Number of Partners

Have you ever seen the trick that the clowns do in the circus with the little car? The car drives around the main ring, looking like it has barely enough room for one person inside; the next thing you know, 25 clowns, big feet and all, come pouring out. Well, you have to conjure up that exact image when you look at a potential partner. The more sexual partners a person has had, the more trouble that spells for you.

When you have sex with someone, not just the two of you are in the bed. Hiding under the covers is every partner with whom that person has ever had sex, and the partners of those partners. Although you may not be able to see their large red noses glowing in the dark, you can be sure that any viruses that they may have left behind inside the warm, naked body presently in your bed are making a bee-line for any openings in your body.

To a virus, you're nothing more than a host — the perfect place to reproduce and multiply — and if the process destroys you, well, all I can say is that their consciences aren't as well developed as their ability to reproduce.

Don't Rely Solely on Your Instincts

Some people have honesty written all over their faces. You just know that if you lend them your car, you'll get it back exactly at the time they say they'll bring it back. But what if they have a split personality, and the half of them who's the thief takes off with your car for parts unknown? You trusted your instincts and you got burned, that's what.

The problem with trusting your instincts when it comes to sexually transmitted diseases is that many people out there really believe that they are disease-free when, in fact, they are not. Some sexually transmitted diseases invade a host's body and cause absolutely no symptoms, so when these people tell you they've never had any diseases, they give the appearance of being absolutely honest, because they *are* being absolutely honest. The difficulty that your never-failing instincts face in such a situation is that these people's honesty isn't worth a hoot. They have a dark side that they are unaware of having. They truly believe that they can't infect you, but in fact they truly can.

When dealing with sexually transmitted diseases, it's much better to be safe than sorry. Instead of trusting your instincts, put your faith in the rules of safer sex. In the long run, you won't regret it.

Never Dull Your Senses When You're with Strangers

I often recommend to people that they have a glass of wine or two to help loosen them up, which can then lead to better sex. But that suggestion only applies when the two people involved are already a couple. In certain situations, any dulling of the senses caused by alcohol or drugs can prove very dangerous.

Many people have wound up having sex because they were high, under circumstances that they would never have said yes to had they been sober. If you're in your local pub with a few friends and you have a few beers too many, the likelihood of the situation turning into a sexual scene is slight. But if you get invited to a party at somebody's house and you don't know the host that well or many of the guests, and you then start to imbibe too much, you may regret the consequences.

If a bedroom is just down the hall, you may well find yourself in it, with your clothes off and somebody doing some very intimate things with you. Under such circumstances, you will not be thinking safer sex, assuming you're capable of thinking at all. And the same goes for the person you're with, too.

To practice safer sex you have to be responsible. And to be responsible, you have to have all, or at least most, of your faculties operating. So if the situation calls for keeping your wits about you, order a soft drink — or one of those nonalcoholic beers, if you don't want anybody to realize that you intend to remain sober.

Discuss Safer Sex in Advance

If you're dating someone and the relationship is moving forward, don't wait to talk about safer sex. The closer you get to the point where having sex is just on the horizon, the harder delaying going ahead will be.

Certainly, if you already have your clothes off, it's far too late to suddenly think about safer sex. But I believe that you should have that safer sex discussion long before you reach that point. If you plan to insist that this potential partner get tested for AIDS, then you can expect a six-month waiting period before you can engage in intercourse. So the sooner you bring the topic to the table, the sooner you can begin having sex (see Chapter 6).

I'm sure that you find many aspects of a person's character, such as his sense of honesty or her ability to give of herself, so important that you wouldn't consider getting involved with that person without knowing them. So just add sexual history to that list, and you'll wind up a lot safer.

Use Condoms

Condoms do not offer absolute protection against sexually transmitted diseases. If used improperly, they can leak. Once in a while, they break. And certain viruses, such as hepatitis B, can actually pass through the latex. But compared to having intercourse without a condom, they are like the brick walls the third little piggy used to keep the wolf away.

You have no valid excuse not to use a condom. Men don't lose their ability to have an orgasm by wearing a condom. They may like sex better without a condom — I can't deny that — but having intercourse using a condom is still better than not having intercourse at all. When it comes to safer sex, there can be no exceptions to that rule.

To use a condom, you have to have one with you. Although young men have long stuck one in their wallets for "emergencies," you should know that heat and age do affect condoms, so make sure that any condom you use is fresh. But in this day and age, not just men should carry condoms. Any woman who is sexually active should be prepared to keep herself safe, not only from an unintended pregnancy, but from sexually transmitted diseases as well.

Develop a Relationship Before You Have Sex

Some people get paranoid about safer sex, and I don't blame them for taking every precaution imaginable. But for many people, safer sex is just not something that is always on their minds. If they're in a special situation, if the stars are shining very brightly, if the chemistry is just perfect, and no condom is available, well, they may give in to the moment. Scolding someone who does that is pointless; face it, sex is part of human nature. None of us is perfect, and everyone gives in to temptation now and then, whether it involves a moonlit night or a container of Häagen-Dazs.

The key to safer sex is to not have sex with anyone until you have developed a relationship with that person. If you get to know someone really well, if you've been dating for a while, if you've had long talks about life and love and know their sexual history — if, after all that, you really believe that having sex (using a condom, of course) is reasonably safe for the two of you, then you may decide to go ahead.

Sadly, some people are liars, and every day they infect innocent people with dreadful diseases. Even a marriage license is no guarantee against sexually transmitted diseases. But you have no absolute guarantees in life, and every day you must make choices, the outcome of which you can't know in advance. You can't let the unknown paralyze you entirely. Sometimes you just have to take a leap. However, if you take every possible precaution, the odds of success are a lot higher.

Don't Engage in Risky Behavior

The chance of passing on HIV during anal sex is greater than during other types of sex. Unprotected oral sex is not safer sex. Having sex with someone you meet at a bar or bathhouse is dangerous. Going to a sex club is far from risk free. Wife swapping does not promote good health. Sharing needles is an invitation to sharing the HIV virus.

Most people don't even think about trying such risky behavior, but others are attracted to living on the edge. These people seem to dare the fates to strike them down, and, more often than not, they do.

At the time that you engage in risky behavior, a certain thrill may come with the moment. But when you're lying in a hospital dying, that thrill will not be a happy memory but a nightmare that you'll live through over and over until the end.

- ✔ If you can't keep yourself from going to a gay bar or bathhouse, masturbate while watching others, but don't do anything risky.

- ✔ If seeing what goes on at a sex club is too much of a temptation for you to resist, go with a partner and don't have sex with anyone else.

- ✔ If you're a drug addict, go get help right this minute (see Appendix B).

You can find the willpower to avoid risky behavior — I know it. If you can't do it by yourself, then go for help.

Don't Forget about the Other STDs

While AIDS has grabbed all the headlines, AIDS is only one of many sexually transmitted diseases. Most of these STDs have been around for hundreds of years (see Chapter 19).

Some think that Columbus may have brought syphilis back to Spain with him from the New World. Whatever the exact method of its spread throughout the world, syphilis has plagued mankind for a long time, and it killed many people before medical science found a cure.

Some forms of syphilis and gonorrhea have become resistant to the normal types and doses of antibiotics, which means that they are no longer illnesses that you can just shrug off. Hepatitis B is much more contagious than most STDs; luckily, you can get a vaccine that prevents you from catching it. Doctors have no vaccine against herpes; nor do they have a cure. Usually, the partner of the person who has herpes ends up getting the disease as well. Some STDs, such as chlamydia, are raging across the country. And now that cervical cancer has been linked to HPV infection, women need to remember that having sex with a high-risk partner can put them at higher risk for developing cancer.

Although you may be with somebody that you suppose doesn't have AIDS — and you may even be right — that doesn't mean that you are safe from catching an STD. The sexual scene is a bit of a war zone, so be careful. Please.

Don't Sell Your Other Options Short

If the main reason that you have sex is to have a baby, then intercourse is surely the only way for you to go. But if you seek pleasure and not progeny, then you have plenty of other ways to get sexual satisfaction without undertaking the risks of intercourse.

What makes intercourse dangerous is the exchange of bodily fluids, which can contain viruses of various sorts. But orgasms don't depend on an exchange of fluids. You and your partner can both wear full rubber body suits, so that not even a drop of sweat would be exchanged, and still give each other orgasms.

Hands and fingers are wonderfully agile and can give a lot of pleasure. (Oral sex, while safer than intercourse, cannot be considered a form of safer sex because people exchange bodily fluids.) If you want to be creative, you can even substitute your big toe. A man can rub his penis between a woman's breasts, and a vibrator can give fabulous orgasms without passing on a drop of anything liquid.

If you really feel the need for sexual release, but you don't know the person all that well, don't sell these safer-sex practices short. You can get sexual satisfaction without having any regrets later on.

Chapter 26

Ten Things Women Wish Men Knew about Sex

*I*t amazes me that many men say that they want to have sex with women so badly, but then don't put any effort into finding out what it takes to have good sex with a woman. So all you guys who complain that you don't get enough of "it," read the following tips closely. I know how you men often resist asking for directions, but if you've lost that loving feeling, then read on with an open mind and force yourself to accept some guidance on how to get to the Tunnel of Love.

Chivalry Isn't Dead Yet

Apart from a handful of ultrafeminists who get insulted if a man holds the door for them or takes off his hat in the elevator, I believe most women still enjoy being treated like ladies. Although this idea also holds true for total strangers, who may only reward you with a wide smile for your efforts, it most definitely applies to the woman with whom you share a relationship, where the rewards can be of far greater consequence.

Bringing a woman flowers or chocolate, taking her out to dinner, calling her during the day — all these little details are important not because of what they cost in terms of money, but because they show that you care, that you are thinking of her, and that she matters to you.

Now some of you men have discovered how to make all the right moves, but your hearts aren't really in it. You have a goal in mind — getting the woman into bed. If you are one of these men, you are not looking for a relationship but are only putting another notch in your gun. Although you may be proud of your conquests for a while, a time will come when you realize what a lonely life you have led.

Empty gestures are not chivalrous, and they won't earn a man his rank of knighthood, either. You not only have to show you care, you have to feel it, too.

Appearances Do Count

Although many men do worry about their hair (mostly because they know that their relationship with it may be rather fleeting), when it comes to the rest of their appearance, many men are not so careful. Now I understand that, if you have to wear a tie and jacket all day for work, you'll be eager to fling them off the second you walk through the door. Working women are no less eager to remove their heels and business suits. But always putting on the same ripped T-shirt and paint-stained jeans turns women off.

As a man, you are probably very conscious of how the women around you look, whether that woman is your partner or someone else. True, you may be more concerned with the length of her hemline than whether or not her shoes match her bag, but you can't get away with saying that you don't pay any attention to the way that women dress. Although most women take care to look as presentable as possible to their men, many men won't return the favor.

Perhaps you're one of those people who doesn't perceive yourself as being sexy, but you are — especially to your partner — so try to look the part.

If you're the type of guy who complains that your wife doesn't make love to you enough, my guess is that you'd have more success in that area if you started dressing more like Casanova than Pigpen.

You Can't Hurry Love

The notion that men get turned on a lot faster than do women is very true. One can speculate on the reasons for this, but the reasons are irrelevant because knowing why won't change anything. Women need time to prepare themselves for sex, and I'm not just talking about the type of foreplay that goes on when you already have your clothes off and you're in bed (or in the hot tub or on the kitchen floor).

What women wish that men would realize is that, if a man wants to have sex, he has to put romance first. He doesn't have to make things complicated. Sure, dinner at the best restaurant in town would be great. But so would any opportunity for some quiet conversation, a moment to throw off the worries of the day to let her get in the mood for lovemaking. So even if you're champing at the bit, you have to be a tad more patient.

If you're like most men, you had no problem giving your partner some of this quality time before you got married or moved in together. You would call ahead, make appointments (called *dates*), go out to dinner, take her for long walks, and look into each other's eyes. As a result, she'd begin to be ready to have sex with you. Now, if she felt the relationship still needed further development, she may well have said no, but that doesn't *necessarily* mean that she wasn't thinking yes. (Some of you men are probably saying "Huh, you mean she was ready but she said no anyway?" Yes, but she knew that if she gave in too soon, you'd have been off chasing someone else the next night, so what choice did she have? And the fact that she was ready doesn't mean that she was sure the time was right.)

You men have to learn that those patterns of romantic behavior must continue after you've said "I do" — not necessarily every time, but often enough to show that you really do care.

A Clitoris Is Not Just a Small Penis

Although the fact that men and women are built differently should be obvious, many men think of a clitoris as just a small penis. These men know that if a woman touches their penis it gets hard, and if she rubs the penis a bit more, the man has an orgasm. And many men think that the clitoris works just the same. They've grasped the point that the clitoris is the seat of a woman's ability to have an orgasm, but they haven't figured out that a clitoris is a lot more delicate than a penis. Many women can't bear to have the clitoris touched directly because it hurts. They need only to have the area around the clitoris caressed and rubbed to give just enough stimulation so that the clitoris doesn't actually hurt. So guys, store this fact away in your memory banks: just because a clitoris grows bigger when the woman gets excited doesn't make it a penis.

Some men take the same attitude toward a woman's breasts as they do to the clitoris. They knead them as if they were dough, forgetting that they're made of tissue, are sensitive, and can even be bruised. The partners of these men would also appreciate it if they took a little more care with their knees and elbows, and if they'd make a serious effort not to lean on her hair. Otherwise, both partners can end up bald.

For the vast majority of women, rough sex is a total turn off. If you're concerned with giving your woman an orgasm, work at it gently, and you'll have a great deal more success.

Women Need to Bask in the Afterglow

Women have many different complaints about the way men make love, but the one that gets the most votes is that men are too quick to go to sleep right after sex. Women take longer to get aroused than men and longer to come down from that aroused state (see Chapter 12). If you roll over and fall asleep (or get up and go home, or go to the basement to watch the ball game), she will feel abandoned. And leaving her feeling alone is not a good way to end a session of lovemaking.

I'm not asking you men to spend as long on afterplay as on foreplay. But, come on guys, admit it, if right after "doing it" you got a call from a friend with tickets on the 50-yard line to a game starting in an hour, would you tell him you were too sleepy to go? Of course not. So isn't your wife or partner worth an extra ten minutes of consciousness? (Hint: The answer to that question is yes.)

Afterplay has an extra benefit — if you play your cards right, the afterglow will last right up until the next day and become the start of foreplay for the next session. And don't tell me that you'll be too tired then!

Kinky Sex Isn't Sexy Sex

I receive many categories of letters from people who write to my column, and one category is women asking why men always want them to do something kinky. Probably the most frequently asked request is for the husband to watch his wife make love to another woman. Some men just want to watch, while others plan on joining in. Some men don't care if the other person is a man or a woman, they just want to take part in a threesome. Other men want to join a wife-swapping group or visit a sex club.

Now I'm not saying that you can't find any women who instigate this type of behavior, because you can, and sometimes their husbands are the squeamish ones. But for the most part, men are the ones who have these unusual sexual appetites.

One thing the wives of these men want to know is why, and I can't give them a good answer. It may be that men have more active imaginations, or maybe they've watched too many porno movies. Whatever the reason, most women want no part of these scenes. They're quite content with having sex with their man, without anyone else looking on or joining in.

I am all in favor of fantasies, so I would never tell you men to stop fantasizing. And if you want to ask your wife or girlfriend about a particular fantasy, go ahead. Just don't try to pressure her if she says no. Instead, pretend you are doing whatever turns you on when you are with her. If you keep pestering her, all that will happen is that you will turn her off and, rather than getting kinky sex, you'll have no sex at all.

Wandering Eyes Mean Less Sex

Men like to look at women, and women usually don't mind being looked at. But there's a time and a place for everything. If you're out on a date, and you see a beautiful woman walk by, and you gawk at her so that your date or wife can see your tongue hanging out, that situation will not sit well with her. She will get angry at you, you'll have a fight, and for the next few hours the odds of the two of you having a sexual encounter will be slim to nil.

Women like attention, and, when they're with a man with whom they're having sex, they expect as much of his attention as possible. (Under certain circumstances, such as when you're driving a car or putting the ice tray filled with water back into the freezer, you're excused from this rule.) Women don't find fighting for your attention particularly sexy, and that includes competing against televised ball games, sports cars being driven down your block, and, most of all, pretty women walking by.

Your lover wants to think that you consider her the most desirable woman on earth. Can she really be expected to do that when you're busy staring at the body of another woman? Of course not. So if you consider yourself a macho stud, don't think that looking at other women needs to be part of this role. Real macho men like to engage in sex, not just fantasize about it, and ogling will not get you where you want to go.

Slam-Bam-Thank-You-Ma'am Doesn't Cut the Mustard

Okay, now I'm getting down to the real nitty gritty. Obviously, if women need time to get themselves sufficiently aroused to have an orgasm, a man who can't "keep it up" (that is, sustain an erection) will cause them problems.

Premature ejaculation is the term used in the sexological literature for this particular affliction, but you really have nothing to worry about if you happen to deserve the label premature ejaculator, because the condition is nothing more than a learning disability.

If you're wondering whether or not you fall into this category, don't go pulling out a stopwatch. I don't classify a man as a premature ejaculator by some predefined amount of time that he can last before ejaculating. All you need to ask yourself is whether or not you are dissatisfied with your performance. If you want to last longer and can't, then you need to do the homework assignment I give in Chapter 20. If, on the other hand, you come as quickly as a jackrabbit, but neither you nor your partner much care because you can do things with your big toe that only a chimp can duplicate, then don't worry about it.

I often get asked why men have this problem, and the answer is no one knows. But as long as men have a cure, the reason really doesn't matter, does it?

Changing Diapers Is Sexy

How many of you fathers do or did change diapers? Whatever your answer, I'm sure that you never thought of it as a sexy experience. Heaven forbid, I'm certainly not suggesting that the sight of a naked baby's bottom should arouse anything more than the urge to thank God for such perfection, *but,* if you never realized how important a role changing a baby's diaper has in your sex life, then you don't deserve the title "terrific lover" just yet.

Mommies change a million diapers, but just because they do doesn't make the task any more pleasant. Too many Dads think that, because Mom changes diapers all the time — even if she works at a full-time job outside the home — she likes doing it. Believe me, changing diapers is not a job anybody can really like. Oh, sure, babies are fun, but there's still an element to the diaper-changing chore that is offensive to all of us.

So when Dad offers to do the dirty job — key word, *offers,* and with a smile on his face too — that makes Mom feel very good. So good that later that night she'll still remember it, and Daddy may get his reward.

Now, of course, this idea applies to any task that always seems to fall on Mom — doing the dishes, folding the laundry, dusting the bookshelves. Don't do it just because you expect something; but if you volunteer for some of the dirty work, I guarantee that you'll earn your reward.

Just Because You Can't Doesn't Mean You Won't

I want to talk to you older gentlemen. I know that you can't always perform the way that you used to. That doesn't mean that your sexual life is over yet; it most certainly isn't, but you do need more time to get ready for the next sexual episode. But remember this truism that many of you either don't want to admit or just never realized: You do not need an erection to satisfy your wife.

Very often, if a wife feels "in the mood," and the husband does not, he'll either ignore her desires, or he'll try to have an erection. Then, when he can't, he'll give up on the idea of sex altogether. But no law says that you have to have an erection to have sex. You can please your wife in a variety of ways. You can give her fabulous orgasms with your fingers, your tongue, or a vibrator.

Don't be selfish. Just because you're not in the mood doesn't mean that she has to be frustrated. And remember, no good deed goes unrewarded. So if at another time you need a little more help from her to obtain an erection, your helping her during her hour of need will go into an account that you can draw on later.

Chapter 27

Ten Things Men Wish Women Knew about Sex

- -

In This Chapter

▶ Making sure your signals are clear

▶ Leaving the light on

▶ Giving him a hand — or a mouth

▶ Letting his eye wander without feeling jealous

▶ Understanding his changing body

- -

Ladies, if any of you still believe that the way to a man's heart is through his stomach, then you have a lot to figure out about men. Between fast food franchises, pizza, and Chinese take-out, men can easily feed themselves. But they're not so crazy about taking care of some of their other needs by themselves — and I'm not talking about sewing on buttons.

Now, just because a man's apparatus is on view doesn't mean that operating it is all that simple. And while you can hire an auto mechanic to look under the hood of your car, I don't think you want anyone else changing the oil (tinkering with the cylinders, lubricating the ball joint, lifting the valves) of your man. So pay attention to these tips if you want to get the most from your relationship.

Try Not to Give Mixed Signals

Turning men on doesn't really take much; if you're not careful, you can do it accidentally. Although, as a woman, getting in the mood takes a while, a man can have an erection in what seems like milliseconds. And with those light-ning reflexes hard-wired into his brain, it's easy to confuse a man by some gesture that you aren't even aware you made.

Imagine that you just had a tough commute home on a hot day. When you walk through the door into your apartment, the last thing on your mind is sex. You feel sweaty and confined and, without thinking, you kick off your shoes, hike up your skirt, and pull down your pantyhose. Ahh, relief. Now your partner, who had gotten home a few minutes before you and was just popping the tab off a can of beer, watches all this. To him, what you're doing is not a cooling off gesture, but a striptease . . . and right in his living room, no less. He may be conditioned to seeing you change clothes in the bedroom without getting excited by it (or maybe he does there, too; you never know), but seeing this sudden exposure of bare flesh where he least expected it will definitely get his blood surging south of the border.

Now he's thinking hot while you're thinking cold, as in shower. He starts sidling over; you see that look in his eyes, think "What is he, crazy?" give him a stiff arm, and make a beeline for shower. If you're really in miscommunication mode, after the gushing waters have had their refreshing effect, you'll start thinking about "it," and, after you pat yourself dry, you come out of the shower wearing only a towel to see what reaction you get. But having just been rejected, he figures that if he reaches out, he'll only get his hand slapped. So instead he plays King Couch Potato and asks what's for dinner, which makes you furious.

Mixed signals such as this happen to couples all the time. You can't always prevent them, but it helps if you're aware of what type of behavior can trigger them. Is it fair that you can't get undressed in your own living room? I wouldn't worry about losing your freedom. Pretty soon you may have kids, and you'll be lucky if you can have sex at midnight under the covers.

Lack of Sex Really Can Hurt

The term is *blue balls,* and whether or not a man's testicles actually turn any colors I don't know, but they can absolutely ache from the need for sexual release. Now, the pain is not so acute that a man can't stand it, and, if no one else is around, all he has to do is masturbate to bring needed relief. But he's also not putting you on when he says that his testicles hurt.

This is another reason not to give mixed signals. I'm not talking about the type of instant erection a man gets from seeing your anatomy, but one that lasts a longer time and really causes his hormones to stir. If you get a man that excited and then change your mind about giving him sexual release, he won't be pleased. Men really don't like women who tease, because not only their egos suffer, but their testicles as well.

While I'm on the subject of pain and testicles, do be careful with the family jewels — even if you don't want them making any part of your family. Testicles are highly sensitive, and if you're too rough on them, or accidentally hit them in some way, then it causes real pain. So unless you're dealing with a would-be rapist — in which case, please be my guest and kick hard where it'll hurt the most — be gentle.

Sometimes Wasting Electricity Is Okay

As demonstrated by the success of magazines such as *Playboy,* men get turned on visually. And although I do urge modesty at those times when the last thing on your mind is a roll in the hay, men would really appreciate it if you would drop those force fields when the time comes to make love. I know that you like to cuddle and be cozy, and that a dark room with the covers drawn up to your chin helps you feel safe enough to get aroused, but for the sake of your man, how about leaving the lights on once in a while?

Now, I'm not asking you to cover your room with mirrors, not even on the ceiling, because I understand that you have to be able to look your mother-in-law in the eye when she visits. But as long as the room temperature is warm enough not to cause goose bumps, give your man the visual stimuli he desires.

Teamwork Is Important

So many of you women are sick to death with sports. Having your man spend Sunday afternoons watching some men toss around a football and then hit each other seems like the most boring way imaginable to pass the time. Although I'm not going to suggest that you try to become a sports fanatic — though many women have decided to join their men in front of the TV or in the stands and love it — I believe you can learn a lesson regarding sex from sports.

To you women, verbal communication is very important. You need to talk to the most important person in your life. Because men, in general, don't talk as much — especially the strong, silent type — it seems as if they don't communicate to each other. But many men would prefer to bond not by talking but by doing something together, as a team. Having played sports as young men and discovered how to appreciate the benefits of teamwork, men find that watching sports has a great attraction.

So how does this idea affect your love life? For one thing, the more teamwork you have in your sex life, the more communication you will have between the two of you, and the happier you'll both be. So don't just lie still and expect him to do all the work.

- ✔ The simplest thing you can do is to initiate sex once in a while if you tend to leave that task to him.
- ✔ Buy some sex toys, edible underwear for example, and present them to him one night.

> ✔ Suggest writing up a game plan for the night's sexual activities. Include starting time, which positions, and which room of the house.
>
> ✔ Buy a team uniform, maybe matching T-shirts, that can serve as a secret signal between the two of you that — if you're both wearing them — then that night, or that afternoon, is reserved for sex.

Take an active part in sex and score some points that put you right at the top of his standings.

The Playboy Playmate Is Not a Threat

I actually do like the articles in *Playboy,* but I know that many women wouldn't care if every issue won a Pulitzer Prize for journalism, they still don't want to see that magazine — or any other publication that features naked, nubile women — in their homes. Such women feel threatened by these pictures because they themselves are not a "perfect" 36-24-36, they don't get the benefits of an air-brush around their cellulite, and they refuse to shave their pubic hair into a well-shaped "V."

Now, I don't want anyone to do anything that makes him or her feel threatened, so you must decide whether these magazines have a place in your bedroom. But this chapter is here to let you women know how your men feel, and I would be remiss to omit this common complaint just to preserve your feelings.

And, you know, in reality, *Playboy* is just the opposite of a threat. Very few men ever get to even meet a centerfold, much less go to bed with one. The man who gets turned on reading — or, if you prefer, ogling — *Playboy* isn't going to rush out of the house looking for Miss October. Instead, he's going to come over to your side of the bed and look for you. He knows you don't look like a centerfold, but he loves you for all your qualities, one of which may even be that you *don't* look like Miss October, whom he may actually be too scared to go to bed with, fearing he couldn't live up to the moment.

And another thing, do romance novels ever turn you on? Does watching soaps ever give you a tingle? A Mel Gibson movie, perhaps? What if your husband told you that he never wanted to see another romance novel on the bedstand? Would that be fair? The sexual content of *Playboy* is more blatant, and you certainly don't want little children peeking between its pages, but if he's discreet about his magazine habit, I know that your man would really appreciate your tolerance — if not understanding — of his choice of literature.

The Day 1 Stop Looking 1s the Day 1'm Dead

In my tips for men, I tell you that women hate it when they're out with a guy and he gapes at other women. Although men should definitely exercise caution when looking at other women when they're with a partner, that's not the same thing as saying that they shouldn't look.

Men will always look at other women; you can't stop them. Now, although I suggest discretion on a man's part when he's around you, at the same time, I have to tell you women not to make a big fuss when your man looks, unless he's being obnoxious about it. Remember, if your man stops looking at other women, it probably means he's also stopped looking at you. It may mean that he has lost all interest in sex, and that idea's certainly not a bonus.

Now we all know that women look at men, although they're much more likely to want to look into a pair of soft eyes than at a passing crotch (though many women report looking below the waist as well as above). And, as far as two partners in a close relationship are concerned, looks aren't the only thing that keeps them together, so looking around is really not that much of a big deal. The key to keeping both partners happy is not to force anyone to wear blinders but, instead, to use discretion.

If You Really Loved Me, You'd . . .

This is not an open question. I just felt a little prudish about putting what this tip is about right in the title. Most of you ladies can guess what I'm talking about, I'm sure, and certainly many of you do keep your man happy by performing that certain act.

Right, you guessed it, the topic here is fellatio — oral sex on a man.

Now, although I'm speaking on behalf of men here, I must put my cards down on the table and state categorically that I absolutely do not want any woman to do anything that really repulses her. But before you go on to the next item, ask yourself this: Is it really that repulsive? I'm not saying that you have to necessarily swallow his semen, but is just kissing and licking his penis that big of a deal?

If you're concerned about cleanliness, then go get a washcloth and clean his penis. He won't object, unless you use cold water.

I really do not believe that men who crave this sex act see it as degrading to women. Rather, they want it because they enjoy the sensations. And maybe you do, too, when he does it to you. Even if this never becomes a regular part of your sexual repertoire, you can at least make his birthday special . . . or even use it just to mark the decades.

The Way to a Man's Heart Is Not through His Stomach

I don't know where that saying that the way to a man's heart is through his stomach started, but ask 100 men if they think that idea is true. Unless all those men are residents of a senior citizens' home, I don't think you'll find the majority in agreement. And I'm not sure that even the seniors would give their vote.

Men like to eat, but if they have to do something for themselves, they'd prefer to feed themselves. Some women, after a few years, or maybe after they've had a few kids, seem to withdraw from sex. Such a woman may think that as long as she puts down a good meal in front of her husband and maybe irons his shirts, that's all he really needs from her.

That idea may work for a while, but then he'll get a new secretary, or go to a convention in Las Vegas, or just look differently at the neighbor's wife, and all of a sudden his attention is permanently drawn elsewhere.

You don't have to be a courtesan, but you definitely shouldn't be disinterested in sex. As a man ages, the urges may come further apart, but they're still there. If, for some reason, you seem to have lost your sexual desire, don't just assume it happens because you're a woman. That's nonsense. Loss of sexual appetite is almost always caused by something specific, so find a specialist — a sex therapist or marital therapist — who can help you overcome this problem (see Appendix B).

To a Man, Sex Is Different than Love

I don't want to make any excuses for men who fool around on their wives, especially in these days when he can catch a deadly disease and then infect his innocent wife. But in general, men and women are different when it comes to sex. Most women need romance to become aroused, which means that their emotions are almost always involved, but most men can have sex without the act triggering an emotional response in them.

This is the reason that prostitutes have always been doing business with men on a quickie basis, while the few *gigolos* (male prostitutes for women) that exist almost always perform for the long term.

The reason knowing this fact is important is that, if you ever catch your man having sex with another women, don't throw away a long-term relationship without doing a careful evaluation. If it really looks like he was only in it for the sex, and if you both love each other, you may be able to save your relationship. I'm certainly not advocating sticking around with a philanderer, the guy who does it over and over again. But in some instances you'd be better off forgiving and forgetting (although you can never totally forget).

When it comes to sex, don't assume that he reacts the same way that you do, because you'd be making an error. But if, upon careful consideration, you know that you can't stay with him, even if he had only a casual fling, then I wouldn't discourage you from moving on. Just don't make the decision in a fit of anger.

The Older a Man Gets, the More Help He Needs

Not every man knows that, at some point in his life, he loses the ability to have a *psychogenic erection* — an erection that comes by itself, without any physical manipulation — but it's a fact. This problem does not signal the end of your love life; instead, it means that your partner now needs foreplay as much as you do.

Some of you women may decide that this is the moment to pay him back for all the times that he didn't give you enough foreplay, but I'm telling you not to play those games. When this change first starts to happen to a man, he gets pretty upset about it. The first few times he runs across a situation where his penis used to take off for the races by itself and now just lies there can be downright scary. So have mercy on him and don't add to his plight.

When a man loses his ability to have erections spontaneously, oral sex can definitely become even more desirable, and if you haven't done oral sex much before, do consider it. At least one positive change occurs over the years — your man will probably have gained more control — so he can almost definitely keep from coming to orgasm in your mouth. Many women find that, after they deal with that fear, they don't mind performing fellatio.

If your man experiences these types of difficulties, definitely read Chapter 20 on male sexual problems to find out as much as you can about what is happening to him and how you can help.

Chapter 28

Ten Tips for Truly Great Lovers

nybody can teach you how to make love, but I, Dr. Ruth, want you to become not just any kind of lover, but a truly great lover. I want you and your partner to have *terrrrific* sex, and to do that you have to find out how to roll your *Rs* and heed the following tips.

Don't Make Love on Your First Date

Sex feels great, doesn't it?

You may think that, because you can find nothing else like it, you want to have sex as often as possible and as soon as possible. But sex isn't a toy to be played with by children; sex is a serious act to be shared by responsible adults. A great lover integrates sex into an overall relationship and never has sex with someone he or she barely knows.

Giving into the temptation of having sex before you really know each other can only lead to problems. One of the more serious problems may be that you end up catching a sexually transmitted disease. But even if you do escape with your health intact, you won't be having great sex.

In life, the more time, effort, and intensity you put into an activity, the more you'll get out of it. If you wait until you've developed a relationship with someone you're attracted to, if you devote your energies to finding out enough about that someone so that you grow to admire, respect, and love the person, then — and only then — can you have great sex.

Set the Mood as Far in Advance as Possible

A common myth says that great sex has to be spontaneous sex — but in most cases, the reverse of that is true. Now, I'm not saying that spontaneous sex can't be great — it most certainly can — but rarely do two people hit their peak sexual mood at just the same time without some planning.

Part of the reason for this idea is that women take a longer time to get aroused than men do. So the further ahead you set the mood for lovemaking, the more aroused she can become. Don't be in such a rush. The more planning and preparation time you invest into making the evening (or morning or afternoon) as romantic as possible, the better the sex that will result.

So send those flowers ahead of time, instead of bringing them home with you, so that they'll have plenty of time to work on her libido. (If you want to know more about how sending flowers can get your partner in the mood, sneak back to Chapter 9.)

Give your full attention to your partner the moment you walk through the door and don't wait until just before you get into bed. Spend time caressing and massaging the rest of her body before reaching for her clitoris. And start the lovemaking process early enough so that you don't feel as if you have to go right to sleep or head back to your apartment as soon as you've had your orgasm.

And ladies, if you know that you want to have sex with him, don't be coy about it. Let him know that the answer will be yes as soon as you know it yourself. That way he can feel free to give you the best foreplay he can, without worrying about whether or not he's going to have his advances rejected.

So don't limit foreplay, or afterplay either. By setting the mood as far in advance as possible and taking your time after you're together, you can show off your prowess as a great lover.

Find Out What Your Partner Needs

I hope that you're not under the misapprehension that sex is a selfish act. Just because no one else can feel your orgasm the way you do doesn't mean that they can't share in your pleasure, or you in theirs. If you want to have the strongest orgasms — the kind that make your heart beat wildly, your breath grow short, and your toes curl up — then you have to work together as partners and give as much of yourselves to each other as you can.

To be more giving, you have to know what the other person needs: more foreplay, a certain touch around the anus, the sensations of oral sex, maybe a thousand little kisses. Whatever your partner's needs, you must find out how to please your partner to the best of your ability. And if your partner does the same, through this teamwork you can have the greatest orgasms and the best lovemaking possible.

To be the best lover you can be, do ask and do tell each other what you want. You've taken your clothes off, so what's the big deal about stripping away some of that shell still covering your psyche? Sex isn't a private act; it's an act of sharing — and the more you share, the more there will be to share.

Protect Yourself and Your Partner

Sex has never been risk free. Having an unintended pregnancy carries serious consequences, both in terms of your health and how society looks upon you. And in this era of AIDS, the risks have multiplied tremendously. If you're not careful, if you don't act responsibly, whether you are a man or a woman, you may actually be putting your life on the line.

If you have the misguided notion that protecting yourself takes away from the pleasure of sex by ruining the spontaneity and placing barriers of latex between you and your partner, then you've been missing out on truly great sex.

The most important sex organ does not reside below your belt, but between your ears — where your brain is. If your brain worries that, as a result of having sex, an unintended pregnancy may occur or some disease be passed on, then it won't allow you to really enjoy yourself. These types of worries actually keep some men from having an erection and some women from having an orgasm, and they can lessen the pleasure for anyone.

Safer sex isn't only less dangerous; it's also more enjoyable. So if you want to be the best lover you can be, always practice safer sex.

Don't Fall into a Rut

The first 10, 20, or maybe even 100 times you have sex with someone, you'll experience a certain excitement that comes from the newness of it all. But after a time, that newness begins to wear off.

For some people, the familiarity brings a certain type of comfort that makes sex more pleasurable, but for others, the sameness makes sex begin to wear thin. Instead of anticipating a certain caress, they begin to dread it. And so, instead of wanting to have sex, they start avoiding it, which can spell not only the end of a couple's sex life, but the end of their entire relationship.

Variety comes in all sorts of packages:

- A different sexual position
- Making love at a different time of day
- Having sex someplace you've never done it before
- Doing it fast when you usually take your time
- Making a point of prolonging the act as long as you can possibly stand it

Even if you find yourself going back to your old ways, because they do bring you a lot of pleasure, force yourself to try something new once in a while. The patterns you and your partner develop can make for great sex, but if you try some new things, you can appreciate the old ways even more. And perhaps you'll find some new ways of having sex that will make sex better than ever.

Make a point of initiating these changes together. Sometimes surprises are nice, and sometimes they can shock the other person into losing the desire for sex altogether. Talk ahead of time about the different ideas that you may like to try, and have those discussions outside of the bedroom. If you need help coming up with new ideas, look at a book (maybe even this one) together, or watch a tape, and then talk over which of the new positions that you just discovered may be fun to try out. Never put pressure on each other to do something that the other person really doesn't want to do, but also don't be so quick to say no.

Think of your sex life as a building that you're constructing as a team. You can't have a building without a solid foundation — but after that foundation's laid, if you want to reach the greatest heights, you'll have to take your chances climbing that ladder.

Do Something about Your Problems

Nobody is born a perfect lover. Everybody needs to practice and work at being the best lover he or she can become . . . even you.

Now, you may have a particular problem that causes you difficulties. Maybe you're a guy who is a premature ejaculator. Or maybe you're a woman who has problems getting sexual satisfaction.

Whatever problems you may have, be they major ones that keep you from enjoying sex altogether or minor ones that prevent you from reaching your peak sexual performance, don't ignore them, don't expect them to go away by themselves, and don't spend your whole life suffering needlessly. In most cases, help is available (see Appendix A).

For some problems, you can find the answer in this book and work it out by yourself or with the help of your partner. If that approach doesn't solve the problem, either because you tried and your solution doesn't work or because the problem is too severe to handle by yourself, make an appointment to see a specialist. And don't dilly-dally. Do it today.

When it comes to most physical problems, be it a toothache or the need for a new eyeglass prescription, you probably don't waste a minute going for help. But if the issue is sexual in nature, you become too embarrassed to talk about it. But take it from me, as someone who's been practicing sex therapy for more than 20 years, sex therapists have heard it all. Sex is what we talk about all day long, and we won't think of you as strange because you have a sexual problem.

And if you're worried that going to a sex therapist will bleed you dry, the techniques that we therapists all use are short term. Sometimes even only one or two sessions can work wonders and would be well worth the investment.

You have no excuse for allowing sexual problems to fester to the point where they not only keep your own sexual pleasure below par, but probably do damage to your partner's enjoyment of sex as well. Thanks to the pioneers in sexual therapy, therapists have the solutions you need, so pick up a phone and make an appointment.

Use Your Sense of Touch

Researchers have done experiments in which they've left baby monkeys alone in a cage without any other monkeys, and the baby monkeys soon went crazy. Just giving those monkeys a soft cloth doll that they could cuddle up to was sometimes enough to get them through this solitary confinement. You are not a monkey, but you and your partner do have the same need to be touched.

Part of that touching should take place while you're having sex. Remember, though, that the art of arousing your partner through foreplay doesn't mean just touching their genitals. You should pay attention to every square inch of them. Touch them, stroke them, caress them, rub them. You can both enjoy the tactile sensations.

But this touching has to be a continuous process. You have to touch each other every day, several times a day, without any thought to having sex. You have to hug each other. Hold each other's hands. Rub each other's shoulders.

Wash each other. All that touching will bring you closer so that, when the time comes to actually engage in sex, the experience will be heightened for both of you.

Don't limit this touching to your hands. Play footsie and feel how sensitive your feet can be. Lie on top of one another and feel your lover with your whole body. Put your cheeks together — both sets! Don't be afraid to explore. You can build an entire map of each other's bodies, finding out all the places where you like to be touched the most, and then use that information to have the best sex possible (see Chapter 9).

Become a Great Kisser

You may have noticed that, in the preceding section, I didn't mention touching your lips together. The reason is that the lips deserve a section all to themselves.

The sensations caused by kissing can feel so good, so intense, that some people can kiss each other for hours. Many people have a pleasure zone centered on oral activity. While I despise chewing gum and would never permit it in any classroom over which I presided, I do recognize that humans have special feelings toward oral activities.

Kissing, by the way, is a gentle art. Oh, you have moments when passions run high, and you may even feel like nibbling on each other, but for the most part being too rough with your kisses can spoil the moment rather than enhance it. Also, although many people enjoy French kissing (that is, deep-mouth kissing), some do not. You shouldn't try to force your way into these people's mouths, because doing so only breaks the mood.

Kissing is an important part of sex and one that you should not neglect, especially because you can do it almost anytime and anywhere. So go for it!

Satisfy Your Partner Even If You Don't Feel Like Sex

You know the saying, "If I've said it once, I've said it a thousand times"? Well, if I've said one thing ten thousand times, it's that two people in a relationship are not Siamese twins. Each person has a different sexual appetite, so no couple is perfectly matched. One person always wants more sex than the other. And as the years go by, those roles may even switch, and then switch back again.

What should you do about this? Help each other out, that's what. You're supposed to be lovers, right? So just because you don't feel in the mood for an orgasm yourself doesn't mean that you can't help your partner reach sexual satisfaction. No law says that both of you have to have an orgasm every time.

Now some women "fake it." Sometimes faking it is okay, as long as she has orgasms at other times. But you don't need to fake it. You can very simply, out of love for your partner, help him or her to have an orgasm in whichever way suits you best. If you're a woman, and you want to just lie back, that's fine. If you're a man and you don't want to have an erection or can't, you can use your finger, or your tongue, or a vibrator.

The point is, don't force your partner to be sexually frustrated on a regular basis just because your sexual appetites are different. Remember, the Golden Rule applies to sex just as much as to every other aspect of human life.

Learn to Adapt to Your Circumstances

If you put on some weight, do you go around with your pants unbuttoned or do you buy a new pair? If you've reached the limit of how far your arms can hold the newspaper from your eyes, do you stop reading or get reading glasses?

As the years go by, your body changes, and some of those changes can affect the way you have sex. You can refuse to adapt; you may say: "If I can't have sex the way I used to, I won't have it at all." And then you'll join the long list of people who no longer enjoy one of life's greatest gifts. But that idea's just as ridiculous as wearing your pants around your knees or giving up reading. You can continue to have good sex, even great sex, up into your 90s, but you will have to make some changes in your sex life.

As they grow older, men lose their ability to have psychogenic erections, which means they'll no longer have erections just by thinking about something sexy, and instead will need *physical* stimulation. But is asking your wife to fondle your penis really that bad? Instead of being ashamed, let yourself get carried away by it, learn to enjoy it, and work it into being a pleasant part of foreplay.

Women who've gone through menopause will no longer lubricate the way they used to, and this problem can cause intercourse to become painful for them. This lack of lubrication is no calamity, however, because every drugstore sells very good products that can take the place of your natural lubricants and make sex just as enjoyable as it was before menopause.

No matter how well the years treat you, your body will undergo changes. But rather than letting those changes have a negative impact on your sex life, find out how to adapt to them and make sure that you continue to enjoy great sex your whole life through.

Appendix A

Step into My Office

Again and again throughout this book, I recommend that, if you have a problem of a sexual nature that you can't deal with yourself, you should make an appointment to consult with a sex therapist. You don't even need a partner (although if you are part of a couple, therapy works better if you both receive counseling).

You probably wonder what visiting a sex therapist entails. We sex therapists know this fear of the unknown keeps many people who have sexual problems from making an appointment with one of us. I hope that, by the end of this appendix, any of you in that situation will know enough about the experience of sex therapy that you can pick up a phone and make that appointment as soon as possible.

Baring All for the Sexual Status Exam

When it comes to the subject of sex, embarrassment is always an issue. Now, if I told you to go to a doctor, you wouldn't be shocked if you had to remove at least some, or maybe even all, of your clothing. It wouldn't really bother you because you know that a doctor has seen plenty of naked bodies and that he or she is used to it and doesn't think twice about it.

When you visit a sex therapist, you will never be asked to remove your clothes — certainly not by anybody reputable. If you are, and if that therapist is not also a medical doctor (which very few sex therapists are), then immediately walk out of that office.

But your sex therapist *will* ask many questions dealing with some very private subjects that you may never have spoken about to anyone. Just the way medical doctors are used to seeing naked people, sex therapists are used to hearing about the most intimate details of the lives of those who consult them. So try not to get all worked up; just accept that you shouldn't hold anything back if you want the therapy to be successful.

These questions form what is called a *sexual status examination,* during which the sex therapist tries to discover exactly what issues you are grappling with by asking many different questions, including some about your past that you may not find relevant.

To explain to you why these questions are vital to the success of the exam, let me return to the more familiar ground of a doctor's examination. Say you go to the doctor because you have a particular problem involving one of your body's functions, but the doctor determines that your problem is only a symptom of something else that is wrong with you — something that has to be treated first. For example, you may go to the doctor because you experience shortness of breath, but, after finishing the examination, the doctor tells you that your symptom has nothing to do with your lungs. The real problem may be that your arteries are clogged. The same thing happens in sex therapy, which is why the therapist must ask so many questions.

A typical example is the couple who visits me because the man complains that they don't have sex often enough, and they both assume that the problem has to do with the woman having low sexual desire. Very often, I discover that the problem has nothing to do with sex, but rather that she's angry at him for something entirely different, such as never helping her with the housework even though they both work full time. Until that problem is fixed, the couple's sex life can't be improved.

I know that answering all these questions can be embarrassing, but you've discovered how to cope with the embarrassment of removing your clothes for the doctor to get better, and so you shouldn't let any such feeling stop you from visiting a sex therapist. After you get started, you may find that being open and honest is not all that hard because of the relief you can feel at unburdening yourself in front of someone who can help you fix your sex life.

Take a ticket; one at a time, please

When a couple comes to see me, I almost always interview them separately first. This way, I get to hear both sides of the story, neither one of which may actually be the whole truth. But, by hearing both sides, I can usually at least begin to spot the real source of the problem.

During this first session, after seeing each partner alone, I then see the couple together. Sex therapists try to get each partner to understand the concerns of the other one. I always see some couples together after that initial visit. With other couples, however, I may have additional separate sessions.

I am not a medical doctor

As you probably know, I answer many people's questions, either on radio or TV or in the newspapers, and one thing that I need to say over and over again is that I am not a medical doctor. That means I get plenty of questions that I can't answer, because they are of a medical nature. However, when a client comes to see me, although I can't answer medical questions myself, I absolutely need to have those questions answered to proceed.

So in addition to the first ethical issue involving sex therapists — keeping your clothes on — here's another: ruling out a physical problem. Any time that the problem is physical in nature, such as a man who cannot obtain an erection or a woman who experiences pain during intercourse, the first thing that the sex therapist must do is send that client to a medical doctor for a checkup. Even if I am almost certain that the real problem is psychological in nature, I know that my responsibility is to make sure that a doctor rules out any physical problem first.

Why not try to heal the psychological problem first? The main reason is that, if an underlying physical problem exists — say, worst case, a tumor which is affecting sexual functioning — then any delay in treatment may end up being a fatal mistake. The other reason is that I may be wrong in believing that the problem is all in my client's head, and, if he or she does have physical problem, why waste everybody's time and energy trying to cure a psychological problem that is not at the root of the situation?

The medical doctor informs me of any physical problems that he or she may have found, as well as any treatment. After the client gets a clean bill of health, I can then begin to try to help that person by using the techniques of *behavioral therapy,* which is what sex therapy is — changing your behavior.

Sex is natural

A basic, underlying principle of sex therapy is that the sexual response is a natural process, like a sneeze. Sexual response is not something that you have to learn. If you have problems with your sexual functioning, my first assumption will be that something is going on that is keeping you from doing what comes naturally.

By talking with you about your problems, I should be able to find out what that something is, and, after we've identified it, your anxieties about it will lessen. That is an important first step in bringing you back to your natural condition. We sex therapists call it *giving permission,* either to partake in sexual pleasure — by having an orgasm, for example — or not to engage in a particular sexual activity.

Sex Therapists Give the Best Homework

You know what my favorite part of sex therapy is? Giving my clients their homework assignments. After the clients and I have talked about the problems they face and identified the causes, we have to take some action. Now this action doesn't take place in my office, but in the privacy of their own home.

If I've seen several clients in one day and given them all homework assignments, later that night I can sit back and picture in my mind what all of them, per my instructions, are doing. And that's one of my favorite parts of my profession — that and the thank yous from the people whom I've helped to overcome a sexual problem.

Assignment 1: The start-stop method

Many of the problems that people bring to me have to do with sexual illiteracy. One or both partners just don't know some very basic things about their own sexuality. For example, if a man has problems with premature ejaculation, he doesn't know how to recognize the *premonitory sensation,* that point of his arousal that if he goes beyond, he cannot stop himself from having an orgasm and ejaculating (see Chapter 20).

To cure himself of his problem, the man has to learn to recognize that moment when he can't stop his orgasm. And how does he do that? By practicing getting right up to that point and then stopping. If he has a partner, I tell him to go home that night and practice what is called the *stop-start technique.* In this method, his partner arouses him with her hand or tongue (at this point in their treatment I usually forbid intercourse), he signals to her when he feels that he is getting to the point of orgasm, and she stops. The more the couple practices this technique, the better he can recognize the sensations and stop himself. (I describe this process in greater detail in Chapter 20.)

So that you don't think I'm mean, I do let the man have an orgasm after one of these sessions; he's just not allowed to do it through intercourse. The reason is that I don't want him feeling the added pressure of having to perform well at intercourse, which is the problem he came to me with in the first place. By forbidding intercourse, I have removed a certain amount of the pressure from him, and this may help him to discover his point of no return much more easily. Eventually, after several practice sessions without intercourse, I have the couple try out the man's new-found skills during intercourse.

Assignment 2: Sensate focus exercises

The start-stop method described in the preceding section is certainly one of the assignments I give the most. Another is a series of exercises, called *sensate focus,* which teaches couples how to touch each other. Masters and Johnson developed this technique, and it is quite useful because it helps to reduce anxiety and increase communication.

The sensate focus exercises are very simple. The couple gets undressed and touches each other, one at a time. Aha, you say, sensate focus is like foreplay? Wrong, it's just the opposite. The person doing the touching is not doing it to please his or her partner, but to please him or herself. The goal is for the toucher to focus on how he or she reacts to the sensations of touching the other person's body. The person being touched remains quiet, unless something happens to cause discomfort, in which case the person can say, "That tickles," for example.

The partners are not supposed to touch the main erogenous zones, the genitals or the woman's breasts, in the beginning, but graduate to those parts of the body.

Do I need a partner?

You don't need to have a partner to visit a sex therapist. Many people come to see me because they have broken up with someone, in part because of a sexual problem, and they don't want the same thing to happen with their next partner. In those cases, my homework assignments may be different, but I can usually still help.

I always have these people call me when they do find a new partner. I give them a pep talk and then have them report to me how things went. Sometimes they need to come see me with their new partner, but, because they're prepared — they know their problem, and they don't allow it to drag on — I can help many of them with their new relationships.

Using psychosexual therapy

I trained under Dr. Helen Singer Kaplan at New York Hospital–Cornell University Medical School, and her method goes one step further than just the behavioral treatment described in the preceding sections. Some people have more deep-seated problems, and they may literally be stopping themselves from enjoying sex.

In that case, we sex therapists have to delve a little bit further into our clients' backgrounds to see if we can spot the source of what keeps them from functioning well sexually. The problem may be something that happened to them as children, including their relationship to their parents, or it may have to do with their relationship to their spouse. Whatever the problem is, after the client and the sex therapist have identified it, we should be able to resolve it. As far as I am concerned, if I feel the trouble is too deep-seated, I often refer that client to a psychologist.

What about sex surrogates?

A *sex surrogate* is a person trained to help people overcome a sexual problem by actually having sex with them. A sex surrogate would speak with the sex therapist to know what the problem was and what they should do, and then report back. Sex surrogates were especially useful for helping people without partners. Because sex surrogates get paid to have sex with people, their profession has always been illegal, but because their "hands-on" approach sometimes worked better than merely talking about how to have sex, many sex therapists were willing to overlook this legal aspect.

With the appearance of AIDS, most sex therapists have dropped the use of sex surrogates, because therapists don't want to place their clients into a potentially dangerous environment. Because they have sex with so many partners, sex surrogates are prime targets for disease.

Some people still advertise their services as so-called sex surrogates in papers such as the *Village Voice*. Without a referral from a sex therapist, however, you'd be hard put to tell whether this person was really someone out to help you with your sexual problem, or just a prostitute looking for a different way of luring clients. Whatever the case, take my advice and do not have sex with anyone who claims to be a sex surrogate. Having sex with anyone who has multiple partners, whatever their motive, is just too risky. A good sex therapist should be able to help you solve whatever sex problem you may have without resorting to any such dangerous third parties.

Finding a Sex Therapist

Many people assume that, because I am a famous sex therapist, I know every other sex therapist in the country, or at least one in every part of the country. The truth is that, although I do know other sex therapists, I never recommend them unless I know them very well. I am just one person, and I cannot keep track of what every sex therapist does. And I don't want to take the responsibility of sending a person to a sex therapist who spoke to me at a convention or lecture but who may not be up to par.

"But if I can't ask Dr. Ruth, then who can I turn to?"

I'm glad you asked. I have several answers, two of which I've been giving regularly for years, and some others that are new because of the arrival of the Internet:

✔ First, call the largest hospital in your area. The best ones are often the teaching hospitals (those associated with a medical school). These hospitals almost always have a referral list of specialists, including sex therapists. At the very least, the people there can tell you whether a particular sex therapist has ever had any complaints lodged against him or her. And, if the hospital recommends many people to sex therapists, you may be able to get even more information about their training, fees, and whether insurance will cover the costs.

✔ Another source in your search for a sex therapist is the association of sex therapists, called the American Association of Sex Educators, Counselors, and Therapists (or AASECT). Its address is P.O. Box 238, Mount Vernon, IA 52314. If you write to this group it will recommend some sex therapists in your area who have qualified for AASECT certification. Anyone recommended will have gone through the proper training.

✔ As far as Internet resources, you can try:

- The Mental Health Net's Clinician's Yellow Pages (www. mentalhealth.net/mhn/yellowpages)

- Find-A-Therapist (www.findingstone.com/find-a-therapist)

- Therapist Director (www.psychology.com/therapy.htm)

- Mental Health Infosource Professional Directory (www.mhsource. com/referral/docsearch.html)

- The Internet Care Directory (www.caredirectory.com/ main.html)

- The Anxiety Disorder Association of America (www.adaa.org/ consumerresources/findaprofessionaltherapists)

- The American Board of Sexology (www.sexologist.org/ index.htm)

Choosing a Sex Therapist

If you have several sex therapists from which to choose, I recommend seeing a few of them before making your selection. Each sex therapist has a different style, and you want to find someone who gives you the confidence to talk in a very open manner.

Some therapists specialize in certain disorders. I, for example, do not treat people who are sado-masochists — who like to inflict and receive pain during sex. So, when someone who has difficulties in these areas comes to me, I refer them to someone I know who specializes in this area. But I do handle just about every other sort of sexual disorder, among both heterosexuals and homosexuals.

If you go to a sex therapist, or any therapist or counselor for that matter, and you find that you are not being helped, then feel free to seek out another. The problem isn't necessarily that your therapist isn't good; it may be that your personalities just don't mix properly. Whatever the cause, you shouldn't have to suffer just because you've had a bad experience. Sex therapists have helped millions of people, and you can be helped too — you are no less deserving of sexual happiness than any of the others who've been helped. Just keep working at it.

Appendix B

Terrific Resources

● ●

Counseling

American Association for Marriage and Family Therapy, 1133 15th Street NW, Suite 300, Washington, DC 20005; 202-452-0109; www.aamft.org

American Mental Health Counselor's Association, 801 N. Fairfax Street, Suite 304, Alexandria, VA 22314; 800-326-2642; www.amhca.org

American Psychiatric Association, 1400 K. Street NW, Washington, DC 20005; 202-682-6000; www.psych.org

American Psychological Association, 750 First St. NE, Washington, DC 20002; 202-336-5500; www.apa.org

Association of Gay and Lesbian Psychiatrists, 4514 Chester Ave., Philadelphia, PA 19143; 215-222-2800; www.aglpnat.aol

American Association of Pastoral Counselors, 9504A Lee Highway, Fairfax, VA 22031-2303; 703-385-6967; www.aapc.org

Sex Therapy

AASECT (American Association of Sex Educators, Counselors, and Therapists), P.O. Box 238, Mount Vernon, IA 52314; www.aasect.org

American Board of Sexology, www.sexologist.org

Sexually Transmitted Diseases

Centers for Disease Control and Prevention's National STD/AIDS Hotline, English 1-800-342-AIDS or 800-227-8922 24 hours a day; Spanish 1-800-344-7432 from 8 a.m. until 2 a.m. (Eastern)

Sexual Orientation

National Gay and Lesbian Task Force, 1700 Kalorama Road NW, Washington, DC 20009; 202-332-6483; www.ngltf.org

Parents, Family, and Friends of Lesbians and Gays (PFLAG), 202-638-4200

Sexuality and Family Planning

Diocesan Development Program for Natural Family Planning National Conference of Catholic Bishops, 3211 Fourth Street NE, Washington, DC 20017; 202-541-3240

Planned Parenthood, 810 Seventh Avenue, New York, NY 10019; 212-541-7800; www.plannedparenthood.org

Sexuality Information and Education Council of the United States (SIECUS), 130 West 42nd Street, Suite 350, New York, NY 10036-7802; 212-819-9770; www.siecus.org

Sexual Toys

Adam & Eve, 1 Apple Court, P.O. Box 800, Carrboro, NC 27510; 1-800-765-ADAM; www.adameve.com

Condomania, 1-800-9-CONDOM; www.condomania.com

Eve's Garden, 119 W. 57th Street, Suite 1201, New York, NY 10019; 1-800-848-3837; www.evesgarden.com

Good Vibrations, 938 Howard Street, San Francisco, CA 94103; 1-800-289-8423; www.goodvibes.com

The Townsend Institute, P.O. Box 8865, Chapel Hill, NC 27515; 1-800-888-1900; www.bettersex.com

Protecting Children

National Center for Missing and Exploited Children, 800-843-5678

National Runaway Switchboard, 800-621-4000

Support Groups

American Cancer Society, 1-800-ACS-2345

US-TOO (International Support Network for Prostate Cancer Survivors), 1-800-82-USTOO; www.afud.org

Index

• •

• A •

• *N* •

• *O* •

Notes

Notes